Romesh C Dutt

LIFE AND WORK OF ROMESH CHUNDER DUTT C.I.E.

BY
J.N. GUPTA, M.A., I.C.S.

WITH AN INTRODUCTION
BY

HIS HIGHNESS
SAYAJI RAO GAEKWAD
MAHARAJA OF BARODA

Gian Publishing House
29/6 SHAKTI NAGAR · DELHI-110007 · INDIA

GIAN PUBLISHING HOUSE
PUBLISHERS OF BOOKS ON HUMAN CIVILIZATION
29/6 SHAKTI NAGAR, DELHI-110007

First Reprint in India, 1986

*Printed at Goyal Offset Printers, Delhi-110035
and published by Smt. Gayatri Garg
for Gian Publishing House, Delhi-110007*

TO

HIS CHILDREN

WHOM MR. DUTT LOVED SO DEARLY

THIS WORK IS AFFECTIONATELY INSCRIBED

BY

THE AUTHOR

INTRODUCTION

In introducing this life of an eminent intellectual leader of modern India, there is no need for me to dwell upon particular events in his life, or upon the literary achievements which have made the name of Romesh Dutt widely known in the West as well as in India. I wish rather to call attention to certain traits which seemed to me—and I had opportunities of knowing him intimately during his most mature period—to mark him out as a man at once of great capacity and great character.

And first of all I would mention his astonishing power of work. Romesh Dutt came from a province the climate and traditions of which are commonly supposed to discourage, in a peculiar degree, the exercise of physical and mental energy; but there were surely few men of his time, whether Western or Eastern, who laboured more continuously and to greater purpose than he.

The claims of the Service to which he gave the best years of his life were in themselves exacting, and it might well have seemed that such strength as was left over from the discharge of official duties would have been wholly absorbed in such researches as those rendered necessary for the writing of the "History of Civilisation in Ancient India."

Yet, as the world knows, his work as a Government officer and as the historian of Early India formed only a part of his manifold activity. He made himself an acknowledged master in the field of Indian economic history and administration; he became the interpreter of the heroic Epics of his country to English readers; he carried through, mainly during his periods of leave from official duty, the gigantic task of rendering into his own mother tongue the sacred wisdom of the "Rig Veda." His labours in the cause of Social Reform are well known. He was after his retirement one of the acknowledged pillars of the Indian National Congress; and his political views were so well-considered and broad based that during the years of his residence in Europe, he was accepted as the most distinguished advocate, by speech and pen, of the Indian reform programme.

The mental grasp, the power of will, and the habit of industry which enabled Romesh Dutt to do all these things, during and after his long term of service under the Government of India, gave him the unmistakable character of a man fashioned in a large mould. There was nothing small about him. It was well and truthfully said that among any company of leading men in any part of the world he would have stood high. The impression he made wherever he went was of a great personal force, a mind habitually taking broad views and working for fine public ends. And this impression was strengthened by his big genial presence and overflowing humanity, and by the frank enjoyment of friendly intercourse which made him, in England as in India, the centre of a large and animated circle.

It is, of course, desirable that in this brief prefatory note to Mr. Gupta's biography, a word should be said of Mr. Dutt's relations with Baroda.

For many years past the policy has been to open the high offices of the State to men of proved ability without distinction of race or creed. That policy has been justified in many instances; but it will, I think, cause no surprise when I say that Baroda has never had greater cause for satisfaction than in the results attained by the appointment of Mr. Romesh Dutt, first as Revenue Minister, and afterwards as Dewan.

His experience in the Imperial Civil Service had led him to the conviction that certain reforms in the government should be introduced for the benefit of the people, more especially the peasants; and it was his belief that the administration of a Native State furnished, by its comparative simplicity and elasticity, a more favourable ground for experiment than is offered by the more rigidly organised system of British India.

In Baroda he worked hard to give practical effect to his theories, and the story of his efforts is told in the series of Administration Reports for which he was responsible during his tenure of office in the State.

May I here express the great loss that the State has been put to on account of Mr. Dutt's untimely death so soon after his appointment as Prime Minister. Had Providence vouchsafed to him a longer span, I am inclined to believe that his administration would have been a still more glorious success. His great experience, his tenacity of purpose and strength of conviction, as also his firm belief in the ultimate triumph of Truth, are facts that might well serve as an example and inspiration to the younger generation of Indians.

SAYAJI RAO, GAEKWAR.

25*th September* 1911.

CONTENTS

BOOK I

BOOK II

Contents

BOOK III

LIST OF ILLUSTRATIONS

PHOTOGRAVURES

HALF TONES

Dear Sir I thank you for your work on our position & duties in India & I trust that from year to year we may come to feel less inadequately the immense burden and the commensurate weight & responsibility of the charge which we have undertaken in that great country

Yours very faithfully

WEGladstone

Jul 20. 97

The destinies of our Indian Empire are covered with thick darkness. It is difficult to form any conjectures as to the fate reserved for a State which resembles no other in history, and which forms by itself a separate class of political phenomena; the laws which regulate its growth and its decay are still unknown to us. It may be that the public mind of India may expand under our system till it has outgrown the system; that by good government we may educate our subjects into a capacity for better government; that having become instructed in European knowledge, they may in some future age demand European institutions. Whether such a day will ever come I know not. But never will I attempt to avert or retard it. Whenever it comes, it will be the proudest day in English History.—Macaulay's speech on the Bill renewing the East India Company's Charter, House of Commons, 10th July 1833.

What I seem to discern are not at all the symptoms of crisis. I do not see or hear demands for violent or startling new departures. What I do see is a stage reached in the gradual and inevitable working out of Indian policy, which makes it wise and in the natural order of things—and I do not at all despair of securing the agreement of the noble Lord opposite to this—that we should advance with a firm, courageous, and intrepid step some paces further on the path of continuous, rational improvement in the Indian system of government.—Lord Morley's Budget speech, 1906.

Gentlemen, I believe more in our fitness for self-government than in any gifts and concessions which we may receive from our rulers. If we are prepared by our devotion to work for self-government, no power on earth can withhold it from us. Nations shape their own destiny, and our future is in our own hands. Let us forget those petty jealousies and differences which sometimes divide us. Let us keep the great object before us. The path of progress is thorny, but in spite of many disappointments I still believe that the path is as clear before us as the noonday sun. This is Dharma; it is the duty of every nation to strive for progress, as it is the endeavour of the plant to seek for light. If we are true to ourselves in education and social reforms, in industrial and political endeavours, our future is assured. Every act of self-seeking and untruth holds us back; every act of self-sacrifice and devotion sees us farther on our onward march.—R. C. Dutt: speech at Lucknow, February 1908.

PRELIMINARY

I

To present a critical estimate of Romesh Chunder Dutt, while standing so near in time to his life and achievements, is a task beset with many difficulties. That, at any rate, is not the sole object of the present biography. But there are stages in the history of every nation, and modern India may at least be conceded to be a nation "in transition," when the life of the strong individual, the leader, forms but a chapter of the larger life of the nation itself. It is from this standpoint that the life of a representative Indian, a recognised leader of Indian thought and opinion, is of especial interest. Such a life faithfully narrated; the sources of its intellectual and moral strength, its aspirations and ambitions, the bed-rocks of its faith clearly exposed to view; its limitation of vision, the moments of its despair and gloom mirrored by a faithful hand; above all, its subtler hues, the play of sentiment, the leaven of occidental culture and energy, the heritage of oriental feeling, all painted with a truthful yet sympathetic brush, cannot fail to serve a useful purpose and find an answer to many heated controversies. Would you really know what advance India under British rule has made in the path of true nationality, would you peer into the future and catch a glimpse of the far-off haven to which this ancient argosy of the East is slowly winning her way? Then, the study of the life of a great Indian cannot fail to deepen your interest and clear your vision.

II

The closing years of the nineteenth century and the opening decade of the present, mark perhaps the most momentous chapter in the history of modern India. For the historian of the future will have to record in these years, if not the birth of a "New India," yet a determined and signal advance in that long and weary path over which it is the appointed task of the people of India to travel, before the goal will be reached and a true political personality will emerge from the heterogeneous mass who inhabit the vast continent. The most reliable and competent observers, both amongst Englishmen and Indians, have not been slow to read the signs of the times, and to detect in the storm and stress through which we are now passing the true portents of a great national upheaval in the country, the parturial pains heralding the birth of a nation. To confine ourselves to English opinion only, what a marked revulsion there has been. Professor Seeley, who was one of the first to make a critical study of the political aspects of the British occupation of India, observed in 1883: "There is no Indian nationality, though there are germs from which we can conceive an Indian nationality developing itself." Even so late as the closing years of the last century, Meredith Townsend declared the impossibility of an Oriental nation advancing in the path of Western civilisation, and held that "the chasm between the brown man and the white is unfathomable." But even in those days preachers of the rival school of thought were not altogether silent. Only two years after Seeley's book appeared, in 1885, Mr. (now Sir Henry) Cotton, one of the ablest and most sympathetic English officials serving in India at the time, saw "a New India rising before his eyes, and a nation in the real sense in actual formation."

The currents of political life in India have moved swiftly since the days of the first publication of "New India," and landmarks which were then dim and unformed have now taken more definite shape and emerged clearly to view, till to-day, the greatest living political thinker of England has himself analysed for us the sources of the present political illumination in India. In the memorable speeches delivered while he was in charge of the India Office, Lord Morley has on more than one occasion made a searching analysis of the inevitableness of the present-day "intoxication of educated Indians with ideas of freedom, nationality, and self-government, and the irresistible and mighty influence which such great teachers and masters of England as Milton, Burke, Macaulay have exercised in India." And it is not only the political philosopher who has seen this. The far-sighted Viceroy, who with Lord Morley has shared the high honour and lasting glory of building the foundations of real autonomy in India, and who had the amplest opportunity of gauging the potency and true character of the new forces at work, recognised the birth of a new spirit almost as soon as he assumed his high office. From his throne in the Council Chamber, Lord Minto, in 1907, declared that "a change was rapidly passing over the land, and new and just aspirations were springing up amongst its people." Still more forcibly, in his remarkable speech in the Council of 1909, introducing his memorable reforms, he pointed out that he "had to deal with political forces unknown to his predecessors, which it was no longer possible for British administrators to ignore, while the trend of events in the far East had accentuated the ambitions of Eastern populations." His Excellency must have remembered the noble exhortation of the Hon. Mr. Gokhale, when, in the course of his speech on the Budget of 1906, he said: "Moreover, my Lord, the whole East is to-day throbbing with a new impulse, vibrating with a new passion, and it is not to be expected that India alone should continue unaffected by changes that are in the very air around us. We could not remain outside this influence even if we would. We would not so remain if we could."

It is hardly necessary to repeat that the central motive

power of this unifying process, this fusion of many races, is the solidifying principle which underlies the British domination of India. "There is no determination more fixed and immovable in the will of England," to quote the words of another great Viceroy, "than eventually to evolve from its present intricate and imperfectly adjusted mechanism a homogeneous community so well-balanced and co-ordinated, so united in its material interests and its moral convictions as to form a loyal, patriotic, and compacted whole."[1] And the heart and core of this movement, the real solvent which is working this miracle, is unquestionably the introduction of English education in India, which, according to Seeley, "remains the great landmark in the history of the Indian Empire, considered as an institution of civilisation."

And the representative Indians of to-day, the children of this Western civilisation, "trained in Western education," are striving to win for their country "Western institutions," and thus fulfil that mission which Macaulay pictured for them in 1833, and which, according to that wise and beneficent prophet, "would herald the proudest day in the annals of England." And a study of the career and achievements of the great Indians who, since the days of Raja Ram Mohan Ray, have devoted their lives to the service of India, abundantly proves that their labours have contributed in no small measure to the uplifting of their motherland. "The last half-century has seen the erection of a mighty edifice in India. Englishmen have placed the bricks, but Indians themselves have supplied the mortar."[2]

III

Nor are the leaders of Indian thought, the pioneers of the Indian national movement, unaware of the complexities of the present situation, or oblivious of the claims of England and of those noble-hearted Englishmen who have made the regeneration of India the primary duty of their lives.

[1] Speech of Lord Dufferin, Feb. 1887.
[2] "Glimpses of Hidden India," by "John Law," p. 231.

How to reconcile the claims of racial nationalism with the claims of that imperial and composite patriotism, which, according to Lord Curzon, "the Indian may share with the Englishman," is a problem which will have to be grappled with not only by all genuine Indian patriots, but also by all those noble Englishmen who set the good of India above the mere perpetuation of their own national predominance. And the key-note of the life and labours of Romesh Chunder Dutt, the driving energy which impelled him to such unremitting and ceaseless toil, is to be found in his unswerving devotion to the cause of his motherland—not in subordination to, nor at the sacrifice of, his loyalty to the British Crown, but in a harmonious and reasoned co-ordination of the two sentiments. On the one hand, to lead India in the path which will end one day in her taking her place among the nations of the modern world, and, on the other, to bring home to the rulers of the country the wisdom of associating educated Indians more and more in the task of the administration of their own country, and thus effectually deepening and broadening the foundations of the Empire, were the twin inspirations of his life.

Amongst the band of noble and strenuous workers who have laid the foundations of true nationalism in India, there is hardly a more commanding figure or a more unremitting worker than he ; and from few Indians has the motherland received such high, unselfish, silent, and enduring service as was offered at her shrine by that gifted son. To the Government, whose servant he was, he rendered equally lasting service. Through him, more than through the medium of any other Indian, has India learnt the value of the rarer gifts of the English character—the love of independence, truth, patriotism, and an unflagging devotion to duty ; and his whole life was a living demonstration of that true "intermingling of the East and West," the attainment of which is perhaps the highest mission of England in India.

IV

Of John Stuart Mill, Lord Morley has written : "From the beginning to the end of his career he was forced into the polemical attitude over the whole field ; into an incessant and manful wrestle for what he thought true and right against what he regarded as false or wrong." The same polemical attitude obtrudes itself in most of Mr. Dutt's political writings. In all the important questions of administrative reform for which he waged such ceaseless war, he was far too anxious to uphold the Indian position to aim at the speculative calmness of a political philosopher. He was far too deeply engrossed in the interests at stake to rise to the clear vision of an impersonal critic. His impatience to secure a hearing for his side of a case not seldom obliterated a true sense of proportion, and he returned to the charge time after time over the same field, but always with unexhausted and inexhaustible vigour. Style and literary brilliancy were sacrificed in the all-absorbing desire to drive home a point, or vindicate a just grievance of the Indian people. Yet he was never blind to the claims of an opposing view, and there was no publicist of his age engaged in the discussion of Indian problems, who took such infinite trouble to study and master details, and to gather first-hand information from the people themselves, whose cause he fought. At the time when Mr. Dutt died, there was hardly another man who excelled him in the knowledge of the real needs and aspirations of the people of India as a whole, and who was so thoroughly at home with the different aspects and vicissitudes of all the great Indian administrative questions which have agitated the public mind during the last half-century. Nor was his view of Indian subjects parochial or dwarfed by a regard for considerations of the hour only. He was a ripe scholar, and was as familiar with the social and political institutions of ancient and modern India as with the political literature and institutions of modern and mediæval Europe.

V

A man is but the product of his age. It is not in every country and during every age that truly great achievements are possible. What type of a great man is India during this transition stage capable of producing? Has the Indian citizen of to-day a better chance of shining in the sphere of action or of thought? Is true statesmanship, the worship of the goddess of political wisdom, within the reach of the sons of a subject nation? In the field of literature, too, are the doors of the shrine of true literature really open to him? In what language is he to clothe his thoughts, if his productions are not to share the fate of ephemeral exotics? What language is destined to be the national language of India of the future? A critic must weigh these and similar questions before he seeks to assign a place for Mr. Dutt.

What, after all, is the true essence of greatness in a man? Is he to be judged by his achievements alone? Or is it the power of his will, his character, the loftiness of his purpose, his resistance to the tyranny of self, and an unswerving devotion to duty against many odds and difficulties, that deserve our truest admiration?

The inspiring beacon-light of Romesh Chunder Dutt's life cannot be better described than in his own language, when, standing on the top of the North Cape in July 1886, "and gazing over the sublime and limitless ocean beyond the last frontier of human habitation," his imagination raised before his mental vision the picture of the India to come:—

"I will not conceal the pain and humiliation which I felt in my inmost soul," he wrote, "as I stood on that memorable night among representatives of the free and advancing nations of the earth rejoicing in their national greatness. Champagne was drunk on the top of the hill, and Germans and Frenchmen, Englishmen and Americans, pressed us to share their hospitality. I accepted their offer with thanks on my lips, but I felt within me that I had no place beside them. May we, in the course of years, progress in civilisation and in self-government, in mercantile enterprise and in representative institutions, even as the young English Colonies in Australia are doing year by year. And may our sons' sons, when they come to Europe, feel that India can take her place among the great advancing countries of the earth. Let us trust to the future, but trust still more to our honest work and hard endeavour. There is not a race in Europe, or in the whole world, but has gained its place by hard, severe, unremitted struggle and toil. And if we too, each individual among us, learn to work honestly and truly for our country, we cannot fail."

And nobly did Romesh Dutt play his part. Along nearly every avenue of intellectual and material progress did he seek to show the way to his countrymen. And in order to awaken a true spirit of nationalism amongst them, and to stimulate their highest and noblest aspirations, there was no labour, however arduous and exacting, which he did not manfully and cheerfully undertake. Nor must we judge him only by the results as we see them to-day. In many spheres he and the noble band of workers, English and Indian, with whom he worked, have only sown the seeds. Who can foretell what the tree will be?

BOOK I

LIFE AND WORK OF
ROMESH CHUNDER DUTT

BOOK I

CHAPTER I

FAMILY

I

ON the night of the 3rd of January 1757, following the day on which Clive retook Calcutta and thus laid the foundation-stone of the British Empire in India, was born Nilmoni Dutt, the first reputed ancestor of the well-known family of the Dutts of Rambagan. The coincidence was one of some significance, for of all the distinguished families of Bengal which have made the attainment of Western culture and illumination the chief object of their ambition and endeavour, the Dutts of Rambagan are without question the foremost. The genealogy of the family goes back to at least four generations before Clive, and Kamalakanta, the great-grandfather of Nilmoni, must have lived about the time when Bengal was under the sway of the Moghal Emperors and the English were establishing their first factories in the country.

The original home of the family was at Ajapur, three miles south of the railway station of Memari, on the East Indian Railway, in the Burdwan district. There is a curious tradition connected with this village and its Buddhistic-looking temple. Tradition has it that one of the ancestors of the Dutt family built seven temples at

Ajapur in order to pay off the debt which a man owes his mother. No sooner, however, had he expressed this desire than the temples began to tumble down, one after another, for the *shastras* say that it is not for man to pay the debt he owes his mother. When six had already fallen and the seventh was about to crumble down, the unlucky man repented and retracted his words, on which the last temple relented and remained in the oblique position to which it had got. There is no authentic information to show when the Dutts left Ajapur for Calcutta, but it seems that a branch of the family migrated to Burdwan, whilst Nilmoni's father settled down in Calcutta.

Nilmoni had three sons; the youngest, Pitamber, born in 1799, was the grandfather of Romesh Chunder Dutt.

II

But before we go on to speak of Pitamber's talented sons—Isan, the father of Romesh Chunder, and Shoshee Dutt, his uncle—it will be well if we let Mr. Dutt himself speak of his ancestor Nilmoni and Nilmoni's well-known son, Rasamoy. With Rasamoy's still more famous family, who were Mr. Dutt's contemporaries, he would seem to have been on terms of intimacy, and he entertained for them feelings of lively admiration.

Nilmoni Dutt, better known as Niloo Dutt, was a well-known resident of Calcutta in the latter half of the eighteenth century, *i.e.* in the days of Clive and Warren Hastings. I have often heard my grandfather (a younger son of Niloo Dutt) say, that Nilmoni kept an open house, and was known for his hospitality. Brahmans and pious men who went every morning for their bath in the Hughli River assembled at Niloo Dutt's house on their return, and were welcomed and entertained with refreshments. The foremost men of Calcutta reckoned Niloo Dutt among their friends; Maharaja Nava Kissen of Sobhabazar esteemed him; and Maharaja Nand Kumar visited him in his house. Liberal and catholic in his ideas, he was equally well known to many prominent Englishmen of the day, and was a friend of Christian missionaries. The preaching of Christianity was prohibited at that time; and the missionary Carey, when pursued by the agents of the East India Company, found shelter with Niloo Dutt, who concealed him for a time. A well-known, well-beloved, hospitable, and charitable man, Niloo Dutt lived the life of the highest class Hindu of the eighteenth century, and passed away in the early years of the nineteenth century, leaving his property much involved.

His eldest son, Rasamoy Dutt, was a stern economist; he cleared the debts left by his father, and reared a fortune and a reputation as one of the foremost men of his day. The British Government sought the co-operation of able Indian gentlemen in spreading English education and in other liberal measures, and soon recognised the splendid abilities of Rasamoy Dutt. Rasamoy was appointed Secretary to the Sanskrit College of Calcutta; he was afterwards appointed a Judge of the Small Cause Court of Calcutta, then a position of highest trust and honour; and he took a leading part in all the great public movements during the first half of the nineteenth century. He had a splendid collection of English books in his house, and infused in his sons that strong partiality for English literature which distinguishes the family to this day. Liberal in his ideas, and also in his expenses, he set his face, however, against that extravagance in the matter of Hindu *pujas* and ceremonials which had involved his father in debt; and this gave him a bad name with many Brahmans and orthodox men. Rasamoy Dutt's life marks a transition in Hindu society, under English influences. He died shortly after the middle of the nineteenth century.

Among the cultured sons of Rasamoy Dutt, Govin Chunder was the most distinguished. He held a high appointment under the India Government in the Accounts Department, but soon resigned service, and devoted his leisure, in retirement, to literature and to religious studies. Early in life he had published a volume of English verses; and these productions, together with some poems written by his cousin Shoshee Chunder Dutt, received the deserved compliment of a favourable review in *Blackwood's Magazine* in England. After his retirement he embraced the Christian religion with his wife and children, his brothers and nephews; and his wife and two daughters accompanied him to England in 1869. There he brought out his maturer poems, with those of his two brothers and a nephew, in a handsome little volume under the title of the "Dutt Family Album." And his talented daughter, Toru Dutt, won a still higher distinction by her own English verses and her translations from French poetry. But the climate of Europe had told on the young poetess and her sister; and both the girls died within a few years after their return to India. Govin Chunder himself followed them not long after.

I have vivid recollections of the visits which I used to pay, as a boy, to Govin Chunder, then living with his wife and children in retirement, in their garden-house at Bagmari, in the suburbs of Calcutta. It was an extensive garden covering many acres of land, and shaded by fruit-trees; and there was a rustic bridge over a canal, which was the delight of our boyhood. We had the run of the whole garden, and Govin Chunder's only son, Abju, showed us his favourite secluded places. Poor boy, he died early, and his loss was an abiding grief to his parents. In the midst of this forest of fruit-trees rose the comfortable and spacious one-storeyed bungalow-house—a perfect picture of repose! There was a good collection of choice books in the house, for study was Govin Chunder's only recreation.

I have recollections also of the time when we met in England. I was a young man then, and had passed the Open Competition for the Civil Service of India in 1869; and shortly after, Govin Chunder arrived in England with his wife and his two accomplished daughters. I secured rooms for them at the Grosvenor Hotel, and shortly after they took a furnished house at Brompton. It is needless to say that I often visited them there, and spent many pleasant hours with my young cousins. Literary work and religious studies were still the sole occupation of Govin Chunder and his family, and they made the acquaintance of many pious Christians. When the "Dutt Family Album" came out, Govin Chunder presented me with a copy, marked out the poems which were his own, and read, almost with tears in his eyes, the verses he had written on his deceased son.

I saw him also, pretty often, after we had all returned to India. I think it was the state of his daughters' health which had cut short his stay in England. They had now left the Bagmari garden-house and lived in a newly-built house in the town, close to their ancestral residence. They were as kind, as gracious, as courteous towards me as ever, and their hearts are full of piety. But the fatal illness of which the germs were brought from Europe declared itself. First the eldest daughter, Aru, and then the talented Toru, fell ill and died. Toru's verses were praised in England by Edmund Gosse, and admired by a select circle of readers; had she lived to a maturer age, she might have left a name in English literature. Govin Chunder survived them a few years, and his widow followed him after some more years.

Of Toru Dutt, Mr. Dutt's cousin and the author of "A Sheaf Gleaned in French Fields," "Ancient Ballads of Hindusthan," and other poems, who died at the early age of twenty-one, before her splendid gifts had time to mature, no less a critic than Mr. Gosse has said:—

> It is difficult to exaggerate when we try to estimate what we have lost in the premature death of Toru Dutt. Literature has no honours which need have been beyond the grasp of a girl who, at the age of twenty-one, and in languages separated from her own by so deep a chasm, had produced so much of lasting worth.

III

Isan Chunder, the father of Romesh Chunder, was born on the 1st of March 1818, and was educated at the Hindu College, Calcutta. He was one of the pupils of the renowned Captain Richardson, of whose reading of Shakespeare Macaulay said, "I can forget everything of India, but not your reading of Shakespeare." Richardson's unique personality did not fail to impress itself on the mind of Isan Chunder, as it practically moulded the whole future career of the greatest poet of India—Michael Madhu Sudan Dutt. Isan's essays and poems, written while he was a student of the Hindu College, and afterwards published in 1872, show his love for literary pursuits. He was a prominent member of the band of students who started the *Hindu Bartabaha*, a monthly magazine of some merit. He left the Hindu College in 1833 and entered the Medical College, where he completed his course of studies, and in 1837 obtained the final diploma and earned a gold medal. Dr. H. H. Goodeve was so impressed with the sterling qualities of the student that he proposed to take him to England, but the idea was not carried out. He was one of the band of noble and fearless workers who did so much to stay the fearful ravages of cholera, which raged in Calcutta during 1837–38. In 1838, through the influence of his cousin Kailash Ch. Dutt, who had already taken service under Government as a Deputy Collector, he joined the public service. He was employed chiefly in survey work, and during the course of his official duties visited Midnapur, Birbhum, Murshidabad, Bhagalpur, Jessore, Khulna, and Pabna. He was personally known to Sir Frederick Halliday, the first Lieutenant-Governor of Bengal, and was present at the Durbar held by the Lieutenant-Governor at Murshidabad in 1854. He met with an accident in the course of his official duties, and was drowned near Kustia on 8th May 1861, when he was forty-three years of age only. His father, Pitamber Dutt, survived him, and died on the 15th April 1868, at the ripe age of seventy. He was married when he was twenty-one years of age to Thakamani, daughter of Ram Ratan Bose. His wife died in 1859, and thus preceded him by a few years only. They had four sons and two girls. The eldest, Jogesh Ch. Dutt, was born in July 1847; Romesh Ch. was born on the 13th August 1848; and Abinash Ch. was born on the 14th May 1854. His biographer describes Isan Ch. Dutt as a man of great determination, and a laborious and self-respecting government servant. In his private life he was a devoted father, a fond husband, and a generous friend. We shall see hereafter how some of the most notable characteristics of the son were inherited from the father.

IV

The man who exercised the most far-reaching influence in shaping the life and career of R. C. Dutt was undoubtedly his uncle, Rai Shoshee Ch. Dutt Bahadur.

Among the many students of the old Hindu College who became known by their command of graceful and idiomatic English, Babu Shoshee Chunder was one of the most distinguished. His Essays in English, published nearly sixty years ago, called forth the admiration of English critics, and received the deserved compliment of a lengthy review in *Blackwood's Magazine*. Shoshee Babu never gave up his studies, and almost to the last day of his life was busy in revising his former Essays or in the production of new works. Among his historical works, "The Ancient World," "Modern World," and

"Bengal" are the best written; among his minor works, "The Reminiscences of a Kerani's Life," are the most interesting; while "Shankar, a Tale of the Indian Mutiny," startled Sir Erskine Perry and Sir Ashley Eden by its strange disclosures, and there was some correspondence with the Government on the subject. Shoshee Babu also left some verses, which are spirited and bold. His connection with the Bengal Secretariat as a Head Assistant is well known. His able services for thirty-four years were recognised by successive Lieutenant-Governors. Sir Frederick Halliday was aware of his merits, and frequently took notice of him; Sir John Peter Grant was much pleased with his work; Sir Cecil Beadon thanked him especially in a Government minute; Sir William Grey proposed to the Government of India the appointment of two native assistant secretaries, Shoshee Babu being one of the nominees. But Sir George Campbell practically superseded him, and Shoshee Babu gave up his appointment and retired as a protest. Sir George, however, expressed his appreciation of the able assistant by conferring on him the title of "Rai Bahadur." A stern integrity, an unswerving uprightness, and the most uncompromising independence marked his character, and made him honoured and respected wherever he was known. The success of Shoshee Chunder Dutt as a writer lay, said the *Indian Echo*, in the extreme ease and felicity of his style, directness of narrative, brilliant anecdote, quiet humour, and chaste sentiment. He died at the age of sixty-one, on 30th December 1885.

Babu Shoshee Ch. Dutt acted as the guardian of Romesh Chunder and his orphan brothers after the death of their parents. It would appear, however, that there was some misunderstanding between the uncle and his nephews, just before the departure of Romesh Chunder to England, brought about chiefly by the jealous and quarrelsome disposition of Suresh Chunder Dutt, the son of the Rai Bahadur and cousin of Romesh Dutt. But the impropriety of keeping up strained relations with his benefactor and nearest relative appealed so strongly to the better judgment of Mr. Dutt that, soon after his return from England, he addressed the following letter to his uncle :—

My dear Uncle,—It is with feelings of sincere regret and sorrow that I now reflect on the unpleasant terms on which I stand with regard to yourself; and the reflection becomes day by day more painful, as I feel that my conduct towards you has been somewhat undutiful and improper. I venture therefore with some diffidence to write to you, in the hope that past differences may be forgotten, past errors forgiven.

I will not here retrace the unfortunate circumstances which have brought about differences between us, far less attempt to justify my own conduct throughout this transaction. There was a time when I did so; but after the calm reflection of three years I feel a painful conviction that my action in harbouring resentment at some hasty and perhaps unjust words from one who was the guardian of my boyhood and the instructor of my youth, has been ungenerous, undutiful, and improper.

I seek reconciliation because I feel my past conduct has not been what perhaps it ought to have been, because it would afford me lifelong consolation to think that in my mature years I had the sense to rectify the mistake of my early youth; because it would give me lifelong pain to think that I never made my peace with one whom, next to my father, I ought most to love and to revere. I seek reconciliation because, in spite of unfortunate differences, I have never failed to admire and hold in high esteem a character the many noble traits of which it will be my lifelong study to imitate; because, in spite of our misunderstandings, I have sincerely grieved over the many misfortunes which are crowding upon you in this old age. I hope to receive from you a kind reply; but, should you decline a reconciliation, I will still, believe me, dear uncle, never fail to think of you with admiration, esteem, and love, to the end of my life. —Believe me, yours affly. ever,

Romesh Chunder Dutt.

The following was the uncle's prompt and generous reply. The misfortune to which reference is made in this letter, and which was looming over Babu Shoshee Chunder, was his son's threatened insanity.

17 Musjid Bari Street,
25th July 187–.

My dear Romesh,—I have received your note of the 22nd with great satisfaction; I would have said with great pleasure, if it were possible for me to be pleased with anything at this moment. The sky is closing darkly around me; I always knew that the storm at sunset is fiercer than the storm at noon, but was yet quite unprepared for such a storm as has burst upon me. I have never repelled the hand of kindness when offered to me by any one. I could not under any circumstances have repelled it when coming from you; I receive your advances with earnest affection.

I do not remember what the words were which gave you offence; I cannot remember anything now. I know that my father was hurt at your defection. All my efforts then were directed towards removing the load of misery which was weighing him down, and I have no doubt that I said many things of you, both to him and to others, that were equally severe and unjust, but which I did not suppose would be so understood. My life has been very dreary; I have had much to bear, and have borne them manfully. But what I have not been able to bear well is that it has been my misfortune to be misunderstood by most of the nearest and dearest to me—in fact, by all except two of the very nearest, one of whom fortunately has been spared yet to bless me with her attachment. Solitariness I have not complained of; I have enjoyed it in my own way, and would have been happy in it, if Raman and Suresh had been happy. My greatest trial has now come in the misfortune that has overtaken Suresh. It was this that I had apprehended most.

You speak of imitating some traits of my character. Do not do so; you will not be understood; what is more, it will make you thoroughly unhappy. Do as the world does, and you will be idolised; even Providence seems to require that we should act so, or, at all events, oftener with the world than against it.

I am alone. For myself personally I care little that it is so; but you, and Jogesh, and Abinash must befriend Suresh's son when I am gone, should Suresh become permanently unfit to help him. On this condition I accept thankfully the reconciliation you ask for; and this condition you cannot refuse.—Ever your most affectionate uncle,

SHOSHEE CHUNDER DUTT.

CHAPTER II

EARLY DAYS

THE following is a reminiscence of their boyhood from the pen of Mr. J. C. Dutt—the eldest brother and lifelong friend of Romesh Dutt :—

Romesh was born on the 13th August 1848, in Calcutta, in a house which no longer exists, but which stood just to the west of his father-in-law's house to the east of the temple of Kali. Romesh was about four years old and I five, when an auspicious day was found to give us *hate khari* in a *pathshala* (village school) which then existed in our neighbourhood. In this *pathshala* we used to write first on palm leaves, and then on plantain leaves, according to the good old style. All the time that we were at school we were attended by a servant named Judhistir, whom we used to call "Jostay." He utilised his opportunity by learning to read and write along with us. He was a native of Mondolghat, near Tamluk. From the *pathshala* we were removed to a Bengali school which has long ago ceased to exist; and thence to the Hare School. I have no recollection of earlier incidents. I, however, remember quite distinctly our journeys to Bhagalpur and Suri, where father was posted on duty. It was during our journey to Bhagalpur by river that an amusing incident occurred of which I have preserved the following note :—

It was about the middle of the last century that a Deputy Collector was proceeding by a boat up the river near Bhagalpur. In those pre-railway and pre-steamer days journey was slow both by land and water, and sometimes dangerous on account of *dakaities*, which had not been altogether then suppressed. The robbers used to attack boats by night with torch-lights. Now it so happened that the boat of the officer was overtaken by night at a place which had the bad reputation of being infested by *dakaits*. He therefore ordered his boat to be anchored in mid-stream and instructed his servants to be on the alert and to awake him in case of any suspicious appearances. He then retired to bed.

Midnight had passed when a noise was heard in a village on the shore, and lights were seen moving to and fro arranging themselves as for a procession. The procession marched towards the river. It was time, thought the men on the boat, to wake up their master. The officer saw the procession with a large following coming towards the river opposite to the place where the boat was moored. Some thought it was a marriage procession, others were of opinion that it was a gang of *dakaits*. There was no time for discussion, as the men had reached the river bank and were about to step into the water. The people from the boat warned them not to do so as a "Company Bahadur's" boat was anchored there. The men on shore paid no heed. At last the Deputy Collector ordered a blank fire. Now among his servants there was an up-country boy who had the handling of a gun, a fine muzzle-loader of those days. It so happened that the ramrod of the gun had been lost and a small bamboo stick had been made to do the duty of the rod. The up-country boy had put an extra quantity of powder into the gun, and rammed in the powder with the bamboo stick. The stick got jammed in the barrel and could not be pulled out. What was now to be done? The men on shore had already reached the water. Finding that there was no time to lose, the up-country boy fired the gun. It was a rash act, for the barrel might have burst. It produced a loud report disturbing the stillness of the midnight air, while the bamboo stick shot out of the barrel, flaming and blazing across the dark sky, a veritable *Agniban* (arrow of fire). This seemed to terrify the people on the shore, and they scampered off in all directions. If *dakaits*, they might very well be alarmed, for they had never seen such a strange missile fired from a gun before!

Our stay at Calcutta and our studies at the Colutolla Branch School were not continuous. We paid another visit to Suri, but I cannot say whether it was after being admitted into the Colutolla School or before it. This is, however, certain that we went to Kumarkhali and thence to Murshidabad.

At Kumarkhali we lived in a thatched house, and for want of accommodation in the inner apartment my brother and I occupied the room in the outer, under the care of our faithful servant Jostay. Jostay used to entertain us in the evenings by reading from the Bengali "Ramayana." One day he happened to read of Lakshman's "Saktishela," and my brother, although he felt so sleepy as scarcely able to keep his eyes open, would neither himself retire to bed nor allow Jostay to stop till Lakshman had been revived.

From Kumarkhali we went to Murshidabad. There we occupied a splendid house between the sepoy lines and those of European soldiers, and we used frequently to see the parade of both the sepoys and the European soldiers. During our stay at Kumarkhali and Murshidabad, we read at the schools of those places.

From Murshidabad we returned to Calcutta, and were again admitted to the Colutolla Branch School. I do not remember to have again left Calcutta before about 1857, when we went to Pabna.

At Pabna we were placed in school soon after our arrival there, where we studied for about a year. In the annual examination my brother obtained, I believe, the first prize in our class. After the examination we were withdrawn from school, and a private tutor was employed to teach us. At Pabna we learnt to ride. We had a horse, but no saddle. We used to ride after the fashion of the country, on *gadis* (cloth-saddle). At Pabna we witnessed the assumption of government by Queen Victoria from the East India Company. When we were on the eve of leaving Pabna, an incident happened which showed my brother's presence of mind and pluck even when he was a child. We and two other boys were playing with a small wooden trunk into which one of us got and the lid was closed from outside. When my turn came, my brother was at a little distance from the place, the other two boys closed the lid and fastened the chain. In a little while I began to gasp for breath and called aloud to have the lid open, and at the same time pushed up the lid from inside. This only tightened the chain which the other two boys could not unfasten. My brother heard my cry and ran up and pressed the lid down, and so unfastened the chain and opened the trunk, to my great relief.

This is the right place to interpolate Mr. Dutt's own reminiscences of these early days.

I had occasion in early life to visit various districts in Bengal with my father, who was employed as Deputy Collector; and the recollections of those early days are among the pleasantest reminiscences of my life. Those were happy pre-railway days, when a journey from district to district was performed by *palki* or by boat, and it took a longer time to travel from Calcutta to Jessore than it takes now to travel from Calcutta to Lahore or to Bombay! But though one travelled less, one saw more of the country in those days, more of the villages, bazars and towns, the rivers, ghats and temples, which he passed.

MEMBERS OF THE ROYAL COMMISSION ON DECENTRALISATION IN INDIA

It was in this fashion that we went to Birbhum, and lived in that delightful district for some time; and I accompanied my mother, who was a pious Hindu, on a visit to the far-famed hot springs of Bakreswar.

Later on, we went first to Kumarkhali and then to Berhampur, and I joined the schools at both these places. Sir Frederick Halliday, the first Lieutenant-Governor of Bengal, held a Durbar at Berhampur, and my father was invited with the other officials of the place to attend the Durbar. Durbars and official matters, however, did not attract my boyish wonder or attention; my pleasantest recollections connect themselves with the green fields and the quiet village scenes in which it was my privilege and my delight to pass my early days. Those were happy days, before malaria had appeared in its terrible form in Bengal, and residence in the outlying districts conduced to health, as it refreshed and strengthened and educated the mind.

Later on we went with our parents to Pabna, and we remained there for two years. Those were eventful days, for the Mutiny had broken out in the North-West, and every week brought fresh news about the incidents of the war. A company of British soldiers was stationed in Pabna, and occasionally these soldiers committed outrages in the place which gave rise to much complaint. It was a relief to the town when the Mutiny was over and the soldiers left the place. Before leaving they had a theatrical performance, playing "Macbeth." I had learnt the story from my father, and I shall never forget the interest with which I witnessed this theatrical performance for the first time in my life.

The East India Company was abolished and the transfer of the Empire of India to the Crown was proclaimed in Pabna, as elsewhere in India, amidst great cheers and peals of cannon. I was present in that impressive scene; cries of "Long live the Queen" in English and in Bengali rent the air; Hindus and Musalmans joined in the wish; and Brahmins held up their sacred thread and blessed the name of their gracious sovereign.

For the rest, I did fairly well in Pabna School, and carried away a prize, but can scarcely say that I deserved it. For we were wild boys, my elder brother and I, and delighted in play and mischief the whole day long! We rejoiced in open-air exercise and often walked from our house to the shores of the great Padma River, and watched with wonder its vast sea-like expanse, its rapid current, its waves and whirlpools. It was generally pretty late in the evening before we returned home, tired with the long walk, but refreshed in body and mind.

To resume Mr. J. C. Dutt's narrative :—

From Pabna we returned to Calcutta in 1859, and soon after our mother died, on 4th September 1859. Our father was obliged to join his duties in the *mufussal*, but as already some interruption had taken place in our studies by frequently accompanying him, he did not like to take us with him; so he left my brother and myself in Calcutta in charge of two faithful servants, Jostay and Sampad Ojha, the last a Brahmin *darwan* from Shahabad district.

In a few months father returned to Calcutta. It was now that we began to taste the sweets of English literature. We read several books with father in the evenings, and Lane's "Arabian Nights' Entertainments" was one of them. My brother enjoyed these stories immensely. But the evenings were not spent in the study of books alone. Discourses and conversations on literary subjects helped to keep us both amused and instructed. One evening father expressed his wish to send my brother to England to complete his education. On my wishing to go also, he said: "What is the use of your going to England? You have not the brains, but after your brother Romesh returns, you can go to see the place." My father's wish was more than literally fulfilled, for not only did my brother finish his education in England but passed into the Civil Service.

On the expiry of his leave, father returned to his work very reluctantly, this time leaving all his children in Calcutta. He was loath to part with us, as he said he had to attend to our education, and intended to apply for pension when he returned next. This he did not live to do. He was drowned on the evening of 8th May 1861, in the Chamrool Khal near Kustia, while returning from tour in a country boat which halted for the night at that place.

On the death of our father, our uncle Babu Shoshee Chunder Dutt came to live in our house in order to bring us up. He too used to sit at night with us, and our favourite study used to be pieces from the works of the English poets. Two very important lessons my brother learnt from our uncle—independence of character and thirst for literary fame. Nothing disturbed the life we led with our uncle. In December 1864, my brother passed his Entrance examination from the Hare School, standing first among the students who passed from that school, and obtaining a scholarship of 14 rupees a month. After my brother's marriage our uncle left our house, and we had to look after ourselves. He was admitted to the Presidency College, the best college in Bengal. Two years later he passed the F.A. examination, standing second among all the students who appeared in that year, having scored only one mark less than the boy who stood first. He obtained a scholarship of 32 rupees. He left Calcutta on the 3rd March 1868 for England to compete for the Civil Service.

Of his college days in India Sir Gurudas Banerjea, himself one of the foremost men of Bengal, remembers a characteristic incident:—

I made the acquaintance of Romesh Ch. in the year 1865, when he was a student in the first-year class of the Presidency College. I had just been appointed an Assistant Professor of Mathematics. I used to set a few questions for the students to answer at home. On two successive occasions Dutt had not done his home task. On my asking him the reason of his failure, he told me that he had no taste for mathematics and found the work uncongenial. I took him aside and spoke to him gently: "For the mathematics you have to do," I said, "you do not really want the genius of a Newton or Laplace. You have only to make up your mind to get through your work and it will be done." He said nothing in reply, but I saw my rebuke had sunk deep. From that day I noticed that the young student showed very satisfactory progress in my subject. I was very young myself, and had just been out from college, and for Romesh Chunder to take my advice in such good part and turn it to such good account, was to my mind a proof of his good sense and strength of purpose. It struck me then that the young student had in him the stuff of which great men are made.

In January 1864, when Romesh Dutt was only fifteen years of age, and before he had passed his Matriculation, he was married to Matamgini (Mohini) Bose, second daughter of Babu Naba Gopal Bose of Simla, in Calcutta. Both the bride and bridegroom were mere children at the time, and the match was arranged by their guardians according to strictly orthodox Hindu ideas. Nevertheless the marriage brought them more real happiness than falls to the lot of most people, and during their long married life of nearly forty-five years, Romesh Dutt and his wife knew of no serious disappointments or misfortunes. Six children were born to them, five daughters and a son. The eldest, Kamala, was born in 1866, her sister Bimala in 1867, before Mr. Dutt went to England. After Mr. Dutt's return from England his third daughter Amala was born in 1872, and the fourth daughter Sarala in 1873. His only son, Ajoy, was born in 1879, and his last child Susila in 1882. Romesh Dutt had not to suffer any bereavements, and when he died he left behind him all his children and his wife.

MR. ROMESH C. DUTT AT THE AGE OF TWENTY

CHAPTER III

EUROPE AND CIVIL SERVICE EXAMINATION (1868-71)

I

In March 1868, Mr. Dutt and two of his friends, Mr. Surendra Nath Banerjea and Mr. B. L. Gupta, sailed for England to compete for the Indian Civil Service. He was at the time only nineteen years of age. Mr. Surendra Nath Banerjea had the permission of his parents, but Mr. Gupta and Mr. Dutt had actually to run away from home under cover of night. Even their berths in the steamer had to be engaged in the name of Mr. Surendra Nath Banerjea and "two friends." But Mr. Gupta's father, Babu Chandra Sekhar Gupta, was not to be so easily eluded. He followed his runaway boy to the steamer on which the friends had embarked. But the minds of the young men had been fixed immovably, and not even the entreaties of a father would turn them back. In his first home letter to his brother Jogesh Chunder, Mr. Dutt describes the voyage. His thoughts naturally turn to the hazardous step he had taken.

We left you all, and the town of Calcutta, at 8.30 A.M. on the 3rd March, and steamed down the Hughli to meet the mail steamer *Mooltan* at Diamond Harbour. The Hughli widened as we went down the river, and we bade a long farewell to the huts and fields and villages of our native country—to the palm trees, the dates, and the green woods which stood on both sides of the river—luxuriant and beautiful. At 1.30 P.M. we came to the *Mooltan*. In the afternoon the *Mooltan* weighed anchor, and we soon came to the mouths of the Ganges. We stopped again, and did not weigh anchor till the next morning at 4 A.M., and by 10 we were on the wide wide sea. We could distinctly see the line between the reddish Hughli and the greenish sea, and the water became deep green and then deep blue, as we came out into the open sea. And now we had nothing around us but the deep blue sea and the deep blue sky. The sight was novel to me, specially at night, the waves rolling eternally on all sides, the milk-white foam sparkling a moment under the cloudless moon, and then blending away in the blue waters, and a starry summer sky formed a scene of which it is hardly possible to give an adequate description.

But as we sat for hours together on the deck watching this still nightly scene, other thoughts than those suggested by the scene oft arose in our minds. For we have left our home and our country, unknown to our friends, unknown to those who are nearest and dearest to us, staking our future, staking all, on success in an undertaking which past experience has proved to be more than difficult. The least hint about our plans would have effectually stopped our departure; our guardians would never have consented to our crossing the seas; our wisest friends would have considered it madness to venture on an impossible undertaking. Against such feelings, and against the voice of experience and reason, we have set out in this difficult undertaking—stealthily leaving our homes—recklessly staking everything on an almost impossible success. Shall we achieve that success? Or shall we come back to our country impoverished, socially cut off from our countrymen, and disappointed in our hopes, to face the reproaches of advisers and the regrets of our friends? These thoughts oft arose in our minds in the solemn stillness of the night, and the prospect before us seemed to be gloomier than the gloomy sky and the gloomy sea around us, without a ray of hope to enlighten the dark prospect.

Well might the veil of the future look dark and threatening to these adventurous spirits who had staked everything on the one supreme experiment of their lives.

It seems [writes Mr. G. A. Natesan in his excellent sketch of Mr. Dutt's life] as if the hand of Destiny impelled them to the bold venture which shaped their future life. The name of Surendra Nath Banerjea is a household word to-day all over India as a patriot, an orator, and a statesman. He has nobly performed his life's duty. Bihari Lal Gupta has also had a distinguished career, and retired from the Indian Civil Service, full of honours, a few years ago, as a Judge of the High Court of Calcutta. Romesh Chunder Dutt has also retired from the same service, but has won fame and distinction by his varied labours in other lines. Who could have imagined, over forty years ago, when these three young Bengalis were sailing over the blue ocean on a difficult and arduous venture, that their work, their character, and their life would leave an impress on the history of their native land? Who could have foreseen that they would live to direct the progress of their country?

In a letter to his brother, Romesh Dutt has described his studies in England, and how he went through the great ordeal of his life.

A year of hard study has passed, and we at last appeared at the Open Competition of 1869. I need scarcely tell you that never before did we study so hard and so unremittedly as during the past year. We attended classes of the London University College, and also took private lessons from some of the Professors of the College. I shall never forget the kindness which we have received from them; they have been more like friends than teachers to us. I wish specially to mention the names of two gentlemen to whom we are under deep obligation. I have never known a kinder, a more genuine and true-hearted Englishman than Mr. Henry Morley, Professor of English Literature. We attended his classes, we took private lessons from him, we shared his hospitality, and we benefited by his kind, friendly, and ever-helpful advice. His house is as well known to us as our own, and his study—the walls of which, on every side, are lined with books—has been the scene of many a pleasant hour of instruction and advice. Not less are we indebted to Dr. Theodore Goldstucker, a profound German scholar, whose Sanskrit class we attended in the University College. But his kindness was not confined to the classroom; he was ever ready with his advice and help whenever we needed it. A profound but eccentric scholar, fond of dictating and contradicting, but really kind-hearted and true, Dr. Goldstucker is quite a character, and is respected and esteemed most by those who know him most intimately.

We passed our days in the University College, either in the classrooms or in the library. In the evening we returned to our lodging-houses, took our dinner, went out for a stroll, returned and took a cup of tea, and then resumed our studies, which we kept up as long as we could. And in the morning, after a hasty bath and breakfast, we went to the College again. We had some introduction letters to some families living in or near London, and we also made the acquaintance of some others.

But our time was mostly passed in our own lodgings or the classroom during the past year.

At last the time for the Open Competition arrived. It was impossible to form any sort of conjecture what the result in our case would be, for over three hundred English students appeared in the examination, and the first fifty would be selected. We did not know where the three hundred odd students had been educated, where they had prepared themselves for the examination, and whether they would score higher marks than ourselves. Many of them had no doubt attended, like ourselves, classes in colleges in London or Oxford or Cambridge, but many had been specially trained for this particular examination by Mr. Wren, who passes many men from year to year. Others had come from schools and prepared themselves under other private teachers.

The examination, one of the stiffest in the world, lasted for a month or more. The subjects are various, but no one is compelled to take all subjects or any particular subject; each candidate takes what subjects he pleases, and candidates are judged by the aggregate marks they obtain in the subjects they take up. I had taken only five subjects—*i.e.* English (including History and Composition), Mathematics, Mental Philosophy, Natural Philosophy, and Sanskrit.

On each subject there is a paper examination and a *viva voce* examination. You will be interested to know something about my *viva voce* examinations. In English I had given a long list of books which I had read; every candidate had to do the same. My examiner looked over the long list and smiled, and inquired, "Have you read all these books?" I answered in the affirmative, but felt for a moment that I would have been wiser if I had mentioned only those authors whose works I had thoroughly and carefully studied. But my examiner was very fair; he did not test my memory about details, but sought to know if I had generally appreciated what I had read. "Which do you think to be the best of Shakespeare's plays?" "Why do you think so?" "What characters do you admire most?" "What do you see in this and that character to admire?" "Some say Gray's style of poetry has something in common with Milton's; what is your opinion?" "Do you find anything in common between Milton and Wordsworth?" "What do you think of such and such pieces of such and such authors?" And so on, with all the best English poets, until he came to Rogers. "I see you have included Rogers's 'Italy' among the pieces you have read. What do you think of Rogers as a poet?" "What is there that you admire in his style of writing?"

> "'Of all the fairest cities of the earth
> None is so fair as . . . ?'"

my examiner inquired. "Florence," I said, to his entire satisfaction. I felt that I had done fairly well in English, and even when I differed with my examiner in opinions about authors, he was fair enough to allow me to uphold my opinions and give my reasons, and was pleased with the same. I also did well in the paper examination, and when the result was out I was delighted to find that among about 325 candidates I stood second in order of merit in English, and had scored 420 marks out of 500.

In Sanskrit, Mr. Cowell, formerly of the Sanskrit College, Calcutta, was our examiner. I did remarkably well in that subject—by mere luck. I guessed the meaning of a passage from Sankaracharya's "Philosophy" and translated it, which my two Hindu fellow candidates—better Sanskrit scholars than myself—had not been able to do. I scored higher marks than they did, but I felt that I did not deserve it, for they really knew the language better than I did. I scored 430 out of 500 in Sanskrit. But here we are at a disadvantage as compared with English students. For they take up Latin and Greek—the full marks in those subjects are 1500—and English students easily get more marks in those subjects than we can possibly do in Sanskrit. In Mathematics, Todhunter, the writer of many text-books, was one of my examiners. He is a very fair examiner, but I was not very well up in Higher Mathematics, and did not score high marks. In Mental Philosophy I got fairly good marks. In Natural Philosophy Dr. Carpenter took Zoology, and is a very good examiner. The examiner in Electricity was not a fair examiner. However, I got good marks in Natural Philosophy on the whole.

We had to wait over a month before the result was out. It was a time of anxious suspense. When the result was out I found I had not only been selected, but that I stood third in the order of merit. I cannot describe the transport which I felt on that eventful day. My friends, too, had passed. The great undertaking on which we had staked everything in life had succeeded; the future of our life was determined, and a path, we ventured to hope, had been opened for our young countrymen.

The list of successful candidates contained the names of four Hindus—Messrs. Gupta, Dutt, Banerjea, and Sripad Babaji Thakur of Bombay, who had taken his B.A. degree from the Elphinstone College. This was a notable performance, for since the commencement of the competitive system of recruitment in 1853 only one Indian, Mr. Satyendra Nath Tagore, had succeeded in winning his way into the Indian Civil Service in 1863. Mr. Dutt was admitted unreservedly into the service. But his other two friends and Mr. Thakur were not so lucky. Difficulties arose about their ages, and the Commissioners accepted the explanation of Mr. Gupta only; but Messrs. Banerjea and Thakur had to go to the Court of Queen's Bench to establish their claims. Mr. Dutt worked hard to help his friends. They all received most generous assistance from their professors and other friends; and in Mr. Henry Morley, their large-hearted professor, they found their staunchest champion. He wrote a spirited letter to *All the Year Round*, which is of interest, not only for its generous advocacy of the case of the Indians who had been declared ineligible by the Civil Service Commissioners, but also for its valuable introductory history of the Civil Service Examinations, with special reference to the prospects of Indian candidates.

In this letter Professor Morley wrote of his pupils :—

These gentlemen reached England in April 1868, entered themselves at once to classes in University College, London, and worked hard during vacation with those professors and teachers who had time to spare for them. Wherever they became known, they made friends. *They came to this country well educated, were liberal of mind, most friendly to England, amiable, upright, and indefatigably hardworking men, in character and general attainment answering to the best class of English students.* They worked steadily for at least twelve, usually fourteen, fifteen, sixteen hours a day, as men well might who had staked so much as they were staking on success in the required examination. It was against their coming that they must break caste, oppose religious prejudices of their friends, cut themselves off in many things from their own people, travel four thousand miles, and maintain themselves alone in a strange country, for the chance—which experience declared to be a bad chance—of beating two or three hundred Englishmen on their own ground in their own subjects of study.

Among the many letters of congratulation which he received from his friends, Mr. Dutt preserved one from Mr. Luke Burke :—

MY DEAR MR. DUTT,—I have just seen your name and that of Mr. Gupta and Mr. Banerjea, in this morning's *Telegraph*, in the list of successful competitors at the Civil Service Examination, and it is, I assure you, with the most sincere pleasure that I congratulate you all on your success. This is one of those struggles in which no one, however well prepared, could feel sure of success, for what with youthful nervousness on the one hand, the inherent accidents of the case on the other, it might so happen that the most deserving would fail. I am therefore delighted that yourself and your friends are relieved from this great anxiety which has so long hung over you, and now I trust you will allow yourselves an ample holiday after all this desperate working, and a holiday, if possible, with some definite object which may fully but pleasantly occupy your minds, for otherwise you are in danger of sinking, when the mental strain is suddenly removed.

. . . .

The overworked students wanted some change and rest, and we find them at the seaside at Eastbourne.

We have at last left the crowded streets of old London for green fields and the seaside. As I am writing this letter to you, I am enjoying an extensive view of the deep blue ocean, a cool and refreshing sea-breeze, and the ceaseless music of the waves. Yesterday we went by sea to Beachy Head, which is four or five miles from Eastbourne. Beachy Head is 575 feet above the level of the sea, and when we ascended the top, we had a beautiful view all round. To walk in the green pasture lands and fields covered with the luxuriant verdure of spring, to scale the chalky cliffs of South England, or saunter on the green hills in the evening, silently watching the quiet windmills on the tops of hills, to hear the skylark pouring forth "harmonious madness" from its aerial height, to spend an evening on the pebbly beach, and hear the wild and ceaseless song of the restless waves which lull you not to sleep, but to gentle thoughts and meditation; to have a pleasant row on the green sea, or a pleasant trip to a neighbouring village, such has been our occupation since we left London, and a most delightful occupation it is, I can assure you, after a long and weary year spent amidst the smoke and toil and dust of old London.

II

Though Romesh Dutt realised to the full the primary obligation of devoting most of his time to preparing himself for the Service Examinations, he utilised his leisure moments to the best possible advantage. Although the time at his disposal was short, and his purse by no means long, he managed to see a good deal of the British Isles, including Ireland, and also something of the Continent, before he returned home. His great fondness for travel and his acute powers of observation were developed quite early in life. He was ever on the alert to assimilate new phases of social and political life, and there was no pleasure dearer to his contemplative mind than to dwell on the memories called up by places memorable in the political history of Europe, or marking the birthplace of some great man, famous in the annals of European literature or politics. He had an equally keen eye for the sublime and beautiful in Nature and Art.

The summer of 1868, from July to September, was spent in visiting the Scottish and English Lake Country. He was fascinated with Edinburgh. From Edinburgh he went to Linlithgow, and visited the ruins of the old palace. Here is an account of his visit to Stirling Castle :—

Stirling Castle is built on a high and precipitous rock, and must have been impregnable before firearms and artillery were invented. There is a room in the castle called the Douglas Room, where James II. invited a Douglas to a feast, and then stabbed him and threw the corpse out of a window.

"Dread towers within whose circuit dread
A Douglas by his sovereign bled."
—(*The Lady of the Lake.*)

The very corner in which the nobleman was stabbed, as well as the window through which the body was thrown out, were pointed to us. We also saw the strong tower where, we were assured, Roderic Dhu was really imprisoned by James V. and where he breathed his last! But the chief interest lies not in the rooms within the castle but in the celebrated fields surrounding it. Standing on the highest point of the castle with your face to the south-east, you see on your left the field of Stirling—the scene of Wallace's greatest victory—while on your right, about three miles off, is the scene of Bruce's greatest victory—the field of Bannockburn. About an hour's walk brought us to the field of Bannockburn. We sat on the "Borestone" on which the Scottish standard is said to have been erected, and looked on the fields where the Scots who had bled with Wallace, and whom Bruce had often led, found, not a gory bed, but a victory glorious indeed. In a few moments a noble commander and a noble army secured the independence of their country.

He left Stirling and reached Callander, whence he travelled by stage-coach to the Trossachs.

Slowly our coach rolled on over hills and by lakes and deep ravines, and through beautiful glens. During the first part of our journey we saw nothing around us but bleak ridges of high mountains like giants guarding the land. Mountain brooks we crossed without number, with their pure crystal waters foaming and clattering on their beds of rocks.

The Trossachs Pass and Loch Katrine and Loch Lomond are certainly the most beautiful spots in the world. Crag over crag, hill over hill, and high peaks towering over all, with mountain trees and plants waving in the breeze, form a noble scene indeed; while little river streams rumbling and leaping, now from a mass of rocks and now through a shady glen, add to the wildness of the scene.

In about an hour's time we came to Loch Katrine, and a beautiful panorama suddenly burst upon our sight. On all sides high rugged hills rise abruptly from the banks of the lake, while beneath, the calm waters of the lake stretch out in a thousand gulfs and bays and inlets. Mountain rills roll down in crystal torrents, glistening and leaping and dancing from crag to crag, and seeming almost like a continuous shower of diamonds and molten silver, and at last mingling with the tranquil waters of the lake.

And so on, his contemplative mind revelled in the beauty and splendour of Scottish scenes.

Then he visited Glasgow, Oban, Iona, Glencoe, Ben Nevis, Aberdeen, Rosslyn, and Melrose. While at Melrose he would not, of course, miss Abbotsford.

> Next morning we went to see the seat of Sir W. Scott, at Abbotsford, about three miles from Melrose. The beautiful and extensive building stands on the banks of the Tweed. In his study room there is still the chair as well as the table used by Scott when he wrote his novels. His library contains about 20,000 volumes, which have been preserved with great care. In the drawing-room we saw the likeness of Scott, as well as those of his eldest son and three daughters. Among the many curious things which we saw in this room was a collection of beautiful presents which Sir Walter had received from various quarters. In his armoury there were arms and weapons of warfare of different countries and different ages, including the Persian scimitar and the Indian sword, as well as a large number of arms connected with the border warfare of the Middle Ages—a subject in which Scott took such a deep interest, and which he has depicted so well.

From Melrose he went on to Carlisle and Penrith, and through the Lake Country. On the way southward he visited most of the places of interest.

His impression of the general election of 1868, and his reflections on the political institutions of the British people, will bear repetition.

> During the last fortnight (5th to 20th November 1868) London and in fact the whole of the British Isles have been in a state of great excitement on account of the Parliamentary elections going on. The amount of excitement in London on the day of the election was simply incredible. Booths were erected every here and there, and voters came to these booths to give their votes. The streets were crowded with people, those who had votes and those who had not, and all engaged in the one absorbing topic of conversation, while the candidates for election could be seen going about from place to place, and from booth to booth with an agitation of mind which can easily be imagined. All the voters were to give their votes on that particular day, and as the day advanced the public could guess pretty correctly what the result in the evening would be, for the number of votes given for each candidate was published hourly in a hundred newspapers to satisfy the insatiate anxiety of the people.

To a reflecting observer this interest which the English take in politics has a meaning and a significance. Every man in this country considers himself as a constituent of a great nation, prides himself on his nationality and the glory of the nation, and therefore keeps an eye on the welfare of his country. Go and speak to the commonest tailor, the commonest green-grocer, the commonest bootmaker in London, and he will tell you the amount of the national debt, he will tell you who introduced such and such a bill, and what likelihood it has of passing, he will argue with you as to the good or evil effects of a bill lately introduced in Parliament. Your cabman will tell you that this bill will pass and t'other bill not, and your boatman will inform you that "them Conservatives are no good." Among such a people, as may be expected, *most improvements emanate from the people, for the people are the government.* Societies are formed by the persons desirous of bringing on some reform; they have their sittings, their lectures, their pamphlets; they write articles in newspapers, they publish books to support their cause. Thus they go on influencing the public mind and convincing the people that a reform is needed. When they are strong enough they make a representation in Parliament, they have a bill introduced by some Member who may be of the same opinion with themselves. The bill may be defeated once, twice, three times, perhaps, but that does not matter; they go on quietly with their work with a patience and perseverance which is almost incredible. They know that the will of the people is the law of the land, and if the people show increasing interest in their cause they are sure to succeed, otherwise their cause must of course be given up. Societies and leagues of this kind exist in England without number, and it is really a wonder how patiently and perseveringly they work. Sometimes the generation which started an association may pass away, but new members come in, the next generation takes up the cause, and the association lives and works on still trying to influence the public mind. *For public opinion is the law of the land which sways the country without a rival, and before which the Queen, the Lords, the Commons must all give way.* The Queen and the nobility do not oppose it, and if the Commons act contrary to it, another set of Members are sure to be returned at the next election who are of the same opinion as the public. Such is England, a country where the people govern themselves —what wonder if such a people have secured for themselves an amount of political liberty which is nowhere else to be found on the face of the globe, America alone excepted. . . .

Is it to be wondered at that the man who had realised so clearly the wonderful vitality and power of British constitutional agitation should have such undying faith himself in its efficacy?

During the winters of 1870 and 1871 the sufferings of the London poor naturally attracted his sympathy. Here are his observations on perhaps the most important as well as the most difficult problem of the English social fabric.

The problem of the condition of the poor engages the attention of Englishmen, and is, in the present cold season, exciting deep interest. Notwithstanding many noble qualities, the lower classes of England are in many respects very far from what they ought to be, and their character is soiled by some of the worst vices of human nature. Drunkenness and cruelty to wives prevail to a fearful extent among them, their independence often borders on insolence, and their remarkable imprudence necessarily makes them wretched. They form the only uneducated class of people in England, and their want of education makes them incapable of improving their condition. What is wanted for them is education, and effective steps are being taken to spread education to all classes of people in England.

Would you step into their dwelling-place? You see a small room in a smoky lane, crowded with members of a large family, an elderly mother with children from the girl of fourteen or fifteen to the baby in her arms, all huddled together in one uncomfortable room. The broken panes do not keep off the wintry blast, and want of sufficient food, sufficient clothing, and of coal to warm the room, presents a sight of misery compared to which the poorest classes of people in our own country are well off. The paterfamilias is troubled out of his wits to support such a large family; the misery and sufferings he gets familiar with make him callous in his feelings, and a cheerless home impels him to seek comfort elsewhere. Where is he to seek such comfort? Why, London is swamped with public-houses, blazing with volumes of gas, with comfortable seats and comfortable fires to invite the poor labourer to a few glasses of beer. These public-houses are the resorts of the London labourer, and out of his scanty earning he learns to spend something on intoxication. Thus flying from a cheerless home he learns to become a drunkard. What follows?—A scene, the horrors of which it is difficult to picture. Drunkenness brings out the most brutal passions of the human mind, and cruelty such as is unheard of among the poorest families of our country, disfigures the conduct of the London "rough" towards his own kith and kin. Pestered and bothered by a hungry wife and starving children, the drunken husband and father often has recourse to violence, the accounts of which, emanating every day from the police courts, fail to startle the people only on account of their frequency. Death is a frequent visitor of such homes, and little boys willingly leave them to turn "street arabs," running about with naked feet and uncovered head to beg a few pence from the passers by.

In 1870 he went to Cambridge, Brighton, the Isle of Wight, Windsor Castle, Eton College, and then paid a visit to the country.

No foreigner should leave England without passing a few days in the country. Immediately before leaving for Ireland I passed a few days with a gentleman at his country seat, and an English country seat is a thing of itself worth seeing. The neat and well-built country house of the landlord, well known to the peasantry all round, the wide portico and beautiful gardens and croquet lawns adjacent to it, the ornamental waters and the darksome shrubbery delightfully cool in summer, the fresh, open country prospect all round with distant hills seen far off on the horizon, the beautiful glades and long avenues and extensive country parks with deer grazing by hundreds, the village hedgerows with wild flowers blooming on them, and taking the traveller by surprise by their sweet scent, and last though not the least, the neat huts dotting the country fields, and the village church lifting its modest spire from among them—these are scenes really worth seeing. But this is not all. In the country you find Englishmen from altogether a different and a new point of view. Freed from the conventionalities of London, the Englishman in his country seat is much more free and unfettered, much more jovial, and at home with every one whom he comes across. It is a delight to see him mixing freely and almost familiarly with the poor villagers, asking them kind questions about their homes and lands, and the prospects of the year, and stretching out a helping hand to them in times of need. Every village girl too knows well the familiar faces of the landlord's wife and daughters, and kind questions and inquiries on the one side and a confiding and respectful regard on the other sweeten their acquaintance, and in some cases ripen it into almost sisterly affection.

Mr. Dutt was certainly not lacking either in imagination or openness of mind to appreciate the best traits of English character.

In June and July of 1870 he undertook a journey through Ireland and Wales. He reached Dublin on the 21st June, and from Dublin went to Avoca. He then visited Bray and Boyne, Drogheda, Belfast, Londonderry, and Enniskillen. He would not, of course, miss seeing the "deserted village," where he saw the ruins of the village preacher's modest mansion. From Athlone he went to Limerick, and from Limerick to the "magnificent lakes" of Killarney, "the pride of Ireland, and equal in picturesque beauty to the most beautiful lakes of Scotland."

> We took a long drive in a car, and then had a ride through one of the wildest valleys that I have ever seen, the "Gap of Dunloe." Emerging from that valley we came to the lakes and took a boat. The scenes through which we then passed defy all description. Enough be it to say that it is the wildest and the most picturesque scene that can be made up of mountains, rivulets, lakes, islands, creeks, promontories, and wild vegetation.

From Killarney he went to Cork. In concluding his letter on Ireland he makes the following observations on the Irish peasantry :—

> As for the villagers, they are poor indeed. Man, wife, and children, a good round number in all, are often seen working in the same field, in sun and rain, and are housed together in the night, probably with their pigs and geese, in the same wretched hut. This is not the only fertile country in which the cultivators are exceedingly poor.

Then he paid a visit to Bristol, where he saw the grave of Raja Ram Mohan Ray. He visited Milford Haven, Carmarthen, Aberystwyth, Carnarvon, Snowdon, and Conway in Wales before returning to London, which he reached on the 14th July.

On his way home from London he travelled through the Continent and embarked at Brindisi, thus taking the opportunity of seeing most of the important places that lay in his route. He left London on the 14th August and reached Paris on the 15th, just after the conclusion of the Peace of Versailles.

Paris, the most splendid city in the world, is now in ruins. The Hôtel de Ville, which was decorated with finest specimens of art, and was in fact the national hall of France, has been utterly demolished and burnt down. The splendid Palais Royal is in ruins, the column of Vendôme, which commemorated the victories of the first Napoleon and was a monument of the glories of France, has been thrown down, and only the base remains, on which you see beautiful carvings. Even the Tuileries, the residence of the kings and emperors of France, has been seriously injured, and in some places totally demolished, and one feels a strange sort of feeling as he walks about these deserted gardens and lingers near the desolated walls and statues.

He saw most of what was to be seen in Paris—the Arch of Triumph, Notre Dame, Napoleon's tomb, St. Cloud, and Versailles. On his return from Versailles he and his friends met with a curious adventure.

When we came to the railway station to book for Paris, we were required by a police officer to show our passport. We did so, and he seemed to be satisfied. Soon after, however, he came up to us and asked us to follow him to the guard-house to have our passport examined! I believe our foreign costume had aroused his suspicions, and he took us for Communists! He seemed to be polite enough, and informed us on our way to the guard-house that Paris and Versailles swarmed with Communists, and that he had therefore considered it his duty to conduct us to the guard-house to have us examined. At the guard-house we were met by the officer in charge, a petty *hakim*, who in a rather insolent manner required us to produce our passport. Though it had been *viséd* by the French Consul, he seemed to have his doubts about it. As we did not know French sufficiently well to enable us to carry on conversation in that language, he put us a few questions on paper. He wrote down that we had been arrested as strangers without proper papers, and inquired if we had anything to say in reply. In answer to this we wrote down that the passport, which we had produced, had been *viséd* by the French Consul. He treated the passport with contempt, and peremptorily demanded proofs of our identity! Any satisfactory evidence on this point it was, of course, impossible to produce on the spot. We produced what proofs we could, including some letters addressed to one of us which we happened to have with us. This, of course, was not considered satisfactory, especially as they were in English, and we were sent under an escort to the police bureau. The commissaire not happening to be in, we were, without any further ceremony, locked up for the night in a miserable cell, and with no better accommodation than a wide wooden bench for bed! We were kept in that place for twelve hours, and about ten o'clock in the morning we were brought before the police commissaire. He read the report of the officer who had arrested us, examined our passport, and failed to discover why we had been arrested! We were at once released, and on our expressing our desire to bring the matter to the notice of the higher authorities, he unhesitatingly gave us a note certifying that we had been arrested without any proper cause having been assigned. We went with this paper to the Police Prefecture, represented the circumstances of the arrest, and were asked to put them down on paper. The officials expressed regret for what had happened, and assured us that the officer who had arrested us would be dismissed from the service. With this assurance we had to be content. We were fortunate that we were not tried and shot on mere suspicion, as many an innocent man has been in these dark days!

On the morning of the 18th August Mr. Dutt and his friends left for Cologne, and from Cologne they travelled to Bonn, and thence to Baden-Baden, the Falls of Schaffhausen, Zürich, and Lucerne. From Lucerne he wrote:—

An old town situated by the lake of Lucerne, perhaps the prettiest lake in Europe. This charming lake glitters in the midst of high mountains whose snowy tops glisten in the sun. The view from the top of the Rigi is certainly one of the best that I have ever seen. Beneath us we saw the lakes of Lucerne and Zug, blue as emerald and calm and beautiful—as beautiful as they could be—while the towns of Zug and Lucerne situated on their respective lakes glistened in the sun. The steamers or sails floating on the calm blue surface of the lakes looked like small specks from the height, while field after field with small elevations and declivities, which could scarcely be marked from the top of Rigi, seemed stretching on as far as the eye could reach. All this was, however, on the north and east. Towards the south and west you would see mountains, nothing but mountains, magnificent peaks penetrating through all mist and cloud, and

"Throning eternity in icy halls."

So noble a scene I had never seen before, and a more magnificent one it is certainly impossible to conceive.

Berne, Lausanne, Chillon, and Geneva were then visited. The following is his impression of the Swiss peasantry :—

As one travels through this beautiful mountainous country one cannot fail being struck with the happy condition of even the lowest classes of the people. Go to the poorest villages and you will see the beautiful and neatly varnished and painted wooden huts which are peculiar to Switzerland, with carefully cultivated fields and lawns adjoining them, and a happy and contented peasantry, passionately fond of their homes and country. In neatness, in intelligence, and even in a gentlemanlike sense of politeness, the Swiss peasant presents a marked contrast to the peasantry of most other European countries, and notably of England. Women comfortably seated outside their huts and sewing their linen in the sun, and healthy little children neatly dressed, and running about in the neat and garden-like fields, form an interesting sight to be seen only among the peasantry of this happy Republic.

Through the St. Gothard Pass he emerged into Italy. He saw Como, Milan, and Venice. At Venice he saw the prison, containing miserable holes, completely dark, with an almost suffocating atmosphere, and with pieces of wood for beds, and small holes in the walls for food to be thrown in.

We felt a chill of horror as we conceived the pangs every prisoner must have undergone in those cells, when the massive doors were closed upon them, perhaps not to be opened for years to come. We passed by these, and then came to the political prisons—if possible still more terrible than the prisons for the criminals. The cells of the political prisoners were closer than the others, and even the pieces of wood which served as beds to the criminals were denied to the political prisoners. Miserable, damp, dark, dirty cells, without seat, without bed, with hardly air enough for breathing, without one ray of the light of heaven, such are the places where many a noble-minded prisoner has lingered away his existence.

III

Mr. Dutt and his friends had been furnished with introductions to many English families, and during their stay they were welcome guests at many English homes. The stir and excitement which Mr. Dutt witnessed at the general election of 1868, which returned the Liberals to power and made Gladstone for the first time Prime Minister, has already been referred to. He secured admission to the House of Commons, and listened to the speeches of Gladstone and Disraeli, and had personal introductions to John Bright and Henry Fawcett, the greatest friends of India in those days. He attended meetings where John Stuart Mill spoke or Charles Dickens gave readings from his novels; he was present at receptions at the India Office, given by the Duke of Argyll, then Secretary of State for India.

Among his own countrymen, he was acquainted with Mr. Dadabhai Naoroji, who was even in those days the recognised leader of Indian constitutional agitation in England. It would appear from the following letter, preserved by Mr. Dutt, that he was not an infrequent visitor at the sittings of the East India Association.

MY DEAR MR. DUTT,—Of course you should attend to your studies first. You cannot and ought not to let anything else jeopardise your position on the list, or your ultimate success at the final examination. If you could conveniently attend the meetings of our Association I shall be glad. There is some chance of the education question coming before the Association, but I am not sure yet. Kind regards to Mr. Banerjea.—Yours truly,

DADABHAI NAOROJI.

Romesh Ch. Dutt, 4 Charles Crescent, Primrose Hill.

Even in his student days he could not resist the temptation of entering the lists and taking up his pen in the defence of the threatened rights of his countrymen. We find a letter from his pen appearing in the *Asiatic* of the 19th August 1870, against the proposal of the Duke of Argyll to make the income-tax permanent in India, and the proposal of the Government to withdraw aid from higher education, and to teach the masses through the medium of the vernacular only. With his usual promptness and vigour, he followed up this letter by having a memorial of the then residents of Bengal written out for presentation to the Secretary of State. This, however, was never submitted.

The *Asiatic* published some views opposed to his, and Mr. Dutt again returned to the charge, and another lengthy letter appeared from his pen on the 20th September. The following observations which occurred in this letter have a more than passing interest :—

I may here add that even for the extension of vernacular education there can be no more efficacious means than English education. The natives of Bengal who are educated in English are naturally desirous of imparting the benefit they receive to the mass of the people—are naturally desirous of extending education to their fellow-countrymen—but mass education must always begin with the vernacular, and thus those who are educated in English are the means of a rapid extension of the vernacular education. This is not merely an idle theory, but is borne out by statistics. In 1856 the number of vernacular schools in Bengal was only 54; in 1869 the number had increased to 2962, and this increase of number is mainly owing to the "exertions of native gentlemen educated in English under the fostering influence of the grant-in-aid system." Further, this is the period of the formation of the Bengali language and literature, and during this period the Bengali necessarily borrows vastly from the English literature, as the English did from the Latin and the Italian during the period of its formation, viz. during the fourteenth, fifteenth, and sixteenth centuries. As a consequence, the best books in Bengali have, during the last twenty years, been written by men who were or are thoroughly well educated in English, and the improvement of the Bengali literature will, for years to come, depend on the extent to which English is taught in Bengal. So that from whatever point the question may be viewed, it is impossible to escape the conclusion that the cultivation of the vernacular languages will necessarily depend on the extent to which English is taught in Bengal, and that, therefore, one of the ostensible reasons for withdrawing state aid from English Education, namely, to facilitate the cultivation of the vernacular languages, is evidently one of the strongest grounds for its future maintenance.

The discussion of this important subject both in England and India evoked a comprehensive article on "Mass Education in Bengal" in the columns of the *Asiatic*. Mr. Dutt considered it his duty to still further emphasise his position by another letter, which appeared on the 29th November. The letter is important as being the first record of Mr. Dutt's ideas on the larger question of British administration in India, and is marked by the comprehensiveness of view which always characterised his political utterances. In fact, what he says in this letter contains the essence of most of his later appeals for the adoption of a higher standard and a more liberal outlook in the discussion of the administrative problems of India.

That India has derived incalculable benefits from the British rule—that she is better governed now than she was under any of her preceding rulers, are facts which will not be denied, and for which the people of India cannot be too grateful to the English. But those Englishmen who plume themselves by instituting a comparison between the enlightened English rule and that of Muhammadans, *do injustice to England by adopting so low a standard of comparison.* The question is, not whether India is better governed now than under the Muhammadans, but whether India could not be still better governed if English legislators had thought fit to direct a part of their attention in that direction. For the sake of the permanency of the British rule, if for nothing else, a closer union must be contracted with the natives of the country than, I am grieved to say, has yet been done. The time has surely arrived when the fair principle of representation may be introduced in the Indian Government; when the many obstacles to Indians holding respectable situations may be gradually removed; when an Indian militia and a corps of volunteers may be raised to guard the soil; and last, though not the least, when by a wider extension of English education (not simply vernacular, as is proposed), the people of India may be better convinced of the numerous advantages resulting from the British rule, and therefore more willing for the continuance of the same.

On the 7th June 1871 the list appeared of the gentlemen who were called to the Bar, and the names of both Romesh Dutt and B. L. Gupta were in it. The list of the successful candidates of the final examination of the Indian Civil Service appeared on the 5th July; Mr. Dutt's name stood second. And now the time for the return to India had come.

I have now done my three years' work in England [he wrote to his brother]—I have gone through the four "further examinations" which we have to pass in Law, Political Economy, and History and Languages of India, after being selected at the Open Competition. I have been called to the Bar after keeping twelve terms at the Middle Temple. I have seen different places of interest in England, and have, I hope, learnt some lessons that will be useful to me in life from the everyday life and manners, the characters and virtues, of Englishmen. We in India have an ancient and noble civilisation, but nevertheless we have much to learn from modern civilisation. And I hope, as we become more familiar with Europe and with England, we shall adopt some great virtues and some noble institutions which are conspicuous in Europe in the present day, and which we need so much. Our children's children will live to see the day when India will take her place among the nations of the earth in manufacturing industry and commercial enterprise, in representative institutions, and in real social advancement. May that day dawn early for India.

The record of the hard work done by Romesh Dutt during his three years' stay in England, and the unflinching resolution with which he accomplished all the objects that he had set before him, must for a long time to come remain an example for his young countrymen.

And here we may anticipate the home-coming of the three conquering heroes. In October 1871, the three successful young men returned to their country, and received a warm welcome. A garden party was organised at the Seven Tanks garden-house, and an address was presented to them. At the close of the ceremony, Mr. Dutt replied in the following terms:—

I am not aware that we have done anything for our country. If, indeed, we have done anything to merit your approbation, we shall consider ourselves amply rewarded if my countrymen were to follow our example. I do not, indeed, wish you to slavishly imitate everything English, but I do think that there are many things estimable in English manners which we may with advantage introduce into our own social institutions. I would therefore beg of you, gentlemen, to try your best to send as many young men as possible to England, for there they would imbibe ideas of liberty and equality between men and women.

CHAPTER IV

OFFICIAL APPRENTICESHIP (1871–1882)

I

ON the 28th September 1871, Mr. Dutt was appointed Assistant Magistrate of Alipur. After about a year, on the 7th November 1872, he was sent to Jangipur in Murshidabad as subdivisional officer, and after a few months' stay there, in the February of the following year, he went to Bongong. While in charge of that subdivision he took a special interest in helping the schools and *pathsalas* of the place. For the construction of a new house for the local school he himself contributed Rs.150. On the 8th of May he was transferred to Meherpur.

The famine of 1874 found him employed as a Relief Officer in the west of Meherpur, in the neighbourhood of the famous field of Plassey, and his name appears in the list of officers who did commendable work in connection with the famine. But about this time he had some differences with the Naddea planters, and he feared that in consequence his official prospects would suffer.

> But one has no resource [he wrote to his brother from Karimpur] but to receive fortune's smiles and buffets with equal grace. My own prospect is not very bright. When I was last at Krishnaghar Mr. Stevens informed me that I had a fair chance of being an Officiating Joint Magistrate within a year. The representations of the planters have, I have reasons to know, prejudiced both the Magistrate and the Commissioner, and it may be years before I am recommended to be a Joint. But I feel a pride at being thus a martyr to my duty. I was not born to wealth or to good fortune, but I live to do my duty, and that inspires me with an exaltation to which rich men's pleasures are nothing.

There is, perhaps, a vein of sentimentalism in this mood; yet even here, at the beginning of his service, Mr. Dutt was schooling himself to that firm adherence to duty at all costs which distinguished him throughout his official career.

In November 1874, after the abatement of the scarcity, Mr. Dutt was sent back to Bongong, where he remained till 1876. In that year came his first great opportunity. He was sent to Dakhin Shahbazpur to fight the combined ravages of famine and pestilence in that unfortunate island. The following account of this dire visitation of Nature occurs in his "Rambles in India":—

A more terrible calamity than the famine of 1874 visited Bengal in 1876 in the shape of the cyclone and storm-wave of the 31st October, and it is estimated that a hundred thousand people were drowned in that memorable night by the waves which swept over villages, towns, and districts.

The subdivision of Dakhin Shahbazpur, which is an island in the mouths of the Ganges, suffered most terribly from this dire visitation, and forty thousand of its population are estimated to have been drowned in that night. The waters, piled up by the tide and the storm, rose above 20 feet in the eastern parts of the island, and the wonder is that any one survived in those parts. But habitations in those places are surrounded by clusters of betel-nut trees, and the thatched roofs of houses floated and clung to those trees, and many were thus saved. Death made little distinction of age; strong healthy men were washed away and drowned, and little infants were found the next morning floating with their mothers on thatches, uninjured and unconscious of the danger they had escaped.

The poor Deputy Magistrate of the subdivision, and his wife, survived by clinging to trees all night, but they lost all their family, four sons and two daughters, I believe, and some grandsons. The Deputy Magistrate went on leave immediately after, and I was transferred from Krishnaghar to take charge of the subdivision amidst these circumstances of calamity and distress.

The railway line from Calcutta to Khulna had not been laid then, and it took me six days to go in a Green Boat through the wilds of the Sundarbans to Barisal. I did not regret this delay, for the Sundarbans have a beauty of their own. Much of that great forest has been cleared in these late years, but twenty years back the route lay through interminable woods and silent creeks which were imposing in their solitude. It is said that the country was higher in some past age, and was the seat of villages, towns, and forts, the remains of which are still discovered from time to time in the jungles. By a strange freak of nature the land has subsided, human habitation is now impossible, and the royal tiger has established his unmolested rule in these vast solitudes of nature. Emerging from these forests, I at last came to the district of Backerganj, a very remarkable district in many ways. The people are mostly Muhammadans, a fine and stalwart race, but much given to fighting and litigation.

I reached Dakhin Shahbazpur about the close of November 1876, and the scene which the island presented was one which can never be forgotten. No battlefield could be more dismal and more shocking. The huts of the people had been swept clean away, and the remnants of the population were living under temporary sheds or under trees. Numerous families had disappeared altogether, and there was scarcely any which did not lose some of its members. Grief itself was silenced, for the calamity had been so awful, so instantaneous and so universal, that the survivors were rather stunned than given to sorrowing, and I heard no sound of wail or lamentation. The land was sprinkled with the dead, and dead putrefying bodies caused no emotion, no disgust. Dead bodies hung on trees, floated on tanks, were strewn in the fields, and came floating up, past my boat, at every tide; and the dogs which had survived the storm-wave fed on the carcasses without molestation. To bury tens of thousands of the dead was impossible; the survivors would not touch them at this stage of putrefaction. People were busy in constructing temporary sheds, in procuring food for the surviving members of their families, in looking for their lost properties. The subdivisional building had been swept away, the police were disorganised, the Chaukidars would not do their work. Everything was out of joint.

No Communist could wish for a more general redistribution of property than was caused by this great storm-wave of 1876, in the island of Dakhin Shahbazpur. Herds of cows and buffaloes had been floated twenty or thirty miles from their villages, wooden boxes containing utensils and silver ornaments had been carried away miles from the homes of their owners, and every one kept what he found, and gave up what was lost. Some search was, however, made from time to time for lost property, and occasionally a box of silver things or of brass articles was found by its owner in the keeping of a villager living perhaps ten miles off. Complaints were brought before me, but it was impossible to treat as "criminal misappropriation" a practice which had become so universal, under circumstances so unique. It was decided by the people themselves that property so found should be restored to its owner, but the finder would keep one quarter of his booty, if he honestly rendered up all the rest. I tacitly acquiesced in this decision, which was neither legal nor very just, but which suited the circumstances and the notions of the people. Hundreds of complaints were withdrawn, all disputes over properties found were amicably settled, and the people thought a Daniel had come to the judgment seat of Dakhin Shahbazpur!

More serious disputes however ensued in another way. As might naturally be expected, many more women than men had perished in the great catastrophe of the 31st of October, and among the survivors, especially in the eastern and southern parts of the island, which had been most exposed to the storm-wave, there was a great disproportion among the sexes. Widowers found a difficulty in getting new housewives for themselves either in the island or from outside it, as few parents cared to send their daughters to such an island, after such a calamity. And many a fight was fought by eager candidates for the hands of the women who had survived and been widowed by the catastrophe.

The island was now overtaken by another calamity scarcely less fatal than what had preceded. The numberless carcasses of men and of cattle had polluted the air and contaminated the tanks, and a cholera epidemic broke out, the like of which I have never witnessed, nor would like to see again. It spread in every village and affected almost every homestead, and created a universal alarm. It swept away the survivors of the storm-wave in many homesteads, and the homesteads became deserted. It drove the population from many villages to others which were supposed to be more healthy. Fires were lighted in every house, as it was supposed to kill the infection, and men and women and children sat round the fire in that dismal winter, and refused all work for the time. Men clung to their homes and almost suspended all business, and Chaukidars often resigned their appointments, rather than go on with their ordinary duties under such trying circumstances.

All that it was possible for the authorities to do was done to relieve the sufferers. A great many Native Doctors were sent, and cholera pills, in which the people had great faith, were distributed to the people through all possible agencies. But in spite of every endeavour there was a great mortality, and it is supposed over twenty thousand people were swept away within a few months in this island by this terrible epidemic. Nor did cholera abate till the rain set in and washed away all impurities from the soil, and replenished the tanks with good drinkable water.

It was from scenes like this that I was called away to Barisal, the headquarters of the district, on the 1st January 1877, to assist in proclaiming in that district that Her Gracious Majesty had assumed the title of Empress of India.

I returned to my subdivision, and worked there throughout the year 1877. I have promised not to inflict on my readers an account of my work, and it is enough to say that the Musalman population of Dakhin Shahbazpur, a sturdy and self-reliant race, faced the worst season with admirable courage, and helped themselves under the most trying circumstances. Their crops had perished, or been seriously damaged by the storm-wave, and the peasantry of the island lived on what they had saved, or sold their things and silver jewellery to import rice from other places. A small and helpless section of the community needed relief, and obtained it for a month or two, and when at last the winter paddy of 1877–78 was reaped, all danger was past and all distress was over. And I left the island in April 1878, after passing an eventful year and a half in this island subdivision.

The following extract from the letter of a local correspondent, written to the *Hindoo Patriot* on 28th July 1877, shows how Mr. Dutt's services were appreciated by the people of the subdivision themselves :—

Fortunate it was that the charge of the subdivision was in the hands of an able officer of the covenanted Civil Service. A more worthy and able officer could not have been found. His broad sympathy for the people, and a high sense of the trust placed on him made him really fit to remain in charge of affairs. Since December he and his assistant Babu Surjya Kumar Sen, Deputy Magistrate, have exerted their best in organising the subdivision. They have gone from village to village, house to house, and inquired into the state of the people and the crops. They have acted with great energy during the prevalence of cholera, and done immense benefit to the inhabitants.

Mr. Dutt himself is inspecting the three relief centres on the north every week, and taking every pains to make himself acquainted with the real state of the people. Every machinery or agency at his command is being utilised for the purpose, and all concerned seem to be anxious to help the people out of the present difficulty. With the greatest economy and least noise, he is carrying out a scheme which would have cost others double the amount, and we only hope that Government will support him in his generous endeavours. Calm, considerate, and bold, Mr. Dutt is a quiet sort of a man, and has his work uppermost in his heart. But for him this subdivision would hardly have recovered. We earnestly hope his endeavours will be crowned with success. We pray to God that he may live a long life, and earn the approbation of Government and his countrymen.

Well did Mr. Dutt deserve these flattering encomiums of his countrymen. It is hard to imagine circumstances more likely to try the utmost resources of mind and body than those which met this young officer of only five years' standing when he went to Dakhin Shahbazpur, and it was only his genius as an administrator that enabled him to overcome all difficulties, and to restore peace and order in the stricken island. The cyclone had practically swept away all vestige of the administrative machinery of the subdivision, and what was wanting in the work of destruction and demoralisation of the people caused by the cyclone, was completed by the frightful epidemic of cholera which followed.

In 1883, when he was appointed Collector of Barisal, Mr. Dutt visited Bhola again, and in his letter to his brother, written in July 1883, he thus described his visit and the memories which it awakened in him :—

My visit to Bhola was pleasurable to me in other respects. Everywhere I saw my own handiwork—the embankments I had raised, the court-houses I had built, the trees I had planted, the things I had selected and arranged after the disastrous cyclone. It was an unfeigned pleasure for an official too, to learn that his services have not been forgotten by a grateful people. My name is on the lips of every resident of the island, and I received a perfect ovation—far more sincere than many ovations which are got up and organised in more civilised places for higher officials. A theatrical performance ("Sarojini" was the piece chosen !) came off last night, and this morning I could scarcely extricate myself from the people, who surrounded me previous to my departure. One enthusiastic admirer said in pure simplicity, that the Egyptians of old fasted six months, gazing on the face of a certain prophet or king, and that he (the speaker) could starve himself for three days at least to have a sight of me again !

II

After a short leave Mr. Dutt was appointed to Tippera, and from Tippera to Katwa, a subdivision of Burdwan; and thence he went to Bankura in 1880. From Bankura he wrote to his brother in March 1880:—

> I suspected when I saw my transfer to this district gazetted, that Government would give me this district if my turn for a district came within this year. The reason of my suspecting this was, you know, that the district is a light one, and that there is no European subordinate to the Magistrate except the Police Superintendent. It now seems that the intentions of Government are of a more thorough-going nature, and that they intend to try here the experiment of a purely native administration of a district. For the English Judge of this district has been transferred, and in his place we shall get a Bengali Additional Judge who would be the judicial head of the district. The doctor here is a Bengali, R. L. Dutt, and the Police Superintendent is about to retire, and a Bengali may possibly be sent in his place. Then there will be no single European official in the district left except the Magistrate, Mr. Anderson, and should my turn for a district come within the year, Mr. Anderson may be removed elsewhere and I may get this district. Of course much of the above is surmise only, but the surmise is a likely one. I for one will rejoice if Government makes this experiment; and though I feel the heavy responsibility which will rest on me, nevertheless I shall willingly stake my reputation and my prospects in service on the success of the experiment.

A justifiable confidence in his own powers, and an ambition to prove himself worthy in whatever sphere it might please Government to place him, were characteristic traits of his official career. The suspicion which appears to have troubled his youthful mind was not born without some cause, and the humiliation of this differential treatment the more noble-minded amongst English civilians of his day were themselves generous enough to acknowledge openly. In his memorable speech in the India Council on the 9th March 1883, on the occasion of the introduction of the Ilbert Bill, Sir William Hunter observed:—

The native civilians have now reached a stage in their service when they must become, in the natural course, District Magistrates and Sessions Judges. We have guaranteed to them equal rights with their English brethren, yet they must be excluded from those offices in the more eligible districts, where English private enterprise exists, and they must be turned out of those offices in any districts into which English private enterprise comes. Let me illustrate this by two examples; one taken from Bengal, the other from Bombay. On the 17th January last, a native civilian was, in the ordinary course, appointed Joint Magistrate, with powers of a Magistrate of the first class, at the important station of Dacca. On the 23rd January, he received a letter from the Secretary to the Bengal Government, cancelling the appointment and transferring him to a less eligible district, on the ground that the opening out of the Dacca and Mymensingh railway was bringing a number of Europeans into Dacca district.

And this unfortunate civilian was Mr. Dutt himself.

But the experiment was tried, and a native of India was for the first time placed in executive charge of a district. Mr. A. Baruah officiated as Magistrate and Collector in Dinajpur for a few months in 1880, Mr. B. L. Gupta acted as Magistrate and Collector of Rangpur for a month in 1881, and Mr. R. C. Dutt officiated as Magistrate and Collector of Bankura for three months in 1881, and again as Magistrate and Collector of Balasore for three months in 1882. After this, in December 1882, Government in their official letter approved of Mr. Dutt's and Mr. Baruah's election of the executive line, and thus formally opened the appointment of District Officer to natives of India. Naturally this experiment aroused some hostile criticism in the columns of the Anglo-Indian journals. Of these the most sober and thoughtful were the following reflections, which appeared in the *Pioneer* of the 20th October 1882:—

A striking fact is recorded in the last number of the Bengal Civil List. Mr. Romesh Chunder Dutt, C.S., is entered there as Officiating Magistrate of Balasore. We believe this is the first occasion on which a native of India has held executive charge of a district; and inasmuch as the appointment of Mr. Romesh Chunder was dated the 18th of July last, so that plenty of time has elapsed to allow of bad consequences being developed, if these were in any way bound to flow from the arrangement, it may be assumed that no embarrassments have ensued. Certainly, if public attention had been called to this appointment at the time it may only have been in contemplation, a good deal of hostile criticism would have been evoked. Is it possible that the greatest change that could be made in the principles of Indian Administration has thus been introduced—unnoticed and unattended with any remarkable results whatever?

The present Government has, for some time past, been alive to the fact that, before long, it would practically have to choose between one of the two courses forced on its election by the progress of time. It would either have to deny promotion to native civilians, however fairly they might have earned it—however pressing their claims, as derived from ability combined with seniority—or it would have to violate the principle on which the British Administration of India has so far been founded, and put the executive political authority of the State into the hands of native officials. The administration of districts means the government of the country. Hitherto every argument on the subject has stopped short at this point. People have pleaded for the employment of natives in all other ways, but the warmest partisans of the movement have generally conceded that it would be premature to put natives in charge of districts. All reasonable men know, of course, that natives are perfectly well qualified to be Judges. And no political difficulties arise in connection with their tenure of judicial appointments. But the executive line is another matter altogether. It may be doubted whether the literature of the subject would yield any serious defence of the position that natives ought to be put in charge of districts. The thing has never been debated: it has only been done. However, one swallow does not make a summer, and the appointment of the officiating Magistrate of Balasore has raised—not settled—the great question to be decided.

Mr. Dutt's own future career as a public servant is the best answer to this challenge. In the *Statesman* of the 28th October, the matter was discussed in the following terms:—

The *Pioneer*, which has lately, very much to its credit, assumed an attitude of justice and even generosity towards the natives of India, draws attention to the fact that for three months a native gentleman, Mr. Romesh Chunder Dutt, has officiated as Magistrate of Balasore. It is easy to say that natives are not fit for certain posts so long as they are not given an opportunity of proving their fitness. But when the necessary reform of the Civil Service is accomplished, when its doors have been thrown open in India to all who can distance their competitors in the exhibition of qualifications, and when promotion within the service is put equally within the reach of all its members, it is impossible to doubt that many native members will show at least equal fitness for high executive employment with Mr. R. C. Dutt.

During the short period Mr. Dutt held charge of Balasore, nothing of any importance happened. But as an example of the care and thoroughness with which he examined every question on which his opinion was asked, we may refer to his very able report on Local Self-government, which was printed in the *Calcutta Gazette*, along with other important reports on the same subject. A few extracts will be interesting, as being his earliest recorded opinion on self-government, a subject so dear to him, and for which he broke many a lance in after life.

I beg at the commencement of this report to state that I have found it impossible to recommend the bestowal of the same degree of independence in the matter of district administration by boards as I have recommended in the matter of municipal administration. Education has not spread in the interior of the district to the same extent that it has in municipalities, and the people in villages are far less familiar with the objects and principles of administration than the people in towns. The management of a district too is a far more difficult and responsible task than that of managing a town; and it is necessary therefore to be extremely cautious in placing the work of district administration in the hands of persons who have hitherto had little experience of such work. While therefore it is most desirable to try, in the generous spirit in which the Government Resolution has been conceived, to induce the people to have a practical share in the administration of local matters, it is also essential, to the very success of the scheme, that they are not suddenly entrusted with a task which may be at first beyond their ability. I have kept this twofold object in view in making the following suggestions.

Thus even in his younger days Mr. Dutt was no blind advocate of impracticable reforms.

The system of election [he continues] is indeed foreign alike to the genius and instincts of the people, and to the system of rule which has obtained since the British power was established in India. *Nevertheless, the simple idea on which the elective system is based is neither unintelligible nor unknown to the people of India.* To select a man to protect or advocate his interests, or represent his claims, or transact his work, is what the Bengal villager does as often as he names a *salees* to settle a dispute or appoints a *mukhtear* to do his work. To people who are so familiar with these customs, the idea of election cannot be unintelligible. It is only necessary to divest the elective system of its unnecessary surroundings, and to put it in a simple form before the people, and the better class of them will not only understand it, but will give their vote with the same degree of intelligence and interest with which they now appoint a *salees* or a *mukhtear* to transact their business. If therefore it is necessary and desirable, as undoubtedly it is, to introduce this system in order to induce the people to take an interest in their own concerns, no difficulty need arise from the fact that the people have hitherto not been acquainted with the system.

Much of the popularity of the proposed measure, however, is likely to be impaired if the District and Subdivisional Boards are authorised to impose a tax. The degree to which the ignorant people of this country are liable to suspect increase in taxation as the ultimate object of many government measures is not unknown to you, and even in taking the last census it was found necessary to explain to the people that an increase of taxation was not the object. Should the District and Subdivisional Boards be empowered to levy a tax, it would be difficult to prevent the ignorant people from identifying the beneficent scheme of self-government with the tax itself, and the scheme itself would be proportionally unpopular.

Even in those earlier days he evinced the same cautious discrimination and far-sighted wisdom which characterised his opinions of later years.

It is curious that in those days even a Bengali

member of the Service did not consider himself committed to the absolute silence about public questions which he would certainly observe to-day. Accordingly, we find a most remarkable letter from the pen of Mr. Dutt to the *Statesman* (April 24, 1882) on such a ticklish subject as the career of the retiring Lieutenant-Governor, Sir Ashley Eden. The letter itself affords a striking example of his independence, candour, and impartial judgment.

Sir Ashley Eden is a great man and a good man. He has worked steadily for the good of my country and my countrymen for thirty years, and has sometimes valiantly fought for our good, even against his superiors and countrymen. His first great work was the battle he fought for the oppressed raiyats against the planters, at a time when the planters were in high favour with the official classes. Bengal will never forget this generous battle for her voiceless millions. His last great work is the draft of the Bill about landlords and tenants, which he has sent up, and in which he has boldly proposed to confer the right of occupancy on the majority of the cultivators of Bengal. This will be a boon to the millions of Bengal, and he has advocated this in spite of the strong, powerful, and persistent opposition of the zamindars, who frightened him and flattered him by turns, but failed to make him swerve an inch from his path of duty. There is not another man in India who had the strength, the practical knowledge of details, and the talent to do this work, and it were well if "the Bengali" (a correspondent), in his sweeping strictures on a great man, had remembered what we and our country owe him.

His real sympathy for the people—his real desire to do them good—deserves mention even in this very brief review. He never missed an occasion to do them substantial good when he could; and if I am permitted to cite one instance, I will cite the instance of his exempting thousands of traders with small incomes from the operation of the Licence-Tax. He fought for this, and he obtained the concession from the Indian Government. No man is freer from race prejudice; he has never failed to rebuke an Englishman when he deserved it by presuming too much on his belonging to the ruling race, and he has never failed to do justice to a native officer in spite of opposition from his countrymen. His ability and practical good sense and candour scarcely need mention.

In spite of these great qualities he has made a series of great blunders, any one of which would have ruined a lesser reputation than his. The reason lies in a nutshell. His first impressions were formed in Bengal as he found it a quarter of a century ago, and being a man of strong convictions, he never changed his first impressions. With the new feelings and the growing aspirations of the people, he has no sympathy; he has tried to trample on them, to hold them to derision, to extinguish them. Patronage and personal rule are the weaknesses of the old class patriarchal rule, and no man is more wedded to them, or has abused patronage more, than Sir Ashley. He likes to see the people come to him and to *salām* him; he likes to oblige them and to favour them with a benign smile, or with posts for their children. This is his way of doing good. He learnt it when he was a young man, and he knows no other. Agitation for rights he hates; supplication for favours he understands and rewards. Representative institutions he hates of course, and his opposition to the Calcutta Municipality is one of his most frightful blunders. A greater blunder was his trying to crush the vernacular press. It were well if the *Hindoo Patriot* did not try to whitewash these acts by stating that Sir Ashley was simply obeying the orders of his superiors. Sir Ashley himself takes up no such line of defence; he did not give a silent vote for the Press Act, but took upon himself the responsibility of the vote in language as strong and forcible as even he has ever used.

Such are the good and bad phases of Sir Ashley Eden's career and administration, and in reviewing it, we have one consolation. His good and great works will last and will fructify; his defects will vanish with him. The good he did to the oppressed raiyats over twenty years ago—the good which he is trying to do the cultivators now, will live, and will bear fruit. His personal rule, his attempts to crush a young press however wayward, his efforts to stamp out the young aspirations of Bengal—will all vanish with him. The car of progress will march onwards, and year after year our legitimate aspirations will increase, and Young India obtain an ever-increasing share in the government of the country.

What a fine character sketch, and what wisdom in the concluding reflection!

CHAPTER V

LITERARY APPRENTICESHIP

I

"LITERARY fame," as he often wrote to his elder brother, was Romesh Dutt's "first love," and literature remained all through life his engrossing passion. But the pursuit of literature was to him only a means to an end—only one, though perhaps the most powerful, medium for revivifying the national mind of India, and restoring to her sons their lost faith in her past. The "cardinal idea" which Mr. Dutt saw running through the memorable literary achievements of such men as Iswar Chunder Vidyasāgar, Madhu Sudān Dutt, and Bankim Chunder, who worked during the latter half of the nineteenth century, was "service to the Motherland." His own aim was to be a votary at the same shrine, and his proudest ambition was to belong "to that band of noble-hearted patriots and gifted men who have taught us to regard our past religion and history and literature with legitimate and manly admiration. For our first and greatest indebtedness for the progress of this half-century is to those who have brought us to have faith in ourselves."

So, even at the threshold of his career, when most of his energy and time must have been devoted to the arduous task of making his mark as an administrator, he still found leisure to turn to literary pursuits. But literary work, as he himself said in his memorable farewell speech, delivered in Calcutta on 3rd February 1900, was to him not a task, but a recreation and a joy.

> That work has beguiled my saddest hours, solaced me in lonely hours, and refreshed me in the midst of overwhelming work of a different nature. I remember the solitary evenings

when I was encamped in the midst of the rice-fields of Dakhin Shahbazpur, a sea-washed island in the mouth of the Ganges, when I read Grant Duff's inspiring work on the history of the Mahrattas, and spent my nights in dreaming over a story of Sivaji. I remember the days when I travelled over Tippera, and occasionally crossed over to Hill Tippera, with Tod's spirited "History of Rajasthan" in my knapsack, and when I ventured to compose a story of Pratap Sinha. I remember how, after weary days spent over official work and official bundles in the heavy district of Mymensingh, I sought recreation and rest amidst the countless volumes of European and Indian scholars who have written on Indian antiquities, and I conceived the idea of writing a connected history of civilisation in ancient India. In my long furloughs, and with the help of many pandits whose learned names grace the pages of my works, I placed before my countrymen, in original and in translation, the substance of that vast body of sacred Hindu literature which is the noblest heritage of the Hindu nation. And I did not consider that task complete till I was able, after my retirement from service, to place before the modern world, in a condensed and readable form, the great epics of India. This, gentlemen, has been the recreation of my life; it has strengthened me and sustained me amidst multitudinous work, and I hope it will continue to help and sustain me in all my labours during the remaining days of my life.

We have already noticed his first essays in journalistic literature. He now took seriously to literature, and tried his pen both in the domain of fiction and in the field of economics. The "Literature of Bengal," a critical and historical study, and "Three Years in Europe," containing his reflections on the social and political institutions of the countries he had visited, appeared during this period.

II

The first published work of Mr. R. C. Dutt, his "Three Years in Europe," appeared in 1872. As the title shows, the book originally contained the story of his travels during his first stay in Europe, from 1869 to 1872. But considerable additions were made as the author was able to extend his travels to different parts of Europe in after years. To a biographer the book has great interest, as revealing the keenness of his vision, and his thirst for knowledge and information, which were the dominant traits of his character. As a traveller, his predominating idea was the study of the existing political and social institutions of the most advanced nations of the world, but his scholarly mind revelled not less fondly in the breath and memory of great historical scenes and episodes of the past. Nor was he wanting in an eye for the beautiful and the picturesque. I have quoted several of his fine descriptions of the scenes which he visited in Scotland and in Switzerland. His observations on the social and political institutions of the people he visited are broad and scholarly, and will well repay careful study by his countrymen. His sympathy with the sufferings of the poor was as keen and sincere in foreign countries as in his own home, and formed an abiding feature of his character throughout life. His style is simple and direct, and altogether free from effort and artificiality. But his travels were hurried, and it is a pity that he did not devote more time to writing his impressions and experiences. As it is, there are pages in the book which are not far removed from the commonplaces of ordinary guide-book literature, and might well have been left out. In fact, too great a proneness to method and completeness in his literary compositions somewhat detracted from the value of the productions of even his maturer years. It is true that he has himself said in the preface to his first edition, "that the book professes to be simply extracts from letters sent from Europe, and as such, they cannot, the writer is but too well aware, come up to the standard of books specially written on the subject, or even of notes taken with an eye to publication." And even in the last and complete edition of this work, the author remarks:—

> But nevertheless I am but too well aware that my accounts of these places are slipshod and careless, often penned in the saloon of a steamer or the smoking-room of a crowded hotel. To revise or re-write what I had written eighteen or twenty years

ago was out of the question, and indeed was scarcely worth the trouble; and thus the little book goes before the public in a somewhat mixed and composite character! Extracts from letters written by a young and enthusiastic student will appear herein, side by side with the notes of an older and sadder, if not a wiser tourist.

Even so, but no man of letters has the right to give to the world anything but of his best.

Of contemporary criticisms of the work we may quote the opinion of the *Friend of India*, of 11th July 1872. "These notes are marked by English thought, a thorough appreciation of English literature, a knowledge of English history, and a sympathy with English civilisation." The *Hindoo Patriot* of 22nd July, edited by the redoubtable Kristodas Pal, was appreciative, but distinctly patronising. "But a little more of living Europe," concluded the notice, "combined with what we have of Europe in ruins, and the work would have been supremely interesting." Mr. Croom Robertson, in the *Dublin Magazine*, June 1874, had a flattering review, and observed: "The work is, on the whole, extremely creditable to the observation and reflection of a stranger who, when he penned it, was still in his minority."

III

"The Peasantry of Bengal," which came out in 1875, was Mr. Dutt's first characteristic work. In fact it is one of the first serious contributions from the pen of a native of India to the discussion of the economic and agrarian problems of the country. Several of the articles had already appeared in the columns of the *Bengal Magazine*, and had obtained a favourable reception. The book appeared at a particularly opportune moment, as the agrarian disturbances in Naddea and Pabna had already attracted public attention to this important subject, and it thus succeeded in creating a very deep impression on the minds of both officials and non-officials. An ardent and whole-hearted sympathy with the raiyat is the key-note of this work. Critics have pointed out that in befriending their cause, Mr. Dutt perhaps failed to do sufficient justice to the claims of the zamindars, and he was thus led to make observations about the Permanent Settlement which he had somewhat to modify in his later years. But whatever faults of youthful enthusiasm and immaturity may be found in his reasonings, the position he took up in the defence of the long-suffering raiyats was altogether praiseworthy, and was a striking vindication of both the ability and the desire of truly patriotic Indians to fight the cause of the voiceless millions of India. A perusal of this book makes one somewhat sceptical about the orthodox official view, that the movement in Bengal for legislation in favour of the raiyat owed its origin entirely to official initiation. Mr. Dutt was apprehensive, and it is to be feared with some reason, that the publication of these unorthodox opinions might lead to his getting into the bad books of the Government. In a letter on this subject he writes to his brother J. C. Dutt :—

> I think I can depend on Omes Dada's story about the authorities not liking my publishing B. P. Civilians are not allowed to speak aloud on the subject of politics; R. H. Wilson was gagged and Geddes was degraded, Mr. Stevens told me about one or two others who were also gagged; and I think to pass judgments on the policy of the English legislators is considered too bold a step; and to advocate the cause of the raiyats against the zamindars may be viewed in a still worse light. Yet I cannot and I will not put fetters on my tongue, promotion in the service I do not much care for, and I will not be sorry if the publication of the B. P. injures my prospects somewhat. At the same time it is fortunate that the other books I intend to write ("Literature of Bengal," "History of Civilisation") do not concern Indian politics.

It is unnecessary to describe the ground covered in this work, and it will suffice if we come at once to the solution which Mr. Dutt offers of the difficulty. After describing the spirit of unrest which had come over the peasantry, he says :—

> There are two ways open to Government: to put down the general awakening and to leave the raiyats once more at the mercy

of the zamindar, as has been done times without number from 1793 to 1859, or to take a more enlightened and intelligent view of the general rising, and to newly create, in a more satisfactory manner than has yet been done, a definite status of the raiyat and a definite status of the zamindar.

After denouncing the first step as illiberal and short-sighted, our author concludes that :—

There is then one, and only one, way left before the Government; to estimate the importance of the general rising correctly—to grapple with the problem intelligently—to newly create the status of the zamindar and the raiyat in a definite manner—to enact a Permanent Settlement between the zamindar and the raiyat as a Permanent Settlement has been enacted between the zamindars and the Government.

In the face of the crisis that is staring rudely at us, half-hearted legislation would be useless and worse than useless. Our rulers will not, cannot, once more degrade the raiyat to his pristine position of servitude under the zamindars—the only other measure then to heal the ill-feeling between the two classes, and to put a stop to the mass of litigation that is eating into the very vitals of an agricultural population, is to raise the status of the raiyats. Let the rates of rent now payable be carefully ascertained after an extensive survey, and let such rates be declared fixed for ever.

This would be a bold step, but we believe it would be one truly beneficial to the country. We know such an arrangement would disturb a nest of hornets, but the Government of India has before now shown itself capable of boldly serving the country in spite of masses of selfishness and class interests that may block the way. We are stating our simple conviction that we cannot think of one valid reason that may be brought forward against this sort of arrangement.

This bold advocacy of the cause of the raiyats created widespread alarm in the ranks of the zamindars, and the great Kristodas Pal, the champion of vested interests, took the field against the daring iconoclast. A scathing criticism of the work appeared in the *Hindoo Patriot* with a broad headline—"Revolutionary." The review is of much interest as embodying the views of the best-informed Conservative of Bengal, whose influence both with the public and in the official world was paramount at the time.

Babu Romesh Chunder Dutt is full of promise of future excellence [wrote the veteran journalist], but we are sorry to observe in him the same spirit of radicalism that marked the thoughts and utterances of the first alumni of the Hindu College. The change which had overtaken these was too sudden, too rapid, and too great, and the result was a most revolutionary spirit in them. In the same way our young men who lived a few years in England have returned to India with new-fangled ideas and opinions, and although the complexion of the present time is different from that which heralded the first alumni of the Hindu College into the world, still we see now and then some outrageous symptoms of the change which has come over the spirit of their dream. We do hope that the change on the whole is one for the better, and we believe that, as in the case of the first students of the Hindu College, so in that of the returned Indian pilgrims from England, age will sober down the excesses of youth.

Coming to closer quarters, the same critic pointed out:—

There are now practically no tenants-at-will, for do they not after twelve years' occupation acquire a right of occupancy under Act X. of 1859 unless there be a specific engagement to the contrary? Our author [he goes on] would give rights of property to any person who may choose to squat on the land. He says, let the rates of rent now payable be carefully ascertained after an extensive survey, and let such rates be declared fixed for ever. So that any man may come and take possession of land at rents fixed for ever.

But the Indian press was not altogether silent in recognising the courage and wisdom of those who refused to be browbeaten by the supporters of the privileged classes, and boldly stood up for the poor cultivators.

We think we are not mistaken in stating [wrote another journal], that it is the first work of its kind—that it is the first attempt in a permanent form hitherto made by a native of this country to advocate the claims of the peasantry against the powerful claims of the zamindars. That the cultivators have their grievances is not denied by any one, and is proved beyond question by their risings in many parts of Bengal at fearful risks of danger, and with the prospect of the penal law being applied in all its rigour against them. How is it, then, that those grievances have never till now been ventilated—that those cultivators have never found a champion among their countrymen?

The reason for this, according to the writer, was to be found in the fact that the champion of the poor raiyats got nobody's support and was "jeered and ridiculed by the élite of the country as a hot-headed reformer," and exposed "to the wrath of the Government."

If, then [concludes the article] there be such, who, in spite of the contempt and ridicule of our community, in disregard of the allurements held out to them to leave the cause of truth and justice, venture to say a word in favour of the oppressed agriculturists, every true well-wisher of the country will no doubt join with us in honouring them and applauding their exertions. We are proud to be able to state that there are such men in the country, though their ranks be thin. Babu Bankim Chunder Chatterjea, in his brilliant essays in the *Banga Darsana*, endeavoured to do justice to a class of people to whom justice is never done. The Rev. Lal Bihari Dey has, in a novel recently published, ventured to evince this sympathy for the same class of people—the poor agriculturists; and, lastly, the author of the book under notice has boldly stepped forward as the champion of the industrious poor. We fervently hope that such writers will think and work together and co-operate in the cause of the poor; and we have no doubt they will succeed in bringing about a change in the public opinion of the country, and in inducing the Government to recognise the claims of the masses against the all-devouring claims of the zamindars.

The extent to which the agitation in Bengal in favour of the raiyats, which culminated in the Bengal Tenancy Act of 1885, gathered strength from Mr. Dutt's writings will be clear from the fact that his book led the Government to order careful inquiries to be made into the matter.

I have indeed reasons to congratulate myself [wrote Mr. Dutt to his brother] if the L. G. has really ordered an inquiry as to whether the facts narrated in my book are true. If I were asked what I myself most heartily wish for my book, I could name nothing better than that it should be the cause of an inquiry being instituted into the practices of the zamindars. Sir George Campbell did institute such an inquiry, and the result was that a long list of the illegal exactions of the zamindars was published, but nothing else came out of it. I hope Sir Richard Temple's inquiry will bear some fruit!

The book was favourably reviewed by many journals and newspapers in England. *The Examiner*, in its issue of the 25th September 1875, had a long critique on the book, of which the opening paragraph is quoted:—

This is a much more important book than might be inferred from its humble exterior and its modest preface, and may be commended to those whom the approaching visit of the Prince of Wales has inspired with a desire to know something about India and her varied and numerous population. It is a description of the cultivating classes of Bengal, and an appeal on their behalf written by one of the few native members of the Bengal Civil Service, whose eloquence flows as easily and idiomatically in English as if it had been his mother tongue. So completely, indeed, has Mr. Dutt mastered his Queen's English, that one cannot help wondering what new developments our language may undergo when it has spread more widely in India, and become the chief medium of expression for the subtle activity of the Hindu brain—the organ of new veins of humour, fancy, imagination, and eloquence.

IV

The little book on the "Literature of Bengal" is perhaps the most notable performance of Mr. Dutt in English during the period of his apprenticeship. In undertaking this work, Mr. Dutt, as in other fields, set up before him a "national" standard. "To trace as far as possible the history of the people, as reflected in the literature of Bengal," was his object. For it was a favourite contention of his that the "literature of every country, slowly expanding through successive ages, reflects accurately the manners and customs, the doings, and the thoughts of the people. And thus, although no works of a purely historical character had been left behind by the people of ancient India, it is possible to gain from their works on literature and religion a fairly accurate idea of their civilisation, and the progress of their intellect and social institutions." The wider and more comprehensive task of reconstructing the history of ancient India, on the basis of her past literature, he took up later in life. For the present he confined himself to a humbler sphere.

The first edition of the book came out in 1877, and the author assumed the *nom de guerre* of Ar. Cy. Dae. To his uncle, Rai Shoshee Ch. Dutt Bahadur, to whom, as we have seen, he owed so much of his literary predilections, he gratefully dedicated the work as a token of esteem. A much improved and enlarged edition, under his own name, appeared later on, in 1896.

The great merit of the work is that it was the first scientific attempt to write a history of our national life and literature. And we have only to compare this book with the previous work on the same subject in the vernacular, by Pandit Ramgati Nyaratna, to appreciate the great advance made in critical method. It is true that the work does not bear the impress of much original research either in the field of the vexed question of the origin of the Bengali language or the disputed authorship of the works of the earliest period of that literature, nor is his canvas large enough to enable him to do justice to even the most important figures of his narrative. But nevertheless the book is marked by a breadth of vision, and a firm grasp of the main stages of the intellectual life of Bengal from the twelfth century to the present day, and of the outstanding factors which have moulded that life.

According to Mr. Dutt, the history of Bengali literature, as of the Bengali people, naturally divides itself into three distinct periods, viz. :—

> First, the period of lyrical poetry, extending from the twelfth to the end of the fifteenth century of the Christian era. The representative men of this period are Jayadeva, Vidyapati, and Chandi Das. A host of other poets of smaller note flourished in this period.

Second, the period of classical influence, extending from the beginning of the sixteenth century to the end of the eighteenth century. The representative men of this period are the great Chaitanya, Krittibas, Mukunda Ram, Kasi Ram Das, the great Raghunath, and Bharat Chunder Ray.

Third, the period of European influence, being the period in which we are living, and commencing with the nineteenth century. The central figures of this period are the great Ram Mohan Ray, Akhai Kumar Dutt, Iswar Chunder Vidyasagar, Iswar Chunder Gupta, Madhu Sudan Dutt, Hem Chunder Banerjea, Dina Bandhu Mitter, and Bankim Chunder Chatterjea.

The first period presents us with a mass of love songs about Krishna and Radhika, composed with deep feeling. The second period presents us with more earnest thinking and work, with the rise of a new religion, the cultivation of literature in the classical style, and investigations into Sanskrit philosophy. The last period strikes us with an outburst of multifarious feelings and the display of a free, daring intellect. The second period is an improvement on the first, and the third beats all. For we do not hesitate to say that the "Meghnad Badha Kavya" leaves Chandi and Vidyasundar as far behind, as Chandi and Vidyasundar leave behind the simple though sweet strains of Vidyapati and Chandi Das.

Up to the end of the fifteenth century our literature consisted simply of songs feelingly sung, about the amours of Krishna and Radhika. But the national mind was now awakened. The first effect of this change was the introduction of a new religion, deep and earnest in its character, and far-reaching in its consequences. In literature, too, there was a hankering for something vaster and nobler than what had been inherited from the preceding ages; there was an energy capable of something greater than the composition of songs. At such a crisis, the nation turned its eyes to the hitherto virgin mine of Sanskrit literature, and that was a mine which satisfied the highest aspirations, and rewarded the utmost endeavour. From this time forward then, we find our authors producing not simple songs as hitherto, but big tomes of poetry, all in the classical style. The two great epics in Sanskrit, the "Ramayana" and the "Mahabharata," were translated into Bengali, and original epics like the "Chandi" of Mukunda Ram and the "Annada Mangal" of Bharat were written in the classical style. Nor was the national mind satisfied with poetry alone. The abstrusest questions of law and metaphysics, and deep and subtle problems of psychology, engaged the attention of the great Raghunath and other earnest workers of the school of Naddea.

Thus the revolution of the sixteenth century had a threefold effect, viz. religious, literary, and philosophical.

But it is his observations on the latest period that deserve our closest attention.

> The conquest of Bengal by the English [says he in the first edition of his work] was not only a political revolution, but ushered in a greater revolution in thoughts and ideas; in religion and society. We cannot describe the great change better than by stating that English conquest and English education may be supposed to have removed Bengal from the moral atmosphere of Asia to that of Europe. All the great events which have influenced European thought within the last one hundred years have also told, however feeble their effect may be, on the formation of the intellect of modern Bengal. The independence of America, the French revolution, the war of Italian independence, the teachings of history, the vigour and freedom of English literature and English thought, the great effort of the French intellect in the eighteenth century, the results of German labour in the field of philology and ancient history—Positivism, Utilitarianism, Darwinism—all these have influenced and shaped the intellect of modern Bengal. In the same degree all the great influences which told on the Bengali mind in previous centuries, the faith of Krishna, the faith of Chandi or Kali, the preachings of Chaitanya, the belief in the truth of Hinduism and the sacredness of the Shastras, the unquestioning obedience to despotic power in all its phases, the faith in the divine right of royalty and in the innate greatness of princes and princesses—all these ancient habits and creeds have exercised feebler and yet feebler influences on the modern Bengali intellect. In habits, in tastes, in feeling, freedom and vigour and patriarchal institutions, our literature therefore has undergone a corresponding change. The classical Sanskrit taste has given place to the European. From the stories of gods and goddesses, kings and queens, princes and princesses, we have learned to descend to the humble walks of life, to sympathise with a common citizen or even a common peasant. From an admiration of a symmetrical uniformity we have descended to an appreciation of the strength and freedom of individuality. From admiring the grandeur and glory of the great, we now willingly turn to appreciate liberty and resistance in the lowly.

These passages he omitted from his second edition, and rightly, for although they define accurately his own mental outlook and his position in the hierarchy of Indian thinkers and writers, yet they can scarcely be said to present a correct view of the Bengali literature of the nineteenth century.

> Every revolution [he goes on to say] is attended with vigour, and the present one is no exception to the rule. Nowhere in the annals of Bengali literature are so many or so bright names found crowded together in the limited space of one century as those of Ram Mohan Ray, Akhai Kumar Dutt, Iswar Chunder Vidyasagar, Iswar Chunder Gupta, Madhu Sudan Dutt, Hem Chunder Banerjea, Bankim Chunder Chatterjea, and Dina Bandhu Mitter. Within the three quarters of the present century, prose, blank verse, historical fiction, and drama have been introduced for the first time in the Bengali literature, and works of imagination have been written which leave the highest and best efforts of previous centuries far behind.

In his second edition, he added a brief but searching summary of the wonderful intellectual revolution which followed the first introduction of English education into Bengal.

> The Hindu College, which was established in 1817, effected a revolution in the ideas of the young Hindus of the day. They imbibed in that College a warm appreciation of Western literature and Western civilisation, and brooked with impatience the unreasoning restrictions which modern Hindu customs had imposed on them. Trained under teachers like Derozio and D. L. Richardson, the first young men who came out from the Hindu College were fired with an ambition to reform all that was unhealthy, and to reject all that was hurtful, in Hindu customs and rules. The reaction against the restrictions of ages went perhaps a little too far, but we can scarcely regret this reaction, to which is really due all the steady improvement and reform which have been effected in this century. One may laugh at the Anglicised young collegiates of the first half of this century, but it was those young collegiates whose advanced ideas and training leavened the society in which they lived, and made the sober reforms of later times possible. Men like Kashi Prasad Ghosh, Ram Gopal Ghosh and Rama Prasad Ray, like K. M. Banerjea, Debendra Nath Tagore and Prasanna Kumar Tagore, were among the early students of the Hindu College, and the ideas which they received with their English education permeated the society in

which they lived. The writings of Akhai Kumar Dutt reflected the progress infused into Hindu society through the Hindu College. The reforms effected by Iswar Chunder Vidyasagar were possible only after Hindu society had been permeated with advanced ideas through a healthy English education. For a time the alumni of the Hindu College stood aloof from directly taking a part in improving their national literature; they still indulged in dreams of distinguishing themselves in English. But the dream was dispelled in time, and when the ardent young collegemen espoused the cause of their own national literature, they achieved results which silenced their critics and astonished their best friends. The present century has produced nothing in verse comparable to that of Madhu Sudan, and nothing in prose comparable to that of Bankim Chunder.

Of his critical estimates, the best is his appreciation of Raja Ram Mohan Ray, and he is generally on firm ground when he deals with kindred spirits like the great Raja or Iswar Chunder, or in a narrower sphere, Akhai Kumar Dutt. But his estimate of Madhu Sudan as the greatest literary genius of Bengal will hardly be shared by most competent critics, for it is doubtful whether Madhu Sudan possessed the supreme gift of inspiration, the inevitableness of true art in the same degree as did Bankim Chander, who is by many acknowledged to be the king of Bengali literature of the nineteenth century. In his best creations like "Chandra Sekhar," or "Krisna Kanta's Will," Bankim Chunder gave us unalloyed gold; but there is not a page in the "Meghanath Badha" where the purer metal is not alloyed with tinsel of a baser stuff.

The book received a warm welcome, and a scholar like Sir William Hunter quoted freely from it in his standard work on the "Indian Empire." On the appearance of his second edition the *Englishman* published a most appreciative notice.

He has now returned [said the *Englishman*] to his first love, the love of his native country, and, with increased knowledge and wider experience, gives us an almost rewritten and greatly improved second edition of his history of the "Literature of Bengal." It will surprise many to learn that Bengali has a literature worth writing about. To most people it consists of one insipid and lubric work, the Vidya Sundar of Bharat Chunder, the writings of Vidyasagar, of Bankim Chatterjea's modern novels, of a few examination text-books, and of the native press. We fear that of these the only ones ever read by such persons are the examination text-books, read once and then worthily abandoned for ever. The others are forgotten or ignored, and much is lost thereby. But Bengali has a literature, dating from the fourteenth century, full of interest not only to the student, but also to the general readers. We need not follow Mr. Dutt through the other chapters of his interesting volume. It is sufficient to refer to those of our readers who wish to know the inner life, the thoughts, the feelings, the real life of Bengal—not the bastard imitation of English habits and, too often, English vices, which floats like a scum on the surface of our great cities—to his book. After all, the songs of a people have more power than its laws, and a young civilian can learn better to gain the hearts of his people from an hour's study of the "Literature of Bengal" than from years of application to the history of the fortunes of A. and Z. in the Penal Code.

Its influence reached even England, and shortly after the publication of this book a very appreciative article on the "New Literature of Bengal" appeared in the columns of the *Times*.

One of the striking products of British rule in India is the vernacular literature of the provinces. With the English and French works of Indian authors, some of them of considerable merit, the European world is more or less acquainted. But we scarcely realise the fact that such works are altogether insignificant compared with the vast and vigorous growth of literature in the native language. That growth is not confined to one part of India or another; where it has found literary dialects ready for its use, it has developed them; where it has not found literary dialects, it has created them. Varieties of human speech never reduced to writings have been furnished with alphabets and printed types. Rude or poor dialects only used for song have been amplified into prose. Better furnished dialects have been still further enriched from the classical languages of India, and now supply vehicles for the complex problems of philosophy, science, and modern thought. Nowhere has the activity been greater than in Lower Bengal.

To those who would study this subject as a whole, and who desire to understand the intense activity of the Indian mind under British rule, we could recommend Mr. R. C. Dutt's recently published volume on "The Literature of Bengal." Mr. Dutt springs himself from a distinguished literary family, and he has well maintained its reputation both in prose and verse. The conspicuous merit of his book is its frank acknowledgment that no literary success which an Indian can make in English or any exotic tongue, is to be compared as regards its value to his countrymen with first-class work in his own language. It is this instinct of literary patriotism which animates the best Bengali writers, and which has within a century created a prose literary language for Bengal.

CHAPTER VI

HISTORICAL NOVELS (1874–1880)

I

As the special correspondent of the *Times* so aptly points out, the highest proof of Mr. Dutt's critical faculty lay in his realising, although the bulk of his own literary productions is in English, that except as a medium for imparting information to the West of the riches of ancient India, the ambition of an Indian to produce anything enduring in English is foredoomed to failure. Early in his career, therefore, his thoughts turned to his own mother tongue. He has himself described how he naturally came under the influence of the master mind of the great Bankim Chunder Chatterjea. Bankim Chunder was a close friend of his father, and since his childhood Mr. Dutt had the highest respect and affection for him. On his return from England he discussed his plans and ambitions with Bankim Chunder, and the latter suggested that he should contribute in Bengali to the *Banga Darsana* magazine, then in the noonday of its influence and fame. "Write in Bengali!" exclaimed Mr. Dutt; "but I hardly know the Bengali literary style." "Style!" rejoined Bankim Chunder; "whatever a cultured man like you will write will be style. If you have the gift in you, style will come of itself." This was a memorable episode in the life of Mr. Dutt, for from that day he turned to Bengali literature. His inmost ambitions he always laid bare to his brother, and in a letter written in 1877 he says: "My own mother tongue must be my line, and before I die I hope to leave what will enrich the language and will continue to please my countrymen after I die." And whatever may be the final verdict on his Bengali novels, there can be little question that his countrymen to-day love and revere his memory for nothing so much as for his own love for his mother tongue. After his demise I received visits from numerous Indian gentlemen, who had all a great deal to say about his great qualities of head and heart. An old Muhammadan gentleman, however, made perhaps the most touching observation: "I admire Mr. Dutt," said he, "for his successful administrative work, and for all his other achievements in England and India, like every other Indian; but what I admire in him most was his love of his mother tongue. It is because he honoured and loved the Bengali literature that I love and honour him so much."

The natural bias of his mind was for history. Writing about his favourite authors in 1905, he said: "Sir W. Scott was my favourite author forty years ago. I do not know if Sir W. Scott gave me a taste for history, or if my taste for history made me an admirer of Scott; but no subject, not even poetry, had such a hold upon me as history." And next to Bankim Chunder we notice the predominating influence of Scott in his historical novels. Not only various scenes, but characters, remind one of the immortal creations of the author of "Ivanhoe." And it would be surprising if the classical literature of his own country had failed to exercise some influence. In the severe repose and grandeur of such characters as Jay Sing and Akbar, and specially in their sage-like and solemn counsels, one is reminded of Bhisma and other characters of the "Mahabharata," while the angry glare of the eyes of Sivaji in the moments of his frenzy is reminiscent of the flame which shoots from the eyes of Siva the Destroyer in the immortal work of Bharavi. But, above all, it is his own passion for the past glories of his country that is the parent of these novels. "Gentle reader," he exclaimed in one of his novels, "my sole object has been to narrate the glories of our past and the greatness of our national heroes. If I have succeeded in kindling a single spark of love and admiration for our national heroes, then not in vain did I take up my pen."

II

His four historical novels cover a period of a hundred years, from the middle of the sixteenth century to the reign of Aurungzebe, and at one time were published as a quartette in the same volume entitled "Sata Barsa." "Banga Bijeta" (the conqueror of Bengal) and "Madhabi Kankan" (bracelet of flowers) relate to Akbar's conquest of Bengal, and the heroes, Noren and Surendra Nath, are two scions of noble families of Bengal. The third is woven round the story of the heroic struggle of Rana Pratap for the freedom of his beloved principality of Mewar against the overwhelming might of the Moghal Empire. In the praise of this prince, a historian who was not his countryman has recorded the following panegyric :—

But the magnitude of the peril confirmed the fortitude of Pratap, who vowed, in the words of the bard, "to make his mother's milk resplendent"; and he amply redeemed his pledge. Single-handed for a quarter of a century did he withstand the combined efforts of the empire; at one time carrying destruction into the plains, at another flying from rock to rock, feeding his family from the fruits of his native hills, and rearing the nursling hero, Umra, amidst savage beasts and scarce less savage men, a fit heir to his prowess and revenge. The bare idea that "the son of Bappa Rawul should bow the head to mortal man" was insupportable; and he spurned every overture which had submission for its basis, or the degradation of uniting his family by marriage with the Tatar, though lord of countless multitudes.

. . . .

Had Mewar possessed her Thucydides or her Xenophon, neither the wars of the Peloponnesus nor the retreat of the "Ten Thousand" would have yielded more diversified incidents for the historic muse than the deeds of this brilliant reign amid the many vicissitudes of Mewar. Undaunted heroism, inflexible fortitude, that which "keeps honour bright," perseverance, with fidelity such as no nation can boast, were the materials opposed to a soaring ambition, commanding talents, unlimited means, and the fervour of religious zeal; all, however, insufficient to contend with one unconquerable mind. There is not a pass in the Alpine Aravali that is not sanctified by some deed of Pertap—some brilliant victory, or oftener, more glorious defeat."[1]

The fourth, "Maharastra Jiban Prabhat," depicts the rise of the Mahratta power under Sivaji, unquestionably the greatest military genius that India has produced within historical times. It was Mr. Dutt's intention to write a fifth historical novel, which would have for its subject the break-up and downfall of the Moghal Empire and the succession of the Mahratta Confederacy to the chief political power in India. This ambition, however, he did not live to realise.

As one of the acutest critics of the day has observed, "the mixture of history with romance, of real actors and known events with avowed fiction, has not always been a successful experiment"; and Mr. Dutt's novels, though they abound in stirring scenes, moving interests, and fully-developed dramatic situations, yet fail to take high rank as works of art because of their lack of organic fusion. The central characters are purely historical, like those of Akbar, Sivaji, and Rana Pratap. Then come some other characters which, though based on history, afford greater scope for invention and the play of imagination. The chapter in which Jay Sing gives sage counsel to Sivaji about the supreme duty of a soldier to keep his personal honour untarnished, and his plighted word unbroken at any sacrifice, reaches a high level of inspiring narrative. Perhaps more impressive and fraught with far-off significance is the death-scene of Jay Sing, when the aged warrior scans through the gathering mist of death the Mahratta warrior sitting on the ancient throne of Prithi Raj at Delhi. In the same novel there is a brief and penetrating character sketch of Aurungzebe, which will do credit to any writer of historical romances. But the moving interest of the plot is sustained chiefly with the aid of the deeds of the young soldier of fortune, a Noren, a Surendranath, or a Raghunath Havildar, who, like Scott's Quentin Durward, carves out a fortune and a career for himself, and wins the object of his affections with the help of his own

[1] Tod's "Annals and Antiquities of Rajasthan," vol. i. pp. 32 and 350.

sword and the prowess of his invincible right arm. A great charm of these books is that they help one to realise to some extent the stir, the excitement, and the atmosphere of romance and adventure which pervaded life in the India of those days. "It would be hard to explain to an average Englishman," observes Meredith Townsend, "how interesting Indian life must have been before our advent; how completely open was every career to the bold, the enterprising, or the ambitious. The whole continent was open as a prize to the strong." The story of the career of Sivaji, who began life as the son of a petty jagirdar and died a mighty sovereign, and of the high eminence to which a subject like Todar Mull ascended in the service of the Empire, help us to picture those days.

But his greatest success are his female characters—beautiful types of the Oriental feminine, who, to borrow the language of Sister Nivedita, one of their most ardent Western admirers—"grow like the tall white lilies of annunciation set in the dimness beside some altar screened from the very glances of the faithful at their prayers." The scene in the commencement of the "Rajput Jivan Sandhya," where Raghunath Havildar casts his glance on the cypress-like form of the fair Rajput maiden, Sarajubala, in the gloaming shadows of evening, when the incense burning at the altar of the temple mingles with the fragrance of the intoxicating flowers of the East, is a scene not easily to be forgotten. Of great beauty and wide human interest is also the scene in the "Madhavi Kankan," afterwards translated by him into English as "The Slave Girl of Agra," where Noren meets the woman he has loved all his life, and through her persuasion uproots from the depths of his soul his vain longings for her who has become another man's wife.

The midnight hour sounded from the Golden Temple, and the light of the moon fell on the inspired face and the glowing eyes of the proud woman who had done her duty in life. Noren, a soldier for nine years, felt that he was but a deserter and a coward whom that woman was calling back to his duty. And as he raised his eyes they fell on the North Star, and a legend of constancy and of duty came back to his mind.

"I will do thy bidding, Hemlata," he said softly. "I will return with thee to Bengal, and may Heaven help me to do my work."

"Spoken like the son of thy father. Thou hast always helped me, Noren, since childhood. Help a woman, who has perhaps her sufferings too, to do her ordained task on earth."

A silence ensued. Noren never knew the silent sufferings that patient woman had borne and conquered.

"One word more before Saibalini comes to meet us, for her devotions must now be over. Dost remember the last time thou sawest me at Birnagar?"

Noren remembered it.

"Dost remember the grey cold morning, the misty lake, the lonely temple surrounded by trees?"

He did.

"Dost remember the jasmine plant we had planted and the flowers that grew on it?"

Noren remembered all.

"Then thou rememberest this token thou didst leave with me nine years ago." And Hemlata bared her white, slender arm, and Noren saw on it the withered remains of the jasmine bracelet, his last present to her before they had parted. It had gone to pieces, but the pieces had been carefully stitched together by a thread, and Hemlata had put it on once more before she came to the temple to-night.

"It was thy gift, Noren. Undo it, for thou alone hast the right to take it back." Her voice trembled a little.

"It was a token," said Noren, "which would keep me in thy mind. Dost thou forget me, Hemlata?"

"Not while life will last, my brother. But that token meant more. It has often troubled my heart when I sought for peace. It has often blinded my eyes when I sought to do my household work. Take it back, Noren, I may not wear it. I am a true wife to my husband."

Neither spoke, but both understood. Noren's heart heaved within him, and the soldier's eyes were blinded with tears, as he slowly undid that bracelet and consigned it to the waters of the Jumna.

Hemlata and Noren silently watched it on the rippling waters till it was lost to view, for ever.

III

The contemporary criticisms of these novels were many. The *Bengalee*, of the 15th March 1879, published a long article, in which it compared the relative merits of Bankim Chunder and Romesh Chunder, who were described "as the only two writers of fiction who have risen to distinction and fame in Bengal." The palm is justly given to the elder novelist. "In imagination, in pathos, in diversity of character and situation, in invention as in description, in all that makes a great novelist, Bankim Chunder excels the younger writer." But the critic does not fail to give Romesh Chunder his due meed of praise :—

> But in one respect at least Romesh Chunder excels all living writers in Bengal. The singleness of aim, earnestness of purpose, a manly devotion to duty, a burning and zealous enthusiasm in its performance; these high notions illumine every work and almost every chapter of the young and enthusiastic writer. Characters drawn from history and characters drawn from the imagination are alike inspired by this noble feeling, and Jay Singh and Sivaji display the same noble devotion to duty which inspires the younger heroes, Surendra Nath or Raghu Nath Ji Havildar, in their lifelong struggle and endeavour. "Do your duty" seems to be the noble motto of Romesh Chunder's novels; and the lesson is repeated in burning chapters and in burning pages.

The *Hindoo Patriot* of the 11th August 1879 published a review of "Jiban Probhat, an historical romance of the times of Emperor Arungzebe, by Romesh Chunder Dutt, C.S." Here also judgment is passed on the relative merits of the two greatest novelists of Bengal :—

> Comparisons are always odious [remarked the writer], and we would therefore like to avoid them, but as Babu Bankim Chunder Chatterjea and Mr. R. C. Dutt excel in quite distinct branches of the same department of literary composition, we do not think we are overstepping the bounds of propriety in saying that the productions of the former have

a more useful tendency than those of the latter. Mr. R. C. Dutt, however, yields to no writer of our day in the flights of his imagination, in the loftiness of his conceptions, and in the symmetry and consistency of the scenes and events unfolded by him. But he deserves high credit for a very valuable trait which his performances in his mother tongue exhibit. The literary career of this writer proves, what we never thought improbable, that it is quite possible for a native of this country to travel thousands of miles by sea, visit the seats of the highest civilisation which this age can boast of, and yet not forget his nationality, not forget the language in which he was cradled, not forget the inmost thoughts and feelings of his countrymen and countrywomen. We need scarcely say that Mr. R. C. Dutt is an English writer of no ordinary merit, but because he visited England he does not consider it a disgrace to cultivate his mother tongue.

As already noted, his "Madhabi Kankan" was translated by him into English much later in life as the "Slave Girl of Agra," and the following extracts from reviews in the English press of this work will be of interest, as not only showing the warm reception which this work received, but also indicating the keen demand that there obviously exists for genuine Indian romances.

The *Scotsman* of the 3rd May :—

Britons have a habit of surveying the vast pageant of India through the keen eyes of Mr. Rudyard Kipling, and, by way of a contrast, this Indian historical romance by one of the blood will come by way of a useful corrective. The European, with his futile strivings after comprehension of the ways of the mysterious East, never crosses the author's path, and one has a succession of picturesque views of the India of the sixteenth-century days, when "the great Akbar was building up a rich and prosperous empire in the East." The hero is the young chief of an ancient Bengal house, and in his company one is introduced to the scene of native festivals and royal courts, and dabbles in royal intrigues, in which a Persian of matchless loveliness, an amorous prince, and a vindictive eunuch have a hand. Of romances there are several in the book, and the princeling, after a disappointment, has a brief but adventurous affair with a Tartar beauty of many charms, who introduces our hero into the residence of Begums, and whom he helps to escape after she has broken the palace rules and knifed the chief eunuch. She is a will-o'-the-wisp heroine, whom readers will find as elusive as the hero did, and as fascinating. Thoroughly wholesome in tone, as a story the book lacks the pulsing interest which drives the reader from chapter to chapter, but as a glimpse of the many-hued empire it will be scanned with interest.

Liverpool Daily Post:—

It is a fine story, full of vigour and historic incident, and the narrative is clothed with all that picturesqueness and grace of style of which all critical writers are masters. The book is, moreover, one which at the present time may be read with considerable interest. The graphic picture which it gives to us of manners, life, and thought in India in the days of the great Emperor Akbar is peculiarly illuminative, and the attention of the reader is fully maintained to the end of the book.

Western Morning News (Plymouth):—

Probably more history has been learned from Scott's historical novels than from the old type of matter-of-fact text-book, and we believe many will be tempted to gain a better idea of Indian history, in this country, by Mr. Dutt's romances than by Blue-books or Parliamentary oratory. We compliment the author on the success he has achieved in this work, and trust that many other books of a like type may be issued. Anything that leads to the increase of our knowledge of India will lead to increased sympathy with India, and, as the Prince of Wales said when visiting that fascinating land, "it is only as we have sympathy with India that we can hope to keep her love and loyalty."

We cannot conclude this section better than by quoting from the very illuminating and thoughtful letter which Mr. Dutt received from his famous compatriot, Prince Kerala Varma, of Madras, on his "Slave Girl".:—

I have just finished reading your really excellent historical romance, the "Slave Girl of Agra," a second time. Alike in point of language and matter, it stands on a supremely eminent level. The honest boldness of your style often reminds me of Bulwer Lytton; your description of mediæval manners and customs is not less thorough and accurate than Scott's; your character-sketches compare favourably with Thackeray's, and your narration of incidents has all the fertility and charm, without the prolixity, of Alexandre Dumas. Indeed, from no other part of India than the premier Province of Bengal can such masterpieces in literature afford to appear for decades to come. On your shoulders, as the author of this romance and "The Lake of Palms," the mantle of the immortal writer of "Durgesanandini" and "Vishavriksha" has deservedly fallen, and I sincerely hope that the "Slave Girl of Agra" will have many sisters and brothers in the nearest future.

. . . .

I doubt whether the old name "Madhabi Kankan" is not more suited to the work as the development of the plot stands at present. The character of Jelekha stands in need of a little further development, and I am glad to learn that this point has already attracted your attention.

The permanent educative value of historical romances is very much more than that of social and domestic novels. Long after the tomes of Zola and Sand have begun to sleep in their graves, Dumas and Hugo are sure to be read by Frenchmen, and whatever contemporary fame Marie Corelli may be able to command, the lives of "The Master Christian," and "The Sorrows of Satan," cannot, in the nature of things, be half as long as those of "Ivanhoe," and "The Last of the Barons." The history of our country is much more stirring, and bristles with much more attractive incidents, than that of Great Britain or France; and yet where are the Indian romances that challenge comparison with "The Talisman," and "The Three Musketeers"? You and Bankim Chunder stand almost alone in the field, while in my opinion there should be hundreds of young men to follow your lead. The latter days of Shahjehan, the strife between Vijayanagar and the Bhamani kingdoms, the history of the Mahrattas subsequent to the death of Madhava Rao Peshwa, &c., are interesting periods, from the novelist's standpoint, though few have cared to tap these perennial springs so far. We cannot look up to authors like F. A. Steel for supplying this want, as they take up only Anglo-Indian stories which have little interest for the masses of India. I am sorry that though there are many novels in Gujrati, most of them are social and have only ephemeral value. This is probably due to the fact that all the writers are Parsis. Whatever it is, the time is come when better insight into our past history is a condition precedent to political advancement, and nothing can more easily or successfully achieve this end than the constant perusal of healthy historical romances.

CHAPTER VII

DISTRICT MAGISTRATE (1883-1892)

I

THE appointment of Mr. R. C. Dutt to the charge of Backerganj, and his sway of two years in that district, form perhaps the most brilliant episode in the whole of his administrative career.

My appointment and administration in Backerganj on this occasion [he wrote in his " Rambles in India "] attracted considerable attention. Previous to this I myself and some others of my countrymen had acted as District Officers for short periods—*i.e.* for one, two, or three months. But this was the first instance that a native of India was kept in charge of a district for a considerable length of time, and the step was spoken of as a doubtful experiment. The district too was one of the heaviest and most turbulent in all Bengal, and the period was one of excitement, for the Ilbert Bill agitation greatly exercised the public mind and embittered the public feeling during these years. All's well, however, that ends well; there was not a whisper of discontent or agitation in the district; everything went on smoothly and well, and I peacefully laid down the reins in 1885, after two years of administration.

Not only was there no hitch or complaint, but great progress was made by the educational institutions of the district under his fostering care, several new roads were constructed, and steamer communications greatly developed. But his most signal success was in the department of criminal administration. By his vigilance, his close and intimate touch with and knowledge of all parts of his district, by his tact in bringing about the amicable settlement of differences between rival zamindars, and by his policy of associating village panchayets and headmen in the work of the arbitration of local disputes and the suppression of bad characters, he succeeded in greatly reducing crime in the district. As a result, serious riots were fewer then than they were for a long time either before or after him. The Commissioner, the Inspector-General of Police, the Local Government, and finally the Viceroy himself, most generously recognised the sterling merits of this capable, strong, and sympathetic administrator. In the Government Resolution on the administration report of the Dacca Division for 1883–84, Mr. Dutt was the only District Officer whose name was specially mentioned for "his administration of a very heavy district." The Inspector-General of Police, in his review of the police administration of the province, remarked very favourably about the reduction of riots in the Backerganj district, which were fewer in that district than "in either Faridpur or Dacca," and the Lieutenant-Governor (Sir Rivers Thompson) in the resolution on the police administration, also remarked that the reduction in serious crime was "creditable to the Backerganj officers, especially as this district was formerly notorious for riots." Referring to these official recognitions of his successful administration of the district, Mr. Dutt wrote to his brother: "It gives me great pleasure that my successful administration has been thus publicly recognised, because this was the first instance that an Indian district has been administered by a native of India for about a year, and a failure in the experiment would have been disastrous for the prospects of our countrymen."

As a crowning mark of official goodwill, the Viceroy himself sent for Mr. Dutt, and at a personal interview the Marquess of Ripon expressed his high approval of Mr. Dutt's work in a difficult district, and during a time of great tension of race feeling. "I sent for you," Lord Ripon said, "as I wished to see you and know you, before leaving India. Your work should be known in England; the fitness of Indians for high administrative posts would not then be questioned."

One of the vital qualifications of a successful administrator in an Indian district is tact, and Mr. Dutt possessed this quality to a striking degree. But though he was tactful, he was never guilty of pushing compromise to the extent of sacrificing his own honest convictions, and there was no officer of his time who was a more stern disciplinarian, and of a more uncompromising independence. His official relations with all his subordinates, both Europeans and Indians, were dignified, though at the same time perfectly harmonious. His social relations with the Europeans of the district, officials and non-officials, were also most friendly. He was thus popular with all classes, and when the time came for him to leave the district, the whole community joined hands to give him a fitting ovation. The following notice of this event appeared in the *Indian Mirror* of the 20th March 1885:—

After an able and successful administration of two years, Mr. R. C. Dutt made over charge of the District of Backerganj to Mr. Fasson on Saturday last, and will shortly proceed to Europe on furlough. It gives us great pleasure to add that his departure from Barisal was marked with demonstrations such as were seldom witnessed in Backerganj before. The relation between Mr. Dutt and all the European residents in the station, official as well as non-official, was ever marked by an unbroken cordiality, and several Europeans entertained Mr. Dutt at farewell dinners. Mr. Bradbury, the popular Judge of the district, gave Mr. Dutt the last farewell dinner on Saturday last, and the Hon. Mr. Prinsep, Judge of the High Court of Calcutta, who was present at Barisal at the time, graced the occasion with his presence. After the dinner was over, Mr. Dutt was entertained at a magnificent supper and evening party by the entire Indian community in the government school-house. All the European residents, including the Hon. Mr. Prinsep; the Judge, Mr. Bradbury: the new Magistrate, Mr. Fasson; the District and Assistant-Superintendents of Police, Messrs. Wilcox and Fullerton; the Joint-Magistrate, Mr. Shirres; Zamindars, Messrs. Brown and D' Silva, were present on the occasion, and heartily joined the Indian community in doing honour to Mr. Dutt, and in wishing him a long life and prosperous journey, over brimming cups of excellent champagne.

On Monday morning the road from his house to the steamer was lined by crowds of school-boys as well as of official and non-official gentlemen. The new Magistrate, Mr. Fasson, the District and Assistant-Superintendents of Police, the Joint-

Magistrate, and all the highest native officials accompanied him to the river bank and bade him a hearty farewell. The steamer left Barisal at 8.30 A.M. amidst deafening cheers.

Before concluding this section I must quote the following letter written to his brother, which will show the earnestness and devotion to high ideals which animated the performance of all his official duties.

BARISAL, *17th June* 1884.

MY DEAR BROTHER,—I was amused to read your letter of the 15th June, in which you are so anxious about a certain affidavit which a certain prisoner has made in the High Court! Prisoners of influence and money when checked in their high-handedness always make such affidavits, and they do not go against the magistrate in the smallest degree! Of course I am exceptionally careful in my work here, and though the High Court may find sometimes that I am legally or technically wrong, they will never find that I am unjust, or oppressive, or high-handed as a magistrate. In the case which you allude to, the appellants based their appeal on a deliberate falsehood which I have exposed, and Mr. Manomohan will find it pretty hard to win his case even if he avails himself of the lying statements made by the appellant!

One or two letters have also appeared in the *Daily News* (the Calcutta paper of that name) speaking of my strong measures, also inspired by men whom I have checked; but my slumbers are perfect in spite of newspaper correspondence and affidavits! There is not a single point in my administration where they can really find fault with me.—Yours, R.

P.S.—Just after I had finished writing to you I received a letter from the Legal Remembrancer that the appeal against my order has been rejected by the High Court, as I expected. I have written all that I have written above so that you may not be nervous again when you hear of representations, &c., against me. Such representations will be made from time to time against me, as it is my duty to check influential men when they are wrong; but as I am never consciously wrong, the representations can do me absolutely no harm.

It may be mentioned here that Mr. Dutt obtained the Honours Degree for eminent proficiency in the Sanskrit language, in 1886.

II

Returning from Europe after his furlough, Mr. Dutt was appointed to Pabna, in 1887. He wrote in his "Rambles":—

I was glad to revisit the place where I had passed my boyhood thirty years ago. The school where I was educated was still standing, and the headmaster whom I had known in my boyhood was an old retired pensioner, and recognised me with pleasure. I found out the house where I had lived with my father; it was still standing, but considerably altered. And as District Officer I was occupying the very house where I had seen the play of "Macbeth" acted by European soldiers nearly thirty years ago.

> "I flew to the pleasant fields traversed so oft,
> In my life's morning march when my bosom was young."

The past came back to me as a dream, and my memory of those who had cast a sunshine over my early life often rose and filled my mind in hours of solitude. I remained only six months in Pabna, and was then transferred to Mymensingh, one of the largest and heaviest districts in Bengal.

But within this short time he succeeded in leaving an indelible impression on the minds of the people of Pabna. The following extract from an appreciation of his brief administration in this district, which appeared in the columns of the *Indian Mirror*, brings out almost all the salient features of his administrative work in the different districts of which he held charge:—

It rarely, or never, falls to the lot of a District Magistrate to be popular. But Mr. Dutt was, during his short stay at Pabna, literally idolised, and his approaching departure is now universally mourned. Magisterial high-handedness reached its boiling point during the last local régime, and Magistrates were objects of terror. In Mr. Dutt the community found a sympathising friend, a ready adviser, and generous administrator. The Municipality loved him and respected him. The Local Board considered it an honour to listen to his counsels. The local officials honoured him, not in methods conventional, but such as is due to a patriarch, and it was difficult to determine whether, in their feeling towards him, affection or regard preponderated most. He was more the object of love than reverence. His amiable manners, kindliness of disposition, and generous nature constituted a halo of attraction which should afford an example to "England-returned" Indians to follow.

As an office-master, Mr. Dutt was stern and inflexible. Diligent and untiring in the execution of work, his relations with his subordinates were extremely cordial and always friendly. He was to them not the taskmaster we read of in Biblical history, but a sympathetic co-worker, always smiling an encouraging smile in their uphill toils, and his smiles extorted more willing work than the frowns of his brother Magistrates. Mr. Dutt was quite an adept in managing the police. Not a single case of police oppression or high-handedness happened during his régime. There could not have been a warmer feeling than that which subsisted between him and the District Superintendent of Police.

As might naturally be expected, Mr. Dutt is a staunch advocate and supporter of Local Self-Government. Whereas in other districts magisterial interference with matters municipal is eyed with jealousy, Mr. Dutt's advice was courted by the civic authorities. He infused new blood into the Local Board's deliberations, and stimulated its members to take a more effective part in the task of Self-Government.

But if there was any matter in which Mr. Dutt took more than ordinary interest, it was in the cause of education. Being an ex-student of the Zillah School of Pabna, Mr. Dutt's personal example spoke with greater eloquence in the interest of education than anything else.

II

When Mr. Dutt was called upon to take charge of Mymensingh, the administrative machinery of that district had got very much out of gear. The District Magistrate had passed orders in connection with a fair in Jamalpur, which was not approved by Government. The Magistracy and Police in Tangail had got discredited, a case had been instituted against the Subdivisional Magistrate of Netrokona, and difficulties had also arisen in Kishorganj. At this critical time the Government of Sir Rivers Thompson decided to send the Indian Magistrate to Mymensingh. This was a most flattering recognition of his merits, and a signal token of the trust imposed in him by Government. He was not sent to Mymensingh till October 1887, but early in September he met the Lieutenant-Governor and Chief Secretary at Saraghat, when the party were on their way to Rangpur. Of this visit he thus wrote to his brother:—

I dined with the Lieutenant-Governor and slept on board the *Rhotas* last night, and will stay on here to see the Lieutenant-Governor off to-night. Sara is in Pabna district. Edgar told me that the Magistrate of Mymensingh has failed to bring that district to order, and the Lieutenant-Governor wishes to send me there in the hope that I shall be able to bring it to order. Mymensingh is probably the most difficult district in Bengal both for rioting and for revenue work, and I am glad to go there to see if I can't do what my predecessor has failed to do. Besides, Mymensingh is now connected by rail and steamer with Calcutta, and is an interesting district; while I am quite tired of Pabna, where there is enough work to worry you, but not enough to bring you any reputation.

After his appointment, the Chief Secretary, Sir John Edgar, wrote as follows:—

I have nothing to say to you at present except to express my confidence that you will justify my recommendation to the most difficult district, in many ways, that there is in Bengal.

Of his administration of the district he made the following notes:—

I thoroughly enjoyed my work in Mymensingh during two years and a half, for Mymensingh is a district where there is plenty of work for a District Officer to do. The area of the district is over six thousand square miles, and the population over three millions. There are four subdivisions, beside the Sadar, and every subdivision is large and important. Backerganj is a district of absentee zamindars and the raiyats assert themselves. Mymensingh is a district of rich resident zamindars, and the zamindars have great influence. Female zamindars display much tact and aptitude for business, and often distinguish themselves by acts of public charity and liberality.

Mymensingh is growing in population and in agriculture, and much of the land which was waste in the earlier part of the century has now been brought under cultivation. The demand for jute which has grown up within the last forty years has been a great impetus to the reclamation of fresh lands. Before the Crimean War of 1855, Russian flax supplied the European markets, and there was little demand for jute. But that war stopped the importation of Russian flax into England, a new fibre was wanted, and Bengal supplied it. Since then the cultivation of jute has gone on increasing, and nearly half the lands of this extensive district are under jute cultivation. Fortunes have been made and lost by jute trade, new trade centres of the first rank, like Narainganj and Serajganj, have sprung into existence. Large firms and steamer companies find occupation mainly in this trade, and factories with thousands of looms have been started in the country. In fact, the demand for jute in Europe has affected peasant life throughout East Bengal in a manner which is highly gratifying. And if the people of Bengal can learn to spin and weave for themselves the jute and the cotton which so plentifully grow in their country, they will have recovered in some degree the ground they have lost in the world's manufacturing trade.

As in other districts, his administration was marked by repression of crime, increase of prosperity amongst the people, and by a great development of roads and other communications. He is specially remembered for the road which he made from Mymensingh to Kishorgang. The new District Boards and Local Boards worked satisfactorily under his sympathetic guidance, and did a fair amount of useful work. The public hall at Tangail was called Romesh Chunder Hall, after him, and the High School at Netrokona was christened the Dutt High School. The local Technical School at Mymensingh also owes its origin to the efforts of Mr. Dutt. He was the first to propose a scheme for the supply of filtered pipe water to the town, although he was not there long enough to complete it. He took great interest in the local associations, "the Saraswat Samaj" and the "Zamindar-Sanmilani," of which latter institution he was president. His object in associating himself with these associations was to encourage zamindars to settle their disputes by arbitration, and to establish more cordial relations between zamindars and raiyats. Indeed, one of his principal claims to public recognition was his anxiety to bring about amicable relations between some of the most turbulent and litigious zamindars in the whole of Bengal, though his efforts in this direction were only partially successful. And the zamindars concerned were not slow in recognising his services. On the eve of his departure from the district, Janhavi Chaudhurani, one of the best known woman zamindars of the district, wrote to him as follows :—

HONOURED SIR,—I shall remain always grateful to you for the trouble which, impelled by your own generous instincts, you took to bring about a settlement of the disputes between myself and Bindu Basini Chaudhurani. I had hoped that both parties would act up to the lines of the agreement which you had taken from us. I, therefore, humbly pray that before leaving this district for Burdwan, you may be graciously pleased to finally settle all the points about which no action has yet been taken by the opposite party.—Yours *nibedica*,

JANHAVI CHAUDHURANI.

Her rival, Bindubasini, had the following letter written in English :—

DEAR SIR,—I hope you will be pleased to excuse me for addressing the following lines to you. I hear that your services have very recently been transferred to the district of Burdwan. Although this transfer from such an out of the way place as Mymensingh to one of the metropolitan districts must have been the result of a due appreciation by the Government of your excellent administration of the district, the people of Mymensingh will almost deplore the event as a great misfortune to them. It was your sincere desire to promote the welfare of the people of the district entrusted to your care, and you have been most successful in your endeavours.

As for myself, I can only assure you that your transfer from the district will deprive me of one of my best and most sincere well-wishers. During the time you have been administering the affairs of the district, I had always looked up to you for kind advice and assistance, and I have always been favoured with both. I can never forget the fact, that it was through your benevolent and sincere exertions that the agreement was arrived at between Srimati Janhavi Chaudhurani and myself. I had hoped that your connection with this district would be much longer, but as the Government has been pleased to remove you to a more desirable quarter, I can only assure you that I shall feel the loss as a personal one, and that I shall always gratefully remember all the kindness and generosity you have been pleased to show me during the time you have been at the head of the administration of the district.—I am, sir, most sincerely yours,

BINDUBASINI.

February 4th, /90,
22 MIRZAFFER'S LANE, CALCUTTA.

The members of the Sherepur Landholders' Association, at a meeting held on the 28th February, passed the following resolution :—

That this meeting deeply regrets to learn that Mr. R. C. Dutt, C.S., the most worthy and popular District Magistrate of Mymensingh, is going away from the district. The members feel it their duty to place on record their deep sense of obligation to him, for the interest he took in the well-being of all classes of people. During his administration, peace has been restored in several subdivisions; and several big families, who would otherwise have been ruined by internal feuds, have been saved by his attention and reconciled to each other. And it is highly gratifying to the Association that his efforts at abolishing the outstill system have been crowned with success. The Association wish him a long life, with happiness, peace, and prosperity.

Here, again, as in other districts, his relations with the other officials remained most cordial. The Commissioner of the division, Mr. C. F. Worsley, before leaving Dacca for Orissa, wrote to him as follows :—

DACCA, *28th November* 1889.

MY DEAR DUTT,—I am to go to Orissa as pucca Commissioner within a fortnight, much to my surprise and pleasure, though I shall be very sorry for many reasons to leave this Division. I hope you will be able to come to Dacca and say good-bye to me. The new chaplain and his wife—Mr. and Mrs. Cole—are staying with me, but I can give you a room on the ground floor. Fix your own day for coming, if you can spare the time, but give me a few hours' notice. I much regret that our official relations, which have been most pleasant and satisfactory to me, are so soon to come to an end. I have felt thorough confidence in your administration of what I take to be the heaviest district in the Lower Provinces, and I think Mymensingh, under your guidance, is making great progress.

Mr. Clay will succeed me, and is to take over charge on the second week of December. I trust you will find him a pleasant Commissioner to work with.

I shall carry away with me most happy recollections of this Division, and of the kindness and consideration of all with whom I have come in contact.—Yours sincerely,

C. F. WORSLEY.

IV

In April 1890 he was transferred from Mymensingh to Burdwan.

In the days of my boyhood [he noted in his "Rambles"] I had always heard of Burdwan as a healthy and flourishing and prosperous district, where one went for a change in order to recoup one's health. How changed the district is now, with its malarial fever! The fever has spread north and south, east and west, over both banks of the Hughli River, and over the whole of West Bengal. It is a national calamity which affects and enfeebles twenty millions of the people, which stops the increase of population, and which bids fair to last, one does not know, for how many years to come.

The change in the course of the main current of the Ganges appears to me to be the main cause why Western Bengal has now become unhealthy, while East Bengal is healthy. The hundreds of small channels and watercourses which brought Ganges water to the doors of villagers, and also effectually drained the country, are now stagnant pools or have been converted into rice fields!

The Census of 1872 showed that one-third of the population of Burdwan town had been swept away by this fell disease. Villages all over the district were desolated, and even the birth-rate was affected; and old villagers will tell you that there were few child-births for years after the disease first appeared in its virulence.

The gradual silting up of the Hughli is the main cause of malaria in West Bengal, but for Burdwan and Hughli districts the Damodar embankment is an additional cause.

In the winter of 1893 and the spring of the following year, after his return from furlough in Europe, Mr. Dutt again acted as Collector of this district. The Raja of Burdwan was then a minor, and his vast estates were under the management of the Court of Wards under the control of the Collector. The talented Raja Ban Behari Kapur, being the father of the minor Maharajah, was appointed manager of the estate and guardian of the ward. In a letter written after Mr. Dutt's death, the Raja said: "The impression I have of Mr. Dutt is that he was a capable worker and able administrator. He possessed a thorough knowledge of the district and its people. He had a noble and high mind, and was a thorough gentleman."

Late in the year 1890 he went from Burdwan to Dinajpur.

Dinajpur is said to have been the headquarters of the ancient Pal kings of Bengal. The large tanks in the district, some of them a mile long, are said to have been excavated by these kings, then the masters of Northern India. But Dinajpur and the whole of Northern Bengal were a great and civilised kingdom many centuries before the time of the Pal kings; for when Houen Tisiang came to Bengal in the seventh century, he found this Pundra land thickly populated, beautified with large tanks, flowering woods and fruit trees, and rich in all kinds of grain. There were many Hindu temples and Buddhist monasteries, and the Jaina ascetics were numerous.

The Dinajpur Raj is also an old territorial house in Bengal, and like all the old houses it suffered in the early years of British administration in Bengal. The maladministration of this district furnished the great Burke with materials for some of the most eloquent passages in his impeachment of Warren Hastings.

From Dinajpur, early in 1891, Mr. Dutt was sent to Midnapur.

Midnapur was another of the ancient districts [he wrote in the "Rambles"] visited by Houen Tisiang in the seventh century of the Christian era. The eastern half of the district is alluvial, cultivated, and thickly populated; the western half is undulating and rocky, covered with sal wood and scrub jungle, and sparsely populated by aboriginal tribes. The sea washes the southern shores of Midnapur, and the tired official is glad to pass a few days in a sea-side bungalow, and to have sea-bath. The Subarnarekha divides Midnapur from Orissa, and many were the battles fought in the olden days in this frontier land, first between the Uriyas and the Pathan conquerors, and then between the Pathan and the Moghal conquerors.

Mr. Dutt's administration of Midnapur is chiefly remembered on account of the vigorous measures he adopted to protect the raiyats from the high-handed conduct of Messrs. Watson & Co., a Calcutta firm, who owned large zamindaries in the western part of the district, in parganas Bogri and Silda, and cultivated indigo, and ran several factories for the manufacture of indigo. The irregular conduct of this company came to the notice of Government on several occasions, and the Commissioner, Mr. John Beams, tried to effect a compromise between the raiyats and the servants of the company, but no tangible results were obtained. Mr. Collier, the predecessor of Mr. Dutt, had on several occasions to adopt strong measures for the protection of the raiyats, and finally, under the advice of Mr. Dutt, Government transferred the subdivisional headquarters from Ghattal to Garhbetta, to enable the District Magistrate to more effectively control the action of the planters. The European manager of Silda was bound down to keep the peace by Mr. C. H. Bompas, I.C.S., the able assistant of Mr. Dutt, whilst his other assistant, Mr. J. G. Cumming, I.C.S., convicted and sentenced to various terms of imprisonment some of the Bagdis of the Company, for severely assaulting some raiyats who were going to the Munsif's court to deposit rents. The case went up in appeal before the Judge, Mr. James Pratt (afterwards a Justice of the High Court), who acquitted some of the prisoners and reduced the sentences of others, but made the following remarks in his judgment :—

> The outrage was brutal and cowardly, and happening as it did within hail of the Amlagora Factory, I think the District Magistrate should take steps to compel the responsible persons there, to range themselves on the side of law and order, and restrain their subordinates from resorting to brute force against inoffensive tenants.

Mr. Dutt was not slow to follow Mr. Pratt's advice, and sent up a long report to Government about this and similar cases, and again impressed upon the Government the necessity of placing a responsible officer at Garhbetta.

It was not to be expected that Watson & Co. would not exert their influence to get rid of such a disobliging District Magistrate, and petitions were sent to Government against Mr. Dutt. But the confidence of Government in Mr. Dutt remained unshaken. In connection with one of these petitions, the Chief Secretary wrote to Mr. Dutt as follows :—

CAMP KHURDA,
Dated 20th Feby. 1892.

MY DEAR DUTT,—The Lieutenant-Governor bids me say that he accepts unreservedly your explanation on the pseudonymous memorial which was sent to you for report by the Commissioner. He has no intention of transferring you from Midnapur, and would be most unwilling to do so. Sir Henry Harrison has lately spoken of your management of the district in high terms.

I shall hope to see you in Calcutta during your leave.—Yours sincerely, H. J. S. COTTON.

But the malarial climate of Burdwan and Dinajpur had undermined his constitution, and Mr. Dutt was compelled to go on furlough in the autumn of 1892. Before leaving Midnapur, the Government, in recognition of his work both as a District Officer and in the field of literature, decorated him and made him a Com panion of the Order of the Indian Empire. The Lieutenant-Governor, in writing to congratulate Mr. Dutt, said "both as a District Officer and as an author you have well deserved this distiction."

His friends and admirers gave Mr. Dutt a dinner on the 27th August, on the eve of his departure from Midnapur, and everything passed off very successfully. All the European officials of the station were present, including Messrs. Pratt, Munro, Maxwell, Buchanan, Halliday, M'Kennie, Marriot, together with Mr. K. B. Dutt, barrister-at-law, and several Indian gentlemen belonging to the subordinate executive and judicial services and to the Bar. At the conclusion of the dinner, Babu Kartick Chunder Mitter, a Prem Chand Roy Chand Scholar, and a leading member of the Midnapur Bar, proposed the health of the guest of the evening in very flattering terms. He alluded to the long and successful official career of Mr. Dutt, and his successful work at Midnapur, and dwelt on the high distinction which Mr. Dutt had attained as a literary man, and as an historian of his country. Mr. James Pratt, the Judge of Midnapur, seconded the proposed toast, and in a very flattering speech referred to the brilliant official career of Mr. Dutt. He said he had known Mr. Dutt in two of the heaviest districts in Bengal, in Mymensingh and in Midnapur, and that the tact, vigour, and ability displayed by Mr. Dutt in both these places were such as he had never seen exceeded. Mr. Pratt alluded specially to the tact with which Mr. Dutt, as the District Officer of Mymensingh, had brought about a reconciliation between two female zamindars, who had been fighting for years past, and whose disputes had been a scandal to the district. "If Mr. Dutt had done nothing more than he had done in Mymensingh," concluded Mr. Pratt, "he would have deserved all the honours which Government had bestowed on him."

This practically closed Mr. Dutt's career as a District Officer. It only remains to note that his name was mentioned for special commendation, in the administration reports of the Board of Revenue, L. P., practically every year from 1883 to 1884, to his appointment as Divisional Commissioner in 1894.

CHAPTER VIII

REPORT ON TENANCY ACT AND OTHER OFFICIAL LITERATURE

I

THERE has been no legislative measure in the last half of the nineteenth century which has caused so much excitement in India, and aroused such bitter and senseless racial animosity, as the attempt of the Government of India to modify the Criminal Procedure Code in such a manner, as to enable Indian Magistrates to have jurisdiction in cases in which European subjects are the accused. The Bill which created the uproar was known as the Ilbert Bill, although it did not originate in any opinion given by Sir Courtenay Ilbert, then Law Member of Council, but was the outcome of a letter of the Bengal Government, 20th March 1882, written under Sir Ashley Eden's orders, and enclosing a note from Mr. B. L. Gupta, I.C.S., which really initiated the whole matter. It appears that when Act X. of 1882 (the Criminal Procedure Code) was before the Council, Mr. Dutt, who was then District Officer of Bankura, requested Mr. B. L. Gupta, then Presidency Magistrate of Calcutta, to exert himself to remove the provision of law by which Indian officers, even though in executive and judicial charge of districts, were disqualified from trying European offenders. Mr. Gupta, who knew Sir Ashley Eden well, saw him on the subject, and Sir Ashley received Mr. Gupta's views favourably, and asked him to submit a note. Sir Ashley Eden's opinion is expressed as follows in the celebrated letter from the Government of Bengal :—

As a question of general policy, it seems to the Lieutenant-Governor right that covenanted native civilians should be empowered to exercise jurisdiction over Europeans, as well as over natives, who are brought before them in their capacity as criminal judges. Now that native covenanted civilians may shortly be expected to hold the office of District Magistrate or Sessions Judge, it is also, as a matter of administrative convenience, desirable that they should have the power to try all classes of persons brought before them. Moreover, if this power is not conferred upon native members of the Civil Service, the anomaly may be presented of a European Joint-Magistrate who is subordinate to a native District Magistrate or Sessions Judge, being empowered to try cases which his immediate superior cannot try. Native Presidency Magistrates within the towns exercise the same jurisdiction over Europeans that they do over natives, and there seems to be no sufficient reason why Covenanted Native Civilians, with the position and training of a District Magistrate or a Sessions Judge, should not exercise the same jurisdiction over Europeans as is exercised by other members of the service.

Mr. Dutt submitted his views on the subject when he was Magistrate of Barisal, and the letter of Mr. Grant, Officiating Commissioner of Dacca, published in the supplement to the *India Gazette*, September 8, 1883, quoted his opinion in full. It contained the following admirable paragraph :—

It will not strengthen a District Officer in keeping peace in his district, for which he is responsible, when he is told, and the people of his district are told, that he has no power over one privileged class of people; that he cannot punish and cannot deal with a disturbance if committed by that class, perhaps in the *bazar* or the station in which he resides; and that for dealing with such cases he must have recourse to the authorities of a neighbouring district. It is clearly not desirable that the people should be told that in districts administered by Indian officers, there is no redress against petty acts of violence by European offenders, unless the complainants choose to seek such redress by submitting themselves and their witnesses to the hardship and inconvenience of travelling to a different district. Unfavourable opinions will be formed by the people of an officer in whom Government seems not to repose full confidence, and who is not empowered by Government to keep all classes of people in his district equally in order. It is to be judged whether it is desirable to weaken the hands of a District Officer who is held responsible by Government for the peace and criminal administration of his district. The real question was decided when it was decided that the Indian members of the Covenanted Service should be allowed to hold executive and judicial charge of districts. This was a generous and a bold concession, for with that concession the vast powers and responsibilities of ruling the people, which had hitherto been exclusively held by Englishmen, were generously shared by them with qualified native gentlemen. Having admitted them to a share of those great powers and responsibilities; having called upon them to administer districts, collect revenue, extend education, and keep down crime; having required from them the same degree of efficiency and administrative vigour and wisdom as has hitherto been manifested by trained English administrators, it is no longer possible for Government to meddle with the powers which naturally belong to that position, and which are necessary for the responsible work which has to be done. Little distinctions, small curtailment of powers, petty disqualifications based on race or caste, are out of place, are virtually impossible, when it has been decided to entrust the administration of districts to the natives of India. Legislation cannot halt where it is; it must proceed or move backwards.

There can, indeed, be little question that the compromise accepted by Government, and embodied in the Bill which actually passed into law, was really a retrograde movement. Sir John Strachey has thus described the result :—

The controversy ended with the virtual, though not avowed, abandonment of the measure proposed by the Government. Act III. of 1884 extended rather than diminished the privileges of European British subjects charged with offences, and left their position as exceptional as before. The general disqualification of native Judges and Magistrates remains; but if a native be appointed to the post of District Magistrate or Sessions Judge, his powers in regard to jurisdiction over European British subjects will be the same as those of an Englishman holding a similar office. This provision, however, is subject to the condition that every European British subject brought for trial before the District Magistrate or Sessions Judge has the right, however trivial be the charge, to claim to be tried by a jury of which not less than half the number shall be Europeans or Americans.

There are many districts in which it may happen, when a charge against a European British subject comes before a District Magistrate, that a sufficient number of Europeans and Americans cannot be found to constitute a jury; the case must then, under the orders of the High Court, be transferred to another district where a jury can be formed. Thus opportunity is offered for the occasional revival of the old scandals and denials of justice and hardship which were common before 1872, when the trial of European British subjects could only take place before the High Courts, and complainants and witnesses were liable to be sent away to great distances from their homes.[1]

II

The report which Mr. Dutt submitted to Government on the proposed Tenancy Bill of 1884 first established his reputation as a capable revenue officer, whose sympathy with the raiyats was only equalled by his knowledge of the actual agrarian conditions of Bengal. As we have seen, he stood up as a champion of the poor and voiceless cultivators against the aggressions of rich and powerful zamindars from almost the beginning of his service, and there was no cause which was dearer to his heart and for which he did such manful battle throughout his whole life as the cause of the poor agricultural population of India.

The course of legislation on this important subject is described by Mr. Buckland in his "Bengal under the Lieutenant-Governors," of which a summary is given below:—

The Bengal Tenancy Act of 1885 may be considered to be the great charter of the raiyats, as Regulation I. of 1793 (the Permanent Settlement) was for the landowners. It is true that, while giving the zamindars permanent rights, Lord Cornwallis specially reserved to the State the right to legislate in the interests of the raiyats when there should be any occasion. Yet, curiously enough, Regulation VII. of 1799—the notorious Haftam, Regulation V. of 1812—the Pancham, and Regulation XI. of 1832, all

[1] Quoted in Mr. Buckland's "Bengal under the Lieutenant-Governors," vol. ii. p. 790.

added to the power of the landlord over the raiyat, and up to the middle of the last century the zamindars exercised an authority over the raiyats far greater than that given to them by the Permanent Settlement. The first tenant law was Act X. of 1859, which defined the class of tenant whose rent was fixed, and conferred a right of occupancy on those who had continuously held the same land for twelve years, either personally or through their predecessors from whom the holding descended. The principal defects of Act X. of 1859 were, that it placed the right of occupancy which it recognised in the tenant, and the right of enhancement which it recognised in the landlord, on a precarious footing. It gave, or professed to give, the raiyat a right which he could not prove, and the landlord one which he could not enforce. The courts of law, with rigid impartiality, required the raiyat to establish his occupancy right by showing that he had cultivated the same plot of land for twelve successive years, and demanded from the landlord the impossible proof that the value of the produce had increased in the same proportion in which he asked that his rent should be enhanced. The party upon whom lay the burden of proof was almost certain to fail. To this evil the Bengal Tenancy Act (Act VIII. of 1885) was intended to afford a remedy. The principle of the Act may be said to be based upon a system of fixity of tenure at judicial rents, and its three main objects are—first, to give the settled raiyat the same security in his holding as he enjoyed under the old customary law; secondly, to ensure to the landlord a fair share of the increased value of the produce of the soil; and, thirdly, to lay down rules by which all disputed questions between landlord and tenant can be reduced to simple issues and decided upon equitable principles.

The necessity for legislation had, indeed, been apparent ever since the occurrence, in 1873, of the serious agricultural disturbances in Pabna. The Bihar famine of the following year diverted the attention of the Government to more pressing duties, but the report of the Famine Commission dwelt strongly on the necessity of placing the relations of landlord and tenant in Bengal upon a surer basis. The Agrarian Disputes Act of 1876 was passed by Sir R. Temple's Government as a temporary measure to meet emergencies like those of 1873, pending the fuller consideration of the whole question. A Bill dealing with the principles upon which rents should be fixed was prepared in 1876, but was not further proceeded with, and in 1878 the Government of Bengal proposed a measure intended to provide only for the more speedy realisation of arrears of rent. This Bill was introduced into the

Bengal Council, but it was found impracticable to confine it to the limited object indicated by its original title. The Select Committee on the Bill recommended that the whole question of a revision of the rent law should be taken in hand, and in April 1879 the Government of India sanctioned the appointment of a Commission to prepare a digest of the existing law, and to draw up a consolidating enactment. Proposals which had been separately made for amending the rent law in Bihar were also referred to the Commission for consideration.

The report and draft Bill of the Commission were presented in July 1880, and, after the whole question had been further considered, the matured proposals of Sir A. Eden's Government were submitted to the Government of India in July 1881. In March 1882 these papers were forwarded by the Government of India to the Secretary of State, with an important despatch, in which the history of the question was reviewed, and the views of the Governor-General in Council, of which Sir R. Thompson was a member, were fully explained. The Secretary of State demurred to the proposals of the Government of India regarding "occupancy right," and consequently a revised draft of the Bill was prepared by the Government of India, and referred to a Select Committee. A preliminary report was presented, including a revised draft of the Bill. The revised Bill was republished, and was subjected to a careful examination by Divisional conferences of the executive officers of Government, as well as by judicial officers, and by the non-official public.

It was on this occasion that Mr. Dutt was consulted, and submitted the able and full report which was published in the *Calcutta Gazette* of October 15, 1884.

The Revenue Secretary to Government, Mr. Antony MacDonnell (now Lord MacDonnell), to whom Mr. Dutt sent a copy of his report direct, in acknowledging it, wrote as follows :—

26/8/84.

MY DEAR SIR,—Your letter of the tenth and your report on the Tenancy Bill have reached me. I have read your report with much interest, and think it one of the most valuable contributions to the literature of the subject we have received. It will be published with the papers of the case. It is probable that the Lieutenant-Governor will adopt, possibly with some modification, the recommendation you make under Section 8 and with reference to registration. The Bengal report on the Bill is now nearly ready, and if it is not accepted as a fair solution of a very difficult question, the question may be regarded as insoluble, at least by us. I should be very glad to receive from you any criticisms on the Bengal report (when published) that may occur to you. You look at things in the light of practical experience, and your observations cannot fail to be of benefit.—Yours sincerely, A. P. MACDONNELL.

The Chief Secretary, Sir John Edgar, writing to Mr. Dutt about this time, said: "I was very glad to hear both the Lieutenant-Governor and the Revenue Secretary speak highly of your report on the Tenancy Bill." Indeed, the Government of Bengal in their letter to the Government of India supported and accepted most of Mr. Dutt's suggestions. The following extracts from the Bengal Government letter will be of interest :—

Paragraph 14. *Presumption of status of tenure-holder from area of holding.*

The Dacca Conference and Mr. Dampier, who even favour a reduction of the area, would change the presumption into an absolute rule, in which case, Mr. Dutt, Collector of Backerganj, hereby meeting several objections, would allow a fee to be levied on the creation of the tenure.

Paragraph 15. *Status, rights, and liabilities of tenure-holders.*

The remarks of Mr. Lowis, Commissioner of Chittagong, and of Mr. Romesh Chunder Dutt, Officiating Collector of Backerganj, are especially valuable, and to them the Lieutenant-Governor would invite particular attention.

Paragraph 17. *Limitation of enhancement to double the former rent.*

Then, as regards section 8, the Lieutenant-Governor, agreeing with the Presidency Conference and the Collector of Backerganj, is of opinion that some amendment must be introduced. In cases of recent reclamation, where land is let at an initial pepper-corn rent, the limit of double rent would be unjust to the landlord; in other cases it would tend to injustice to the tenant.

Agreeing with those who hold that the substantive law should meet all cases, where this can be done, the Lieutenant-Governor would cut out section 212, and provide for such cases in this place, and also under Chapter V., by substituting for section 8 the section in the margin, which he has adapted from the excellent report of Mr. Dutt, Officiating Collector of Backerganj. It will be seen from the observations I am to make under section

45, withdrawing the limitations on the enhancements by suit of raiyats' rent, that a tenure-holder will always be able to raise his raiyats' rents in due proportion to the increase which he himself may have to pay.

Paragraph 18. *Simplified procedure for registration of transfer.* The only other point on the subject of tenures which the Lieutenant-Governor desires to notice is registration, and in regard to it he invites the attention of the Government of India to the remark made by the Collector of Backerganj.

Mr. Dutt recommended the following procedure :—

Parties transferring tenures generally register the deeds-of-sale, and this may now be made compulsory under the provisions of this Bill. Registrars will in such cases take an additional fee of two per cent. on the annual rent of the land, and also the sum of one rupee for service of notice on the landlord. These sums he will remit to the Collector, with an intimation of the contents of the document. The Collector will transmit the fee to the landlord, and also serve notice on him to show cause within a month why the sale should not be declared valid. In case there is no objection raised, the sale will be declared valid after the expiry of the month. In case objection is raised by the landlord, the Collector will refer the matter to the Civil Court, which will then proceed under section 19 of the Bill.

This procedure was accepted by the Lieutenant-Governor as being "at once simple and effective."

Paragraph 33. *Objections to pre-emption clauses of the Bill.* The pre-emption clauses of the Bill meet, as the Government of India will observe, with no approval, and it is in the Lieutenant-Governor's opinion essential that they should be abandoned.

As the Collector of Backerganj says, "a raiyat seldom sells his land except under sudden and pressing necessity. To give the landlord the right of pre-emption under such circumstances, and to compel the vendor to comply with the dilatory procedure laid down in section 32, would be virtually to stop the sale when the necessity is pressing."

It was only natural that Mr. Dutt should be highly gratified at the appreciation of his report by Government. He wrote thus to his brother :—

BARISAL, *16th Oct.* 1884.

MY DEAR BROTHER,—My report, along with other reports, has been published in the extra supplement of the *Indian Gazette* of the 11th instant. I almost blush to read the frequent and favourable notices of my report which the L. G. has taken of my report in his despatch to the India Government. But what makes me more glad is that all my important suggestions have been accepted, and the Bill, if passed in the shape it has now assumed, will do lasting good to the country. Sir Rivers Thompson, in spite of his numerous faults and mistakes, will be a real benefactor to the millions of the country if he can pass the Bill as he recommends it. But will he succeed? Zamindari opposition in the Council will be violent and severe, and there are half-hearted men who will be willing to make low promises, and any compromise in any of the main points will mean ruin. I am still in demi-official correspondence with Mr. MacDonnell on the subject of the Bill, and I will continue to do my utmost to guard against any treacherous tinkering with the present proposals.—Yours affly., ROMESH.

Mr. Dutt's apprehensions, however, proved to be only too true, as will be seen from the following :—

On the 27th February 1885, the Bill was brought forward in Council by Sir Steuart Bayley, who moved that the report of the Select Committee should be taken into consideration. But the Bill was not passed by the Council till the 11th March, received the assent of the Governor-General on the 14th, and became law as Act VIII. of 1885. This Act differed in some important particulars from the Bill which had been introduced into Council two years before. The Bill, as originally brought in, embodied provisions for the sale of *patni taluks;* but it was eventually determined to leave Regulation VIII. of 1819 untouched. The settled raiyat acquired by the original Bill an occupancy right in all land held by him in the village or estate. The Act limited this to land held in the same village. The occupancy raiyat was empowered to transfer his holding, subject to a right of preemption by the landlord at a price to be fixed by the Civil Court. The pre-emption clauses were struck out, and the power of transfer was left to be regulated by local custom. The rent of an occupancy raiyat could not be enhanced, under the Bill, to an amount exceeding one-fifth of the gross produce, nor that of a non-occupancy raiyat to an amount exceeding five-sixteenths, but no limitation of this kind found a place in the Act. In suits for enhancement, the Bill provides that no increase of demand in excess of double the old rent should be awarded; but there was no corresponding provision in the Act. A prominent feature of the Bill was the preparation of table of rates, by which lands were to be classified according to the capabilities of the soil, and rent rates were to be fixed, which should be in force for not less than ten, or more than thirty years; but this chapter was entirely struck out. The Bill provided that the non-occupancy raiyat, if he were ejected from his holding, should receive compensation for disturbance; but no such stipulation will be found in the Act.

While the Act was still under the anvil of the Council, Mr. Dutt supplied fresh information to Government. Two of the letters of the Revenue Secretary written about this time may be quoted here:—

WRITERS' BUILDINGS, The 1-12-84.

MY DEAR MR. DUTT,—I have been away on leave, and also very busy since my return, facts which I trust will explain the delay in replying to your two letters regarding the so-called "tenure holders'" meetings. I have laid both letters before His Honour. They have been of use to us in showing the opposition in its true light. You will be glad to hear that so far as the Select Committee has yet gone with its revision of the Bill, we have no reason to complain of the result. I am also hopeful as to the future. Trusting you are keeping well,—Yours sincerely,

A. P. MACDONNELL.

MY DEAR MR. DUTT,—You will probably have seen from last *Gazette of India* the result of all our struggles to secure for the country a just Rent Law. It will, therefore, be unnecessary for me to reply in detail to your letter, which I was glad to receive. I do not abandon all hope that the Bill may be somewhat improved by motions of amendment in Council, but it is now, I fear, quite hopeless to expect that it can be what we wanted in any of the points noticed by you. This is the more disappointing to me, to people who like yourself think with me, because it seemed but a short time ago that things were going fairly well.

It would be impossible in the short space of a letter to explain the various reasons which have brought about this result; some of them are not even now clear to me: of others I cannot think with patience. The only hope, or perhaps I should say my great source of solace, is that in the long run the just cause must triumph. The landlords of Bengal are preparing for themselves the same sort of bed which a similar short-sighted policy made for landlords in my native country—Ireland. I can only trust that the pains of lying on the bed may be not so great for Bengal as it has been for Irish landlords.

We at all events have done our best, and we can do nothing after the struggle is, for the time, over, but put up, as best we can, against the obloquy we have incurred and the interested misinterpretations of our acts. The future lies with us: and in the future struggle, should it be precipitated by unwisdom on the landlords' part in our time, I hope you and I may be fighting in the same side again.—Yours sincerely,

A. P. MacDonnell.

III

In February 1891, he wrote from Dinajpur to the *Indian Mirror* two letters on the Age of Consent Bill, outlining what he called a "practicable solution of a difficult problem." At the conclusion of the second letter, he made a characteristic suggestion:—

I implore my countrymen, therefore, those to whom we look up for intellectual guidance and real progress, to convene a great meeting on this subject. Let the Bill itself, and the modifications proposed, be calmly discussed, and let suggestions, supporting the principle of the Bill and modifying it into shape, best suited to modern Hindu notions, be adopted. Having thus agreed among ourselves, let us approach the Government, as the Muhammadan community has approached, tendering our services and our help to the cause of progress and the repression of a sin against nature, but safeguarding our existing customs against sudden and violent change. The split which appeared to threaten our unity will thus be healed, and the whole nation and its numerous associations and organised bodies, social, religious, and political, will bless the names of the true reformers and patriots who will thus stand forth to secure our unity, to serve the cause of progress, and to safeguard the customs of the day against a violent change.

Commenting upon this wise intervention, the *Indian Mirror* said:—

The two letters from our distinguished Bengal Civilian, Mr. R. C. Dutt, one of which appeared in these columns yesterday, and the other of which we publish this morning, have been most opportune, and will go far to strengthen the hands of Government, and also to restore harmony among the contending factions. Mr. Dutt is as good an authority as any other on Hindu Shastras and all ancient and modern Hindu writings, and he can claim to speak with the very highest authority. And he has shown conclusively that the early consummation of marriage is a comparatively modern innovation, that it was altogether unknown in Ancient India, for early marriage was likewise then unknown; that the consummation of marriage on the appearance of the first signs of puberty is a modern custom, which has crept into Hindu society within the last few centuries, and that it so crept in after the Muhammadan conquest and when Hindu national life had become extinct. It was then only that Raghunandan and other commentators had their innings. Mr. Dutt's second letter, headed "A Practicable Solution of a Difficult Question," which we publish this morning, ought to command the widest attention. It will be seen that Mr. Dutt enforces our own arguments. He says that the time for mutual recrimination has passed, and the time for mutual suggestions for the modification of the Age of Consent Bill has come. We hope, with our distinguished correspondent, that "the time is now come for the moderate and sensible men from both sides to join hands, and to agree to some common proposal." These are our own sentiments, as given expression to several times in these columns. As we ourselves said yesterday, and on a previous occasion, Mr. Dutt would not regard the opinions of "dishonest men among us who trade, with vast profit to themselves, either in the name of Hindu orthodoxy, or in the name of social reforms." Of course, it is the interest of such men to let the controversy go on indefinitely. But the country cannot afford to play their game. Mr. Dutt has quoted the three alternative proposals, which have been suggested to the Government already, viz. those of Mr. Manomohun Ghose, of Mr. A. O. Hume, and of Sir Romesh Chunder Mitter. It is Mr. Dutt's idea that these moderate proposals should be considered at a great "historical" meeting, to be held in Calcutta, and at which Sir Romesh Chunder Mitter himself may preside. We think that such a meeting, composed of moderate men from both sides, and from which the violent and the dishonest are carefully excluded, might really lead to what Mr. Dutt calls a practicable solution of a difficult question.

IV

The only other official report, submitted by Mr. Dutt about this period of his service, to which reference should be made is his note on Country Spirits. This appeared in the Report of the Excise Commission, appointed by Sir Rivers Thompson in December 1883, to consider and report upon the subject of the Excise on Country Spirits, in all its aspects. The Commission was appointed "in consequence of clear indications of a serious increase in the consumption of spirituous liquors in Bengal, and as there appeared to be reason to believe that this increase was to some extent due either to the outstill system of excise, or to the manner in which that system has been worked." The following quotations from his note express Mr. Dutt's views on this important question :—

The introduction of the outstill system undoubtedly had the effect of repressing illicit distillation of country spirit to a great extent. The evils, however, which the new system introduced were found to be far greater than those which it checked. Liquor was sold so cheap at the outstills that a large proportion of the aboriginal and semi-aboriginal people became consumers. Under the previous system a very small section only could afford to buy distillery liquor, and another very small section habitually evaded the law and distilled for themselves, while the mass of the drinking population contented themselves with *pachwai* or rice-beer. Under the new system the great mass of them gave up *pachwai* and took to country spirit.

For many reasons I consider country spirit a bad substitute for the rice-beer. Rice-beer or *pachwai* is food, it has much nourishment in it, and, while it slightly inebriates, it scarcely does any harm. Country spirit, on the other hand, is pure drink and not food ; it intoxicates much more, and affords no nourishment ; it leads to greater excess, and it tells on the constitution.

My observations in Bankura often reminded me of the two celebrated paintings of Hogarth—one of Beer Lane, and the other of Gin Lane ; the one a picture of comfort and happiness, the other a picture of misery, degradation, and sin.

My remarks about the district of Backerganj will be very brief. The large semi-aboriginal population that one meets within western districts is almost entirely absent in Backerganj, and drunkenness on any large scale is also entirely absent. There is no general demand for drink, and no general supply. In a tract of country 80 miles long and 60 miles broad, inhabited by nearly two millions of the most prosperous and well-to-do cultivators and traders, there are only 75 outstills. The reason is obvious. The great mass of the Musalman and Hindu population will have nothing to do with drink, and it is a matter of no importance to them whether the distillery system or the outstill system is in force, whether the country liquor is dear or cheap.

But more interesting than his remarks on the effects of different systems of excise administration are the observations which he makes at the conclusion of his report on the allegation made in certain quarters that English education has introduced drinking amongst the more respectable and educated classes of Indians:—

I wish to make a few general remarks about drinking among respectable and educated men. It is a mistake to say, as is often said, that English education has introduced drink in India. Drink was well known in ancient India, and we know enough of the facts of the last century to be able to assert that drinking was a fashionable vice among the courtiers and retainers of princely zamindars. Devout *Shakta* worshippers have also been partial to drink for many centuries in Bengal, and semi-aboriginal castes have always been addicted to drink. There can be no doubt, however, that with the introduction of English education in Bengal in the early part of this century a sort of impetus was given to drinking among the higher classes. Educated men who broke through the prejudices against forbidden food disregarded at the same time the salutary restraint against drink. Drinking was regarded as a sort of index to liberal ideas and reformed ways, as a commendable accomplishment in an educated gentleman. When there is a reaction against ancient prejudices and senseless social restraints, it is difficult to confine it within exact and proper bounds, and the first distinguished men from the Hindu College, who took part in all the commendable political and educational reforms a generation or two ago, were generally men who were not admired for their sober habits in private life. The example of these distinguished men was of course followed by a large circle of educated men in Calcutta.

I have noticed with pleasure a salutary change in the Calcutta society within the last twenty years or less. A closer knowledge of English society, derived from a more careful study as well as by the frequent visits of our young men to Europe, has convinced our educated countrymen that drinking is not a necessary accomplishment in English society, and that drunkenness is simply not tolerated. The public men of the present generation, who take a lead in most political and social agitations, and whom the great majority of educated men almost instinctively follow to some extent, are setting a commendable example of temperance, which is different from the example which was set thirty years ago. The thousands of schoolboys who flock to public places to listen to the speeches of their leaders on political and social matters are intimately acquainted with their habits and thoughts in private life, and instinctively adopt many worthy and amiable traits in their conduct. I believe I am right in stating that drunkenness is decreasing among the higher and better educated classes in Calcutta, and the example set in Calcutta spread rapidly among the similar classes in all mofussal towns.

I have made the foregoing remarks in order to show that drinking among the educated classes has nothing whatever to do with the outstill system, and that it depends entirely on other influences on which excise legislation has no control. A great deal of what is wrong or objectionable in the present day is also laid at the door of English education. Thoughtful men and sincere well-wishers of this country and its people often regret that the old patriarchal system in India should be so suddenly and rudely disturbed before another system has sprung up to take its place, and they doubt if it is wise to suddenly enfranchise young members of the society, and to let them act and think in any way that they please. I confess I am somewhat of an optimist in these matters, but in justice to myself I may be permitted to state that I have formed my opinion entirely on my own personal observations. I speak from my own observations when I state that the old system is being slowly replaced by a new system, and that the new conditions of life and thought are healthier on the whole than the old, while they are undoubtedly more suited to the requirements of the present day. We miss in modern Bengal society some of the amiable characteristic features of old Hindu life, like simplicity, obedience and unobtrusiveness, and we are struck at first sight with much that is undesirable or positively objectionable. But a closer examination always reveals the fact that in real kindliness of heart, in real helpfulness to dependants and friends, and in the faithful discharge of the affectionate duties which he owes to his kith and kin, the educated Indian who has broken through the joint family system is not inferior to his forefathers. In many nobler and citizen-like qualities, in integrity, in thought and action, in public spirit and devotion to duty, and in an honest endeavour to serve his country, he is pre-eminently superior to those who went before him. When every one is allowed to speak and to act, much that is foolish, and much that is positively objectionable will be said and done; but the follies which are incident to a sudden change in the social system will be corrected by time, while the real improvement that is taking place in thoughts and ideas will last and will bear fruit. The development of citizen-like and commendable qualities, which is due mainly to English education, has already begun to bear fruit in society, and I may add is already receiving graceful recognition by Government. The Municipal Act which has just been passed, and the Local Self-Government measure which is likely to pass in the next cold season, are instances in point.

V

The statistics of crime for 1890 attracted attention. It was found that an unduly large proportion of crime was not reported, and that police inquiry into a large number of cases proved infructuous, and that a disproportionate number of persons brought before the courts were acquitted. A Provincial Committee was therefore appointed by Sir Steuart Bayley, under the order of the Government of India, to inquire minutely into the causes of the unsatisfactory state of the police work of the province, and to ascertain by what means, whether legislative or executive, remedies capable of being made effective could be devised and applied.

Mr. Dutt, while Collector of Burdwan, submitted an exhaustive report on the subject, which was incorporated in the final report of the Committee published in 1891. Jointly with this report of Mr. Dutt's should be considered his report (September 1891) submitted on the draft Bill to amend the Chaukidari Act of 1870, in accordance with the recommendations of the Police Committee. Subsequently, in 1892, he published a small pamphlet entitled "The Chaukidari Act: A Difficulty and its Solution," in which he still further elaborated his views with regard to the creation of an effective machinery of village local self-government, calculated to bring the Subdivisional Officer and the District Magistrate into closer and more sympathetic touch with the people. In both these reports, Mr. Dutt strongly controverted the view that the rural police should be completely subordinated to the regular police. In his first report he showed that actual experience does not justify the anticipation of any tangible improvements in the detection and suppression of crime by a more complete subordination of the rural police to the Police Department than actually existed at the time. In most of the thanas in Burdwan, he pointed out, although the Chaukidari Act did not apply and the chaukidars were completely under the control of the Superintendent of Police, the rural police force in Burdwan was admittedly more inefficient than in most other districts. Similarly in municipal areas, where the municipal police constables took the place of chaukidars of rural areas, the actual figures showed that crime was much more rife and detection much poorer. In his report on the draft Bill to amend the Chaukidari Act, and in his pamphlet, he developed the idea that an excellent solution of the difficulty would be to organise a system of local self-governing bodies, with elementary powers and responsibilities ; and to subordinate the rural police to these bodies, subject of course to the general control and supervision of the Subdivisional Officer and the District Magistrate. His views on this point are of great interest, and are slowly but surely forcing their way to public recognition.

The panchayeti system has failed [he wrote] because every little village with about eighty houses has been made into a separate Chaukidari Union, and we have sought to find within such small unions, inhabited by ignorant villagers, men fit to carry out the provisions of the law. The panchayeti system will succeed if we form unions with larger areas, including groups of villages, so as to make the selection of intelligent and educated men possible. If a small agricultural village with a hundred families of cultivators be made into a Chaukidari Union, as has been done hitherto, we can only get ignorant cultivators to be appointed as members of panchayets, and the system must be a failure. If, on the other hand, we enlarge our limits and group together ten or twelve villages to form a union, we can find within it men of influence, intelligence, and some education—men who are respected in the neighbourhood and are willing to loyally serve Government in the work of administration. Men of the position of Talukdar, and respectable trader, and Mahajan, a priest, a village physician, a village schoolmaster, a cultivator on a large scale, may be found within such limits willing to come forward for election; and such men are likely to help us in our administration.

We have every reason to expect much help from panchayets so constituted. The District Officer and the Subdivisional Officer will obtain from intelligent and representative bodies much useful local information, and will also obtain from them help in making local inquiries and settling local disputes. The District Board and the Local Boards will utilise them in superintending schools, *pathshalas*, and dispensaries, in reserving tanks in villages for drinking purposes, and generally in the work of village sanitation. On extraordinary occasions, as during a famine or during census operations, such local bodies will be of the greatest help to us. *And on all occasions they will form a link, which does not at present exist, between the Government and the people.* In the absence of such local bodies really representing the villagers, government officers have no real touch with the people; their administrative acts are misunderstood; and their measures and objects are unknown to the mass of the people.

These views were partially shared by other experienced and senior officers in the service. Mr. Cotton, then Chief Secretary to the Bengal Government, to whom Mr. Dutt sent a copy of the pamphlet, wrote :—

I am much obliged to you for your little pamphlet. Although we differ as far as the question of police control is concerned, on all other points in regard to unions we are, I think, in agreement.

In his speech in the Council of the Lieutenant-Governor, Mr. Cotton said :—

I am far from asserting that local self-government may not be extended to villages in this province. I believe that some steps might judiciously have been taken in this direction. I believe that the union contemplated under the Local Self-Government Act might have been established and organised with a view to exercise of particular functions. But those functions are functions of a purely local character. If you extend the principle of local self-government to a village or group of villages, it must be limited in its application to questions in which alone that village or group of villages is interested—that is to say, such objects as sanitation, keeping tanks clean, the provision of good drinking water, it may be the drainage of a portion of a village, the clearing of jungle, and the like. It occurs to me that this latter is one of the first things which may properly and rightly be entrusted to village unions. Again, there is the question of village communications. What can more aptly be made over to local bodies in the mofussal than the control over its village roads, or the control over schools, primary schools, the village *pathshalas*.

In the amended Chaukidari Act which was passed, the control of the rural police was, however, left entirely with the District Magistrate, and public opinion read in this measure a continuance of the old unsatisfactory state of affairs, in which both the panchayets and the rural police are in reality completely subservient to the regular police.

As was to be anticipated, critics were not wanting who questioned whether there are not many difficulties in the way of the practical working out of the scheme outlined by Mr. Dutt. Thus the *Englishman* of the 15th August remarked: "We are willing to concede to Mr. Dutt the position that groups of villages, call them circles or unions, are better suited to the working of a Village Police Act than isolated villages, but we cannot share his enthusiastic assumption that leading and public-spirited patriots are everywhere to be found in any part of rural Bengal, Bihar, and Orissa. Has the experience of the working of Municipalities, and of District or Local Boards in any district in Lower Bengal been such as to warrant such an assumption?"

It is remarkable, however, in how many essential points Mr. Dutt anticipated the recommendations of the Indian Police Commission of 1902–03. In regard to his central position, that the rural police should not be made completely subordinate to the regular police, but should be linked with village agencies, he was fully supported by the Commission, as will be seen from the following extracts from its Report:—

Returning now to the general consideration of the subject, the Commission desire to record the strong impression that has been made on their minds in the course of this inquiry of the paramount importance of maintaining and fostering the existing village agencies available for police work. With reference to this question, the Commission desire to emphasise their conviction that the village police ought not to be separated from village organisation, and placed under the regular force. They desire to see, not a body of low paid stipendiaries or subordinate police scattered over the country, but utilisation of the village agency itself. The village is the unit of administration. Improved administration lies in teaching the village communities to take an active interest in their own affairs. The village community is represented (ordinarily) by its headman, and effective police administration must be based on the recognition and enforcement of the responsibility of the headman. He is the man who can really help the police; his position and influence should be strengthened, and it is to him that the police should look for co-operation in their work. . . . The Commission consider it to be of vital importance to emphasise the responsibility of the village headman, and to hold the village police officer, by whatever name he may be locally known, responsible rather as the subordinate of the village headman and his servant for the performance of police functions. The village headman for police purposes ought, as far as possible, to be the man recognised as headman in respect of the revenue and general administration of the village: where that is impossible, he ought to be a man of position and influence in the village, and the District Officer ought to maintain and strengthen his position and influence. . . . The intimate connection and association of both these men with the people must be maintained. Both should discharge their duties as representing the village community, and as responsible to the head of the district. To place the village police officer under the thumb of the station-house officer would be to subvert the system in its essential principles, to get out of touch with the people in their customs, usages and interests, and often to place the dregs of the people over respectable classes. The village watchman would become the menial servant of the police, and probably become unscrupulous in his methods. He would work apart from, and often against, the village head. His intimate knowledge of village affairs would be lost, and he would become a very inferior police officer. Both the village headman and the village police officer must be regarded as co-operating with, not subordinate to, the regular police.

The main contention of his pamphlet that the key to good government in India is to be found in a careful reorganisation of the ancient self-governing village institutions of the country, a view which he greatly developed in his later writings, also received the full support of the Decentralisation Commission of which he was himself a member. For the Commission recommended "that it is most desirable, alike in the interests of decentralisation, and in order to associate the people with the local tasks of administration, that an attempt should be made to constitute and develop village panchayets for the administration of local village affairs."

In other minor points also, such as his recommendation for an improvement of the existing system of the surveillance of bad characters, with the object of preventing as far as possible unnecessary harassment by the subordinate police; for a more judicious and careful use of the large powers given to Magistrates under sections 110 C.P.C.; for a substantial increase of the pay and prospects of Sub-Inspectors and Inspectors, and for the avoidance as far as possible of police investigation by Head Constables, his views received the support of the Police Commission.

Finally, in his report to the Police Committee he suggested that District Magistrates should have ampler powers than they now possess, to employ pleaders and legal experts both in watching important police investigations, and in advising police officers while they are engaged in making investigations into difficult cases.

At a time [said Mr. Dutt] when the District Bar is daily becoming better educated, and therefore more influential and strong, and when the whole strength of the Bar is practically monopolised for the defence in important cases, the appointment of a legal officer to interest himself in such cases, and to work for the prosecution of such cases from their first initiation to their close, seems to me to be urgently required for the purposes of an efficient criminal administration.

It is safe to say that most District Officers will cordially endorse this view, and steps are already being taken in some provinces to give District Officers much ampler powers in the matter.

CHAPTER IX

"RIG VEDA," "THE LAYS OF ANCIENT INDIA," AND THE SAHITYA PARISAD

I

A SOCIAL novel in Bengali styled "Sansar," and the Bengali translation of the "Rig Veda" were the fruits of his literary labours after he went on furlough in 1885. Of "Sansar," and its sister volume "Samaj," we shall speak hereafter. The translation of the "Rig Veda" belongs to an entirely different sphere of his literary activity. He had a deep-seated conviction that no fallen nation can rise again to greatness unless her sons feel within them the life-beat of the truly great achievements of their forefathers. The poems and hymns of the "Rig Veda," revealing, as they do, a pantheistic scheme of the universe and the immanence of the Supreme Spirit, marked the highest altitude of spiritual wisdom reached by the ancient Hindus. To lay bare to the people the riches of this locked-up and forbidden store of spiritual wisdom was an ambition worthy of this devotee of Indian nationalism, and the industry and courage with which he accomplished this task and successfully overcame all difficulties are deserving of high praise. Mr. Natesan writes in the short biography of Mr. Dutt, from which we have already quoted:—

> If he had promised himself a quiet and congenial literary work, he found himself mistaken. Orthodoxy took alarm at the prospect of the sacred hymns being laid open to laymen; and the idea of a non-Brahmin like Mr. Dutt laying sacrilegious hands on the holiest of holy books raised a perfect storm of opposition. Bengal had seldom witnessed such a violent literary controversy since the days when the venerable Vidyasagar had

stood up for the marriage of Hindu widows and the abolition of polygamy. Furious articles appeared week after week in vernacular newspapers, sarcasm or invective was poured on the devoted head of the daring translator; and the translation itself was condemned and vilified before it had appeared in print! Mr. Dutt faced this opposition in the way in which he has faced all opposition through life. He scarcely deigned to make a reply; he worked silently and laboriously through the hot summer months; and, before the year 1885 was out, his first volume astonished an orthodox world! The very attacks on his book had added to the list of his subscribers; and before he sailed for Europe, early in 1886, the complete translation of the work was in the press. It is the only complete translation of the "Rig Veda" hymns published in the Bengali language.

In carrying out this arduous work, Mr. Dutt received the support of the Local Government, and Sir Rivers Thompson directed a portion of the printing expenses to be borne by Government.

The *Englishman* published the following appreciation on the work:—

Mr. Dutt has not, we think, acted unwisely in adhering mainly to the traditional interpretation of Sayana, except in rare instances where Sayana is obviously wrong, and tries to construe the simple hymns of ancient bards according to the mythological, philosophical, and pantheistic doctrines of later Hinduism. There is a sufficient unanimity of opinion, however, among all scholars as regards the general import of the "Rig Veda." The religion of the "Veda" consists of the worship of the sun, the fire, and the air; of the sky, the dawn, the storm, and all other manifestations of nature which inspired a simple agricultural people on the banks of the Indus with gladness or with awe. We find frequent references also to the wars which these Aryan invaders waged with the black aborigines, while we get occasional hints as to the life and manners of these early Aryans, their pastoral habits and agriculture, their marriage ceremonies and domestic habits. Mr. Dutt has considerably added to the usefulness of the work by drawing attention to these passages in his notes, and by annexing to each volume a sort of index to these notes. These indices will enable the general reader to follow up his inquiry into any particular subject, and to lay his finger at once on the passages in the "Veda" which illustrate that subject. On the whole we consider the work a very useful publication, and it will enable the Bengali reading public to examine for themselves an ancient and sacred work in which they must ever feel an abiding interest.

The *Bengalee* of the 12th March 1887, drew the following inspiration for Indian Nationalism from the verses of the "Rig Veda":—

We would ask our countrymen to reflect for a moment upon the last passage in the last page of the last volume of Mr. Dutt's translation. We render the passage into English for the benefit of the reader:—

> (1) O Fire! Thou art Lord! O Bestower of choicest gifts, thou art indissolubly associated with every being. Thou art burning at the altar. Thou givest us riches.
>
> (2) O Singers of hymns! Chant your hymns in one voice. May your minds be blended in one common object. The present Gods after the example of the ancient Gods share with perfect unity of feeling the offering of Yogya.
>
> (3) Let the recital of hymns of these priests be harmonious and in the same uniform strain. Let their minds and hearts be one and the same. O Priests! I am initiating you in the same Mantras, and am burning incense for your common benefit.
>
> (4) Let your views and aspirations be the same, and let your minds and hearts be the same. And may there be perfect unity among you and in all respects.

The Rishis of the "Rig Veda" in their last slokas enjoin upon the priests and upon the worshippers perfect unity of heart, soul, and spirit. May their views, ideas, and aspirations be the same—may perfect harmony reign among them—so sang the Vedic Rishis of olden times. It is true we are their degenerate descendants, their spirit does not live amongst us. We have fallen, fallen very far, from the high ideal which was theirs. But in the midst of our degradation, we are content to worship their spirit, to sit at their feet, and to derive from them that knowledge, and in rare moments perhaps that inspiration, which translating us into the past imparts to us something of the fire and the fervour of the past. The appeal of the Vedic Rishis, coming down to us through the mystic past and in a language which records the noblest ideas of our own or indeed of any race, has a significance all its own. Here our Indian patriots are straining every nerve, and are preparing themselves to make every sacrifice to further the interests of Indian unity. Only in

December last, all India met from north, south, east, and west, and were in solemn congress assembled. They met in response to their own patriotic aspirations, and to the great lessons which the West has taught them; but they also met in obedience to a still higher call—that which comes to them from their sires of olden times. *Modern India, as it seeks to give effect to the lessons which it has learnt from the West, draws nearer to its own ancient traditions and habits of life.* The translator of the Vedas has rendered a public service by calling attention to this passage, and we join with him in the appeal which he makes that these slokas should be graven on the heart of our people. We know now, such as we never knew before, that in cultivating among ourselves a sense of unity and a brotherly feeling, we are cultivating the spirit of ancient India, that we are drawing nearer to our fathers, and that in our own humble way, and according to the measure of our humble capacities, we are glorifying the spirit of our ancestors. May that spirit deepen and grow in our midst; for it will be the moving spirit of modern, as it was of ancient, India, and it will communicate to the dead forms of our national life that Promethean spark which may yet serve to revivify them. Such is our hope and such is our faith; and we are confirmed in them by the voice which comes down to us from the misty past of ancient India, and from the venerated relics of our revered sires.

Both Professor Max Müller and Professor Cowell wrote to congratulate Mr. Dutt. "It must have been a hard piece of work," wrote Professor Max Müller, "and I congratulate you on having finished it." "My dear friend," wrote Professor Cowell, "I congratulate you most heartily on your having finished the Bengali translation of the 'Rig Veda.' It is an achievement well worth the labour."

Among his own countrymen he received most encouragement from the illustrious Bankim Chunder, who was himself engaged in interpreting the ancient religion and philosophy of the Hindus to his countrymen, and wrote an appreciative review in Bengali in the columns of the *Prachar*.

It is impossible to praise too highly the work of Babu Romesh Chunder. It is not an easy task to translate the "Rig Veda Sanhita." But the thoroughness, accuracy, and rapidity with which Romesh Babu is completing the work would have evoked universal praise in Europe, had he been born there. But the public feeling in these matters is different in this country, and it is to be hoped that he won't be discouraged for that reason.

. . . .

Whatever others might say, we feel certain that this work of Romesh Babu will bring him enduring fame. When the Bible was translated into the modern languages of Europe, the Roman Catholic priests and other scholiasts showed bitter hostility to the work. It is not unlikely that Romesh Babu will meet with similar opposition. But as in Europe the translation of the Bible paved the way for reforms in religion and a general advance in civilisation, it is certain similar results will follow the translation of the "Rig Veda" in this country. The Bengalis will never be able to fully repay the deep debt of gratitude under which Mr. Dutt has placed them.

The erudite Dijendra Nath Tagore, eldest son of the famous Maharshi Devendra Nath Tagore, wrote to Mr. Dutt in Bengali :—

I am much beholden to you for the valuable present of your book. Under what a deep debt have you placed Bengal. The mine of untold wealth which hitherto lay buried under ground, you have now exposed to the dazzled gaze of Bengal. The ancient and priceless jewels are, it is true, ours by our birthright, but, nevertheless, it is through you that we see them again to-day.

II

The "Lays of Ancient India," composed chiefly during Mr. Dutt's furlough in 1893, appeared in 1894. The following review from the columns of *India* is a fair exposition of the merits of the work and the gap which it helped to fill :—

In recent years there have been many learned, poetical and delightful renderings of the matter or spirit of Indian poetry into the English language. Scientific men and poets have vied with one another in giving the inquiring West sweet tastes of the rich beauties of thought and feeling of the East. The British public have taken all greedily; but it must be confessed that the average reader has been bewildered by these samples and failed to grasp their relation to each other, and the general scope and range of Indian literature, the various steps in its development and the special characteristics of each epoch. Mr. Dutt has attempted a useful work in preparing a book of selections which cover the whole period of ancient Indian literature, and give the English reader, in a convenient form, a sort of bird's-eye-view of the thought and poetry of the more than thirty centuries. Of course, in a book of about two hundred pages of large print, it is but little which is actually presented—a few small grains as samples of the great harvest—but they have been selected with taste and judgment, and excellently serve the purpose of not only whetting the appetite for more, but of pointing the way to find it and making it seem easier than before. If Mr. Dutt has made a mistake, it is in trusting too much to his command of English verse. We frankly avow the difficulty he has found in performing his work in a language which is not his mother tongue, and he has no reason to be ashamed of a result which not one Englishman in a thousand could have achieved. His English prose is of a high order, rich, lucid, and vigorous; but his verse seldom rises to the poetical feeling, the dignity and beauty of his subject. He has almost invariably chosen common jingling metres, and more often than not has found it difficult to reach the end of his stanza without false accents, awkwardly transposed phrases, or weak, jarring rhymes. However, these blemishes are but superficial. Through them and behind is the beautiful thought, the rich stirring imagery, and the profound wisdom of his subject matter. He has apparently a strong clear perception of the spirit of the original, which the thoughtful reader can feel, see, and appreciate, and under the spell of which he forgets to criticise fastidiously the dress in which it is presented. Curiously enough Mr. Dutt has been most successful in the metrical rendering of some passages from the Upanishads. His reason for turning these into verse is the less apparent as the originals are in prose; and Max Müller has been content with prose for their appearance in English; but Mr. Dutt has thought verse desirable, and his verses are amongst the best in the book. Following these three great sections are some brief metrical renderings of the Edicts of Asoka, who spread the Buddhist religion throughout India. Thus Mr. Dutt has presented to his readers at a glance a complete outline of the evolution of religion in the East; a story spread over five and twenty centuries, but told in outline in a hundred pages of short and impressive extracts from the literature of successive generations. In the remainder of his volume he gives some specimens of which may by comparison be called the modern poetry of India. A large portion of this is occupied by a translation of a short epic of Bharavi. The story of the "Hunter and the Hero," as he calls it in English, though hundreds of years old, is claimed to be representative of the poems which are the favourite study of the Hindu even to the present day, and to convey the feelings, the ideas, and popular beliefs of modern Hindus. This long poem is considerably abridged from the Sanskrit original, which is again an abridgment of one of the great ancient epics of India. It is typical of the most prolific age of Indian literature. The original depends largely for its charm upon the beauty of its literary form, the glowing imagery, the sweet alliteration, the rolling phrase, as stirring as it is vigorous. Milton himself might have failed to reproduce this in an adequate English form, but Mr. Dutt has done well. He has given us the spirit of the original, the strange Eastern story, the romantic setting of a romanticism as fascinating and as vigorous as that of the Western world, and yet so utterly different. He has done enough to inspire others to undertake a similar work, and has not left them hopeless with the despair which would face them if his workmanship were of unsurpassable merit. It only remains to add that the volume is enriched with a number of notes and introductions to the various sections, which will prove of the greatest value to the reader or student who comes uninstructed to the study of the lays of ancient India.

The *Times* observed :—

Mr. Dutt's graceful translations prove their author to possess no small skill at metrical English composition.

The *Statesman*, which found fault with the title of the book, observed :—

In concluding this notice, after recognising the excellence of Mr. Dutt's motive, his sound learning, and his poetical skill, strong exception must be taken to the title he has given to his volume. "Lays of Ancient India" is obviously suggested by Macaulay's "Lays of Ancient Rome." A false analogy is thus established, for the ordinary reader could expect to find in Mr. Dutt's volume a series of ballads dealing with conspicuous events in early Indian history, either translated from the Sanskrit or catching the tone that a ballad-writer in those days might have assumed. That is exactly what Mr. Dutt's volume does not contain. There is no trace of ballad poetry, original or translated, in it.

III

In the year 1894, Raja Binay Krishna of Sobhabazar wrote to Mr. Dutt, and requested him to become the President of the Bangya Sahitya Parishad, the Academy of Bengali Literature, an offer which he gladly accepted. He soon infused new life and vigour into this assembly, and much useful work was done under his guidance. The society has since published many old works, and collected numerous valuable manuscripts. The well-known poet Babu Nabin Chandra Sen was the first vice-president, and Babu Rabindra Nath Tagore, the foremost literary man of Bengal of the present day, was the second vice-president. Most of the leading men of Bengal soon joined the society. Mr. Dutt was made an Honorary Life Member in 1898. The society still continues to be the only important literary society in Bengal.

CHAPTER X

"HISTORY OF CIVILISATION IN ANCIENT INDIA"

It was during the years 1888–90, when Mr. Dutt was in charge of the heavy and responsible district of Mymensingh, that he undertook and completed the gigantic task of writing a history of civilisation in Ancient India. This was perhaps the most ambitious effort of his life, and it is the one English work, along with his translations of the Epics, by which he will be longest remembered. The scope of his work, the exact object which he set before himself, and the method which he pursued, could not be better stated than in his own words:—

I have often asked myself: Is it possible, with the help that is now available, to write in a handy work a clear, historical account of the civilisation of Ancient India, based on ancient Sanskrit literature, and written in a sufficiently popular manner to be acceptable to the general reader? Scholars who have devoted their lifetime to the study of Indian antiquities, and who have brought out rich ores from that inexhaustible mine, seem, however, to have little time or little inclination to coin the metal for the everyday use of the general public. The unambitious task must, therefore, devolve on humbler labourers. That there is need for such a popular work will not be denied. The Hindu student's knowledge of Indian history practically begins with the date of the Muhammadan conquest—the Hindu period is almost a blank to him. The schoolboy who knows all about the twelve invasions of Mahmud, knows little of the first invasions and wars of the Aryans, who conquered and settled in the Punjab three thousand years before the Sultan of Ghazni.

And yet such things should not be. For the Hindu student, the history of the Hindu period should not be a blank, nor a confused jumble of historic and legendary names, religious parables, and Epic and Puranic myths. *No study has so potent an influence in forming a nation's mind, a nation's character, as a critical and careful study of its past history. And it is by such study alone that an unreasoning and superstitious worship of the past is replaced by a legitimate and manly admiration.*

Ten years ago I collected and arranged the materials then available to me, with a view to write a little school-book in my own vernacular, and the little work has since been accepted as a text-book in many schools in Bengal. Since that time I have continued my work in this line, as far as my time permitted; and when, three years ago, I was enabled by the generosity of the Government of Bengal to place a complete Bengali translation of the "Rig Veda Sanhita" before my countrymen, I felt more than ever impelled to re-arrange the historical materials furnished by our ancient literature in a permanent form. In pursuance of this object, I published some papers, from time to time, in the *Calcutta Review;* and these papers, together with all other materials which I have collected, have been embodied and arranged in the present work.

The method on which this work has been written is very simple. My principal object has been to furnish the general reader with a practical and handy work on the Ancient History of India—not to compose an elaborate work of discussions on Indian Antiquities.

In undertaking this great work, I must once for all disclaim any intention to make any new discoveries, or to extend in any way the limits of Oriental scholarship and research. My limited knowledge of the subject precludes the possibility of such a pretension being advanced, and the limits of the present work made it impossible that any such results should be achieved. I have simply tried to string together, in a methodical order, the results of the labours of abler scholars, in order to produce a readable work for the general reader. If, in the fulfilment of this design, I have been sometimes betrayed into conjectures and suppositions, I can only ask my readers to accept them as such, not as historical discoveries.

This herculean task was accomplished in three years.

Huge packages of books of reference arrived [writes Mr. Natesan] from Calcutta, as there was no suitable local library; and when the District Officer went on his river tours in the rains, his boat was stocked and loaded with manuscripts, books, and proof sheets. Without a moment to spare during the day, he often worked after dinner till past midnight, and sometimes the grey light of the dawn came to him as a surprise, and sent him hastily to bed. It was rash, it was risky, to overwork thus; but the determination, the passion of writing a history of his own country, impelled him to his labours, and the book at last appeared in three volumes.

It would be pretentious for me to attempt to describe either the magnitude or the difficulty of the task so successfully accomplished by Mr. Dutt, or to assign him his place as an Oriental scholar. That story is best told by contemporaries to whose judgment he submitted his work. It was reviewed by almost all the well-known Oriental scholars of the day, and, besides the numerous criticisms which appeared in newspapers, reviews, and journals in India and Europe, numberless letters were received by the author from different parts of the world.

In the *Critical Review*, Dr. Kern, of Leyden, had a long and thoughtful article, from which the following extracts are made:—

Though from the "Veda" no history of states and wars can be gleaned—and efforts in that direction have not been wanting as contribution to the development of the human mind, and especially as an authentic witness of the religious and moral notions of a highly gifted race during the most ancient epoch known of its existence—yet the "Veda" has an historic worth which cannot be too highly valued. Not only the "Veda," but the entire literature which has come down to us in Sanskrit, Pali, or Prakrit, belongs to the most important productions of the human mind. The Chinese excepted, no people on earth can boast of possessing a literature in which its mental and religious development is pictured for more than thirty centuries, as is the case with Indian literature. In the history of human civilisation, India occupies an important place, a place so much the more important that the Indian mind has made its influence felt far beyond the borders of Hindustan, in Farther India, Asiatic Pelago, China, Japan, and Siberia. We are silent here on the discoveries made in the domain of the comparative study of the Indo-Germanic languages and archæology in Persia and Assyria, which but for the knowledge of Sanskrit would have been impossible.

Although in scientific circles the knowledge of Indian antiquity is usually fully appreciated, yet the ordinary reading public is still far from being satisfactorily acquainted with the results of scientific researches. This opinion is shared by the author of the *History of Civilisation in Ancient India*, and he has used his best efforts to supply a want he has felt.

Dr. Kern then goes into details, and his remarks are valuable, both when he agrees with Mr. Dutt, and when he does not. The learned Doctor agrees with Mr. Dutt in thinking that it is possible with our present knowledge to sketch in main outlines the development of Indian civilisation; but there are many gaps which modern researches have not yet filled up. The origin of the idea of Metempsychosis, which appears for the first time in the Upanishads, and of the inhuman custom of *sutti*, which become prevalent after the time of Manu and Yajnavalka (several centuries after the Christian era), have not, for instance, been yet explained. Of the Hindus of the Vedic period, two schools of writers, Dr. Kern says, present us with two different pictures. One school shows us the favourable side of their character, and Mr. Dutt follows this school; while the more recent school is inclined to unearth and place before the public the harsh traits of their character. The truth, in Dr. Kern's opinion, lies midway. Mr. Dutt, differing from Dr. Max Müller and Dr. Rajendralala Mittra, holds that human sacrifice was unknown to the Hindus in ancient times. Dr. Kern does not altogether support Mr. Dutt. The learned Doctor thinks that the majority of the Hindus from the Vedic times downwards disapproved of human sacrifices, but that there were exceptions to this rule. Finally, the Doctor recommends Mr. Dutt's book "to those who, having made no particular study of Ancient India, nevertheless desire to obtain an insight, not altogether superficial, into the general development of the civilisation of India."

Professor Max Müller, in acknowledging the books, said: "I have read both the volumes with great pleasure; they exhibit the history of the Indian mind in a delightful panorama passing before our eyes." Owing to his failing health he could not himself review the work, but his assistant, Dr. Winternitz, published a review in

Trübner's Record, from which the following passages are taken :—

The author is well fitted for his task. He possesses a thorough knowledge of Sanskrit literature, is well versed in the works of European scholars, and, though saturated with Western ideas, is filled with a genuine love for his country and with a real enthusiasm for his subject. Nor can we doubt that this book will serve its purpose, and help to spread a knowledge of ancient India among the Hindus of to-day. But though chiefly written for Hindus, a perusal of it will be found useful and interesting to English readers also. And though the author professes to write for the general reader only without "any intention to make any new discoveries," yet it will be no waste of time even for the special scholar to go over the pages of this book.

. . . .

But while Mr. Dutt hardly succeeds—and there was no chance of his succeeding—in mapping out the chronological outlines of the history of Ancient India, he has been much more successful in drawing his pictures of ancient Hindu life, in sketching the development of Hindu civilisation, the rise of intellectual and the decline of political and social life. It is a real pleasure to read such a chapter as that on the social and domestic life and the position of women in the Vedic age, to hear the author's praises of that age when wives joined their husbands in the performance of sacrifices, and when women were themselves Rishi, and composed hymns and performed sacrifices like men. For there were no unhealthy restrictions against women in those days, no attempt to keep them secluded, or uneducated, or debarred from their legitimate place in society. And a pleasure also it is to read the character on the Vedic Rishis, where Mr. Dutt proves, and dwells upon the fact, that those ancient poets of the Vedic hymns were members of an undivided society, a society without caste.

The well-known savant Monsieur A. Barth had a long notice of the work in the *Revue Critique*. The following extracts will be of interest :—

It is at the same time an essay towards the popularisation of scientific truths and a patriotic work which Mr. Dutt wanted to write, and, to undertake it, none was in many respects better prepared than himself. Placed as Magistrate at the head of a district in Bengal, "Mymensingh, with more than three millions of inhabitants," he has been able to acquire the experience of things and men indispensable to the historian. He has also, better than many of his countrymen, been able to understand the actual present condition of India, which knowledge is so necessary to one who wishes to understand her past condition. Finally, Mr. Dutt knows Europe, where he finished his education. He is well acquainted with the principal works which have appeared on India, in England as well as on the Continent. And what he has gained by this long intercourse does not limit itself to merely temporary results. It has begotten in him the real occidental spirit, with very little difference, the European way of thinking and feeling. The assimilation is so complete, that in admiring him one would wish for less, one would like to find in his book something more Hindu, a little less of what could have been written as well in London, Berlin, or Paris. . . .

The book is written with warmth, in a clear and correct language, without that vain and easy show of learning which tires more than instructs. In short, I know of no work which gives you a better idea of ancient India and forms more agreeable reading. Nothing gives a truer and more comforting idea of the work accomplished by England in India, nothing gives more hope for the future in store for that country.

Dr. H. Oldenburg's notice in the *Deutsche Litteraturzeitung* had the following :—

The entire execution, however, of the work of this finely cultured Indian, and one who is undeniably full of historic taste, and who can claim for himself lucidity and the courage of his convictions (which, if I mistake not, is more particularly apparent in his treatment of Buddhism), may well justify the hope of future success still more complete.

Dr. R. Pischel, of Halle, wrote in the *Göttinger Anzeiger* :—

R. Ch. Dutt has honestly striven to make his countrymen acquainted with the results of European researches, as far as they were accessible to him. He has proved himself to be an enlightened and a clear-headed man, who, with all his patriotism, is not blind to the errors of the people of his time. He has not cared to give the results of his own researches, and numerous errors are not wanting in his work. Nevertheless, it deserves, by reason of the good aim it has in view, and in the entire absence of another similar work for Indian readers, the fullest appreciation and the widest circulation.

In his letter to Mr. Dutt, Dr. Pischel had written: "Books like yours will do much to strengthen the connection between India and Europe, and therefore are very meritorious."

The following reviews appeared in English journals.

The *Athenæum*, 17th September 1892:—

A cordial welcome should be given to Mr. Romesh Chunder Dutt's "History of Civilisation in Ancient India," as a work supplying a long-felt need. The book is primarily designed for the author's countrymen; but even scholars, not to say the general public, have had, since the publication of Lassen's somewhat unwieldy work, none in which the place of an early Hindu king or dynasty could be verified. Though the title-page describes the work as "based on Sanskrit literature," we regard precisely that portion of it which rests not on a literary, but on an archæological basis as calling for the warmest reception. European readers at least have by this time a fairly large number of hand-books for the earlier Indian literature, but what has been so sorely needed for many years past is a work summarising in a convenient form the chief achievements of archæologists and likewise duly co-ordinating the results of sciences ancillary to history, such as numismatics and palæography, for in the absence of a regular historical literature such results become, of course, of redoubled value.

The *Glasgow Herald*, 27th November 1890:—

But perhaps the chief attraction and value of the volumes do not so much lie in the new and varied information which they bring, as in the manner in which it is put before us. With equal patience and industry a European writer might have gathered it from the same source; but his exposition would necessarily have been wanting in that sympathy and living interest which animate the Hindu scholar as he records the early history of his own race, and which lend such a charm to his work. Though based on solid erudition, it is eminently popular; the style is not only clear and picturesque, but also correct and elegant to a degree which reflects the greatest credit on a writer whose mother tongue is presumably not English.

The *Morning Post* (London), 22nd June 1891 :—

Apart from its inherent interest, the study of ancient Indian history is a duty incumbent on those who are called to the government of the country. A knowledge of the past is essential to a successful administration in the present, and students are greatly indebted to Mr. Romesh Chunder Dutt for the assistance he has offered to them in the attainment of that object.

To sum up his arguments and deductions, he looks for an emancipation of religion from the superstitions of the Brahmins, and a regeneration of the Hindu race. National ignorance and caste disunion, social degeneracy and political weakness, have made the history of the Hindus for six centuries after 1200 A.D. a blank. Three thousand years ago they were the only civilised Aryan nation in the world; to-day "they are the only people socially lifeless and politically prostrate, not only among the Aryans, but among all the civilised nations of the earth." But through the darkness the author distinguished a ray of life and hope, and he finishes his book with these words :—

"It may be England's high privilege to restore to an ancient nation a new and healthy life. Under the vivifying influences of modern civilisation, ancient races in Greece and Italy have begun a new intellectual and national career. The influence of civilisation will spread, and the light and progress which has been lighted in Southern Europe will yet spread to the shores of the Ganges. And if the science and learning, the sympathy and example of modern Europe help us to regain in some measure a national consciousness and life, Europe will have rendered back to modern India that kindly help and brotherly service which India rendered to Europe in ancient days—in religion, science, and civilisation."

It will readily be seen that Mr. Dutt is at once an able historian and a sanguine patriot, and his work, which is written in graceful and expressive English, will be widely welcome. His modesty and self-depreciation, though undoubtedly genuine, are wholly unnecessary, for a more exhaustive and learned treatise on ancient Indian history in anything approaching popular form has certainly not appeared.

Amongst the letters received by Mr. Dutt some deserve a place here.

Professor Buhler, of the Oriental Institute, Vienna :—

The appearance of a work like yours in India is always a great pleasure for me, as it shows that we do not work in vain, and that our Indian colleagues and fellow-workers do direct their attention to our labours.

Professor J. Jolly, of Wurzburg:—

Allow me to express to you my sincere appreciation of the excellent plan of this new work, and of the scholarly way in which the plan has been executed. The investigations of European students of Indian antiquities are apt to be confined to minutiæ, and the absorption in philological details occasionally makes one lose sight of the grand aim of all studies of this kind—the elucidation of the gradual growth and development of such a superior and thoroughly original civilisation as your native country can boast of. Therefore it is not only necessary for the wants of the general reader, but refreshing to the Oriental scholar as well, to have the result of philological research collected and arranged in a readable form. Nobody could be better qualified for performing this difficult task than scholars like yourself who are equally acquainted with all the intricacies of ancient Sanskrit literature, and with the wants and notions of the general reader in India and England. It is much to be hoped that these common aims and studies will draw a closer bond of union between scholars of the East and West.

Professor A. Weber, of Berlin:—

Your task of popularising the scientific results of our age is a very meritorious one. Old India is still full of riddles, but a good and broad way has been already cut through all those wildernesses, and we may hope to come to light.

Very dear to him must have been also the appreciations of the members of his own service. The Lieutenant-Governor, Sir Steuart Bayley, wrote a very warm letter:—

THE SHRUBBERY, DARJEELING,
13*th June* 1889.

MY DEAR DUTT,—I have read your first volume with great interest, and am looking forward with eagerness to its successors.

The volume is written in excellent English, and you have succeeded in making a difficult subject very interesting to general readers, giving enough quotations both to justify your generalisations and to interest the reader, without so overloading the book as to render it unacceptable to any but students. I also congratulate you on the tone of the book. You have succeeded in showing sincere respect and admiration for the achievements of the early Hindus, without indulging in the fictitious and unreasoning glorification of everything that tradition fathers upon ancient Hinduism, as is rather the fashion in recent journalism. Above all I value the clear distinctions which you have brought out between the different periods of your history, distinctions which are essential to even an elementary understanding of the subject.—Yours truly, S. C. BAYLEY.

The Chief Secretary, Sir John Edgar, wrote:

MY DEAR DUTT,—Many thanks for your letter of the 4th and the first volume of your "Ancient India." I have had only time to read the introduction and the first four chapters, but have found this extremely interesting. Of course it is not possible for me to make an estimate of the historical value of this sketch. The third and fourth periods are less unfamiliar to me than those dealt with in the present volume, but I am able to appreciate its remarkable literary ability and the fascinating treatment of the subject displayed in the part which I have read. I am very much obliged to you for your kind thoughtfulness in sending me the book.—Yours sincerely,

JOHN EDGAR.

MY DEAR DUTT,—Very many thanks for the third volume of your "History of India." Let me congratulate you on bringing to a close a work of great value and high merit, *which all the members of our service ought to feel proud of as coming from one of the members*.—Yours sincerely, JOHN EDGAR.

A fellow-worker in the same field, Dr. Grierson, also wrote to congratulate him:

MY DEAR DUTT,—Let me write and congratulate you on the issue of your first volume of the "History of India." It has been great pleasure to me to read it, and to think that a brother-civilian was able to write so sound and interesting a work. It is what we have all been wanting for years; and it was a happy thought of yours, with your knowledge of the "Rig Veda," to step forward to supply the want. It is just the thorough and, at the same time, delightful book which one would expect from "Ar Cy Dae."

Do you ever see the *Indian Antiquary* nowadays? I am

trying to let Indian people know what Weber, Barth, and others are doing by a series of papers called "Progress of Oriental Scholarship." What you say about the "Mahabharata" has reminded me of an interesting paper lately published by Weber, of which I send a notice to you by this post. It may interest you. I shall look up any other papers which I have bearing on the subject, and send them at the same time. There may be amongst them all some grain of information which has escaped even your industry.

Are you going to give an index with the third volume? I hope so: a full index would immensely increase the value of the work.

Will you forgive me making one suggestion, and that is to threaten to murder the printer if he makes any more misprints. I hope, and am sure, your book will widely circulate in France and Germany, and the people there are very particular that names are properly spelt, with their full complement of long marks, &c.—*experto crede.*—Yours very sincerely,

A. GRIERSON.

Amongst his countrymen the work aroused a very wide interest, as the following letters show :—

MY DEAR ROMESH CHUNDER,—I have just finished reading the first volume of your history. Perhaps it will not be unwelcome if I tell you a few of my impressions. I have read it through with unabated interest. It has won you a name side by side with Müller and Weber and Williams. It would be no flattery if I say that the work evinces higher constructive and generalising power. The sustained tone of sympathy, eloquence, and enthusiasm is not unbecoming an author who belongs to the nation. Without being superficial, it is eminently readable; charming from beginning to end. It should be in the hands of every Indian student. If it lay in me, it should be a textbook for M.A. in English, Sanskrit, and History.

Some of your views have startled me, as when you demolish the authenticity of the *Sambat* era. But as the evidence *pro* and *con* is more familiar to you, I can say but little against your view, though it gives one a pang when a cherished notion falls. One is apt to cry out when even universally adopted eras turn fictitious: "Truth's a gem that loves the deep." At least, historical truth seems to be so.

Your merciless strictures on the caste system will hardly win you the good graces of the Revivalists. This, you know, has already appeared among us a portent of the times, a form of reaction against Anglicism. Our nationalists, at least many of them, would revive Hinduism in its entirety, with its caste, even with its *sutti*, for the matter of that; though, Heaven knows! Hinduism has not been a constant quantity, as your book will no doubt show to those who are willing to see.

You have spoken out on widow marriage, infant marriage, zenana seclusion, too. There you give expression to sentiments not likely to be palatable to many, even from Justice Gurudas Banerjea downwards. However, these are matters which I don't see how you could have helped. If it is any solace, I may add there is not a sentence in your book which I would not heartily exclaim "Yea" to. Though at my age, it would be an act of daring to say all this, an act of which I would not be equal in the yellow leaf of life. Albeit, however, I suppose I am right in anticipating universal praise for your book.—Yours,

K. K. BHATTACHARJEA.

30th June 1889.

THE *Hindu* OFFICE, MADRAS,
6th August 1890.

MY DEAR SIR,—Your kind letter of the 1st instant. I send you copies of the two issues of the *Hindu* in which a review of your work has appeared. I really think that the publication of your work would mark an era in the growth of public opinion in this country, especially in regard to social matters. But the work should be widely read. I recently read some remarks about your book—I think it was in the *Hindoo Patriot*—which made me suspect that you are like the prophet, not being honoured in your own country. I controverted the *Patriot's* views, and the *Statesman*, without understanding the point at issue, took the *Patriot's* side.

Yes, I had intended to translate your work into Tamil. But for the last twelve months I have been afflicted by several domestic misfortunes, which have prevented me from prosecuting the work with vigour. I have anticipated you in the opinion that the translation must be of an abridgment of the three volumes. In that view I have condensed the first and a large portion of the second volume. I hope to be able to commence the Tamil translation in a month or two.

I shall gladly let you have a copy of the translation when it is printed and published.—With highest regards, I remain yours truly,

G. SUBRAMANIA IYER,
Editor of the *Hindu*.

During his furlough in 1893, he wrote an abridged history of "Ancient India," and in 1894 he brought out a new and revised edition of his great work. He revised and enlarged it once more in his later years, and in the last edition the second volume is styled the "History of Buddhist Civilisation."

CHAPTER XI

TRAVELS

I

DURING the first ten years of his official life Mr. Dutt took advantage of the "privilege leave" he obtained to visit some of the most interesting portions of India. It was not only the great historic places of India that had deep interest for him. He loved to wander through its ruins of a bygone age and its busy centres of present-day life. "How few of our countrymen," he observes in describing his impression of Baroda later on in life, "feel the poetry of Indian customs and life in the various provinces they visit, or appreciate the beauty of temples and mosques, of village festivities and village gatherings, and of that deep faith which is planted in the hearts of the Indian people. An education that is superficial, and a life that is passed in imitation of Western ideals, make us almost blind to much that is interesting in our own land and in our own customs and life. Every spot in India is full of interest to those who have eyes to see and the capacity to feel."

His earliest travels after his return from England were in Upper India.

For a Hindu of Bengal, his first visit to Northern India is an important event in his life. All that is heroic in Indian history and traditions, all that is brilliant in Sanskrit literature and poetry, all that is sacred in ancient Aryavarta, connect themselves with Northern India. Hindu science and philosophy have been developed in this land, Hindu poetry has shed on it the light of its magic lamp, and Hindu history is recorded on its ancient ruins. A visit to Northern India is an education which our schools do not impart; it tells a history which our text-books do not record.

Of Benares he observes :—

As we stroll through these narrow and crowded lanes we seem to be withdrawn for a while from the precincts of modern life, and to live again in the past, and amidst past recollections and past incidents! Ancient learning is still cultivated in the precincts of many temples, and ancient hymns which were chanted by Hindu Aryan settlers in this spot, thousands of years ago, are still chanted by students who come from all parts of India to learn the Vedas.

From Benares he went to Lucknow, where he saw the Residency and other memorials of the dark days of the Mutiny. From Lucknow he went to Delhi, the centre of ancient Aryavarta, the metropolis of ancient India.

Standing on the banks of the Jumna, the thoughtful Hindu calls back to mind the ancient days when the Kurus ruled in Hastinapura and the Pandavas in Indraprastha over three thousand years ago. He recalls all that has been preserved in an imperishable epic, of their ancient civilisation, of their schools of learning, of their valour in war, of their virtue and worth.

He carefully examined the ruins of the old cities which stood on the site of modern Delhi and the many memorials of recent historic events. He went to Agra, and visited the Taj Mahal and other architectural wonders of that famous town. He also visited Fatehpur Sikri and its immortal ruins.

In some respects, Fatehpur Sikri is the most remarkable place that exists. It is a noble and perfect palace with audience halls, lofty chambers, royal offices, and rooms for queens and begams, all deserted and desolate! It is like the city of the dead that we read of in the Arabian Nights, a city, splendid in its streets and houses and public marts, but without inhabitants, without a trace of life!

The Taj Mahal, the tomb of Sekandra, and the deserted but unique palace of Fatehpur Sikri, make the environs of Agra among the most interesting spots in the world for the tourist and the traveller. But the Hindu tourist turns from these interesting places to the far more ancient and interesting spots, Mathura and Brindaban. I visited these places some years after I visited Agra.

My thoughts flew back to the time when Mahmud of Ghazni found it in all its loveliness, and left it a ruin, back to the time when Houen Tisaing and Fa Hian found it ringing with joyous Buddhist celebrations and pompous gatherings, back to those dim ages when Krishna and the Yadavas went as colonists from this spot and Hinduised the far shores of Gujrat! It is difficult to avoid sentimentalising when standing on this spot, for there are few spots which recall to the Hindu more vividly the memories of an ancient world and an ancient civilisation. The nation which has a past has a future also, and the faith and destiny of the great Hindu nation will survive the degradation of the present.

In 1882 he visited Orissa :—

In our younger days we scarcely suspected that the backward province of Orissa had a connected history which goes back fifteen centuries, that it boasts of temples which are among the finest specimens of Hindu architecture. And we were scarcely prepared to admit that over two thousand years ago this province received Buddhism and Aryan civilisation from the West, and that the Buddhist caves of Orissa are among the earliest that we find anywhere in India. And yet such is the case. Wherever we lift the veil of darkness which hangs over modern India, we descry long and glorious vistas into the past, rich with memories of great achievements in war and in peace. And the modern Hindu, whose early education consists in prolonged lessons about his own littleness, has to unlearn this teaching and to learn for himself that he has a past.

Jajpur was the first place of interest he saw, and he was much struck with the ancient Hindu statues of blue chlorite stone; the one of Chamunda, the wife of the all-destroying Siva, struck him as being a powerful work of art.

It is a colossal naked skeleton, with the skin hanging to the bones, and the veins and muscles standing out in ghastly fidelity. The figure attests the boldness of the Hindu sculptor of ancient days.

From Jajpur he went to Cuttack, and thence to Udaipur, Khandagiri and Bhuvaneswar.

Bhuvaneswar was the ancient capital of the Kesari kings, now a collection of magnificent but deserted temples. Seven thousand temples are said to have, at one time, encircled the sacred lake of Bhuvaneswar, and some five hundred still remain, exhibiting every stage of Orissa art, from the rough conceptions of the sixth century, through the exquisite designs and ungrudging artistic toil of the twelfth, to the hurried dishonest stucco imitations of the present day.

The last sentence in his account of his travels in Orissa is well worthy of being quoted.

India is a land of recollections, and there is scarcely an ancient site, or an ancient ruin, which does not open up a vista of ancient history and ancient traditions. The Hindu lives in these traditions, and cherishes these recollections, and he may well exclaim of his native land what the poet has said of Rome:

"The Niobe of nations! there she stands,
Childless and crownless, in her voiceless woe;
An empty urn within her withered hands,
Whose holy dust was scattered long ago."

II

In 1885 Mr. Dutt took furlough for two years after fourteen years of active service, but a good portion of the furlough was spent in strenuous work. It was during this period, as we have seen, that he translated the "Rig Veda," and wrote his first important social novels. But his passion for travel was far too strong to allow him to spend all his holiday at his desk, and he travelled widely both in India and in Europe. During the autumn of 1885, he visited Rajputana and Central India. He was at Jeypur during the Dashara festival, which he thus describes:—

I returned from Amber to Jeypur, and nothing that I have ever seen has impressed me more than the celebration of the autumnal Dashara in Jeypur. The Rajputs worship the sword on this occasion, and in the olden days their chivalric wars, which fill many a bright page in modern Hindu history, commenced after this significant worship. I witnessed the Maharaja performing the worship, assisted by his priests and ministers; I saw the Maharaja going out in a procession among joyous and enthusiastic crowds of people, and I also witnessed the grand military review and festivities in an open plain adjoining the town. Fireworks and illuminations closed the scene, and as I came back to the city among tens of thousands of joyous, enthusiastic, and loyal citizens crowding round their chief, the descendant of a long line of heroic kings who have maintained the independence of the Rajputs of this State through a thousand years, I could to some extent realise their loyalty, their pride, their joyousness.

Of Chitor he wrote:—

After thus visiting Jeypur and Ajmir, Jodhpur and Abu, we at last came to the most famous spot of the far-famed Rajasthan, the hill fort of Chitor. History loves to dwell on the great deeds which have sanctified this spot; legends and songs cling round this ancient capital of the Ranas of the Solar Race; tradition hands down to us the heroism of the chiefs in many a battle and many a historic siege, and poetry and drama immortalise the devotion and determination of the maids and matrons of Chitor who nobly perished on the pyre, when the chiefs fell in battle, and all was lost save honour! Stirring memories are connected with the names of Padmini and the great Lakshman Sinha, who nobly but vainly defended this fort against Allauddi Khilji. A blaze of glory still illumines the name of Rana Sanga who fought with Baber, the Emperor of India, in the memorable field of Fatehpur Sikri. And lofty associations sanctify the lifelong labours of Pratap Sinha, who defended the last relics of Rajput independence against the conquering arms of Akbar.

Of Ujjain, he says:—

If Chitor is perhaps the most famed spot in modern Indian history, Ujjain or Ojein is one of the most famous in ancient Indian history. For centuries before the Christian era it was the capital of Malwa, and Asoka the Great is said to have ruled here as a Viceroy when his father was the Emperor of Northern India, and ruled in Pataliputra or Patna. Later on, Ojein was the capital of Vikramaditya the Great, and poetry and learning have shed a lustre on his name, which has only glowed the brighter in the gloom of succeeding ages. It is difficult for a Hindu, even in these matter-of-fact days, to walk through the bazars, and stony streets, and dark lanes of the ancient city without recalling to mind the glory of Vikrama's court, and the creations of Kalidasa's genius!

III

Next year he made a prolonged tour through Europe.

On the 15th April 1886, I left Calcutta for London. Eighteen years ago I had performed the same voyage. Eighteen years—what a large slice out of one's brief life! What a number of events have crowded themselves within these eighteen years of my life, what great changes have transpired since I last left my home, almost like a truant in pursuit of adventure! In 1868, I had left my home impelled by an ambition which was rashness, and staked my future, staked all, on success in an almost impossible undertaking. I acted as only a young man can act, utterly uncertain as to my chances, as to my prospects, as to my future! But success like charity covers all sins, and success had crowned my undertaking.

Now in 1886, I left Calcutta with greater assurance as to the present, with greater confidence as to the future. But the cares and responsibilities of life had increased, not decreased, with added years. I was not alone now, but my wife and four little ones accompanied me in my present voyage. The children gazed on the blue ocean and on every port that we touched at with much the same elasticity and buoyancy of feelings that I had felt in my first journey. To show them a little of European life and civilisation, to enable them to look around them a little in this great world of ours, was mainly the object of this my second visit to Europe. And my brother too was with us, now on his first visit to Europe. And no pilgrim to Jerusalem or anchorite to Jagannath ever wended his way with a keener ardour than what impelled him at this period of his life to visit the Eldorado of his dreams, the Europe of to-day.

For two days together after my arrival in London I felt as one feels on revisiting an old friend. Every familiar place that I visited, the very streets and squares in which I walked, brought back vividly to my mind the days of my first sojourn in London, eighteen years ago! Old associations and memories came to me, and I felt at times as if I was the careless youngster again,—as if a wide gulf of eighteen years with their weary weight of work and cares and responsibilities had not severed me from the days of my early youth! I walked by the well-known streets and squares and circuses and crescents of London, and scarcely believed that I did not revisit them in a dream!

But no place in London had stronger associations for me than the University College where I had studied so long under some of the ablest of professors and best of men that I have known anywhere. Many a dark, misty, rainy day in autumn, many a frosty, wintry one, had I passed in that gloomy Gower Street, under that dark pile of buildings which I now revisited again after so many years. I knew the Philosophy Class and the Mathematics Class well. I knew where I had worked in the Electricity Laboratory, and where I had studied Sanskrit under that eminent German scholar now no more. And above all, I knew the English Literature Class, and the genial, good-hearted, noble-souled Professor, who is still the Professor in that subject. He had been a real friend to us at a time when we needed friendly assistance and help, and a better man I have never met since.

His observations on the economic condition of the British people have a special interest in these days, when social questions of every kind have taken so prominent a position in the sphere of English politics.

Imagination can scarcely compass the vastness of modern London whose population exceeds that of the whole of Scotland, or the kingdom of Holland, whose traffic and trade are almost fabulous, and whose wealth as displayed in the miles and miles of the richest shops in every direction, and in every part of the town, are almost beyond the dreams of Aladdin!

And yet there is a shady side to this picture. The cry of depression in trade has gone on increasing year after year, and the "better times" so hopefully prophesied and wished for have not come. There is capital in the country which can find no investment, there are goods produced year after year which find no market, there are millions of English labourers in the towns, and in the country willing to work for their bread, but who can find no work and are on the brink of starvation. Clear-sighted if somewhat pessimist thinkers and writers offer an explanation which is sufficiently intelligible, though one is loth to accept it as correct. They say that the insular position of England, her comparative freedom from revolutions and foreign invasions, and the wonderful enterprise of her sons gave them a start in the commerce of the world which cannot for ever be maintained. For a time Englishmen monopolised the carrying trade of the world, they manufactured goods for the great marts of the world, and they alone reaped the profits of this wonderful monopoly. Population multiplied accordingly in England more rapidly than anywhere else in Europe, and far exceeded what the produce of the little island could support. But this monopoly could not last for ever. Other nations have waked to a consciousness of the benefits of trade—steady hard-working nations like the Germans, who deserve to succeed, are competing with Englishmen all over the world, are cutting out the English abroad, and even in England. London tradespeople complain with a bitterness which one can understand, that in London itself there are many thousand Germans who have ousted so many Englishmen from work, who are daily ousting more because they can live on so much less than Englishmen of the same class. Frugal, abstemious, almost stingy in their habits, the Germans work hard and spend little—while even the London shopboy has not yet learnt to save, but must needs enjoy his holiday, and spend his little saving with his chums or his sweetheart in the Crystal Palace. Abroad, there is the same competition, continental labour is cheaper, continental goods compete with English goods even in English colonies and sell cheaper! At the same time all over Europe—the French, the Germans, and other nations are protecting their home industries against English products by heavy protective import duties, and England vainly asks them to be free traders, and to repeal these duties. The United States do just the same thing, and even the English Colonies, Canada, Cape Colony, and the Australian States protect their own goods and keep out English products by heavy duties, and England cannot ask them to repeal such duties as she has made India do. Thus the circle of foreign markets is gradually contracting, the competition of other nations in the old markets is increasing, and even in England foreign labourers are cutting out Englishmen.

In 1886 he visited the House of Commons several times during the memorable debates on the Irish Home Rule Bill, and from a contemplation of the aspirations of the Irish he was naturally led to the following reflections about India:—

Many of us who are young, and even many of us now in their middle age, will probably live to see the day when the people of India will have a constitutional means of expressing their views, and the administrations of their country, when their views will to a large extent shape that administration, and when their hands will to a great extent practically manage that administration. The divine right of conquerors will be as obsolete a phrase in the political dictionary of the twentieth century as the divine right of kings is in the nineteenth, and the people of India will be proud of their connection with England, as are the sons of Englishmen in Australia or Canada.

Fortunate he was to live to see almost the realisation of his hopes.

From London he paid a short visit to Oxford, and needless to say he was much impressed by that most classic of English towns.

Historical associations have always a charm for me, and there is no town in England so redolent of historical associations as Oxford.

At Oxford he made the acquaintance of Professor Max Müller and his family, and ever since that time a tie of scholarly interest and mutual regard grew up which was terminated only by the death of the Professor.

From Oxford he returned to London, and then paid a visit to Norway and Sweden in July 1886.

28th July.—Early this morning we found ourselves in the harbour of the town called Tromsö, and after breakfast we went on shore and walked along the Tromsödale (Tromsö valley). We saw an encampment of Lapps and reindeer about two miles off. We were now in Norwegian Lapland, the region which was at one time almost entirely populated by the Lapps. We went into a Lapp tent built of birch barks and sods of grass, with a hole in the top for the admission of light, and to allow the smoke to escape. A kettle was boiling in the fire, and a couple of babies were sleeping in cradles. And such cradles! The poor babies were tightly encased and wrapped in skin cases of the shape of canoes, so that they could move neither arm nor leg! Their faces only were visible when not covered with cloth.

29th July.—Early in the morning we found ourselves in Hammerfest, the most northern town in the world. Two hours more brought us to the celebrated North Cape, rising boldly and precipitously out of the sea to a height of nearly a thousand feet. Europe terminated here, and the billows of the cold and sublime Arctic Ocean stretched from the foot of this noble hill far, far into those Polar regions which man knoweth not and has not seen! As one gazes and gazes over this sublime and limitless ocean—beyond the last frontier of human habitation—beyond the last traces of man's handiwork—he almost feels himself removed from the round of human actions and feelings, and remembers human life but as a troubled dream, and he contemplates this vast earth as a speck in the limitless universe spreading through limitless space and through endless time. I shall never forget the feeling of enthusiasm and exultation with which, after finishing a substantial supper, we all began our ascent of the North Cape by daylight at 10 P.M. on the 29th July 1886.

At last we were fairly on the top of the hill, after having passed several large patches of snow hanging in crevices. The sun was above the horizon, but it was impossible to see it through the mist which rose and gathered that night, and we could, therefore, only imagine his solar majesty, and know and feel his presence in the broad daylight around us. From the highest part of the North Cape we looked on the vast and limitless Arctic Ocean rolling under our feet. We had come to the end of our travels, we had reached the point where Europe ends, where the habitation of man terminates, and where the great unknown Polar Sea begins. It is impossible to describe the exultation which the tourists felt as these ideas waked in their minds. Groups of Germans sang their national songs until the midnight air re-echoed their voice, and Americans hoisted their national flag—stripes and stars—over a stick, and drank to the formation of a universal Republic of Peace!

He visited most of the important towns of Sweden and Norway, and he thus describes the impression he carried away of the people :—

The artificiality of civilised life and of social manners almost disappears among these simple people, they seem contented and happy as children! Their faces and features are not unlike those of Englishmen, only there is no pride or reserve in their deportment or expression, in their manners or conversation. And they are so obliging, so really anxious to do a kind act to a stranger! A busy man will leave his office and walk a considerable distance to show the way to a stranger, and he takes off his hat and bows when he is thanked. Both in Norway and Sweden, the land belongs not to landlords but to farmers, who live in their own domains and cultivate them. Small farmers own perhaps a hundred acres, or even less, while larger farms extend over three, or four, or five hundred acres, up to a thousand acres. The farmer pays the king's taxes, but no rent to any superior holder.

After his visit to Norway, he returned to England and stayed at Littlehampton with his family.

Out of the three weeks that my family were at Littlehampton, I passed one in the West of England. The trip was not of my own seeking, but was undertaken in compliance with invitations from the Colonial and Indian Reception Committee. Soon after our coming to Littlehampton, therefore, I left my family there and went to Bristol. I cannot describe the magnificent reception which was given to us in all these ancient towns. The Colonials and Indians were received as the sons of old England visiting the old country from ends of the earth. In fact, these receptions were in furtherance of the great idea which underlay the exhibition [1] itself. England is great, not as a military power in Europe, but in her colonies. To display in a focus, as it were, the vast resources of her various colonies, to display to Europe and to the world the strength which she derives from her connection with various nations to the ends of the world, and to draw closer the bonds of sympathy and fellow-feeling which bind these colonies to her; this was the idea of the Exhibition, and of the reception of the Indian and Colonial visitors.

From Littlehampton Mr. Dutt, with his family, went and spent a fortnight in Paris, and saw all the wonders of that wonderful city. Then, leaving his family in London, he made a tour through Germany, Austria, and Italy. On his way through Belgium, he visited Brussels and the famous battle-field of Waterloo. Of Waterloo he wrote :—

There have been greater victories in modern warfare, but probably none more important. For in that battle ended the glory of the greatest conqueror of modern times and the greatest man that the world has ever produced. Alexander conquered vaster kingdoms, because he fought with vast undisciplined forces, and Cæsar won his laurels and victories too against defenceless barbarians. The spectacle of a general fighting against nations, equally great and civilised, equally rich and powerful, equally brave and disciplined as his own, fighting them all round with a

[1] The Colonial and Indian Exhibition, held at South Kensington, 1886.

matchless celerity which baffled all combination, fighting and beating them in every single instance for nearly twenty years, has only once been presented by the world, and that was in Napoleon! At Moscow he met his first disaster, at Leipsic he received his first defeat, at Waterloo he fell, never to rise again.

What a wonderful difference is observable as one crosses the frontiers of Belgium and comes into Holland! Belgium is under French influence, and French in its appearance and associations. French may be said to be the language of Belgium, and even the lower classes who speak Flemish, speak French also. The great towns of Belgium, like Brussels and Antwerp, are beautiful imitations of Paris, the Belgian cafés and restaurants are like French cafés and restaurants, the beautiful and gorgeous cathedrals and churches of Belgium are like the magnificent French churches, and preach the same Roman Catholic religion to the same Celtic people. In Holland the traveller is struck with a vast difference in all these respects. He suddenly comes amidst a vigorous self-asserting long-headed Teuton race, speaking a Teuton tongue, living in the bustle of trade and activity. They don't make much show in the way of fine churches, and have not much pageantry in their religion, but they have by sheer industry, by dykes and drainage, won a great part of their country from the sea; they have intersected their fields by a system of canals which one would think was possible only in small gardens, and in their large towns they have as many canals as there are streets! These towns do not pretend to the beauty of Paris or of Brussels, but are merely systems of canals, successions of quays, wharves and jetties, with hundreds of vessels and ships eternally unloading their cargoes from the far Indies! Towns with regular streets and uniform houses, with canals and wharves and numerous heavy-laden ships, a country protected by dykes intersected by a regular network of canals, and dotted over with thousands of windmills, a population hard-working, pushing, self-asserting, and selfish if you like—that is Holland! That is the tough Teuton race who have ere now contested with England the empire of the seas, and who, next to England, possess the finest and most flourishing colonies, and have in recent years in war and in peace, obstinately pushed themselves forward and made England recoil before her in South Africa.

To the west of Binnenhof is Buitenhof, which is now occupied by some Government offices; while between the Binnenhof and the Buitenhof, and a little to the north, stands the celebrated old state prison of Holland, called Gevangen Poort, the scene of the tortures connected with the Spanish Inquisition. It makes one's flesh creep to go through these dark chambers with the old instruments of torture carefully arranged therein. What exquisite and ingenious inventions of cruelty, what devices discovered by man to torture man! What tales of cruelty, of exquisite and frightful torture, of the breaking of bone after bone, of the wrenching of joints, these cold dark vaults and chambers could tell if they could speak. Imagination shudders to think of what men and women have suffered day after day, month after month, in these dark vaults for the cause of righteousness and of liberty. Let us hope those dark days of ingenious cruelty are gone, never to return again! Modern civilisation has still much of wars and bloodshed, of conquests and cruelty to answer for, but the day of slow, deliberate, ingenious torture is, let us hope, gone for ever, and it is in so far a gain in the cause of humanity.

From Amsterdam he passed on to Hanover, in Germany, and thence to Berlin. As he stood one day adjoining the great statue of Frederick the Great, he saw a large assembly at its foot.

But they were not looking at the statue, but at a perfectly plain and quiet looking building on the south side of the street. There were two soldiers on guard at the gate, and a flag was floating above. The truth flashed on me suddenly then—this quiet and almost humble house, less imposing than many of our houses in Chowringee in Calcutta, is the residence of the greatest of living sovereigns—the Emperor of Germany! The Emperor shows himself to the people at stated hours, and the crowd had collected outside the palace to have a view of their beloved and worthy Kaiser. I stood amidst the crowd for a few minutes. In due time a white face of an old, very old man, was seen behind the window. I had seen the Emperor's face a hundred times in photographs and pictures, but the face I saw now was whiter and older than what I had expected. The Emperor looked at the people benignantly for a moment, bowed to them three or four times, and retired. The loyal people waved their hats, and cheered the Emperor vociferously and repeatedly. And I, too, though a stranger in this land, raised my hat to the most powerful of the sovereigns of the earth, and to one of the best of men.

The following reflections on Germany are worth recording:—

The contributions of the German race to modern civilisation and modern thought are of a very high order, and, if we can believe patriotic German historians, modern civilisation and modern history are German civilisation and German history. After the fall of Rome, and when Europe remained sunk in the weakness and demoralisation which follow upon subjection, it was the Germans who infused fresh life to the Continent and made progress possible. It was the German Anglo-Saxons who introduced new life into Gaul; it was the German Anglo-Saxons who introduced fresh life into Britain; it was the German Visigoths who conquered Spain and checked, and in time drove back, the Moors. It was the Germans who conquered everywhere and sowed the seeds of civilisation. Such is the boast of German patriots—and the boast is not unfounded.

From Berlin he went to Dresden, and saw Raphael's "Sistine Madonna," in the picture gallery in the magnificent palace at Dresden. Then he went on to Prague and Vienna.

His view of the future of the German and Austrian Empires is given in the following passage:—

"We were dreamers before," as a Hanoverian told me; "we are trying to be practical men now." There is more truth in this than one would suppose. The Germans, though among the bravest nations of Europe, have ever been somewhat of dreamers! With their matchless and ancient wealth of intellect, they were wanting in the vigour of youthful political life. Prussia, which formed itself into a kingdom in recent times, exactly supplied this want. The Prussian Germans, whose history during the last 200 years has been a history of vigorous struggles and unscrupulous annexations, were exactly the people who could cement the scattered German races together with their young energy and vigour into one great Empire. Germany represents the intellect and Prussia the will of that great Empire. Goethe and Schiller, Kant and Hegel, and the two Humboldts were true-born Germans. But the rough strong men who, since the time of Frederick the Great downward, have by hard continuous strokes shaped kingdoms and empires, have been mostly Prussians. Union, therefore, is to some extent necessary, and should last if the Roman Catholic South Germans consent to continue under the Protestant North Germans.

But the union of the Austrian Empire is more precarious. Austria at one time was the master of Italy, the rival of France, and the head of the confederation of German races. But ever since the time of Frederick the Great the house of Austria has had less and less influence with the German States, until in our time all such influence was finally extinguished on the field of Sadowa. Italy, too, with the help of France, has thrown off the Austrian yoke, and modern Austria is very unlike Austria of the Middle Ages. But it is not reverses in battle-fields or the loss of territory that make Austria weak. It is the internal organisation of the Dual Government which makes it weak. Modern Austria is composed of three different nations, differing in race, in language, in sympathies and interests. It is possible to conceive a complete disruption of the Austrian Empire, the Germans merging in Germany, the Slavs combining with the Russian and Turkish Slavs, and the Magyar Hungarians forming a little Switzerland of Hungary, guarding their independence like a tiger at bay, by a struggle to death.

Then, towards the end of the year, Mr. Dutt travelled on to Italy.

The sky was cloudless and the sun shone gaily and brightly on the morning of the 28th November 1886, the day I had fixed for crossing the Alps by the Brenner Pass on my way to Italy. I could scarcely believe my eyes when in the morning I saw from my hotel window the snowy peaks dazzling in the sun on every side, like a vast wall of adamant and silver surrounding the gay town of Innsbruck. A little after ten I left the town to cross the Alps, and the scenery that I witnessed during the whole day was glorious.

"Am I in Italy?" asked the poet Rogers of himself in rapture when he came to this classic land; and the same question seemed to arise in my mind as I walked through the streets of Verona on the sunny morning of the 29th November. There could be no doubt, however, in the matter. Everything around told me that I had left the last traces of gloomy Gothic architecture behind, and had come to a land where the very houses spoke of tropical taste and tropical imagination. As I walked through the narrow but cleanly streets with the well-plastered houses and green Venetian windows, I could well fancy myself in some Indian city, in some quiet handsome street in Calcutta! From the doorways I could see square courtyards inside the large houses, not unlike our Indian courtyards, and as portly Italian gentlemen passed lazily by me with the right wing of their loose cloaks flung over their left shoulders, so as to cover their chin and even their mouth and nose, I thought to myself I had seen their not very distant relations of a winter morning in the streets of Calcutta! Inside the numerous churches I saw women kneeling before images of saints or of the Virgin, which would have passed as Lakshmi or Kartikeya if robed in Indian drapery.

But the resemblance, which is not altogether fanciful, goes further and deeper. The same genial climate and fertile soil enabled the peoples of India and of Italy to light the lamp of civilisation at a time when northern nations were buried in barbarism. But as these nations rose in their turn, that ancient civilisation declined. After the tenth century Italy and India were the unfortunate battle-fields of foreigners—India of the Moslem, and Italy of the Frenchman, the Spaniard, the Austrian. The sympathy and help of modern Europe has helped Italy, feeble as she is compared to northern powers, to regain her place among nations and administer her own affairs. That sympathy and help will yet spread beyond the limits of Europe.

In the centre of this square at Verona is a marble statue of the greatest poet of modern Italy. Dante stands in a contemplative mood, with a finger on his cheek, and with that melancholy frown on his forehead which befits the poet of the "Inferno." Not far away is a spot which every lover of English literature must regard with the deepest interest. It is the old palace or family house of the Capulets, from the window of which Juliet is supposed to have given away her soul to Romeo!

Of Florence he notes:—

In the morning as I looked out of my hotel window and saw the classic Arno rolling below, as I surveyed the beautiful houses of Florence and its streets all paved with stone, and as far beyond I surveyed the high wooded hills bounding the horizon on every side, I remembered the lines I had read in my school days:—

> "Of all the fairest cities of the earth,
> None is so fair as Florence!"

In writing thus the poet, however, not only thought of the beauty of the town, the river, and the hills and gardens around, but must also have involuntarily thought of the glorious past of Florence! For when Europe was buried in the gloom of the Middle Ages after the extinction of ancient civilisation, it was Florence which imparted to a dead world the vivifying energy of poetry and literature, of painting and sculpture, of arts and civilisation. And where is the town in Europe or in the world, Athens alone perhaps excepted, which can boast of having given birth to such a galaxy of great men, such a crowd of the instructors of the world as Florence? The names of Galileo and Dante alone would suffice to make a city proud, but Florence displays to the admiring world, almost as great and glorious, Petrarch and Boccaccio, the merchant prince Lorenzo di Medici, Leonardo da Vinci, the father of modern painting, and the matchless Michael Angelo, who were all born in Florence. The devotee who sets out on an intellectual pilgrimage cannot come to a nobler shrine than Florence.

And of Rome :—

From the Capitoline Hill to the Coliseum of Rome, it is scarcely more than five minutes' walk, and in this short walk the modern traveller sees the ruins of an ancient world and an ancient civilisation. It was when sitting on a shapeless stone among these ruins that the historian Gibbon was first inspired with the idea of his matchless history; it was when standing amidst these ruins, Byron composed some of the sublimest passages that even he ever wrote. And the most commonplace tourist cannot survey this spot without, for a moment at least, forgetting the present, and being lost in a reverie of the past.

IV

In September 1892 he took furlough for a year and two months, and as before, spent a good portion of his time in travelling. Travel was almost a passion with him, and he enjoyed it not only for its own sake, for the pleasure of seeing the varied scenery of the earth in various parts, but also as an education.

Every educated man ought to travel to some extent if he can. Travelling opens up our mind, broadens our ideas, enlarges our sympathies, and makes us better fitted to receive new impressions and new incentives to work. For us, who are born and educated in India, it is also of incalculable advantage to see with our own eyes and to study with care the results of modern civilisation in Europe and America, and to assimilate what is good in them with our own national progress. Why should we, by a senseless and self-imposed disability, preclude ourselves from one of the greatest sources of instruction and pleasure, when all the world around us benefits by it?

During the autumn and winter he visited Kashmir, Mussurie, and other places in Northern India, with his friend Mr. Bihari Lal Gupta, and an account of his travels in these parts is to be found in Chapters IV. and V. of his "Rambles in India."

We left Baramula in a boat and went up the Jhelum, which is navigable in its entire course through this valley. We stopped at Supur at night, and the next morning we tried our hand at fishing and shooting, with poor results. For the much-coveted *mahseer* fish had already left this high latitude for the plains at the first approach of the cold season, and the ducks had not come from the higher latitudes yet, as the winter had not set in. So we left Supur at 10 A.M. and reached Srinagar, the capital of Kashmir, in the afternoon.

During a stay of about a week in Srinagar we saw a good deal of the city, its shops and bazars and busy life, its fine walks and lovely chinar avenues, the neighbouring lake and the surrounding hills. The Maharaja was then in Srinagar, and he is idolised by his people. We visited his palace, and also some of the well-known temples and mosques. The manufacture of shawls is declining, but is interesting even now; while the manufacture of cheaper woollen things like carpets, rugs, screens, and cloths still flourishes. The Kashmirians are real artists in manufacturing silver and copper articles and in painting on wood, and hundreds of travellers return from Kashmir every year with some specimens of the art of this country. As in Venice, you go almost everywhere by boat, and we enjoyed our evening trips to the Dal lake, a lovely sheet of water reflecting on its bosom the neighbouring hills.

To the Punjab at last! The land of the five rivers, the land of the ancient Rishis, the land of the "Rig Veda!" One of those sacred lands where man reared his infant civilisation, and first cultivated arts, poetry, and science. Civilisation is the common heritage of modern nations, and it is difficult in the present day to realise that a hundred and fifty generations ago it was confined to four gifted nations, dwelling on the banks of four rivers, and separated by wide spaces of barbarism. The Ethiopian races developed their early civilisation on the banks of the Nile, and have left vast and imperishable monuments which have never been equalled. The Semitic races achieved their earliest results in culture near the mouths of the Euphrates, and made discoveries in science and astronomy which are the heritage of modern Europe. Turanian races reared their early greatness on the banks of the Hoang Ho, and lighted the lamp of civilisation which has burned with unfailing lustre during over four thousand years. And the Aryan nations obtained their earliest triumphs in enlightenment on the banks of the Indus, and have left lasting records in poetry and thought which are the admiration of the moderns. All the world was filled with darkness when these four nations lighted their magic lamps in four isolated spots, in the east and the west, in the north and the south. All the other nations of the earth were nomad barbarians, who roamed with their flocks and tents through the vast regions of the earth, who invaded, conquered, and perished, and who lived and died without leaving a trace of their life, without leaving a mark on the history of human culture and progress.

On the evening of the 1st November we left Sahranpur, and went by rail to the far-famed Hurdwar. The Ganges rolls here by a precipitous and lofty rock, and the place is full of temples and palaces of Indian chiefs, and its streets are full of pilgrims from all parts of India. Beyond this the place does not boast much of natural beauty. For the Ganges does not issue out of mountainous gorges at Hurdwar, but at a place called Rishikesh, some twenty-five miles farther to the north. Thither, therefore, we went, and were amply rewarded for our toil. The infant Ganga is quite a hill stream here, issuing out of the lower ranges of the Himalayas and clattering over its stony bed, and forming into rapids wherever the rocks on the pebbly beach offer resistance to the wild torrent. The waters of the stream are bluish and clear, and the hills around are imposing.

Our return journey from Rishikesh to Hurdwar was truly romantic. Boats are out of the question over this wild hill torrent, and so we floated down in strange vessels. Two inflated skins of nilgais were put together, an ordinary *charpoy* was put over them, and on this I sat while two men, supporting themselves on two other skins managed this primitive vessel over the wild waters. Bihari had another vessel of this kind for him. In this primitive fashion we floated down the stream with almost railway speed, clearing about twenty-five miles in a little over three hours. The tossing on the waves, specially over rapids, was exciting, and the journey was altogether pleasant. It was night, and the moon, nearly full, lit up the sparkling waters of the infant Ganga and the wild hills and rocks all round. As we were pursuing our nightly journey in this romantic fashion, suddenly our boatmen (if they can be so called when there were no boats) stopped and pointed with alarm to a dark object moving across the river in the moonlight. What do you think it was? It was a wild elephant crossing the stream from the primeval jungles on one side to those on the other. We remained in anxious silence for some time; the huge animal slowly crossed over and disappeared, and we continued our journey and reached Hurdwar.

Early in 1893 he sailed for Europe. The inclement spring of England brought about a fresh attack of the malaria he had contracted in Burdwan, and for weeks he was confined to his room by the seaside at Bournemouth. Even on his sick-bed he went on revising his books, till his English landlady had to remove all his papers and books from his bedside. Recovering from this attack, he proceeded to Germany, and went through a course of mineral baths and mineral drinks at Wiesbaden. He amused himself there with German grammars and easy readers, but never made much progress in that language.

V

The following letters to members of his family belong to this time:—

ON BOARD THE "GANGES,"
24th April 1893.

MY DEAREST SARALA,—I was delighted to get your letter of the 10th and your mother's letter at Aden, where we reached on the 20th. We were very lucky in having no hot days in the Red Sea. There was a north wind which gave a pleasant swell to the sea and a lovely "pitching" to our steamer, and made the weather cool and comfortable. As I was walking on the deck while the steamer was pitching, the Captain asked how I liked it. I said: "It is a pleasant change from the tiresome smooth journey we have had so long." "Other passengers don't think so," said the Captain—for some of them, specially ladies, were seasick, or imagined they were, in a wonderfully short time! "There is a nice swell on to-day," I remarked to Judge Beverley. "Yes, there is a swell," he said, "but all people don't think it nice!" Poor Mrs. Geake was quite prostrate in the music room, and other ladies followed her example; and a big strapping Scotch merchant, who sits just before me at breakfast and dinner, suddenly left his seat in a hurry which made me laugh out. I wasn't at all sick; and I thoroughly enjoyed the sight of the long waves rolling towards our steamer from a distance, dashing on her prow, lifting their white crests as in anger, and falling in a sheet of spray and water over the front deck. And as the mighty steamer went up and down over the heaving billows and the cool breeze blew on my face, I enjoyed my walk on the waving deck for hours. The wind and waves have subsided to-day, and have made it cool. I am wearing warm clothes to-day; good-bye to hot weather for some time to come.

We have taken a number of new passengers who came from Bombay to Aden in another P. and O. steamer. There is an English peer among them, Lord Castlemaine, and a live Indian chief and his wife—the Thakore and Thakorani of Gondal (not Rhinoceros!). They have been to Europe before, and their children are studying at Edinburgh. The Thakorani wears a sari and covers her head. They are going only for a fortnight, to be present at the opening of the Imperial Institute by the Queen, on the 10th May. I will be present also.—Your loving father,

ROMESH.

LONDON, 12*th May*.

DEAREST SARALA AND AMALA, BIMALA, AND KAMALA,—Why, bless me, they have not done with me yet. They have elected me Fellow of the Imperial Institute, which means £2 as subscription at once, and that sum every year to come. And they have invited me, as a newly elected fellow, to an evening party at which the Prince of Wales is going to receive us. Bless me, I have not got a decent evening dress. The one I have was made at the time of Kamala's marriage, and has been repaired by a *darzi* lately! And the trousers are altogether by the *darzi*. The Prince of Wales and his party will be greatly edified no doubt by the sight of *Pati's* handiwork.

Sir Charles Bernard has asked me to call on his wife, and he will introduce me to other people. Miss Manning wishes me to appear at her afternoon parties. Appear how? In the suit made at the time of Kamala's marriage? For I have no newer morning suit. With great reluctance I have been forced to order a new frockcoat and vest, and I am afraid I shall be forced to order a new evening dress also. I will write to you about all these parties in my next mail letters.—Your ever loving father,

ROMESH CH. DUTT.

THE COMMISSIONER'S HOUSE, CUTTACK

OXFORD, *22nd June* 1893.

MY DEAR BIHARI,—I wrote to you one or two letters from the steamer, but have not been favoured with any reply yet. Probably you were waiting for a letter from me from England, as I was waiting for your replies.

I left the steamer at Marseilles on the 1st May, and came through France and reached England on the 4th, as you probably know. I went to the India Office, and was very cordially received by Sir Charles Bernard and others, who forthwith managed to get me appointed Fellow of the Imperial Institute.

I have also been busy with my books, as you may imagine. My small school book on "Ancient India" has been brought out by Longmans & Co., and favourably and lengthily reviewed in *India* for June. I hope you take *India*, and have seen the review. My larger work on "Civilisation in Ancient India" is in the press here, and the revised edition will be brought out by Kegan Paul, Trench, Trübner & Co. in a few months. A series of school books, "Bengal Readers," Standards I. to V., illustrated all of them, are in the Clarendon Press, Oxford. I am now trying to abridge Babu Sarat Das's verbose and unduly long account of his "Travels in Tibet," and make it readable, and will then put it in the press. A few other minor works I have in hand, which I hope to finish before I leave England. Dr. Rhys Davids has written to me asking me to be a member of the Royal Asiatic Society, and I have consented.

You will be sorry to learn that shortly after my arrival in Europe I caught a chill somewhere, perhaps in France, and this brought out the malarious fever which is in my system. I was confined to my room with fever and cough for a fortnight, but am all right now. I am so utterly careless and reckless about my health even at this age, and wish I had something of your prudence in this life. But I shall be more careful after this recent lesson. I propose to spend a month in some German baths to get rid of my rheumatism and fever poison, &c., before leaving Europe. My going to Chicago is more than doubtful.—Yours affectionately, R. C. DUTT.

It may be mentioned here, that it was while he was on furlough in 1893 that, besides revising his "History of Civilisation in Ancient India," he published a carefully thought-out article on the separation of the Executive and Judicial services in India. His views were strongly supported by so eminent an authority as Sir Richard Garth, and in the Memorial presented to the Secretary of State on the same subject in July 1893, Mr. Dutt's scheme was forwarded as an annexure. During the same furlough he annotated Rai Sarat Ch. Das Bahadur's accounts of his travels in Tibet, and had it published by the Council of the Royal Geographical Society of London.

He was elected Fellow of the Imperial Institute in May 1893, and Member of the Royal Asiatic Society of Great Britain and Ireland in June of the same year.

CHAPTER XII

DIVISIONAL COMMISSIONER

November 1893—*October* 1897

ON his return from leave Mr. Dutt was posted to Burdwan, and he held charge of that district till April 1894, when, on the retirement of Mr. Power, the Commissioner of the division, he was appointed officiating Commissioner in his place. This was the first occasion on which a native of India had been appointed to so high a post in the service, and naturally the event created a good deal of excitement both in the Indian and Anglo-Indian communities. It has been stated that the question of his appointment went up as far as the India Office, and it was there held that an Indian officer should not be passed over if he was fit. As regards the question of his fitness, very little doubt was entertained in official circles. The head of the Bengal Government himself wrote to Mr. Dutt congratulating him on his promotion.

BALASORE, *April* 10, 1894.

DEAR MR. ROMESH CHUNDER DUTT,—I thank you for your letter of the 4th April. I meant to have written to you myself when the time came to announce the appointment to you, but being on tour it escaped me. I wished to say how much pleasure it gives me to make this promotion in your case, which is, I think, the first instance of the appointment of a native of India to a Commissionership. The post will attract towards you some observation and criticism, and you will need tact and amiability, especially in dealing with your European subordinates in the service, but I have no reason to think there will be any serious inclination on their part to resent your being placed over them, as your record of good work is such that the appointment must have been for some time foreseen. I trust that you will be able to help the Government in what is probably the only new piece of work on a large scale which I shall take up as Lieutenant-Governor, the commutation of Chakran lands, which exist principally in the Burdwan Division.—Believe me, yours sincerely,

CH. ELLIOTT.

The remarks of the *Englishman* on this appointment were characteristic. "Meanwhile it must be pleasant," said the Anglo-Indian journal, "for the European civilians who are placed in subordination to the first Native Commissioner in India. Perhaps they are wondering how Sir Charles Elliott himself would have relished the position in his former days." But all those who, with the *Englishman*, anticipated any trouble or friction were grievously disappointed. As the *Bengalee* pointed out at the time, "loyalty to authority is one of the highest qualities of the Civil Service, and we feel confident that the unworthy appeal of the *Englishman* will fall flat upon the ears of those for whom it is intended." And so it did. There was not a whisper of dissatisfaction amongst Mr. Dutt's European subordinates, and his relations with all his Collectors were as cordial as could have been desired, a fact which is the more noteworthy, as the Collector of Birbhum, one of the six districts of the division, was actually senior to Mr. Dutt in service.

Soon after assuming charge of the division, Mr. Dutt had to submit the Annual Administration Report, and the following extracts from the Government Resolution thereupon will be of interest:—

The Lieutenant-Governor considers the Report which has been submitted by Mr. Romesh Chunder Dutt to be very creditable to that officer, as he only entered on charge of the division subsequent to the expiry of the year which forms the subject of the Report.

Mr. Romesh Chunder Dutt's remarks in paragraph 31 deserve careful attention as giving a correct description of the obstructions to drainage, which are believed to be the main causes of malarial fever in Burdwan, and which the Drainage Bill now before the Legislative Council is intended to remedy. And his aspiration in paragraph 35, that every town should be supplied with filtered water, and every village with a reserved tank, is one towards the realisation of which Government and its officers, as well as all the leading men in the country, should be prepared to give their hearty help. The work done in this direction by the Burdwan District Board and by the Collector, as recorded in paragraph 36, merits commendation, and should be imitated in other districts.

Mr. R. C. Dutt's suggestions in paragraph 54, on the steps required to improve the efficiency of the Police, have the Lieutenant-Governor's concurrence. One of the remedies he suggests —the improvement in the pay of the Sub-Inspectors—has already been partially introduced, and will be carried on further as the funds of the province permit; also a new system of appointment has been initiated, by which it is hoped that a better class of recruits will be supplied. As regards the other remedy suggested —the treatment of the Police with greater discrimination by their superior officers—Mr. Dutt's views agree closely with those of Mr. Nolan, which his Honour has recently quoted with complete approval.

The statement in paragraph 80 that the Tenancy Act does not give protection to raiyats in respect of their homestead lands, and that zamindars in attempting to oust raiyats from their fields often secure their ends by turning them out of their homesteads, is a grave one. The section of the Tenancy Act which deals with the question of homesteads, section 182, has hitherto been supposed to be an effective security for the rights of raiyats, providing as it does, that unless a specific local custom or usage to the contrary is proved to exist, the homestead land is subject to the same conditions as the raiyat's agricultural land. The Commissioner is requested to submit a special report on the subject, together with such statistics as he can collect to prove the existence of this abuse. If it does prevail, and if the law is powerless to stop it, an endeavour must be made to amend the law.

The view expressed in paragraph 114, that District Boards are useful as consultative bodies, and that it is a good thing for non-officials to obtain acquaintance with administrative work, is one which has never been contested. The battle of Local Self-Government—if there is a battle—lies round the question whether any loss of executive efficiency is incurred, and whether, if so, this loss is compensated for by the advantages in which all agree. On this subject, Mr. R. C. Dutt's remarks throw no light. But he is a hearty supporter of village unions, and his views on their utility (paragraph 116) are sound and valuable. The Resolution which issued on this subject on the 1st September 1894, shows how far the Lieutenant-Governor is able to agree with them, and in what manner he proposes to carry them into effect.

In his defence of municipal shortcomings (paragraph 110), Mr. R. C. Dutt goes rather further than his Honour can follow him, in asserting that equal shortcomings existed in the official administration which preceded the municipal law. The District Officer of to-day carries on the administration in a more efficient way than his predecessor of thirty years ago; and the District Officer, with a hundred strings in his hand, cannot give the same attention to any one of them which a body created for the purpose is able to do. On both grounds, therefore, the municipal administration of to-day ought to be superior to the official administration of thirty years ago, and should not rest content with such comparisons as those which the Report adduces; but the Lieutenant-Governor cordially endorses Mr. Dutt's experience that "when we make reasonable and practical suggestions, and indicate the way in which improvements should be effected, Municipal Commissioners show an anxious and sincere desire to accept and act on our advice."

The observations of Mr. Dutt about the police, to which reference is made in the Government Resolution, were as follows :—

Two things are necessary to improve the Bengal Police. In the first place, we must allow the Police Sub-Inspector a pay at which it is possible to get educated and intelligent young men, fit for the great powers and responsibilities of thana officers. When we pay less we simply pitchfork inefficient or dishonest men into these responsible posts. In the second place, the police force ought to be handled more intelligently than it is at present. Sub-Inspectors should be treated with greater consideration than they now receive, their good and zealous work should be more carefully noted and rewarded, and their apparently dishonest or inefficient work should be more promptly discouraged than it is at present. They should feel that they are being judged by their work; they should feel a zeal to show good work, a confidence that their good work will be appreciated. A District Magistrate would be more competent, even in addition to his other work, to deal with the police on these lines than District Superintendents of Police generally are. I have not always found District Superintendents able to discriminate between good workers and bad workers, and competent to train subordinates into zealous workers. And yet I feel sure that this could be done, and that by handling the police force with greater intelligence and with more sympathy, it would be possible to inspire them with an emulation and a zeal for doing good work which at present does not generally exist.

A brief summary of the executive and administrative work done by Mr. Dutt is to be found in the Divisional Report for 1894–95, which was submitted by his successor, Mr. (afterwards Sir) J. B. Bourdillon. He visited all the districts of the division and most of the subdivisions, and carefully inspected almost all the departments of the administration. The sanitary condition of the towns and rural areas, and the working of the municipalities, received his special attention. He set right the incorrect procedure of the Revaluation Deputy-Collectors of Bankura and Midnapur, who "had committed serious mistakes in treating ordinary raiyats as tenure-holders for the purposes of the assessment." The difficult question of the settlement of the *Ghatwali* lands of Bankura and Birbhum was discussed by him with the local officers, and the special circumstances of each district examined on the spot.

As an example of the care and minuteness with which he inspected offices might be mentioned the fact that, when inspecting the Treasury at Bankura, he detected a defalcation by the Treasurer of nearly 3000 rupees. It was discovered that the Treasurer was in the habit of temporarily misappropriating public money by falsifying certain totals of the daily balance-sheet. The matter was reported to Government through the Board of Revenue. The Treasurer was prosecuted and convicted at the Sessions, but was acquitted by the High Court.

In January 1895, Mr. Dutt was appointed a member of the Legislative Council, and I believe it was the first instance when Government appointed a Commissioner of a division away from the metropolis to be a member of Council. During the debates on the Public Demands Recovery Act and the Drainage Bill, Mr. Dutt took a very conspicuous part. On the occasion of the discussion of the Public Demands Recovery Act, the Lieutenant-Governor went out of his way to praise the new member. "I must compliment the honourable member," said His Honour, "on the excellent way in which he put his case, and I think the Council may be congratulated in having an official in their midst who has been practically engaged in carrying out the work of this particular Act, and who has given a sympathetic and intelligent consideration to the matter." And it would be no exaggeration to say, that of all the official members, Mr. Dutt rendered the most substantial assistance to Government in passing the Sanitary Drainage Bill. His gift of marshalling facts, and of bringing to bear on any particular question the result of his unique powers of observation, together with his personal acquaintance with facts bearing directly on the issue, gave unusual weight to all his official pronouncements.

In April 1894, while Mr. Dutt was Commissioner of Burdwan, Bankim Chunder Chatterjea, the greatest literary genius of modern India, died at the early age of fifty-six. We have noticed before how Mr. Dutt was influenced by this great man, his father's friend and his own literary god-father, to write his Bengali novels. Mr. Dutt visited him on the day before his death. At the sound of his voice Bankim Chunder, who was fast losing consciousness, opened his eyes and at once recognised the visitor. By some unaccountable association of past ideas, he even asked for a photograph of Mr. Dutt. The next day Bengal lost her greatest son. To do honour to the great departed, Mr. Dutt called a memorial meeting, at which the Maharaja of Burdwan, the District Judge, and other notable persons were present. Mr. Dutt was the principal speaker. He also wrote about the great novelist in the *Nabya Bharat*, and his highly appreciative article contained many personal reminiscences of his departed friend. Later on he contributed an illuminative notice of the illustrious Bengali's life to the "Encyclopædia Britannica." "For the last thirty years," wrote Mr. Dutt, "Bankim Chunder has been the inspiring genius of the Bengali nation, guiding the national imagination, and shaping their intellectual and religious aspirations."

On the return of Mr. Bourdillon, his senior, from leave, Mr. Dutt was relieved of the charge of the division on the 8th April 1895, and was posted to Hughli as

Collector. In October, however, he was transferred to Orissa, to relieve Mr. Cooke and take charge again of a division. The Commissioner of Orissa is *ex officio* Superintendent of a number of Native States called the Orissa Tributary Mahals, and as such exercises *quasi* political powers. In this division, also, the Collector of Balasore was senior to Mr. Dutt. The general administration report of the division was submitted in the usual course, and the Government resolution remarked : " The Lieutenant-Governor thanks the Commissioner for his efficient administration of the division, and for his clear and concise report." He was also thanked by Government "for his careful supervision of the Tributary States under his charge."

The relations of Mr. Dutt with all the government officials in the division were, as usual, quite friendly. There was only one unpleasant exception. Mr. Dutt took a great deal of interest in the training and education of the chiefs of the Tributary Mahals who were minors, and put them into the Government College. He also arranged that the minor chiefs should ride, play tennis, or engage in some other healthy exercise. One evening the young Raj Kumars of Narsingpur and Pal Lahera were out riding, and met Mr. N. L. Hallward, the Principal of Cuttack College, who was playing golf. Mr. Hallward believed that the chiefs had seen him and had failed to salute him. For this offence they were publicly caned on the following day. Mr. Dutt, as guardian of the minor chiefs, took exception to Mr. Hallward's action, and brought it to the notice of Government. Both the Director of Public Instruction, Sir Alfred Croft, and the Government strongly disapproved of the Principal's conduct, and severely censured him. Mr. Dutt also removed the boys from the Government school, but this action was not approved by Government.

II

While Commissioner of Burdwan, Mr. Dutt submitted important reports on the Sanitary Drainage Bill the Revenue Sale Bill, and the Public Demands Recovery Bill, all of which were much appreciated by Government. But perhaps his most important work as Commissioner of Burdwan was the assistance he rendered Government in abolishing the Ghatwali service in Bankura, and bringing the Ghatwali lands under settlement—a matter which had been hanging fire for some time past. He also submitted a draft Bill for the "abolition of Ghatwali service." His scheme was to assess the lands of the Ghatwals as found in the survey of 1880–87, at rates of rent favourable to the Ghatwals—*i.e.* 25 per cent. below current rates, and then to settle the ghat with the Raja of Burdwan, the zamindar. The Ghatwals were by this arrangement to become raiyats of the zamindar, and the zamindar was to pay the government demand, as a part of the revenue for his estate. He was against the lands being settled directly with the Ghatwals.

In his report he pointed out: "The great recommendation of this scheme is that it is simple and eminently workable, and we can proceed to settle the Ghatwali lands under this scheme without the help of any legislation for the present." His main suggestions were accepted by Government.

As Commissioner of Orissa, he submitted valuable reports on such important subjects as the maintenance of records and the Patwari system, on the question of a tenant's right to transfer his interest in land, and, lastly, the chaukidari system in Orissa. The various settlements of the temporary settled estates of Orissa, including the important Khasmahal estate, comprising practically the whole of the Khurda subdivision, came under his careful scrutiny and review. These reports have only local interest, but his observations with regard to the important question of limitation by legislation of the right of the owners of land to transfer their interests by sale or otherwise, a question which is still the subject of much discussion, will bear repetition :—

The apprehended danger of lands passing from the agricultural to the non-agricultural classes does not exist in any part of Bengal, so far as my experience goes. I cannot speak with authority of Bihar or of Chota Nagpur, as I have never been employed in those divisions. But with regard to the other divisions of Bengal, I am able to state with confidence that the evil apprehended is unknown, and that the remedies provided are not only uncalled for, but would virtually be a confiscation of rights which the agricultural classes have enjoyed for generations past, and which have a pecuniary value.

Part II. of the Memorandum, to which my special attention has been drawn, deals with proposed restrictions on the right of transfer of proprietary rights with regard to land. If the Bengal zamindars of the present day were informed that it was intended to legislate in order to protect their interests and to prevent their estates from going to the non-agricultural moneyed classes, the zamindars would probably listen to the proposal with some degree of amusement. And if the particular remedies proposed in Part II. of the Memorandum were explained to them, the zamindar would certainly reject them, and would very justly protest against them as a confiscation of rights which they have enjoyed for generations and for centuries.

The fact is, the present race of Bengal zamindars do not require the protection which it is contemplated to provide for landed classes. The value of land has greatly increased since the date of the Permanent Settlement, and estates generally bring a handsome profit to their owners after the payment of government revenues. Transfers of large and important estates were frequent immediately after the Permanent Settlement, and in the early years of this century, but they are not so now. One does not frequently hear of large and important estates in Bengal districts changing hands through the indebtedness of the landed houses. In the sales which I have held as Collector, during the last fifteen years in various districts of Bengal for non-payment of revenue, I do not remember to have sold any large and extensive estate. The landed classes of Bengal are not decaying or in a state of indebtedness; lands are not slipping out of their hands into those of shroffs and money-lenders; the remedies proposed to save their interests are not needed, the restrictions proposed on their right of alienation would be hurtful and injurious, not beneficial.

Men who make money by trade or otherwise in Bengal often enter into the status of zamindars by purchasing land. Such purchasers do not generally find large and profitable estates in the market. On the contrary, they negotiate for the purchase of shares here and there often held by old and decayed families divided among themselves, and incapable of managing their properties. In such cases the sales are a benefit to the country, and should be encouraged by legislation. When a family proves itself, by its vices or incapacity, to be unfit to manage the ancestral property, when it is divided in itself and ruined by litigation, it is desirable that the estate, or portions of it, should pass into the hands of abler men, who are better able to manage it. The transfer in such cases need not be regretted either from an economical or from a political point of view. The new landlord is likely to be able to manage the property better than a divided and enfeebled and decaying family. And the new landlord is likely to be as loyal a subject of the British Government, and as alive to the responsibilities of his position as the family he has replaced.

I now come to Part III. of the Memorandum, and to the important subject of restricting the transfer of tenant-rights. So far as Bengal is concerned, the proposed restrictions are uncalled for, and would be a confiscation of rights which the tenants of Bengal are exercising every day. When the Tenancy Bill came up for discussion in the Viceroy's Council, and the question of legalising the right of transfer of tenant-rights was discussed, the Viceroy, who was against the legalising of this right, nevertheless said:—"The evidence appears to me, I confess, to be overwhelming that in the greater part of Bengal the practice of transfer exists under a custom which the Courts have recognised." It is a pity that landlord interests prevailed in the Viceroy's Council, and that the right of transfer was not legalised, but was still left to custom.

The question now is, does the right of transfer, enjoyed by tenants in all parts of Bengal, lead to their holdings passing into the hands of non-agricultural classes? The figures for 1883–84 would show that out of 47,000 holdings sold by registered deeds, 6745 holdings, or about one holding in seven, passed into the hands of mahajans. The highest proportion is in Burdwan Division, where, out of 14,229 holdings sold by registered deeds, 3204, or nearly one-fifth of the holdings, passed into the hands of mahajans. It would be misleading, however, to suppose that these mahajans were non-agricultural classes, and that lands passed from cultivators to shroffs and money-lenders. On the contrary, men who are described as mahajans in the returns were generally well-to-do cultivators themselves who had bought up holdings which other cultivators could no longer hold and cultivate.

Since coming to the Orissa Division, I have had another rare opportunity of observing how raiyati lands are transferred. The whole of Khurda Subdivision in Puri district is practically one large Government estate, and our opportunities of observing the results of the transfers effected by the raiyats are unusually good. And yet while transfers are thus frequent and unrestricted in Khurda Subdivision, there is no evidence to show that land is passing out of the hands of the cultivating classes. On the contrary, there is positive evidence, collected by careful observers, to the effect that the proportion of land-owning cultivators is the same in Khurda now as it was in years before.

In paragraph 3 of the Government Resolution on the General Administration Report for 1895-96, it was observed :—

Mr. Romesh Chunder Dutt, from his experiences in Orissa and elsewhere, infers that the right of transfer possessed and exercised by raiyats by custom in many parts of Bengal has been beneficial to their interest. This important question is separately under the consideration of Government. It is one on which it is dangerous to generalise, and regarding which Government are not in a position to express a decided opinion at present.

III

Some idea of his life in Cuttack is to be gleaned from the following letters :—

CUTTACK, 10*th Oct.* 1895.

MY DEAREST BIMALA,—From Cuttack to Sylhet is like from China to Peru, and this letter will probably be on its way for a week before it reaches your hand. But I feel so relieved to come away from malarious Burdwan and Hughli ! Orissa is healthy and near the sea, and my house overlooks a broad river, with a fine prospect of woods and hills beyond. There is an excellent club here, with racquets and tennis and badminton and whist, so that I have plenty of exercise and games in the evenings. I am already feeling better since leaving Hughli.

In a week's time I go to inspect Ganen's subdivision, and will spin out the inspection over ten or twelve days ! ! Then from the next month I visit the Tributary Mahals and the Jungle Rajas in their hilly and wooded country. There are some sixteen of them, and I have to look after their administration, advise and guide them, decide questions of succession, and put down disturbances when they arise. All is quiet now.

Write to me a long letter telling me all about you. Your

mother has probably gone to Darjeeling by this time.—Your loving father,

ROMESH.

KEONJHAR STATE, 10*th Jany.* 1896.

MY DEAREST BIMALA,—I was delighted to see your well-known handwriting on one of the letters which came to me by yesterday's *Dak*. For you had not written to me for an age, and I was wondering what the matter was with you. I inquired of Amala and of Sarala, and they both told me that they had heard from you recently, and that relieved me of my anxiety.

I have been touring during the last month in the hills and jungles of the Tributary Mahals, doing my marches every day on elephants, visiting the States of the native Rajas, and receiving from them ostentatious ovations which the Emperor of China might envy! This morning I have done 15 miles on elephant, have been received by the Maharaja of Keonjhar, have passed through his town decorated with flags and festoons, and am now in my tent pitched on the high banks of the Baitarini River, the river flowing before me and the hills around and behind me. So you see I am not leading an uncomfortable life in Orissa! And I am enjoying splendid health in this healthy division and in this bracing weather.

I have no idea when I shall go to Calcutta next. My present plan is to stay on in Orissa till November next, when I shall be entitled to furlough, and my qualifying service also will be completed. I then take two years' furlough, and may return to service after two years, or retire on pension, just as I like. Bihari is probably going to England this summer, and has promised to take Ajoy if your mother will allow. Then when I go to England later, I shall see Ajoy there. But these are only vague plans; nothing has been settled yet.—Your loving father,

ROMESH.

CUTTACK, 13*th March* 1896.

MY DEAREST BIMALA,—At last we are all in Cuttack, fairly settled down in this beautifully situated and spacious house. I went to Calcutta last week, and have brought down your mother and Susila and Ajoy, and Pratap is also here for a change. Sarala and her baby are also here with us, so we are a goodly company. How we miss you and Boli, and your dear children.

How they would have enjoyed a run in this park-like compound, with its avenues and grassy lawns and shady trees, actually giving shelter to over twenty deer, who are half tame and residents of this compound! And the broad sweep of the river to the south and the view of the hills beyond form as lovely and open a site as the climate is healthy and pleasant! Kamala and Pramatha are still in 37 Park Street, and will probably be going to Darjeeling next month. We will try to let our Calcutta house then, if we get a decent tenant in this season, for your mother won't hear of giving up the house! Your mother will be here with me as long as I shall be here, *i.e.* till November next when Cooke returns from furlough, and if Cooke does not return to Orissa, then till March next, when we go to England on furlough. It has been settled that Ajoy will remain with us this year, and we take him to England next year when we go on furlough. And it is practically settled also that your mother and Susila will also go with me.

I hear that Boli Narain retires next year; won't it be jolly if you all come to England with us! Boli will, I suppose, get a much better pension in England than if he retired and lived here, and if we settle down all together in some place away from London, your expenses won't be much. These are dreams almost too good to be realised; but yet I do not see why they should not be realised.

Ajoy (to-morrow is his birthday) will be put in the Ravenshaw College here, and may go up for his F.A. Examination from this College (as Bihari's boys did) next January, unless I am transferred from here in November, which is not likely. We have brought Ajoy's riding pony with us, as well as a phaeton and waler for your mother and Sarala's drives, and I have my dog-cart and pony besides. So we expect to make ourselves pretty comfortable. And in April and May, when it becomes very hot in Cuttack, we will live in the seaside circuit-house of Puri, where it is breezy and cool, and have our sea-bathing every day.—Your ever loving father, ROMESH.

CUTTACK, 24*th July*.

MY DEAREST BIMALA,—I have received your loving letter and have sent it on to Ajoy, so that he may learn that you are all doing well in far off Sylhet.

As I am writing to you this letter, the river flowing past my house is in flood. The water has risen 15 feet in two days, and is now within a few feet of my verandah. The flooded river spreads its sea-like expanse before me, so that I can only see this vast sheet of roaring and rushing waters, and the line of green bank and blue hills across, far in the distance. This is the beauty of this house, the best situated Commissioner's house in

Bengal. I suppose the waters will begin to subside now, for they are too well-behaved to actually come into the Commissioner's house. The highest flood known within recent years is, I believe, 28 feet, and the river is now 25 feet.

I have decided to take furlough in November next, and intend starting for Europe at once, if your mother can make up her mind.

With kisses for your dear children, and love for you and Boli, I am your loving father, ROMESH.

CAMP NARSINGPUR IN THE GARJATS,
ORISSA, *17th December* 1896.

MY DEAREST BIMALA,—I was glad to get Boli Narain's telegram informing me of your safe arrival and also that Boli Narain has quite recovered. In that case you might have done this tour with me in the Garjats. I am now in a hilly country (like Dhenkenal, which you saw), and to-morrow I am going to cross a range of hills about 1000 feet high in order to get into another hilly State. I shall be touring the whole of this month, and hope to make over charge to Cooke early in January.

I hope you and Tush and Indur will retain pleasant recollections of your visit to Orissa. To me, who am accustomed to a lonely life, your and Amala's coming to Orissa was real happiness, a gleam of sunshine which brightened my last days in Orissa, possibly the last days of my service, as I may not return to service again.

Hoping to hear from you by return of post how you are all getting on in Sylhet,—Your loving father,

ROMESH CH. DUTT.

PURI, *24th May* 1896.

MY DEAR BROTHER,—I have received your letter of the 20th. I am always willing to give you the best advice I can, but the decision as to what Pratap should do rests with you, not with me.

My advice decidedly is that Pratap should go to England if he gets Mullick's scholarship. With two or three years' continuous study at Wren's, Pratap has a very fair chance of passing, as he is assiduous. Jotsna Ghosal failed at the entrance examination, but is assiduous, so he passed after three years' continuous grind at Wren's. And when Pratap has a fair chance he should not forego it merely through fear of failure.

I ought to have paid the whole expenditure of Pratap's education in England if I could stick to my service longer, but my health is breaking down. Since returning from England in 1893 I had malaria in 1894, had dyspepsia and sleeplessness in 1895, and am just now down with a return of rheumatism. I *must* go to England at the end of this year, and very likely never return to service again. I leave Puri to-morrow for Khurda, and thence go to Cuttack. So address me to Cuttack henceforth.—Yours affectionately ever, ROMESH.

CUTTACK, *2nd June* 1896.

MY DEAR BROTHER,—I returned to Cuttack yesterday and received yours of the 29th. I think the *Indian Mirror* is mistaken in thinking that Government intended to pass me over. The Lieutenant-Governor wanted to bring Bolton in, and he was therefore compelled to send out Buckland as a Commissioner. I never thought of this as an injustice or even an unfairness to me. The difference in pay between a permanent Commissioner and an acting Commissioner is very slight, and I am permanent to all intents and purposes, as there is little chance of my reverting even if I don't take furlough next winter, as I propose to do. —Yours affectionately ever, ROMESH CH. DUTT.

IV

This brings us to the subject of Mr. Dutt's retirement from service. In 1897 he completed the period of service which entitled him to a pension. An official career had always been his second love only; other ambitions, literary and national, had always exercised a far stronger attraction over him. Early in 1897 he again went on furlough, and in October of the same year, after a service of twenty-six years, he retired from the Indian Civil Service. In what esteem he was held by the members of his own service may be seen from two letters which Sir Henry Cotton and Sir Charles Bernard wrote to him on hearing rumours that he was about to retire.

SIMLA, *11th October* 1896.

MY DEAR DUTT,—Thank you very much for your most welcome and cordial letter of the 4th October. I am of course glad enough to go to Assam, but my pleasure is tempered with regret at leaving so many good friends in Bengal. No one has been more dependent than I have been on the co-operation and

support of men like yourself. The better I have known you the better we have worked together, and I honestly hope you will not think of retiring. You hold a very special position in the service, and we can't afford to lose you. You have done good work in Orissa, and I am sorry you are leaving that province, but it can't be helped, I suppose, as both Forbes and Cooke are coming out, and only Luttman Johnson is going home. But I presume you will get the next *pucca* step. You have always utilised your holidays to England well, and I hope you will score another literary success on this occasion. Unfortunately I shall not see you in Calcutta on my way through, but I hope it may not be very long before we meet again.—I am always yours very sincerely,
H. J. S. COTTON.

INDIA OFFICE, WHITEHALL, S.W.,
5th November 1896.

DEAR MR. R. C. DUTT,—I see a statement in the *Homeward Mail* that you are going to retire from the service. I hope your health is not breaking down. If you are well, your voluntary retirement will be a great loss to Bengal, in my judgment. You have now come to the standing when your advice must have great weight. And, of course, you can look at Bengal questions from a point of view which no other C.S. man can command; while at the same time you are as much a well-wisher to the British Raj as any Englishman could be.—I am, yours sincerely,
C. E. BERNARD.

The following remarks on his retirement I know to be quite true, and are here reproduced from Mr. Natesan's sketch :—

Much surprise was felt at Mr. Romesh Dutt's retirement after twenty-six years' service, when under the rules of the service he might have continued nine years more. His best friends thought that he had taken an unwise step in leaving a service so honourable, so well paid, and holding out prospects so rich. And the general public whispered that he must have retired under some feeling of dissatisfaction at some unfair treatment. Those who have heard him speak on the subject know that these last rumours were absolutely without any foundation. Mr. Dutt was treated with perfect fairness throughout the period of his service; he was never once passed over in the regular line of promotion, and on two occasions he was promoted over the heads of his seniors. More than this, his good work was prominently recognised;

even his mistakes were treated with indulgence; he was never once seriously found fault with. He retired from the service with the most lively sense of the fairness and the courtesy of the Government he had served.

The true reasons for his early retirement were two. In the first place he wished to devote himself whole-heartedly to literary pursuits which he always called his "first love." He had formed the ambition of leaving some durable works behind him, which his countrymen would value, even after his death. He was in the fiftieth year of age, and had earned his pension, and he decided to devote the remaining years of his life to earning literary fame rather than to earning a fortune, to serve *Saraswati* rather than to serve *Lakshmi.*

In the second place he wished for greater independence and larger opportunities of striving for that progress in self-government, and those liberal reforms for which the time was ripe. His long experience in administration had convinced him that British Rule in India could be more efficient and more popular by the admission of the people to a share in the control and direction of the administration. And he felt an irresistible impulse to take a part in the national endeavour to secure this share for his countrymen.

These were the two motives which led to his early retirement from service. (Mr. Dutt's biographer might well have added a third—namely, his failing health, to which he refers in his letters to his brother written about this time.) The general public did not then believe that such dreamy reasons could have induced Mr. Dutt to sever himself from a fine career in a fine service. But those who have watched his career since 1897 will now admit that he decided rightly in obeying the impulses which he felt within himself.

Thus closed Mr. Dutt's career as a public servant in the active service of the Government. The head of the Imperial Government, the Viceroy himself, had at a comparatively early stage of his career congratulated him on his success as an administrator, and recognised in his brilliant career a demonstration of the fitness of Indians to fill the highest offices under the State. Successive Lieutenant-Governors had the highest regard for his abilities, and Sir Steuart Bayley after his retirement once said that in his opinion Mr. Dutt was the most capable executive officer of his time in Bengal.

His views on public questions were not always acceptable to Government, but there was never any question that his observations were the outcome of honest conviction, based largely on personal experience, of facts as he saw them, and that they formed by far the ablest exposition of the views of a school of thought which was entitled to very careful consideration. While enjoying in the highest degree the confidence of the Government, and of the more liberal-minded officials of his time, he was held in the highest esteem by the enlightened section of the Indian community. Nor did anything in his career as a public servant shed greater lustre on his name than his staunch and continuous advocacy of the cause of the Indian peasants, and his tireless efforts to improve their position. This part of his work provides a crushing reply to the criticism of those who hold that the educated Indian and the Indian publicist are in no sense the representatives of the voiceless millions of India. We cannot conclude this section better than by quoting a paragraph from the address presented by the people of Kendrapara to Mr. Dutt on the occasion of his visit to that subdivision.

> We do not allude to these works of yours as instances of your literary abilities only; we look at them from a higher standpoint. Who but a true lover of his country, a patriot in the true sense of the term, could devote so much time and energy in improving the language which he learnt on the lap of his mother? . . . Your works have the true ring of the patriot in them, not noisy and boisterous, but quiet, calm and dignified, and therefore the more efficacious.
>
> Your schemes and proposals of administrative reform are admitted on all sides to be based on a true grasp of the situation, and to proceed from a thorough knowledge of existing facts and circumstances, and although you may not have the satisfaction of seeing them adopted at once in their entirety, yet we have not the least doubt that they are such as are calculated to impart great weight to and to influence the judgment of Government whenever the questions arrive at the final stage.
>
> In you we do not know which to admire most, your renowned literary abilities, your silent but ardent patriotic spirit which lies behind them, your advocacy of the cause of your country and its

people, your tact and judgment in your official capacity, or your strict faithfulness to the Government you serve. And what must be our feelings when we come to claim you as one of ourselves? India's sun has set, says the world, but while there is one such star in her eternal firmament, brightening the horizon far and wide, old decrepit Mother India may gladden her heart and cheer up her slumbering sons to action.

CHAPTER XIII

SOCIAL NOVELS

BREAKING loose from the traditions of historical romance rendered predominant by the example of Bankim Chunder, Mr. Dutt turned to a sphere more congenial to his gifts and inclinations, and produced two social novels, "Sansar," and its sequel, "Samaj." The first appeared in the year 1885, and the second eight years afterwards, when he was Commissioner of Orissa. The two together present an admirable picture of the everyday life of present-day Bengal. Amongst the leading characters we find the rich zamindar, who leads a life of luxury and profligacy; the educated young man, who has imbibed the courage, the freedom of thought, and the high ambitions and aspirations which liberal English education imparts; the man of high character and solid worth, who does not find an opening for a career in the limited avenues of present-day life in Bengal; the true ascetic, who has found in the hidden treasures of the Hindu faith high moral teachings of toleration and brotherhood; and the lowly peasant, satisfied with his lot, whose day is spent in trying to please a termagant wife and dodging the money-lenders. These are all admirably rendered, and the author is still more successful in the fascinating delineation of his women characters. They are all characteristically Oriental, faithful and loving, long-suffering and gentle. The chief interest of these stories, however, lies not so much in character-drawing as in the undercurrent of social and intellectual forces, slowly moulding the minds and habits of young Bengal. Indeed, it is such problems as widow re-marriage and the unmasking of the pleasure-seekers who masquerade in the garb of the defenders of Hindu orthodoxy which absorb his deepest interest.

Here, as in his historical novels, Mr. Dutt was writing with a distinctly national object. To exemplify in actual life the true lines on which social and intellectual progress will have to be achieved in India, by an intermingling of the best traditions and teachings of the East with what is most liberal and elevating in the West, was his main object. No other Bengali writer has approached such questions in the same liberal spirit, and with the same intimate knowledge of the life, the troubles, and aspirations of all grades of society from the peasant to the nobleman. It may perhaps be admitted that as works of art these novels do not attain a very high level, being more analytic than constructive and living, yet they make fascinating reading, and fulfil a high and valuable purpose.

"Sansar," the first of the two social novels, was translated into English as "The Lake of Palms," and was widely reviewed and praised by the English Press, as the following extracts show :—

Spectator (May 17, 1902).—All readers who care to know something of Indian life from the native point of view will find it a deeply interesting and pathetic study. The contrast between the peace and affection of a patriarchal household in the ancestral village, and the loneliness, distractions, and temptations which beset those members who leave the country and settle in Calcutta, strikes one as a very close reproduction of the corresponding situation half a century ago in England.

Pall Mall Gazette (May 13, 1902).—The tired reviewer has a very pleasant surprise before him in "The Lake of Palms." It seems an error in nomenclature to call the book a novel. It is so restful, so quiet, so easy in movement that it resembles nothing less than what we in Europe know as a "novel." It is a very attractive country, the East which Mr. Dutt pictures for us here: calm with the calmness not of stagnation but of security; wise with ancient and mystical wisdom, nor troubling overmuch at the acquirement of knowledge; superstitious with the serene faith of the Middle Ages; yet touched, though ever so slightly, by the activities of European modes of thought and methods of action; this wonderful India gives you an impression of solemnity and of immobility that are very well reflected in "The Lake of Palms."

Dundee Advertiser (April 21, 1902).—At present there are plenty of Anglo-Indian novels of a dressy order, in which handsome subalterns make love to the ladies of their superior officers, and the reader derives the pleasurable belief that India is only a hot edition of Bond Street and Hurlingham. Mr. Romesh Dutt's tale presents another view—the vast toiling, passive, superstition-ridden India, not of her romantic, gorgeous cities, but of her thousand villages. The fashionable, frivolous India of Calcutta, Simla, and the cantonments is another matter from this domestic India of patient drudgery and uneventfulness.

Glasgow Herald (April 22, 1902).—The magnificent adventures and luxuriant rhetoric of the Oriental novel are in this case entirely wanting; but the warm domesticities and fresh love-interests of the tale hold the interest of the reader by their absolute sincerity and their delightful fidelity to nature. The life of the farm, of the college, of the temple, of the city, the struggle of the old with the new in social and religious habits, the aspirations and speculations of the Hindu are interpreted with unfaltering accuracy and whole-hearted sympathy. The love story of Sarat, the college student, and Sudha the little widow, is delicately sketched, and the reconciliation of the Hindu squire with his betrayed wife is a piece of work that the practised Western novelist might well envy.

India (April 25, 1902).—Incidentally it is contrived so as to bring readers in contact with the social, religious, and political life of the country—the peasant, the student, the official (Native as well as British), the tributary Raja, the Anglicised zamindar, the priest and the guru, questions of Government and administration, the tragic working of the leaven of social and religious reform, and many other aspects of current life. Mr. Dutt takes care, however, to subordinate his teaching and preaching to the business of his story, except perhaps in the descriptive episodes of pilgrimage, the interest of which temporarily overshadows though it deeply involves the development of the personal fortunes of his people. No one can read the book without gaining a sympathetic insight into the conditions of Indian life, and being drawn powerfully towards the men and women that are struggling in their millions to solve the problems of a new time under the urgency of strange ideas from the West, and yet in accordance with the traditions of a long and splendid historic past. To most British readers at home the perusal of this simple and charming story will probably work a complete transformation of preconceived ideas regarding their Indian fellow-subjects. Mr. Dutt writes with charming simplicity and ease, with profound sympathy as well as with the knowledge of experience, and over all he casts the magic mantle of a poetic flush.

KAMALA, ELDEST DAUGHTER

CHAPTER XIV

HOME LIFE AND PERSONAL ATTACHMENTS

I

NATURE had designed Romesh Chunder Dutt to be an ideal father of a home, and his life in his own family circle perhaps absorbed more of the real man than he was able to give even to his ambition of becoming an ideal citizen of the State. In his nature were combined in a rare degree some of the best traits of the East and the West. His emotions had Oriental depth and richness, but they were restrained by an Englishman's reserve and strength of character. It is difficult to conceive of any father being more devoted to his children than he was, and in his daily communion with them and in the fostering care with which he tried to nourish them and broaden their minds and hearts, he evinced all the tenderness and devotion of an Eastern mother, with the culture and benignity of a monitor of the Socratic type. Yet he was singularly free from any display and sentimentalism, so often a failing of the Bengali character. His home was a perfect temple of freedom, where reigned sweetness, refinement and love. There were no false notes, no exaggerated sense of decorum or undignified familiarity.

But the particular charm of his social nature was unquestionably his geniality, his bright playfulness, the faculty of enjoying the brightness and sweetness of life, and infusing in others the same joyousness of spirit. It was in his home that the true largeness of his heart was most obvious. Nobody who ever came within that delightful circle can easily forget the penetrating influence of his ever-youthful vivacity or the subtle magic of his unobtrusive but lifting and all-embracing sympathy.

Of his five children—his only boy was the fourth—daughters and son alike had an absolutely equal share of the father's heart. His wife, though perhaps not able to keep pace with the intellectual march of the times, was yet always assured of her place as the real mistress of the family and her due share of the love and affection of her husband. It is usually a charge against Indians who have been to Europe that they lose touch with their own people, and what the individual perhaps gains in personal affluence and position is a loss to the family and society. In no case was this charge more completely falsified than in that of Mr. Dutt. Seldom indeed was a man more scrupulously yet naturally alive to the claims of all his relations, in the truly generous style of the Hindus, than he.

His relations with his elder brother, Mr. J. C. Dutt, remained throughout life peculiarly close and sacred. They went far to realise the Oriental ideal which assigns to the elder brother the same reverence due to a parent, brightened by the Westerner's view which regards a brother as one's best friend.

Another striking feature of his emotional life was the steadfast and almost romantic attachment he had for his lifelong friend and companion, Mr. B. L. Gupta, a feeling which was naturally reciprocated by his friend. In fact, it would be difficult to say whether he regarded his brother Jogesh more as a friend, or his friend Mr. Gupta as a brother.

II

The following letters written in his more serious mood are good examples of the tenderness and sweetness of his nature.

His eldest daughter Kamala was married to Mr. P. N. Bose, of the Geological Survey, in 1882, and shortly afterwards he wrote to her from Balasore:—

BALASORE, *August* 11, 1882.

MY DEAREST KAMALA,—I cannot tell you how happy I feel to receive your loving letter. I have been longing to hear from you since some days past, and would have written to you if I had known your new address. Last Tuesday I wrote to your mother asking her to let me know your address, but I have not heard from her yet in reply.

Yes, I learnt from your mother and from Mr. Gupta that you were doing very well in your new home, that you were liked by all of your husband's family, that you had put your house into order, and that you had asked Bimala and the rest of them to see your new house. Every account that I received of you filled me with pleasure. You have always been a good and sensible girl, and I always expected you would make an exemplary wife and a good housewife. That you may be happy in your new home and in the new sphere of your life, and that you may long live to enjoy that happiness is the dearest wish of your ever loving father.

Your *Jathamohasoy* sends you his love and his wishes for your happiness from Darjeeling. You should write to him if you have not done so already. Yes, Balasore is a nice station; I am learning Uriya here, so when we meet again I will surprise you all with my new learning! My affectionate regards for your husband.—Your ever loving father,

ROMESH DUTT.

About this same daughter he wrote to his brother :—

BALASORE, *August* 13, 1882.

MY DEAR BROTHER,—To-day I complete my thirty-four years. My first district appointment, my second district appointment, and Kamala's marriage are the happy events of these last twelve months. . . . I hear more favourable accounts of Kamala, and you must not mind if, with a father's pride, I repeat them to you in every letter. Kamala and Pramatha came last Sunday for a dinner in the Bengali style, at 20 Beadon Street, and this is what Chamatkar (Mr. Dutt's sister) writes of Kamala :—

"I cannot tell you what pleasure it has given me to see Kamala. You have rightly named her Kamala (Goddess of Wisdom). It is impossible to describe her thoughtfulness and good sense. She knows by instinct in what esteem to hold the different relations of her husband, and how to behave towards each one of them. It is a pity you have had no opportunity of seeing her after her marriage. The thought comes naturally to me that a girl of Kamala's pure character ought to be happy through life. She is indeed an ideal of what a daughter should be."

I have nearly forgotten what tender emotions are, but I could hardly read the above without an outburst of emotion and love for my dearest child.—Believe me, yours affectionately ever,
ROMESH CH. DUTT.

His second daughter, Bimala, was married in 1883 to Mr. B. Borrah, then Assistant Engineer in Assam. Her marriage meant removal to a new sphere of life altogether, far away from friends and relations, and it was this which led him to write regularly to her once a week.

BARISAL, *October* 20, 1883.

MY DEAREST BIMALA,—I have just now received with sincere joy your loving letter of the 15th from Gauhati, and have learnt with much pleasure and relief that you are making a comfortable journey to the place of your destination. You have asked me to reply at once, but you have not given me an address, so I am sending this note to Gauhati, and hope it will reach you safe.

Write to me, Bimala, as often as you can, and write me long letters telling me all about yourself, your station, the people you find there, and the incidents of your daily life. You must know how very anxious I am to learn everything about yourself.

I am glad to read your description of your journey up the Brahmaputra. Be sure I will do the same journey in about six months hence, and spend a happy time in Assam with you. You are a poet, Bimala, and I am not. Nevertheless, as I was coming away in my steam launch from Calcutta, I could not but think of our parting at the railway station, and could not help composing some lines. They are not so good as your poems are, but accept them, such as they are, with a father's most sincere love.—Your ever loving and affectionate father,
ROMESH CH. DUTT.

BARISAL, *November* 4, 1883.

MY DEAREST BIMALA,—This is the third letter that I am writing to you from Barisal, and I hope the other two have reached you safe. The first I addressed to the care of the *Assam News*, Gauhati, and the second to Golaghat.

BIMALA, SECOND DAUGHTER

I am delighted to learn from your husband's letter that you are in high spirits in your new station, and shall be still more delighted to have some proof of this in the shape of some beautiful verses such as you so often compose. You must not forget either to write to me all about your station, the scenery there, and the people with whom you mix. And last, though not the least, you must send me a passage from the "Ramayana" at least once a month.

These are my commissions which you must try to execute. Your husband has also very wisely commissioned you to polish up your French and to look after his vegetable and flower gardens. I fancy your *Jathamohasoy* has also sent you a commission or two, so that you will have a pretty busy time of it in Assam! And quite right too. Nothing is so healthy for the mind, nothing cures it so effectually of fancied sorrows and morbid despondency, as hard healthy steady work. At least I have found this to be so.—Your ever affectionate father,

ROMESH.

BARISAL, BENGAL,
9th Nov. 1883.

MY DEAREST BIMALA,—It was with sincere pleasure that I received and read your two loving letters of the 30th and 31st October. I can quite imagine how anxious you must be to receive letters from us. When I was a few years older than you are now, Bimala, I left home for England, and I quite remember the eager anxiety with which I looked for home letters, and the eager pleasure with which I read them. It is with this knowledge that I am writing to you every week, and you can depend upon my replying to every letter that you write.

My photographs are so bad that I returned them to the photographers, and they have not charged me anything for them. When I go to Calcutta again in January, I will have a photograph taken at Bourne and Shepherd's, and I will then send you a copy, or take one with me.

I have every hope of taking a month's privilege leave in January or February, and going up to see you in your new home. I look forward with sincere pleasure, dear Bimala, to passing a few quiet, happy days with you, and I know you, as a good housewife and an affectionate daughter, will make me comfortable. But, nevertheless, I cannot be certain of this, for my privilege leave may be refused; but if it is refused I will take my furlough, so I am sure to see you some time later on in the year. Let us hope, however, that my privilege leave will not be refused, and then we will meet in January or February. How very, very happy I shall be to see you, and I know you will be happy to see me.

It was with the deepest interest that I read your account of your daily life, of the progress you are making in French, of the diary you are writing of your daily life, and of the walks you have in the evening and the music you have at night. The programme is excellent; you have just enough work to keep you busy all day, and your evening walks are absolutely necessary for your health. There is nothing braces one up so completely, and gives a feeling of freshness to the body and mind, as a good long walk in the cool of the evening. I always take it when I am in camp (where there is no racquet or lawn tennis), and I feel a better man afterwards. By the time that I come to Assam you will be a good walker, and we will then see who can walk longest—you or I!

And your French, too; keep up your French by all means, it is a very mine of wealth. I am going to subscribe to the *Revue des Deux Mondes*, which is the best magazine not only in France, but in the world. It is issued every fortnight, and every number contains one or two interesting novels, beside other essays. When I get it I will send on each number to you after my perusal.

And your music too—yes, by all means keep up your music, for I wish to hear it when I go to Assam. Mind you, no hesitation, no nervousness then; no Didi to help you there; you must come out with your full, clear voice, your heartfelt, loving songs, and fill the night and my soul with gladness—

> "Till my soul is full of longing,
> And I cry with impulse strong,
> Bimala, for the love of heaven,
> Teach me, too, that wondrous song!"

There—there is something from your own favourite poet, with one or two words changed. How happy I was to read your pathetic and beautiful poem. I read it over to your Shejokaka last night, and he admired it very much. I will correct it, and send it to you in my next week's letter. You may be sure of hearing from me every week.

And now good-bye, dearest child.—I am your loving and ever affectionate father, ROMESH CH. DUTT.

Then in the winter of 1883–84, he and his friend Mr. B. L. Gupta spent the few days at Golaghat, to which he had looked forward with so much pleasure. On his return he wrote to his daughter from Gauhati :—

GAUHATI, *29th January* 1884.

MY DEAREST BIMALA,—I will not soon forget the heartfelt pleasure with which I saw you, Bimala, after a long absence, with which I stayed with you in your quiet little bungalow at Golaghat, and listened for hours together to your gentle, loving conversation. The recollection of these my delightful days at Golaghat, and of your loving kindness for me there, will recur to me often and often in after life, and will always fill my heart with sincere joy.—Your ever loving father,

ROMESH CHUNDER DUTT.

DHUBRI, *31st January* 1884.

MY DEAREST BIMALA,—It was in this place—in this bungalow and perhaps in this room—that you stopped for a night with your husband on your way to Golaghat. I have read your poem on Dhubri, and as I look round me—on the river before and the quiet scenes behind, I can realise to myself what you must have felt when you suddenly found yourself here, separated from home and the scene of your early life by hundreds of miles in the course of twenty-four hours! . . .—Your loving father,

ROMESH CH. DUTT.

His third daughter, Amala, was married to Mr. K. B. Dutt of Midnapur in 1892. On her birthday, in 1908, her father wrote the following verses :—

Infant, girl, and bride bejewelled,
  She now wears a prouder name;
Mother of a troop of children,
  Matron of unsullied fame!
Still she doth her kindly mission,
  Nobly as in days of yore;
Still he works, an ardent patriot,
  Citizen King of Midnapur!
Oft achieving, often failing,
  Dauntless still in task of life;
Such is manhood's noble mission,
  Mission of true-hearted wife!

'Tis a night in black December,
  And beside an English fire,
Seated in his lonely chamber,
  Lo ! an old man tunes his lyre :
And a troop of laughing children,
  Loving women, lightsome men,
And a home across the ocean
  Burst upon his inner ken.
Oh ! the loves of those we cherish
  Cheer us in our toil and strife,
And the sunshine of affection
  Flings a glamour on our life !

In 1902 he wrote :—

LOUDON STREET, CALCUTTA,
26th March 1902.

MY DEAREST AMALA,—I am so glad to get your loving letter of yesterday. I, too, miss my Midnapur comforts and repose! You made me so happy ; it is a dream of joy when I pass a few days at Midnapur. And I miss Khirod very much, and the moonlight nights in your verandah with Khirod's entertaining talk about the Midnapur people. I could sit up all night on that verandah with you and Khirod in that balmy air and soft moonlight. Calcutta has nothing like that. And when I come to Midnapur again, and it is bright moonlight, it would be a good idea for us to sit up all night—once at least—when you are stronger, and Khirod has a holiday the next day ! Does the world contain any higher joy than that ?

His fourth daughter, Sarala, was married to the present writer in 1894. The following letter, which he wrote to the suitor of his daughter's hand, is so characteristic of the man and his views on important social questions that I may be pardoned for quoting it :—

BURDWAN DISTRICT, *10th February* 1894.

MY DEAR GANEN,—I feel pleased and honoured by your proposal. You know I have liked you since I first met you in England, that I have respected your opinions even when I differed from you most, that I have admired your straightforwardness, and candour, and love of country, even when, as a senior, I have sometimes taken the liberty to rebuke your failings. I cordially give you the consent you have asked for ; and I have no doubt my wife will give hers when I will speak to her. And I hope I shall be of some help to you through life, after we are united by a closer bond.

You are right in thinking that your father should not consent to see you degraded in the eyes of all honest men by undergoing a penance. And while you will refuse to do this, and while you claim to use your own discretion in choosing a partner for life, you should also, as you have wisely decided to do, try your best to conciliate your father, and to retain that love which should exist between father and son. Your wife should help you in doing this, should be dutiful and respectful to her father-in-law, and should, in fact, conform to the Hindu usage in respect to her father and mother-in-law. My other daughters who have fathers-in-law do this; they appear before them veiled, never speak to them, and they do obeisance by touching the feet. They conform to the Hindu usage with respect to their husband's parents, and I like this. We need not in these small matters hurt the feelings of seniors by departing from old Hindu customs. We depart from them only where we should do so on principle. On principle inter-caste marriage is a duty with us, because it unites the divided and enfeebled nation, and we should establish this principle (as well as widow marriage, &c.) safely and securely in our little society, so that the greater Hindu society, of which we are only a portion and the advanced guard, may take heart and follow. I cannot tell you how deeply I have felt this for years past; of my last two novels, "Sansar" goes in for widow marriage, and "Samaj," of which the first few chapters have gone to "Sahitya," goes in for inter-caste marriage.

I will gladly write to your father, and ask his consent to this match with the utmost respect and courtesy. I am sure you will permit me first to consult your cousin, Mr. Gupta of Cuttack, both because I have always consulted him on all serious questions in life, and also because he knows your father and will be able to advise me how I should proceed. I have always found him a true friend during these thirty years that we have known each other, and a man who has one true friend in this world has more than his share of happiness. I have more than my share—all my daughters are true friends of mine, my very images in feelings, sentiments, in their thought and in their heart. No man in the world is more blest in gentle and loving children than I am. I am proud of their goodness and love. I have dedicated my best works to them.—Believe me, yours affectionately ever,

ROMESH CH. DUTT.

In reply to his daughter's first letter after her marriage, he wrote as follows:—

BURDWAN, 21*st May* /94.

MY DEAREST SARALA,—Your first letter to me after your marriage is most dear and welcome to me. You know how much I have loved you and all my daughters; and you are aware I have no greater and truer joy in life than to know that you are happy. That your husband's abiding love and kindness will sustain and bless you among all the cares and troubles of life, that your ministering and never-failing love for him will cheer him amidst all his duties and anxieties, are the dearest wishes of your ever-loving father. I have had more than my share of happiness in this world, more than I deserved, but my truest joy in life has been the love of my daughters and the knowledge that they are happy. I am glad you have seen the Elliotts and the Cottons in Darjeeling. I have written about Ganen's leave, and I believe he can stay in Darjeeling till the end of this week. But he must join on Monday next at the latest.

I went down to Calcutta yesterday, and found every one all right. Kamala and party are probably coming here early in June, and then you can often come up from Hughli and see them.—With my sincere love and blessing to both of you, I am, your ever loving father, ROMESH CH. DUTT.

With what impatience he looked forward to meeting his children, and what childlike joy overwhelmed him in their presence is to be seen from this:—

CUTTACK, 1*st Jan.* /96.

DEAREST SARALA,—My loving new year greetings unto you and Ganen. May you both be ever happy in your love and in your virtues.

I arrived here last night, expecting to see you and Ganen in my house for the Christmas festivals. How bitterly I was disappointed not to find you, specially as I had made my boatman pull twelve hours in the hope of arriving in time to see you. But I am glad to get your letter of the 30th, and to know that you are at Khandgiri. I shall be delighted to see you and Ganen to-day if possible, or to-morrow. I will have a separate tent for you here. I have a lot of things to tell you. Hurry on, start at once—I expect you to-day.—Your loving father, ROMESH.

Beautifully tender is the next letter, which was written to his daughter on hearing of the death of a grandson.

EDINBURGH, *24th Aug.* 1899.

MY DEAREST SARALA,—We are deeply grieved to hear of the great misfortune which has overtaken you. How fondly I had looked forward to seeing your two dear ones on our return to India, and it gives me a bitter pang to learn that one of them is no more. Your feelings, and those of Ganen, I will not endeavour to fathom; your sorrows I will not try to console, for words of consolation are vain when such terrible misfortunes visit us. Yet I hope that by the time this letter reaches you time will have softened your grief, and your good sense and patience and endurance will have helped you to tide over the first shock. Death spares none, neither the infant nor the aged. Your Shejdidi has been a more frequent sufferer than yourself; we must face all these bereavements and bear them as best we may. Accept the heartfelt condolences of those nearest and dearest to you, accept the loves of the living, and dry your tears for those who have passed away. With sincerest grief I have written these hasty lines; accept them from your father whom you have always loved, and who will never cease to love his daughters as long as he is alive.

We are in Scotland on a short tour, and expect to be back to London next week. I have asked Grindlay & Co. to secure passages for us by the *Rewa*, due at Calcutta on 21st December. Boli Narain has purchased our house in Darjeeling, and I hope both you and Ganen will come over there and stay as long as you can with us.—Your ever-loving father, ROMESH.

On a birthday of this daughter, he wrote the following lines :—

. . . .

Five and thirty years have parted,
  How I still recall the day—
Child of light, and love, and beauty,
  When in Bongong's home she lay!
Years went by, with ringing laughter
  How she chased each childhood's toy,
How she picked the shells and pebbles
  On the banks of fair Ajoy!
Years went by with eager gladness,
  How she crossed the boundless sea,
And in happy homes of England
  Lived the maid in maiden glee!

Years went by, and brighter visions
  Stirred her soul in Burdwan,
She had counted twenty summers,
  She in love was sought and won!

. . . . .

I can see the loving faces
  Gathered in my loving home,
I can hear the sounds of laughter
  As across the seas they come!
I can feel their love's young tendrils
  Wind around an old man's heart,
Loves of children true and tender
  Lands and oceans cannot part!
If at times my soul is weary,
  Thoughts like these come from above;
Work is noblest human mission,
  Noblest human bliss is Love!

III

While he was Collector of Backerganj, Mr. Dutt had made a comfortable home for himself at No. 20 Beadon Street, Calcutta, and the following letters written to his daughter Bimala give us an interesting picture of his life in his new home, his daily work, his recreations, and his childlike faculty for enjoying the simple joys of life:—

20 BEADON STREET, *30th March* 1885.

MY DEAREST BIMALA,—I am very glad to receive your letter of the 25th which came this morning. The alterations and additions to my house are nearly complete. I have got a nice large comfortable room upstairs—a flight of stairs leading up to it and a small new bathroom below—all to myself—so that you see I have made myself pretty comfortable. All the rooms in the house have also been white-washed, and I am furnishing the house with some decent furniture and pictures, so that when you come you will see the house bearing quite a gay appearance.

I wish you could come before August or September, and stay a few months with us. But of course you must make your plans according to your convenience. Kamala has decided to buy a piece of land on Beadon Street and build a house there; Chamatkar's house is nearly complete, so that you see we shall be a goodly number here.

I hope you are saving some money now for a suitable house either in or near Calcutta. When shall I get your next remittance for buying a Government security? I expect a few thousands from you this time. Tell Boli Narain there is no peace in life without some competence—as we are all finding to our cost.—Your loving father, ROMESH CH. DUTT.

20 BEADON STREET, 28*th April* 1885.

MY DEAREST BIMALA,—I received your letter of the 19th instant a few days ago. The weather is hot here, with occasional gusts of wind and showers. I fancy the weather is still hotter where you are, and you should not go out to camp in this weather.

Pramatha is not come yet, and there is some chance of his being detained for a couple of months more. But nothing is certain yet, and he may return in May. Kamala and children are here, and are all doing well.

Amala and Sarala are reading "The Lady of the Lake" with me. They like the book very well, and get quite impatient to know the story, though Amala knows the story partly as she heard it from you.

I am going on quietly with my Sanskrit studies. I am not reading very hard for the examination, but am devoting much of my time to a translation of the "Rig Veda" into Bengali which I have taken in hand, and for which I have asked for Government assistance. It is a voluminous work, but I hope to complete it in a year with the help of Noren and some pundits. Then next year we go to Europe.

We all feel your absence very much—specially as we are all together now—except you. There is splendid cooking of *luchi* (Indian pastry) every day in the new cook-room, and one would be startled to see us eat our tiffin. And we have procured a *handi* of *gur* (molasses), and Amala and Sarala (as well as their elders) are showing astonishing progress in emptying its contents. I am much afraid it will not last very long.

Kamala's eldest boy is becoming more and more interesting every day, and joins us at breakfast, tiffin, and dinner, and shows powers of digestion which astonish even his grandfather. He will take bits of meat, rice and pudding till his belly swells out, then he will come up and take his usual quantity of milk, and go to sleep, and next morning he is none the worse for all this over-feeding and comes down with renewed appetite. He chews bits of ice, drinks quantities of water, plays about with Ajoy, whom he thrashes whenever he can and loves all the same, and has, I can tell you, a decided will of his own.

His younger brother is quiet and a very good child—goes to every one known or unknown, sits by himself when there is none by him, and does little else than smile and make himself amiable. Ajoy rides every day, and reads a little with his *meshomahashoy*. The repairs and additions to our house are complete, and we have badminton occasionally and go out for long walks at 4.30 A.M. almost every day to have some little exercise.

So you see we are a happy family. Do tell us when you are coming. If Boli Narain does not take leave, can't you come in July or August and stay here till B. comes in the *puja* vacation.
Your loving father, ROMESH.

20 BEADON STREET, CALCUTTA, 14*th July* 1885.

MY DEAREST BIMALA,—I did receive a letter from you some time ago, and forgot all about it till I received your note of the 8th this forenoon. I am very glad indeed to learn that you are coming next month for certain. We have jolly meetings now and then, either here or at Kamala's.

Kamala's nilgai has grown to be big and strong, and we are trying to break him to a cart. Pramatha has got a cart constructed, but when we tied the animal to the car, the first day the animal ran like fury with the car sounding behind him. Three times he went in and out the portico (in Pramatha's house), and then made a dash right into the garden, breaking through the flower pots and trees, till he broke the rope, and stretching onwards free and far sought the quiet retreat of the Babarchikhana side. We saw this would not do, so we mended the ropes, fixed the hooks again and heaped the cart with bricks till it was so heavy that I could scarcely roll it. Well, we tied the nilgai, and this time, poor fellow, he had to drag it slow. But after two or three rounds the weight was too much for the cart, the bottom gave way, and there ended our adventure for the day.

Last Sunday we began the work again. The cart had been mended—so strong that, as the mistry said, ten maunds would not break it. Well, we tied the nilgai, and everything went merrily as a marriage bell. But at last Pramatha thought the time had come for him to drive in the cart. So he got upon it, and sat on the heap of bricks. This was too much for the nilgai, and he would not pull. A whip was brought, and as soon as I went behind the animal with the whip he made a rush. All attempts to restrain him then were fruitless. I tried to hold back the cart from behind, but could not, and the nilgai madly rushed right into the garden, breaking one of the wheels of the cart (the cart was unbroken—so the mistry was right in what he said), and safely landing Pramatha among rose bushes, and rainy weather mud. Of course we had our dinner there, and came back about 11 P.M. Pramatha and Kamala will probably be coming here next Sunday.

My "Rig Veda" work will keep me engaged for about a year, and I very much fear I shall not be able to leave Calcutta, even for a month, within that time. But I don't mind that—I am making myself pretty comfortable in my house, and like my work. You will see our garden much improved when you come here.

Your *Jathamahashoy* is all right now. There was a proposal of Saraju's marriage, but it has been broken off. Ajoy and Susila [my youngest girl is so named] and Asoke and Aloke and we all are enjoying excellent health.—Your ever loving father,

ROMESH.

I shall add some more letters which give us an insight into his daily life and home.

MYMENSINGH, 30*th May* 1889.

MY DEAREST KAMALA AND BIMALA,—I am very happy to receive your letters of the 27th, and to learn that you made an expedition to Senchal, and enjoyed it so well. Kamala must take care against a return of the fever.

Mymensingh is nice and cool after the late showers. Occasionally it gets a little close and warm, but it is never so hot as Calcutta. I wrote to you from Mymensingh three days ago, and informed you that I have completely recovered now. I propose to go out in a boat towards the latter end of June or in July, and my river trips will go on till the end of September. Boli Narain and Bimala cannot join me, for their leave will soon be up, but if Pramatha and Kamala can come here, I am sure they will thoroughly enjoy these river trips through the green and populous villages of East Bengal. They should stay in Darjeeling say a couple of months more, to shake off the last vestige of malarious fever, but by the beginning of August they will be getting quite tired of Darjeeling, and it will be an agreeable change to come to Mymensingh. If Kamala comes, my wife and children will come, of course, and we will form a pretty large party here!

Tell Amala and Sarala that Mymensingh is as pretty and nice as ever. The Himalaya-like Garo hills loom in the distance, and are visible in clear days! The Rungeet-like Brahmaputra winds its meandering course through green fields and villages. Occasionally I take a stroll through the Birchhill of Mymensingh, *i.e.* through the avenue leading to the jail, and return by the doctor's house! While behind me rises the Jallapahar of Mymensingh, with the barracks of Captain Kallonas and his host. In the Mall of Mymensingh, *i.e.* the riverside road, I often meet the Charleses and the Petersons, and in the evening I retire into the palatial halls of my Shrubbery!—Your loving father, ROMESH.

MYMENSINGH, 24*th July* 1889.

MY DEAREST BIMALA AND AMALA,—How shall I adequately thank you for the excellent collections of ferns which you have so lovingly sent to me bound in frames? And Kamala's collection too is as excellent as her verses are touching. I will keep them carefully as long as they will last, but in this damp climate I am afraid they will not last many years. I did not know what you meant when you spoke of "pictures" in your letters a few days ago. How delighted and surprised, and charmed I was when I opened the box yesterday, and found that the "pictures" were your loving presents, your collections of ferns! Dr. Basu was here when the box was opened, and he was not a little surprised that these presents from you had remained so long unopened in the box? I am sure you must have thought me very cold, but then how could I know the contents of the box?

I will hang up the "pictures" in my drawing-room to-day, and as I have a dinner to-night, I shall have to answer many questions about the givers of these loving presents! But where is Sarala's present? Or does the bottle of Eau de Cologne found in the box represent her present!

Kindly send this letter on to Kamala, as that will save me the time required for writing another letter to her. What with my office work, with the Commissioner's inspection, with the proofs of "Ancient India" waiting for correction, and what with the dinner to-night, my time is pretty well occupied.—Yours affectionately ever, ROMESH.

20 BEADON STREET, CALCUTTA,
28*th December* 1889.

MY DEAREST BIMALA,—You can understand the reason of my not replying to your loving letter of the 12th. Being in Calcutta, not a moment's time is my own. The theatrical performance is most perfect. A real stage has been put up in the dining-room, the decorations are grand, the acting most excellent and beyond all expectations! Kamala and Sarala have really surprised all. I do wish you could be here to see them act; they have surprised everybody, and surpassed the most sanguine expectations! Kamala is king, and Sarala, a sweet girl who is lost in the wilderness, and there is rescued, only to die in a sad scene. Chuni is a most astute and amusing physician; Kali, a most cruel and scheming and unscrupulous priest who does puja; Jogen is the priest's pupil, an honest good-hearted fellow; Protap is a stalwart Durwan; Banka is a wag or fool (which perhaps he is); and Ajoy is a sweet little boy picked up by the King, and who saves the King's life. Read Rabi's "Rajarshi," and you will know the rest of the story. Amala does not act, but is the prompter, and also the betel-seller to the audience!

It is decided that I will either take a transfer or leave in March or April next, so all our family remains here, and I go to Mymensingh alone. Pramatha and Kamala go to Darjeeling next week.—Your ever loving father, ROMESH.

BURDWAN, *7th October* 1890.

MY DEAR BIMALA,—I am very happy to receive your loving letter of the 27th September. Pramatha is here again, and will start with your brother and the children on the 9th October, and reach Darjeeling on the 10th (Friday next). Both your *Jathamahashoy* and Kamala are getting impatient at our delay, but I have informed the gods of Olympus, Jupiter *Jathamahashoy* and Minerva Bose, that it is not very easy for us poor mortals below to run up to cloudland, when one officer is tied to his district (Burdwan), and another to his office (the Museum); when ladies have to travel, and the line breaks in several places so as to make travelling impossible for ladies!! I hear that the line has just been repaired.

I shall probably get my privilege leave from the end of October, but it has not yet been gazetted or officially notified. I don't think I shall get permission to leave my district during the Puja holidays (18th to 29th October) as I had asked for.

I think your plan of visiting Dibrughar and Sadiya (*kana mama* as you call it) is better than doing nothing during the holidays. What shall I do if I can't leave my district during the holidays? Sit at some bungalow in the interior of my district, and write something about the History of India!!

My affections to Boli, and my love and kisses to Biju and Tush.—Your ever loving father, ROMESH.

DINAJPUR DISTRICT,
8th December 1890.

MY DEAREST SARALA,—I was very happy to get yours of the 6th last night. I am getting on very well here. I am already out on my cold weather tour, and am encamped in a place called Patiram! Don't laugh at the name, it is not a (*Ram*) place at all. On the contrary, it is a fine place situated on the Atrai River, which issues out of the Teesta and runs right through this district. My Bhutia pony is very hardy and strong, but very slow—it was a new experience to the pony to be made to gallop. And I did make it gallop, moving my arms about like a windmill, and shouting at the top of my voice to frighten the beast, and now and then hitting him with my bamboo whip to the utmost of my power! But the pony bore all with philosophic gravity—neither my howls nor my gestures frightened him, nor did my blows make any impression on his iron frame! He did gallop, however, about a mile at a time, and then resumed his stately and slow course again, and thus, partly walking, and partly galloping, we did ten miles in two hours. I suppose if I persevere in my frantic efforts to make him run, I will gradually teach him that he has to run in the plains, not walk most of his journey as in the hills! To-morrow I go to a place called Chintamon—quite a wrong name, for I have no kind of *chinta* now in my *mon*. The weather here is mild and pleasant, the work is light, and the health of the district now is good. The Khansama whom I brought from Burdwan wanted to charge me 3 Rs. a day for my food! So I have said good-bye to him, and when he asked for his railway fare to Burdwan, I told him that what he had earned as *upri labh* in two days from me would cover the cost of his journey! I have now got an excellent Khijmatgar here, and my Uriya bearer is as assiduous as ever about taking out and putting back my warm clothes the whole day long. The Bhutia syce I have discharged, and taken on another local man here.

I am anxious to learn that it is getting so very cold in Darjeeling, and that Ajoy had fever. I can make arrangements for your all coming here in January if you like. I have not taken any house yet, but can do so any day if required. But probably you would like to try "Craigmount" before deciding. Have the residents left?

I have heard nothing more about my furniture in Burdwan—except that Ban Behari has removed them to his house. That is all I wanted. My love to all.—I am your loving father,

ROMESH.

CHANDPUR, BAY OF BENGAL,
MIDNAPUR DISTRICT, 26*th May* 1891.

MY DEAREST BIMALA,—Being about eighty miles away from Midnapur town, and on the sea there, I got your letter of the

20th instant only this day. I have thoroughly enjoyed my week's stay in Contai (where your *Mejopishima* and *Barka* were before), and my three or four days' stay on the sea-side. Oh! if some of you were here—how you would have enjoyed the strolls on the sands, and the view of the vast and limitless ocean eternally surging in breakers on the beach. I have not bathed in cold water for years, for fear of a return of fever or rheumatism, but here, I could not resist the temptation any longer! So yesterday I plunged into the sea as the foam-crested breakers came dashing on the shore! I could not go very far, as there is fear of sharks in this coast; but I went some distance into the water and sat down, and the mighty waves went rolling over my head, carrying me back some distance by their velocity! It was the most delightful bath I have had for many a long year, and this morning, I need hardly say, I plunged into the waves again. I will go back to Contai in a day or two, and by the end of this month I shall be in Midnapur. I will then settle everything with Khirod about his marriage with Amala—as you have all agreed to the match.

MIDNAPUR, 13*th August* 1891.

MY DEAR KHIROD AND AMALA,—Many and sincere thanks for your loving and kind wishes. I have had more than the usual portion of success and happiness allotted to men in this life; but, believe me, there is no happiness which I have felt more keenly than to see those who are near and dear to me, affectionate and happy and good. Their love is the best solace, and the best reward of a life of toil and endeavours.

To convince you that I appreciate your goodness, I will come over within an hour and do wonders with the good things which you will no doubt provide for me at the breakfast-table.—Yours ever affectionately,
ROMESH CH. DUTT.

His affectionate anxiety to keep his daughters informed of all that was going on in the family is to be seen in the next letter. The first part refers to a serious illness of his eldest daughter Kamala about this time, which caused him very great anxiety. The illness was the result of a bullet shot from a revolver which her brother, quite a boy at the time, was careless in handling. The bullet got imbedded just above the hip, and was never found again.

HUGHLI, *6th May* 1895.

MY DEAREST BIMALA,—I have just returned from Calcutta, and as the Calcutta people are not much given to writing, and you would be anxious to know something of Kamala and Sarala, I hasten to give you some news.

Kamala is much the same, and all the family will leave for Darjeeling about the middle of this month. Dr. Joubert told Kamala to take *anything* she likes; so Kamala is taking rice every day besides an egg in the morning, and a tonic which Joubert has prescribed. The great thing is to keep up her strength for the journey. Pramatha has obtained a certificate from Joubert to secure an invalid's carriage from Siliguri to Darjeeling.

Both Sarala and the baby are doing very well, and are quite healthy. The baby has the weakness of his *mamar bari*, in devouring more food than he can well keep! He sucks like anything, and is then happy and asleep for twenty-four hours!

Ajoy will be soon admitted in the Presidency College; he is reading Latin and Sanskrit with private tutors. Ganen will be in Calcutta for three or four days now, as his departmental examination takes place there. I have not heard anything about my leave yet.—Your loving father, ROMESH.

After Kamala had been taken to Darjeeling for a change by her husband, Mr. Dutt sent his whole family to Darjeeling also, so that Mrs. Dutt might be able to look after her daughter.

The next letter of a later date, which describes the engagement ceremony of his granddaughter Susama, is a fine specimen of his letter writing.

April 5, 1904.

MY DEAREST AMALA,—I am happy to get your letter of yesterday and to learn that Khirod, Ajoy, and Asoke so greatly enjoyed and benefited by their stay at Puri. Asoke came day before yesterday, and Ajoy arrived this morning. At the ceremony which took place at Dharamtalla last evening, we all greatly missed both Khirod and Ajoy. Your coming with all the children for two days was of course impossible, but Kamala and we all would have been so happy if Khirod and Ajoy could have come.

Everything passed off very well, but how can I describe it all in a letter? From the morning Bimala and her children, and Ganen and Sarala were at Dharamtalla, and helped in all the preparations. It was like a marriage ceremony in miniature. The house was decorated with leaves, &c., the drawing-room was furnished with rugs and carpets, &c., and a part was screened off for the ladies. Food was prepared for the invited guests, and the work of the day was enlivened by Ganen's witticisms at the cost of Pramatha, who met them with his unfailing cool good-nature, while everybody else roared with laughter. We were so glad that Asoke had been summoned back in time; he worked like a horse from morning till evening, and Bhaya too did his best. Your mother and I came to Dharamtalla in the afternoon, and in the evening everything was ready. I decked myself in *Dhoti* and *Chaddar*, and Pramatha in his *Dhoti* and *Panjabi* silk coat, which caused endless amusement to Ganen and all of us! All was ready except the bride-elect; her new pink vestments had not arrived, and everybody was in despair except Kamala, who said that her *Darzi* had never failed her, and would not fail. Right enough, in the evening, the gorgeous vestments came, and then Bimala and others commenced decorating Susama.

Punctually at seven o'clock, or even before, the guests began to arrive. Prasanna Sen in *Gerua*, and Prasanta in his usual *Dhoti* and *Chaddar*, Kanti Babu, and Gour Gobind among the Brahmo missionaries, Nirmal Sen and Subodh, Mahalanavis and other friends of Prasanta, Sucharu and her sister, Mrs. Mahalanavis, and of course all our relations from Rambagan and elsewhere, your *Jathaima*, your *Didima*, your *Mashima*, &c. Pratap Mazumdar was the priest of the occasion, and sat on the *masnad*. Pramatha read out a written promise to marry his daughter to Prasanna's son, and Prasanna read out a similar promise to marry his son to Pramatha's daughter. Then the bride and bridegroom appeared on the scene, took their seats on either side of Pratap Mazumdar, and repeated words uttered by Pratap Mazumdar engaging to marry. Prayers and songs followed, and the ceremony was over by the exchange of rings. Feasting followed—first the men, then the ladies, then the people of the house. Prasanna Sen introduced to me his wife, who is an exceedingly good-hearted and good-natured woman, and I was very glad to know her. Bimala also brought Sucharu, and Moni (Mrs. Mahalanavis) to me, and I liked them both. Susama conducted herself splendidly—with due decorum and humility, but without undue bashfulness, and everybody praised her. Your *Jathaima* and all our people (ladies of course!) were loud in the praise of the handsome face and graceful manners of Prasanta, and everything passed off very well. It was past midnight before we could return home, and while I am writing you this letter, Bimala is still having her rest and sleep here, and I have no doubt every one is having rest to-day at Dharamtalla. I suppose the marriage will take place in Puja time, or at Christmas; we are all against its taking place in this summer or in the rains. Sarala and Ganen had little rest at night, as they were to catch the 5 A.M. train to Bankura this morning.

Do you want more news yet? Boli Narain has left Sylhet, and is expected here on Thursday, and we shall probably leave Calcutta next Monday or Tuesday.

I want to introduce Ajoy to Paltu, who has promised to help him, as he has helped Sisir Mullick. Of course Ajoy cannot expect any practice for two years to come, but he should get a gold mohar now and then as all young barristers do, or he will lose heart. Shall be happy to see Khirod on this subject when he comes here next Sunday.—With love to all, your loving father,

ROMESH.

IV

To no other person did Mr. Dutt lay bare his inmost ambitions and aspirations as he did to his brother Mr. J. C. Dutt, and the letters which he wrote to him have a great deal of autobiographical interest. Those here quoted belong to his youthful and more impressionable years, and there is perhaps a vein of sentimentalism and lack of restraint about them. But there is ample evidence here to show how genuine and deep-seated was his resolve from the very earliest years of his career to devote himself to literary work and the service of his Motherland.

CAMP KARIMPUR, 22/6/74.

MY DEAR BROTHER,—Yesterday I had to go about a long distance (in a *palki*, I am ashamed to say, for I apprehended rain) on some survey work. I wish you could have a view of the country prospects about this time of the year. For miles and miles together you see the young *dhans* spreading a sea-like expanse on all sides of you, and covering the earth with a velvet as it were of waving green. This fine cheerful prospect is dotted here and there with a shrub or a tree, and bounded far off by a deep green hazy line of trees, which mark the villages. The cultivators view with unspeakable delight and joy this fair prospect, point to the *dhan* as Ma Lakshmi, and are ever and anon doing something for the better growth of the harvest. And living among, and speaking with, cultivators, I confess, I have become so much of a *chasa* that my heart dances within me at the prospect of such unbounded rural wealth.

As I expected before, a great storm is gathering around my head. The Planters have combined and petitioned, and have resorted to underhand means, and, as might be expected, their representations have been accepted as true, and I have received hints from my superior officers. But I will tell you more of this when I go to Calcutta. The conviction that I have always done justice, quite regardless of class interests and party feelings, that there is nothing whatever in my actions which may even for a moment be pointed out as wrong, fills me with confidence and courage, and I feel pride and exultation at my own position surrounded by difficulties.—Yours affectionately,

ROMESH.

BONGONG, 17/3/75.

MY DEAR BROTHER,—Robertson's opinion of my book ["Bengal Peasantry"] is certainly very reassuring. England is indeed a free country, and every one is free to give his opinions; in India all free thought is strangled by red-tapeism, officialism, party feeling, class interests, the tyranny of the high officials, and the corresponding servility of the officers of the lower grade. Such servility shall never be mine, let the bigwigs say what they like and do what they like.—Yours affectionately, ROMESH.

BONGONG, 7/4/75.

MY DEAR BROTHER,—I have named four books which you have to send me. I am sure you will not find all of them in the public library. In that case send me the new book which the public library ought to have received by this time. It is called "Lectures on the Early History of Institutions." I am very anxious to read this.

It is impossible for me to devote as much time to reading, under the present circumstances, as I should like to do, or as would enable me to write something worth writing. When I think of this, I get perplexed and don't know what to do. Shall I let the chance—feeble as it undoubtedly is—of doing something great and noble slip from my hand without one effort? Shall the want of an independent fortune, and the consequent necessity of clinging to a service, prevent me from making any endeavour towards greatness when I feel in me constant aspirations, and at times confident hopes, on that subject? When I read the works of such great thinkers as Darwin, when I think of the great ferment of bold speculations and free thoughts now prevailing in the scientific circles of free England, how fervently do I wish to cut myself from society, and family, and service, and bury myself for years in the library of the British Museum, and make at least one attempt to do something great and glorious! Will this opportunity be ever denied to me?—Yours affectionately,

ROMESH.

CAMP KASBA, 11/11/75.

MY DEAR BROTHER,—Your blood need not boil at such a simple thing as a newspaper criticism. There are many low Anglo-Indians in London who are always but too glad to get an opportunity to vilify Indians, specially such as have succeeded in entering into the sacred ranks reserved so long for Anglo-Indians. Low remarks from such low quarters should be taken at what they are worth. The time may come when I shall be able to silence scoffers and vilifiers. If I fail in that—if I fail to write anything really good and meritorious—what matters it if such trashy things as "The Three Years" and "The B.P." are slightly praised or condemned in *toto?*—Yours affectionately,

ROMESH.

. . . . . .

We have faults and weaknesses, and where is the man who has them not? But we are prepared to forgive each other. Disagreements, even unpleasantness, may occasionally arise, but we shall drown them in the love which we bear towards each other. I can truly say that there is not another thing in this world in which I feel richer or happier, of which I feel prouder, than the love you bear to me and I bear to you.—Yours affectionately ever,

ROMESH CH. DUTT.

DIST. BACKERGANJ, 13*th August* 1877.

MY DEAR BROTHER,—To-day I complete my 29th year. If I compare what I have done with what I hoped and aspired to do, how little, how very little, has been done! Where are the great achievements and works, the European reputation, which were the dream of our younger years? But I have well-nigh outlived those dreams and discontent, and disappointment forms no part of the present state of my mind. I have worked according to my humble powers; I have written a few English books which have, for the time, pleased my countrymen for whom they were written. I have composed two Bengali novels which will probably live after my death. I have seen bits of Europe and

India, and have secured a place in a coveted service. I have health, I have a good income, and I am not unknown to my countrymen. It would be ridiculous to compare this with what I once aspired to, but I have learnt it is still more ridiculous to make myself unhappy because I cannot do more than what I can do. I have long since given up the idea of "European reputation." I shall write more books, which I am confident will be acceptable to my countrymen, and will increase my reputation such as it is; and when I die, I shall die a happy, contented man who did what he could do, and did not make himself unhappy because he could not do more.

I am labouring with as much perseverance as ever at my principal English work, "The Study of History," which, according to my present plan, will be completed in three volumes. It may make me known in England or it may not. In the one case I shall be happy; in the other, believe me, not for a moment unhappy. My own mother tongue must be my line, and before I die I hope to leave what will enrich the language and will continue to please my countrymen after I am dead. Is this not a more desirable plan than to make myself miserable because I cannot do more than I can?—Yours affly., ROMESH.

CAMP KOICHOR, 1st *January* 1880.

MY DEAR BROTHER,—At last we are in 1880, and on this day one naturally turns back on the decade of his life which has passed since 1870. For me this decade has been one of hard, uninterrupted work, of endeavour to get settled in life. This work has, I think, been achieved. I have cleared my debt and got a house; I have secured a name in the literature of my country, and I have fixed the plan and tenor of my future life. Everything was unsettled ten years ago, even as regards the place and the manner in which I would live; everything is settled now; I have chosen my sphere and fixed my plans, and am at last settled down in life.

Thus the first decade (or rather twelve years) of my life, ending 1860, may be described as boyhood passed in fresh village scenes, mostly under the affectionate care of parents; my second decade may be described as a hard and studious scholastic career, culminating in the success at the Open Competition of 1869 at London; my third decade may be fitly described as a harder struggle to get settled in life, to choose my sphere and make my mark in the world. This struggle is now at an end, and I may fairly hope the next decade to be one in which the strain on my energies will be less, in which my difficulties, pecuniary and otherwise, will be less, and in which my work will be interrupted by repose and enjoyments, among which last I reckon a fresh visit to Europe as a principal one. But, of course, men propose, circumstances dispose.—Yours affectionately ever,

ROMESH CH. DUTT.

MYMENSINGH, *28th September* 1888.

MY DEAR BROTHER,—I have received your letter of the 25th, and two letters of the 26th. The dream of our passing the latter days of our life in England is one which comes to me as often probably as to you. I did not think of an appointment in the India Council, but of a readership in Indian History or in Sanskrit, in Cambridge, Oxford, or London, if my "History of India" makes a name for itself. Anything which will give me a position and some little income over and above my pension, and will enable me to organise an Indian party to represent Indians' rights in England and in Parliament. But it is foolish to think of these things now.—Yours affectionately ever, ROMESH.

GERMANY, *24th August* 1893.

MY DEAR BROTHER,—I have received yours of the 1st August. I know I am risking something by supporting the Congress party in one of their proposals, viz. the separation of the Judicial and Executive services. The "powers that be" will not be pleased with me for this, and they may even go so far as to stop my expected promotion to a *pucca* commissionership, giving some false reasons for it. But I am willing to risk so far. It does not matter very much to me whether during the next three years of my service they keep me as a first-grade Collector, which I am, or make me a Commissioner. On the other hand, I have felt an intense joy, not merely in serving the interests of my country, but also in making my power felt by the Indian Government. They have treated me on the whole fairly, but not with any special favour. The doors of the Secretariat have been kept closed to me, I have not been employed for a day in any special post, and I have seen my juniors appointed as Secretary to the Government, as Senior Secretary to the Board, as Inspector-General of Police, and in other special and highly paid appointments. I do not complain of this, but I only state these facts to show that if Government is not disposed to repose any real trust and confidence in me, I am free to utilise my powers and abilities, such as they are, to the benefit of my country in other ways. And Government will feel this when they see me co-operating with Sir Richard Garth and Mr. Reynolds to press for a reform in the system of our administration. —Yours affectionately ever, ROMESH CH. DUTT.

GERMANY, *8th September* 1893.

MY DEAR BROTHER,—I have received your letter of the 15th August with your very kind wishes on my completing forty-five years. From you such wishes are most welcome, because you mean all that you say and more than you say. For I have ever found in you a friend who has helped me when I needed help —sympathised with my aims, appreciated my endeavour, and triumphed in my successes. And my labours and successes have been doubly pleasant to me because I know you appreciate them and are pleased with them. Let us work on thus, together, with mutual sympathy, during the brief remainder of our lives, and we shall have thus doubled the happiness and lightened the grief which falls to the share of all mortals.—Yours affectionately ever, ROMESH CH. DUTT.

His confidences to his brother in the later stages of life we shall have occasion to note hereafter. But one of his letters to his brother is so vibrant of genuine emotion that it must find a place here.

BARODA, *9th April* 1907.

MY DEAR BROTHER,—I have received your touching letter of the 6th April. So far from having done much for you, the painful thought often comes to me that I have not done my duty in life to those who are near and dear to me. To you specially, who first helped me to go to Europe, I have been able to give very little help in life, to poor Apara also very little. I often regret the want of wealth, not for its own sake, but because it would have enabled me to make some people comfortable in life.

I sincerely trust this dry weather will improve your health. I am quite well, but dread the work of the next two or three months in this dreary friendless place before I have my leave.— Yours ever affectionately, ROMESH.

His brother's letter to which the above was a reply was equally touching.

CALCUTTA, 6/4/07.

MY DEAR BROTHER,—I had lately an attack of fever from which, though I have recovered now, I feel very weak. I can barely walk half-an-hour during the whole day, and my voice has become feeble, so that I feel some difficulty in dictating letters, I cannot speak loudly, and the writer cannot catch my words rightly. However, do not think I am very ill, for besides weakness I am pretty well, and I hope to recover a little during these dry months.

As regards the money you have sent to Pratap, I feel very grateful to you—more grateful than I can well express. In fact, in all the good things of life that I have enjoyed I find your helping hand, and I die deeply indebted to you.—Yours affectionately ever, JOGESH.

The failing health to which his brother refers in this letter was the result of a touch of paralysis, which gradually attacked his whole body and confined him to his bed for the remaining period of his life. The man who was so active, fond of travel and the joys of life, died a slow lingering death for nearly eight years, and yet never uttered a single word of complaint and had always a smile for those who went to see him. Indeed for sweetness and saintliness of character he reminded one of the Rishis of old. In a touching poem, "Sixty years have come and parted," Mr. Dutt has well described his brother's heroic fortitude :—

> Yet if patience in our woe,
>   Trial and trouble silent borne,
> Sanctifies this life below,
>   Saint's white garment thou hast worn :
> Thine is sweet-souled resignation,
> And thy life,—a dedication ! "

It was strange irony of fate that the bedridden invalid survived his younger and far stronger brother. It was indeed the sad news of his beloved brother's death which blew out the flickering flame and released Jogesh Dutt's soul from its mortal prison. Though his body had been practically dead during his long illness, yet his mind remained unimpaired almost to the end. He inherited the literary instincts of the family, and composed some beautiful poems, and he was also the translator of the "Rajatarangini" ("History of the Kings of Kashmir") into English, a work which betrays considerable historical erudition.

We cannot better conclude this section on "his noble-hearted friend and brother" than by quoting the verses, suggested by Longfellow's "The Day is Done," which he wrote in 1894.

TO MY BROTHER

The day is done, and darkness
  Closes round our earthly strife,
Side by side, in joy or sadness,
  We will stand till close of life.
What though lights of earthly gladness
  Gleam not through this mist and rain,
Living souls that cheered our sadness
  Parted from this world of pain,
What though all unfriended,
  We are left in toil and care,
And a deeper gloom o'erwhelms us,
  And a tempest in the air,
Brother's love hath powers to quiet
  Toil and trouble, ceaseless care,
And comes like the benediction
  That follows after prayer.
That love shall wake a music
  O'er the closing of our day,
Until our life, like the Arabs,
  Silently shall steal away.

V

And with me a friend true-hearted
Silent from his parents parted,
Shared with me my hopes and fears,
Stood by me in joy and tears,
Stood by me these forty years!
Life is sweeter, life is dearer,
When true friendship links us nearer,
Heart to heart and hand to hand,
As in youth, in age we stand!

The above lines were written of his friend, Mr. B. L. Gupta, the companion of his youth and youthful ambitions, his constant comrade in after life, and one of those who stood by him when he drew the last breath of life. I shall find place for only two letters referring to the romantic attachment of the two men. The first is from the pen of Mr. B. L. Gupta's father, for whom Mr. Dutt had the highest respect and affection. The second is Mr. Dutt's reply to a letter of appreciation received ten years later from the same gentleman.

My dear Mr. Dutt,—Your last letter, as also your present to me of a copy of your latest edition of your work on the ancient civilisation of India, overwhelm me with kindness. Though my acquaintance with you commenced when you were a school-fellow of my son Bihari, my knowledge of you over thirty-five years has deepened into a genuine feeling of love and esteem for you, and I hope and trust my children may deserve and cultivate your and your family's friendship long after I am gathered to those who have gone before me. Yes, your relation to Bihari is an unique one. It is not one of ordinary friendship, but a union of destiny more wonderful than the wildest fiction. You know it all. To me it is still a dream. Stern reality has not been able to dissipate it, and I still delight to recall my anxious thoughts when I, with those who felt for me, took both of you for lost. You, though an orphan, had yet a modest competence to back you, but Bihari was the youngest of your party, and the son of an humble and poor man. You, however, allowed him to cling to you through thick and thin, and shared with him your last loaf of bread. All the same your prospects of success were still quite remote and gloomy, while all your possible trials in a strange and unsympathising country were vividly present in my troubled mind. But by the grace of God you both succeeded beyond expectation and returned to your country with honour, and ever since your return have filled with credit the highest posts to which any native could aspire. To you Bihari owes everything, and, though with your natural goodness you may disown it, I am glad of this opportunity given me of disburdening my heart of what I so deeply felt.

May God sustain you both throughout life is the earnest prayer of yours ever sincerely,

Chunder Sekhar Gupta.

Baroda, 31*st October* 1904.

My dear Chundersekhar Babu,—Your appreciation of my work is more than a reward of my labours,—it is a joy and sincere gratification to me. I have written nothing for years past—prose or verse, history or economics—which has not found in you a most friendly judge and appreciative reader. This is not merely owing to the great love which you bear towards me—as towards Bihari—but it is greatly owing to your large-mindedness and to the many-sided, comprehensive intellect with which you approach, grasp, and assimilate all subjects, however divergent from each other. Novel or poetry, history of civilisation or history of economics, ancient religious thought or modern administrative questions, nothing comes amiss to you. If there is any worth in a book, your penetrating intellect gets to the kernel, your comprehensive mind grasps and assimilates it. I do not flatter you when I say that I know of few intellects so keen in its power, so universal in its sympathies. It is therefore that I appreciate your friendly criticism, and treasure it as a precious object.

You have perhaps forgotten that you wrote me such a kind letter ten years ago, when I sent you a copy of my "Civilisation in Ancient India," London edition. I preserved it; I have it by my side now. I have re-read it to-day after receipt of your present letter. The same friendly judgment, the same kindly sentiment, the same blessings and love! . . . God has sustained us both these ten years, and we have both tried to do our duty, each in his own line. What is more, our friendship, "more wonderful than the wildest fiction," has deepened within these ten years, and we can both look back on more than forty years of uninterrupted love without one day, one moment of serious difference or disunion. Sons and grandchildren have been born unto him and to me; but there is no man living whom I hold closer to my heart than the friend of my boyhood, and I believe there is no man living whom Bihari holds dearer than me. And may we thus pass through the remaining years of our lives, hand in hand, never ceasing to love each other, never separated in our hearts, till we earn our final rest!

"May God spare long your precious life" is the concluding wish of your present letter. I sincerely hope and trust that, ten years hence, you will be still in the land of the living, and that I may live to quote this line again, with some account of my endeavours during this period. My endeavours are humble, as my scope is limited; but I do believe every honest effort, every humble endeavour for one's country, brings its harvest in time. Bihari will have told you that the offer of my present appointment at Baroda came to me to Calcutta as a surprise, though I knew that for years past the Maharaja Gaekwar had the idea in his head, and had once before asked me to come to his State when I was Commissioner of Burdwan. Of course I declined then, and I am glad his fresh proposal did not come till I had finished my "India in the Victorian Age." Having no other work in hand just now, official or literary, I have accepted this post, as it will enable me to do some good here, gain some new experience, and make me better fitted to speak and write about India in the future, when I am free from official work once more. There is a great deal to be done in this State, and there are great difficulties to overcome—far greater than in Mysore or Travancore—but of these I will speak on another occasion. But I hope, with patience, tact, and persuasion I shall succeed in silently and gradually overcoming all difficulties and introducing large reforms. Though a new-comer, I have succeeded fairly well so far; and two printed memoranda, which I send you by this post, will show you what I have done in the Income-tax and Customs Departments. I believe the Maharaja is shortly going to Europe, and there will be a regular Council to manage the affairs of the State. And I hope, with gentle pressure and persuasion, I shall be able to carry the Council with me to effect great reforms. Great expectations are formed in these parts from my appointment; every one knows here what I have been writing and saying in England and in India these seven years; the entire rural population expect redress at my hands; and I do not think I shall belie expectations. But it is necessary to proceed cautiously, not to be revolutionary, not to excite alarms, in order that I may secure the end in view. In a few years I hope to leave my mark on the administration of this State; and if I can bring a little more of joy and comfort to the homes of the harassed cultivators and the humble traders of this State, I shall have done my duty here.

I am thankful to say I am enjoying excellent health here, as the country is drier than Bengal, and the bracing cold weather is before us. But famine has already appeared in some parts of the State, plague has been reported from many places, and, besides the great task of reform which is before me, relief works and their supervision will take up much of my time. But I feel a joy in this congenial work, and a hope inspires me that I shall not have laboured in this Native State in vain.

Hoping this will find you in the enjoyment of good health, in that quiet peaceful home at which I long to revisit you when I have a chance again,—I am, ever yours affectionately,

ROMESH CH. DUTT.

Alas! only seven years have elapsed since the above lines were written, but although Mr. Gupta, an old man of over eighty-five, is yet living, still for ever is the unquenchable spirit that inspired the above lines. And on his death Mr. B. L. Gupta, in a letter written to the present writer, alluded to their friendship in the following lines :—

> India has lost one of her greatest and noblest sons, and I am deprived of a friend whose society, kindness, counsel, and love formed a rare and choice gift of Heaven to me, and which compensated me for all the disappointments I suffered in life.

BOOK II

B. L. GUPTA

INTRODUCTORY

As we have seen, Mr. Dutt retired from service with a definite object. From the age of adolescence forward, one single ambition filled his heart and inspired all his efforts. This was to serve his motherland to the best of his ability. He now left India and a lucrative and honourable service which held out brilliant prospects, and made his home in a distant land and worked unremittingly for seven years, bringing under requisition his many-sided gifts for the attainment of the cherished object of his life.

He realised that to fight the cause of India to the best advantage, the most effective as well as the most natural policy would be to form an alliance with those noble and generous Englishmen who had spent the best years of their lives in India, and who more than any other agency had helped to mould modern India. He appealed also to the best instincts of the British public, to those ideas of justice and fair play which inspire the political life of England more than that of any other nation on the face of the earth. And, lastly, through the British public he sought to reach the wider bar of the modern civilised world. One of his chief ambitions was to do what he could to bring before the gaze of modern Europe the riches of the past wisdom and civilisation of ancient India. The main objects of his mission to Europe may thus be described to have been :—

(1) To form and organise an Indian party of sympathetic Englishmen in England.

(2) To influence the British Parliament through prominent members of the House of Commons.

(3) To educate the British public in general, and the

democracy in particular, in Indian subjects, and to win their sympathy and support.

(4) To appeal to the wider world of Europe through literature and history.

During the seven years of his life which form the subject of the present section, he sought to attain the above objects by every means in his power—through the medium of the press, from the platform, and through the more permanent medium of treatises and historical and economical works.

As under the circumstances of the case he was obliged to repeat his arguments, and return to the same subject on different occasions and at different stages of his political career, it will conduce to greater lucidity if, after giving a brief and chronological outline of his work during this period, a more synthetic treatment is followed, and a *résumé* given of his most important observations on constitutional and economic problems.

CHAPTER XV

1897

PUBLICATION OF "ENGLAND AND INDIA"

ALMOST immediately after taking leave, Mr. Dutt set sail for Europe, and wrote as follows to his second daughter and her husband :—

ON BOARD THE "MANORA," *January* 26, 1897.

MY DEAR BOLI NARAIN AND BIMALA,—We had a week's work and worry in packing and making preparations. Packing alone was not much work, but we were vacating the house for Mr. B. L. Gupta and his children (now stopping there), and hence we had to pack off our books and some 20 or 30 boxes to Rambagan, beside packing for the voyage. Then there was the visit to Asansole, which took a day and two nights, and also visiting our people at Rambagan, Simla, and Goabagan. Lastly there were other visits to pay and to receive in the Park Street side of the town, and you can conceive, therefore, we had not an easy time of it. Purchases had to be made until it seemed they would never end, bills poured in for payment with the most astonishing rapidity; the goldsmith, the *darzi*, the Lala and other worthy customers seemed to make the Park Street house their own. . . . However, the longest day has its end, and we have finished all work, and now find ourselves comfortably on board the *Manora*, with a good-sized cabin to ourselves. And now we feel we have a little breathing time, and some leisure to sit and write and say good-bye to our friends! . . . Nothing so comfortable as lazily reclining on a steamer's deck, when all your arrangements are done and you have fairly started!

My present leave is for ten months, and very likely I will extend it by a year. What I shall do after that I cannot guess. If I get some congenial occupation, if I do not feel stinted for money, I don't think I shall return to service. But return to India I must, maybe on short visits, maybe for long residence. In the meantime we have cut our moorings and are drifting onwards—

> "Where'er the waves may roll,
> Or tempests' breath prevail."

ROMESH CH. DUTT.

As usual, before settling down to work, he spent some time in travelling. He visited various places in Italy and France. He saw Naples, Rome, Florence, Pisa, Genoa, and Turin. At Rome he was in the thick of the Carnival, and greatly enjoyed "the continuous and promiscuous fight with flowers and sweets and nosegays, between men and women of all ranks." The great St. Peter's impressed him greatly, though this was his second visit "to the noblest and richest edifice of God built by the hand of man."

TURIN, 10*th March* 1897.

Turin, where I am now staying, is the place where Victor Emmanuel was reigning and Cavour was planning the independence and unity of Italy between 1854 and 1860. All thoughts in Italy were directed to the spot, and all the forces were united, until they kindled into a blaze in 1860. Victor Emmanuel was proclaimed King of united Italy at Turin by the Chamber of Deputies on the 14th March 1860.

At Genoa after visiting the endless works of sculpture, I went to the top of the hill and there stood before me the massive and simple tomb of one of Italy's greatest sons, Joseph Mazzini. That immortal patriot, along with the statesman Cavour and the soldier Garibaldi, planned and effected the independence of Italy only the other day, and we heard of the battles of Solferino and Magenta being fought when we were in school. Grateful Italy cherishes the memory of these three men—the patriot, the statesman, and the soldier—and numerous monuments have been erected, and streets, squares, and edifices have been named in all large towns after Mazzini, Cavour, and Garibaldi.

At the end of March he was in Paris, and found that "city also mad with its Carnival festival and its processions."

And yet this gay nation [he goes on to observe] has a sober and intensely practical side in their character, and it is wonderful how they have progressed within the last quarter of a century. When I visited Paris first, in 1871, France was prostrated after her great defeats, the finest monuments of Paris were in ruins, and Europe thought that Frenchmen would never recover completely, at least within this century, from the terrible blow dealt by Prussia. How wonderfully France has falsified all such calculations! She has replaced a corrupt Imperialism by a vigorous Republic, she has paid up her debts honourably and quickly, and she has armed herself slowly and steadily and terribly, until competent judges now think she would be more than a match for Germany, if Germany had not sheltered herself under a "triple alliance" with Austria and Italy. The quiet unfaltering perseverance with which France has repaired her losses and has prepared herself for the coming encounter has astonished Europe. And while she has strengthened herself at home, she has extended her empire abroad; Cochin China, Madagascar, and many large slices of Africa have been added to her colonial possessions. The history of France during the last quarter of a century teaches us the great and important lesson that, so long as a nation has worth and vigour, vitality and perseverance, no external causes, however disastrous, can crush her altogether.

In the beginning of April he reached London and got settled down in Shirland Road. He wrote to his daughters, Amala and Sarala, about his new household.

We are in London at last. I have been busy this week looking after suitable lodgings, and we are at last going to settle down in the house the address of which you will see in the top of this letter. The house is in an open part of London (near Maida Hill), away from the busy parts of Bayswater, and is roomy and nice, and we have been lucky enough to secure two floors entirely to ourselves, *i.e.* the dining-room floor (two rooms), and the drawing-room floor (two rooms). Further, Ajoy stops with his teacher (Mr. Chuckerbutty) in the next street, only a minute's walk from us, and this is a considerable advantage.

Ajoy has passed the University examination, and will enter New College, one of the best Colleges in Oxford. Fancy, he came down to Dover to meet us! We had a rather rough passage across the Channel, and when we reached Dover in wet clothes and were about to land with our luggage, imagine our pleasure and our surprise to see Ajoy rushing on board the steamer, and hailing us joyfully! For a second or two we could not recognise him, then of course we knew him. But he has not changed much; only he is in perfect health and cheerful spirits and enjoys the cold of England, so different from the prostrating heat of India. It actually snowed a little this morning; does it snow in Midnapur or in Khurda in April?

. . . .

Fancy, Miss Manning wrote to me to Italy (getting my address from Ajoy), asking me to read a paper at the National Indian Association in April. I have politely declined.

By the end of April, he was beginning to form his plans. On the 30th of the month he wrote to his daughter Sarala:—

There is little chance of my going back to India this year. I must really make a prolonged attempt in the writing line, and see if I can do something here. And I must have at least two years' time to see what I can do. Did you read a speech which Conan Doyle made last year about his first contributions to the papers? They always came to him, he said, with the faithfulness of carrier pigeons! It will be long, however, before my carrier pigeons (if my first endeavours prove such) will tire me; I will stick to my work, and tire out my pigeons till I can make them find shelter somewhere! Official life has no special charms for me if I can succeed in a more brilliant line, and it will not be for want of steady endeavour if I fail.

He was also slowly cultivating the acquaintance of those friends and congenial spirits whose sympathy and assistance were of such immense value to him in the work which he had set before himself.

I have seen Sir Steuart Bayley and Sir George Birdwood at the India Office, and expect to meet Sir W. Wedderburn and a few other friends to-day. Sir William Hunter has asked me and my wife to come and lunch with them some day next month.

About this time the "Poona outrages" attracted a good deal of attention both in England and India, and, as was to be expected, Mr. Dutt took a prominent part in the discussions on the subject. On the 30th June, Reuter wired that Government had proclaimed the occupation of Poona city by a punitive police force owing to the conduct of the inhabitants. Mr. Dutt wrote two letters to the *Daily News* on the subject, and his views appear to have not a little influenced the opinion of that important organ of public opinion. In his first letter of the 2nd July, in which Mr. Dutt signed himself "Loyal Indian," he wrote :—

The cowardly assassination of Lieutenant Ayerst and the attempted murder of Mr. Rand have aroused the just indignation of Englishmen in India and in England. The most searching inquiries are being made, and every friend of peace and order, be he Englishman or be he Indian, hopes that the perpetrators of the foul deed will be hanged amidst the just exultations of loyal Indian multitudes. The suspicion which hangs on Indian communities will thus be lifted.

The suspicion is unjust and unfair. The Lord Bishop of Bombay, who knows India better than many English officials, vouches for the fact that the deplorable crime committed at Poona is not execrated by Englishmen more than it is execrated by the Indian communities generally. It is panic only which creates a general suspicion against Indian communities, panic by which Englishmen in India should never be influenced.

The matter quickly assumed greater importance. Questions were asked in the House about a memorial, which, it appears, had been presented to the Governor of Bombay, protesting against the manner in which soldiers employed on plague work in Poona had been discharging their duties, while another section wanted to know "whether Government would consider the desirability of adopting effectual means to prevent the inculcation of sedition through the Press." Mr. Dutt wrote a second letter to the *Daily News*, which generally adopted the views expressed in it and observed :—

As "Loyal Indian" says in his second and most excellent letter which we print to-day, "criticism of Government action when rightly understood is a help to good government." "If," adds our correspondent in words which Lord George Hamilton would do well to learn by heart, "if I were plotting against the Government of India, the first thing I would hope for, wish for, ask for, would be the gagging of the Vernacular Press, and of all newspapers conducted by my countrymen. The suppression of such papers will be like the extinguishing of street lights to the burglar."

In the autumn Mr. Dutt went to the south coast, and remained there till the middle of September.

5th August.

My dearest Kamala,—We are still at the sea-side passing our days in luxurious laziness. Once a year your mind requires such rest, and people in this country are very wise in giving themselves such rest. I was working pretty hard in London the last few months on a small book about modern progress in India, which will come out next month, and so I enjoy this rest thoroughly. We all have sea-baths every day, Pratap, and Ajoy, and Romesh Gupta and the Goodeve Chuckerbutty family. And then we have strolls on the breezy cliffs or rides on open omnibuses along the sea-side at something like threepence for three miles. Not ruinous! Your mother appreciates these rides, and also goes out for long walks occasionally. This morning I took Ajoy and Pratap by sheer force to a photographer's, and had them taken. So that next mail you may expect their portraits, if ready by that time.

Lucky we are not in London now, for it must be unbearably close and hot there. In the sea-side you have a breeze, and the sea-baths are so cooling. I remain afloat on the cool delicious water for ten or fifteen minutes or swim about, until I feel perfectly cool and refreshed. Ajoy, too, can swim, and sometimes has a bath twice in the day, morning and afternoon. Salt water is most salubrious and does no harm; I would not venture to bathe in cold water if it was fresh.—Your loving father,

Romesh Ch. Dutt.

Early in September, Mr. Dutt returned from the sea-side, but unfortunately the sea did not cure his rheumatism, and he had to go to Buxton.

Buxton, Derbyshire, *7th October* 1897.

We are stopping here in a delightful hotel, overlooking a hill on one side, and the public gardens on the other. The town is surrounded by hills, and is in the Peak country (you know Scott's "Peveril of the Peak"). It is about a thousand feet higher than London, and the air is cold, and bracing and

AJOY C. DUTT, SON

invigorating. It is the only place in all England where people suffering from rheumatism and gout come for the mineral baths, so I am sure they will do me good.

LONDON, *9th October* 1897.

We have come back to London, and a thick and yellow veil of mist and fog is hanging over this deliciously dirty city these forty-eight hours and more! Ajoy is in Oxford, happy in new scenes and among new friends. We have settled down in a tolerably comfortable house, and have asked Pratap to come and stay with us. Miss Mull will also stay with us as Susila's tutor and your mother's companion and help; so we shall be pretty comfortable during the winter. . . . Your ever loving father,

ROMESH CH. DUTT.

LONDON, *29th October* 1897.

MY DEAR BROTHER,—

. . . .

I asked you last mail to send me "Bhishma" and "Drona" Parvas (Pratap Ray's translation). I now ask you to send the "Bana" Parva also. I am trying my hand at a metrical English translation of the most important portions of the "Mahabharata." But you need not mention this to any one yet. . . .

My hands are quite full now with a variety of work, and by this time next year the English public should have before them five or six uniform and moderately priced and readable volumes on the civilisation, religion, &c., of ancient India, as understood and interpreted by an Indian. But it is foolish to count one's chicken before the eggs are hatched!

"Life isn't a game, once lost, we play again."

. . . I always think of that line as I am struggling to win before life is lost and ended. And it is worth while spending one's last years, not in service, but to win his favourite object, which with me is fame!—Yours affectionately,

ROMESH CH. DUTT.

At the close of the year 1897 an important event of his life happened. On the 14th December he received a letter informing him that the Council of the University College, London, had resolved to offer him a lectureship in Indian History for three years, which offer he thankfully accepted. About this appointment he wrote:—

LONDON, S.W., *16th December* 1897.

MY DEAREST BIMALA,—

. . . .

You will be glad to learn that the London University College has created a chair in Indian History, and has appointed me to that chair. The appointment carries no pay, and I shall only get the fees which the students pay for joining my class. But the appointment is a high honour; it gives me honourable and congenial occupation, and it also gives me a sort of status and position in this country.

If I succeed in forming classes here, then I can only visit India during the long vacation in summer—from July to October—and hence there is the utmost need for my having a house in Darjeeling, not in the plains. I have already written to Boli Narain about it, and shall expect to hear something when you go to Darjeeling next spring.—With love to all, your ever loving father,

ROMESH CH. DUTT.

The first year was thus spent chiefly in recouping his health and making plans for the future. But he had also written his "England and India," one of the most readable books on the subject, and was preparing himself for greater efforts in the future. He was elected a member of the Authors' Club in 1897, having in the previous year been elected a member of the Incorporated Society of Authors.

II

In the August (1897) number of the *Fortnightly Review* appeared his article on "Famines in India," and in September Chatto & Windus brought out "England and India: A Record of Progress during 100 Years from 1785 to 1885." In the concluding chapter of this book, and in the *Fortnightly* article he, for the first time, gave an outline of his constructive ideas on reforms in the Indian Administration, which remained the pivot of his political writings in the future years of his life. A summary of his views will be found in later sections.

"England and India" received a sympathetic hearing in England, as the reader will see from the following extracts from contemporary papers:—

The *Scotsman* (13th September 1897).—What he has written is well written, and if the story of Indian progress which he tells is a good deal less flattering to the ruling power than some other records with which we are familiar, it is well worth study as giving us the points of view of an educated Indian gentleman, practically acquainted with the methods of government, who is loyal, friendly, and in intention just, but yet critical and not seldom condemnatory. Without attempting to sum up his views on past reforms, and on the reforms which he thinks sadly needed, we may say that in his eyes the crying defect of British rule is the lack of representative government and the comparatively small share given to natives of the country in the higher offices of the public service. *To enforce this view loyally and temperately appears to be the main object of his book*, and though it cannot be said that his arguments are conclusive or even always forcible, the style and temper in which they are put forward, as well as the nationality and position of the writer, claim for them serious and respectful consideration.

The *Times* (17th September 1897).—Mr. Dutt attempts to correlate the history of India with that of England during the past century, and to show that the British policy in the East was at each stage the outcome of the British policy at home. There is much to be said for this view at particular moments, but it is a theory which can be easily pushed too far, and which, as a matter of fact, tempts Mr. Dutt to lengths to which impartial and well-informed readers will scarcely find themselves able to follow him. Such a thesis, to be rendered convincing, would require a combined knowledge of the inner history of Great Britain at home and in India to which no writer of repute in our day pretends. But regarded from the essayist's point of view, and not that of the historian, Mr. Dutt's little book is suggestive in a high degree. Within 166 pages he manages to convey an impression, generally correct, of the influence which British political movements have had upon Indian administration during the hundred years from the date at which the Company came under the Board of Control. . . .

Mr. Dutt is a patriotic Indian who has distinctly a theory to establish, and a case to make out. He believes the time has come for a general inquiry into British rule in India; he demands for the Indian races some form of representation in addition to what has been already conceded to them, and a larger share in the control of the government, and in the higher administration of the country. This is the case which he frankly desires to make out. The theory which he seeks to establish is that political progress in India has been regulated, *and ought to be regulated, by political progress in England.* To those who may object that England has worked out her own political salvation by centuries of stern preparation, by the hard discipline of the Norman period, by the cautious semi-enfranchisement of her Tudor kings, and by the long constitutional struggles under the Stuart dynasty, Mr. Dutt has a ready answer. It may be true that the history of India, since her verified history begins, is a record of subjugation by one set of invaders after another. But for more than a century India has enjoyed the blessings of British rule, and the degree of representation and self-government already accorded to her now gives her a right to demand more.

Daily News (22nd September 1897).—We do not suppose any competent critic will dispute Mr. Dutt's general explanation of India's great and increasing poverty. That about a fifth of the Indian population suffer from chronic insufficiency of food, and that the majority of the four-fifths would be reduced to destitution by a single year's failure of the rains, is an appalling fact after all these forty years of railway and canal making, rise and development of numerous industries, commercial progress, and (within the Indian borders) uninterrupted peace. . . . Only, people will disagree about the limits of the possible. Mr. Dutt's own public life is an illustration of the spirit of English rule in India. *The ideal of this rule is the finest, and the least selfish, ever conceived or attempted to be realised by a dominant race.* In spite of mistakes, England has been true to it. She shows no sign of weariness, or of lessening faith in her mission.

CHAPTER XVI

1898 AND 1899

THE BENGAL MUNICIPAL ACT AND OTHER CONTROVERSIES

I

THE next year opened, as we shall see, with fresh ambitions and renewed struggles.

LONDON, 13*th January* 1898.

MY DEAR BROTHER,—Received yours of the 23rd December. "The whole country rejoices," you say, at my success. The feeling which oppresses me personally is that success is yet far off, and I have nothing before me at present but struggle, struggle, struggle! I am struggling to get some literary fame by my translation of the "Mahabharata," though the modern style of English poetry is Greek to me. I am struggling to make myself felt as an authority on Indian subjects, though as yet the journals and newspapers will scarcely condescend to publish what I write; and I am struggling to make my lectures at the University College a success, as you will find from the enclosed prospectus. I am writing all this not from mock modesty, but as I feel. It is a frightfully uphill work to establish your name, and get a footing in the crowded and unsympathetic world of London, especially if your speciality is Indian subjects, which tire Englishmen to death. However, I will see to the end of this struggle, and will even learn public-speaking at this fag-end of my life—for that is the only way to influence masses of Englishmen on politics. It is worth while making an arduous and manly struggle, if only to find out if distinction and fame are or are not possible.

I have got the "Udyoga" Parva which you have sent me. My translation work is somewhat impeded now by my work at the College, and my work for India.—Yours affectionately ever,

ROMESH CH. DUTT.

To his daughter :—

28th January 1898.

My dearest Bimala,— . . . Do you get *India* regularly every week? Last week's *India* had an account of my introductory lecture at the University College on Indian History—and this week's *India* has my speech at Darlington at an election meeting. So you see I am beginning to dabble on English politics! And just now English audiences hear Indian speakers with great attention and interest because Indian matters are attracting attention. I am going to Oxford to see Max Müller, who wants to see me, and I may speak at an election meeting next Saturday.—Your ever loving father, Romesh Ch. Dutt.

It was arranged that a course of ten lectures on the history, civilisation, and religion of the ancient Hindus, as shown in their ancient literature, would be delivered at University College by Mr. Dutt on Thursdays, beginning January 27th. Accordingly a preliminary lecture on "The Study of Indian History" was delivered by him on the 20th January, and the following notice of this lecture appeared in the columns of the *India* :—

Mr. Dutt complained of the little interest taken in ancient Indian history in the educational institutions of Europe, as compared with the interest taken in the history of Greece and Rome. The educational system of the present day was still based on the traditional belief of a past age, namely, that human civilisation and culture began in Greece and Rome—a belief which, he said, the discoveries of the present century had proved to be a myth. To Greece and to Rome belonged the credit of catching the light of a more ancient civilisation from the East, and reflecting it on the West, until it warmed the Western nations into cultured life. . . . The reason for this ignorance of ancient Indian history was that the materials of Indian history had only recently been placed before the European public, and a sufficient period of time had not yet elapsed for embodying these materials in popular works for the general reader.

A second course of fifteen lectures on the same subject began on the 26th October, and it was arranged to have lectures on Muhammadan rule during the second term, with British rule in India during the third term of the session.

Mr. Dutt delivered his first political speech at Cockerton, near Darlington, on the 24th January 1898, in support of the Liberal candidate for South-East Durham, the seat having been vacated by the death of Sir H. Havelock-Allen. Mr. Herbert Samuel spoke on the Home and Foreign Policy of the Indian Government, and Mr. Dutt spoke on the Indian Frontier War. In the course of his speech he said :—

Wherefore these disastrous wars? Wherefore try to maintain forts and valleys and passes beyond India's natural frontier? The advocates of the "forward" policy had not an articulate answer to these questions. They hardly spoke of the danger of a Russian invasion now, because the incidents of the present war had shown a Russian invasion with a large army to be impossible. The ostensible reason for the "forward" policy has ceased to exist, and a cloud of sophistry about keeping routes open, &c., &c., was all that was now urged in defence of an insane policy.

Before the close of the year, Mr. Dutt had spoken at twenty-four different meetings held in different parts of England. The new Sedition Bill, the new Calcutta Municipal Bill, and the Frontier forward policy of the Indian Government formed the subject of most of his speeches. Mr. Dadabhai Naoroji and Mr. A. M. Bose were his fellow workers this year in the task of popularising Indian questions in England, and rousing the interest of the British public in the aspirations of the Indian people.

On the 29th January Mr. Dutt addressed an audience at Swindon in support of the Liberal candidate for the Cricklade Division, Lord Edmond Fitzmaurice, brother of Lord Lansdowne. He spoke on Indian affairs in relation to Liberalism for nearly an hour, during which he was repeatedly interrupted by prolonged cheers. During the course of this speech he maintained that nowhere in the world-wide Empire of the Queen "did her name evoke greater loyalty and affection than among the millions of India, and that India has been won by good government, and was held by good government."

On the 12th of February, he again spoke in support of Lord Edmond Fitzmaurice at Wanborough. In the first part of his speech, which excited great enthusiasm, Mr. Dutt denounced "the Jingo policy of useless, profitless, and wicked wars at the cost of the Indian taxpayer," and in the latter part commented with just severity, and with the authority of an experienced administrator, upon the attempts to gag the Press in India.

About this time Mr. Dutt made fresh protests against the passing of the Sedition Bill, which passed into law in the Governor-General's Legislative Council on the 18th February 1898, and on this subject he wrote several letters to the *Manchester Guardian.*

On his first letter, in which he pointed out that the Bill was discussed in the House of Commons after it had actually become law in India, the *Guardian* observed:—

Mr. Romesh C. Dutt's long experience as a high official under the Indian Government, and his reputation as a writer on Indian affairs, lend weight to his protest against the new Sedition Law, which we print in another column. . . .

What is more important is the reason he gives for believing the law to be unworkable. In Friday's debate the Secretary for India made it clear that the law was aimed at the native press—was devised, as he would delicately put it, for its "guidance." Now Mr. Dutt shows that criticisms of the Government are to be found in the Anglo-Indian press quite as much as in the native papers, and that these criticisms are often quite harsh enough to justify the charge of "bringing the Government into hatred and contempt," while some Anglo-Indian journals indulge in such grossly contemptuous remarks upon the natives as to lay them open to the accusation of promoting feelings of enmity or ill-will between different classes. Is the law, then, to be applied to these Anglo-Indian papers, and, if so, how long will it endure? As to the native press, Mr. Dutt declares that the Indian Government is often misled by extracts made by subordinates into thinking the vernacular papers far worse than they really are.

On the 16th of March, on the occurrence of the Bombay plague riots, he contributed a second letter :—

In the present instance, as in many previous instances, that warning voice, that friendly and loyal and invaluable information about the sentiments and feelings of the people, has been treated with contempt and even with threats. The Government determined to remain in the dark; they declared that "rumours of serious unrest amongst Muhammadans in Bombay are untrue." But you cannot avert danger and disturbance by closing your eyes to it, or silencing the friendly voice of warning. The warning voice was silenced, but the catastrophe came. . . .

Lord Sandhurst wires:—"When I first heard of the disturbance I was engaged in discussing plague operations with native gentlemen, and trying to devise means of combining efficiency with greatest possible regard for native susceptibilities." One cannot read this without feeling the highest respect for the Governor of Bombay; but, nevertheless, one may be permitted to inquire, without disrespect, why the "means of combining efficiency with the greatest possible regard for native susceptibilities" were not devised twelve months ago. The reason does not lie in a want of sympathy on the part of Lord Sandhurst for the people over whom he rules; it is admitted on all hands that the present Governor of Bombay is as distinguished for his kindliness and sympathy as for his ability. The reason lies in the unworthy and undeserved distrust with which the native Indian press and the native Indian public bodies are looked upon by English rulers. When they speak on behalf of the people—and I hope they will never cease to do so, in spite of every discouragement—the first impulse of the rulers is, not to find out if they have a real grievance, but if they are preaching disaffection.

In raising his voice against the Sedition Law he had in some measure to defend the Indian Press, but this should not lead to the inference that his observations were intended to screen even the disloyal and scurrilous section of the Indian Press. In his report on the Indian Press, submitted while he was Commissioner of Burdwan, and published in the Calcutta *Gazette*, he impartially condemned all organs of public opinion, whether Indian or Anglo-Indian, that encouraged racial animosity or preached disloyalty to the Government.

The services which Mr. Dutt was rendering by voicing the views of the educated Indian public were warmly appreciated in India.

Mr. Romesh Ch. Dutt [wrote the *Madras Standard*] has been doing yeoman service to his country in England. He has done much, in concert with Mr. A. M. Bose, to educate the British public on Indian questions. His vast experience as a servant of Government for the last twenty-five years, and his reputation as a historian, entitle him to be heard on Indian affairs; and it is a matter for congratulation that he happens to be in England at a time when so many untruths about the educated natives of India are being assiduously propagated in England by reactionary Anglo-Indian politicians and journalists. Mr. Dutt has both by voice and pen been doing his best to allay the panic and explain the situation.

In Mr. Dutt's letter to the *Manchester Guardian* there is not a superfluous or objectionable word or sentiment. He knows his country and his countrymen, and with the knowledge he possesses he tries to show that the repressive measures, which have since been rushed through the Supreme Legislative Council, are unwise and are the outcome of panic.

In March, April, and May he spoke at several places, including Oxford, at which last meeting Professor Sidgwick presided. But his next important public utterance was on the death of Mr. Gladstone, when he spoke on behalf of India at the annual meeting of the National Reform Union, held at Derby on 20th May. The speech is thus reported :—

He said he had the melancholy duty of saying a few words on the death of one whose name was as lovingly cherished in the hearts of millions of his countrymen as in those of the country where he laboured. The loss which England had suffered in the death of Mr. Gladstone was not alone confined to this kingdom. It was a loss which was felt all over India; it was a loss to the cause of humanity. (Applause.) England was rich in illustrious men, in men of marvellous genius, whose words and thoughts had from time to time gone forth from this land to the remotest corners of the world in favour of justice and liberty. He questioned very much, however, if within the present century there had breathed a man whose heart yearned more for the cause of the sufferer and the lowly, or whose voice pleaded more eloquently for the cause of righteousness, truth, and justice. For the last fifty years Mr. Gladstone's name had been identified not only in this country and in Europe, but all over the world, with all that was free, noble, and generous; and wherever there was a battle to be fought for the cause of liberty and humanity, or the amelioration of the condition of the people, Mr. Gladstone's voice was heard.

. . . .

Standing, if I may say so, by the grave of the greatest statesman of this century, we cannot think that wise government is dead even in the dependency of India. The great heart of England is sound to the core—(cheers)—and England, which is just and true to her colonies all over the world, cannot be unjust and untrue to India—at least as long as England can cherish and love and venerate the name and the memory of Mr. Gladstone.

On the 20th of June a conference of Indians was held in St. Martin's Town Hall, presided over by Mr. Dadabhai Naoroji, to discuss resolutions dealing with the currency question, the new sedition law, the proposal to deprive Calcutta of municipal self-government, and the decision of the Imperial Government to charge the whole cost of the last frontier war to the finances of India. The first resolution was moved by the President, the third by Mr. A. M. Bose, while Mr. R. C. Dutt was entrusted with the second resolution.

Mr. Dutt [said *India*] impressively stated his regret, as an old officer of the Crown, at having to speak to such a condemnatory resolution, but he took the courage of duty from the disastrously reckless and unwise legislation of the Government of India. He said that the proposed law contained provisions so antagonistic to British ideas of liberty that the most powerful Government seen for many years hesitated to bring it before the British Parliament. While in charge of large districts in India, he always felt that his own security and the peace of his district rested on the confidence of the people in the justice of the British Government; but he hardly remembered the time when the confidence of the people in the justice and fair-play of the British Government had been so shaken as in the last two years.

The next important public question to which he devoted his attention was the proposal of the Indian Government to make gold the standard currency of the Empire, and artificially to fix the exchange value of silver. He wrote a letter to the *Manchester Guardian*,

November 1898, in which he summarised his views on the subject:—

With regard to the currency question, the educated people of India, in so far as I have seen their opinions expressed in their journals, are practically unanimous against the closing of the mints and the raising of the value of the rupee artificially. Their arguments are these:—

(1) Virtually all the investments of the millions of India take the shape of silver trinkets and jewellery for their women; and this is the national wealth of India. By artificially raising the value of the rupee the Government has confiscated between 20 and 30 per cent. of the value of this national wealth, estimated in the currency of the land. It is an act of confiscation all the more cruel because it touches the poor millions of India.

(2) All the rent paid by the agriculturists of India (and four-fifths of the population depend directly or indirectly on agriculture) is paid in rupees. To raise the value of rupees artificially is to increase the rental and to impoverish the agriculturists, who are already in an abject state of poverty.

(3) The agriculturists are deeply indebted to grasping money-lenders, and the debt is estimated in rupees. To add to the value of the rupee is to add to the debt, to benefit the well-to-do money-lenders and to crush the already indebted cultivators.

(4) All the taxes paid in India, by the rich and poor alike, are paid in rupees. To add to the value of the rupee is to add to the taxation of the country.

(5) A large portion of the public debt of India is in rupees. To add to the value of the rupee is to add to the public debt of the Government, *i.e.* of the Indian nation—and to give an "unearned increment" to those who hold the bonds in this country or in India.

He gave evidence before the Currency Committee on November 30th, and was examined by the President, Sir Henry Fowler (afterwards Lord Wolverhampton). One of the members of the Committee, Sir J. Muir, observed that the evidence Mr. Dutt had given was "very important," and the President described it as "splendid." Before the Committee he expressed in greater detail the views to which he had already given publicity. They were practically shared by such sound economists as Mr. T. Lloyd, the editor of the *Statist*, who, in an article in the *National Review*, spoke "of the confiscation of the nation's saving by the closing of the mints, of the unwillingness of the Indians to accept the proposed change, of the increase in taxation by raising the value of the rupee, and of the resultant increase of the indebtedness of the poor." He also pointed out that the proposed change would handicap India in competing with China.

In March 1899, the Government of India passed the Sugar Bill. Mr. Dutt strongly supported the measure, and wrote both to the *Manchester Guardian* and the *Times* on the subject:—

> Permit me as an Indian [he wrote to the *Manchester Guardian*] to say a word on the subject of the Indian Sugar Bill which is the subject of so much discussion in this country. In passing this bill Lord Curzon has protected an extensive and important industry from ruin by unfair competition, and has acted in strict consonance with educated Indian opinion. It is not true that this bill is in the interests only of sugar factories managed by European capital in India. It is in the interests of thousands of Indian workmen who find employment in the factories. And more than this, it is in the interests of hundreds of thousands of growers who supply raw sugar to those factories. The area of sugar cultivation in India was becoming contracted by unfair and bounty-fed imports, and the growers of Indian sugar were losing a legitimate means of subsistence. Lord Curzon has saved them and their industry.

It was about the beginning of the year 1899 that he began his memorable campaign about the poverty of the people, famines, and kindred economic topics. In January of that year he wrote two articles in *India*, on "Land Legislation in India," and "Land Settlements and Famines in India." These articles had special reference to the land settlements in Madras.

In the same year Mr. Dutt was made a Fellow of the Royal Society of Literature, and on June 14th read an excellent paper on the "Mahabharata" before a large and select audience at the rooms of the Society in Hanover Square. The paper was very well received.

present time as fantastic and Quixotic! We have changed all that. Rhodes, who has founded Rhodesia somewhat after the method of Clive and Hastings, is the modern hero, and gets his certificate of honour from our modern statesman, Chamberlain; Jameson is publicly condemned for his raid, but is privately admired; Mr. Goschen is almost universally lauded for spending millions on millions in increasing the British navy; and the rampant Tory papers are trying to hound on Lord Salisbury to war with Russia and other Powers in order to secure monopoly of trade and influence in China. Never since the Crimean War, never perhaps since the death of Castlereagh in 1822, has Imperialism been so rampant in England; never have the purely animal instincts of self-love and self-aggrandisement been stronger or more violent; never have the higher instincts of humanity and justice, of respect towards rival nations, and fairness towards subject nations, been at a lower ebb. Do you now understand why the Indian Government has, in recent years, turned to methods of coercion and repressive legislation? Talk to the serried ranks of Tory members in the House, and to high Indian officials, about reposing trust and confidence in the people of India, about extending their privileges, and allowing them a larger share in the administration of their own concerns; you may as well talk Chinese to them! These words and ideas find no place in the vocabulary of their politics, they convey no intelligible sense or meaning to them. The close of the nineteenth century, like the close of the eighteenth century, is marked in England by the coarsest form of Imperialism that the country has ever known, and true Liberalism is at a discount. And yet, if I am not much mistaken, the tide is already turning, and Englishmen are already getting disgusted with blustering and bullying in China, with repressing and coercing in India. There is hope after the next general election.

We may find a place also for his observations on the victory of Omdurman :—

I am proud as any one can be of England's glory and England's triumph and England's world-wide Empire, but I confess this celebration of Omdurman makes me sick, and reminds me too painfully of the demand of the Roman audience at the Coliseum for "more victims!" "more blood!" For there was no real warfare, but slaughter only at Omdurman; the barbarians had no chance against the maxim-guns of our troops, and they hurled themselves against our arms of precision with a bravery and reckless valour which has never been excelled in the history of the world, only to be mowed down and exterminated! Ten thousand of them were killed, and more than ten thousand were wounded, and special correspondents inform us that after the battle was over the Egyptian troops, who had been led under British command, went among the wounded Dervishes, and deliberately shot these wounded and bleeding men to death or killed them with appalling cruelty which the special correspondents decline to describe. . . . It is sickening to contemplate this; sickening to think that we are celebrating the return of the army from these scenes as if they had returned from some real warfare.

Those who remember the impassioned oration of Lord Morley (then Mr. John Morley) at Brechin on the "slaughter of Omdurman" will easily realise that Mr. Dutt had not taken by any means a too serious or too bigoted a view of the situation. Indeed Mr. Morley thought that the English nation was being led into "a course of policy, a spirit and a temper" which he believed to be injurious to the material prosperity of England and her national character.

His comparison of the careers of Sir Antony MacDonnell and Sir Alexander Mackenzie as Indian administrators has a more local interest, but is pungent and far-sighted.

Sir Antony is a thoroughly honest worker, true to his connections, and to the people whom he has been called upon to govern. Bengal will long remember the twin-workers who were in the Bengal Secretariat in past years—Mackenzie and MacDonnell—as the industrious and the idle apprentices of Hogarth. Both were promising young officers, both had abilities, and each had a good start. Sir A. Mackenzie spoilt his chances by his want of sympathy with the people, by his changing his convictions with the change of his masters, by his unworthy endeavour to rob the people of Calcutta of their valued rights, and by his unseemly utterances and unsympathetic speeches. Sir Antony MacDonnell will be remembered for his sympathy with the people, his earnest endeavours to serve the people, and for the honesty and the courage of his convictions. A few weeks ago he told a London audience that the two golden rules of Indian administration were the maintenance of peace and order, and sympathy for the feelings, wishes, and even prejudices of the masses of the people. I suppose the two golden rules for your late Lieutenant-Governor, Sir A. Mackenzie, are to change opinions and convictions with the change of masters, and to abuse and vilify a loyal and grateful nation, whom one is sent out to govern. The ends of these two men are befitting their careers, like the ends of Hogarth's apprentices. Sir A. Mackenzie retires amidst the deep, not loud, groans of the entire Indian nation; Sir A. MacDonnell lives and works amidst the applause of Englishmen and Indians alike.

III

In August 1898 Mr. Dutt began his campaign against the Bill introduced in the Bengal Legislative Council to modify the constitution of the Calcutta Corporation, and he carried it on with unflinching resolution for nearly two years. He addressed his first letter on the subject to the *Manchester Guardian* on the 22nd August. Then he delivered a speech on the same subject at the Westminster Town Hall on the 26th October, and on the 31st of the same month he wrote to the *India* explaining his views in detail. His most important speech on the subject was delivered in Manchester on the 22nd of November, when the Bishop of Hereford (Dr. Percival) presided. On the 28th of November he received a telegram from Raja Binay Krishna, of Sobhabazar, to the effect that the inhabitants of Calcutta had appointed him delegate to represent their opposition to the Bill.

A second letter appeared in the *Manchester Guardian* on the 9th December, and he wrote a further letter to the *Times* on the 13th January following. At the annual Conference of the London Indian Society, held on the 28th December, he moved the following resolution :—

> That this Conference deplores all legislation restricting self-government in India, urges the Government to withdraw the Calcutta Municipal Bill now before the Bengal Council, and affirms the principle that the extension of popular rights and of trust and confidence in the people is the surest foundation of British rule in India.

Of the proceedings of the Conference the *Daily News* said :—

"Our responsibility forbids us to let the people destroy their own lives from pure ignorance. But that object might surely be attained without depriving Calcutta of representative institutions.

The devoted and single-minded way in which Mr. Dutt went to work, and the more than personal interest he took in defending the rights of his countrymen, will be exemplified by the series of letters he wrote about this time to Raja Binay Krishna, who was leading the constitutional agitation in Calcutta against the proposed changes. These letters also disclose the thorough and tactful manner in which he carried on his political work in England.

54 PARLIAMENT STREET, LONDON, S.W.,
22nd December 1898.

MY DEAR RAJA BINAY KRISHNA,—The political sky has cleared a little in England. Sir W. Harcourt has resigned, which means that there is a split in the Liberal party; some of the leaders have seceded from extreme jingoism, especially Morley and Harcourt. This is good news for us; we may have a somewhat better chance of obtaining a hearing.

Thanks for your letter of the 1st December. I will not forget the task which you and my countrymen have imposed on me. I am devoting all my time and all my exertions to this work.

I have reprinted the Calcutta Memorial, as no work could be done without that document, and I could not wait for a further supply from Calcutta. I have sent copies to Sir Arthur Godley and to Sir Charles Bernard, with a strong appeal for their sympathy and help, repeating in writing what I urged verbally when I had interviews with Sir Charles Elliott, Sir Steuart Bayley, and Sir Alfred Lyall, and will present them with the Memorial and urge all that I have to say. I saw Mr. Caine yesterday, gave him a copy of the Memorial, and obtained a promise from him to write on the subject to the *Daily Chronicle*, as I have written to the *Manchester Guardian*. I know Sir Henry Fowler, as he examined me for well-nigh three hours at the sitting of the Currency Committee on the 30th November. By Mr. Caine's advice, I am sending a copy of the Memorial to Sir Henry Fowler, and am asking for an interview with him. If he is amenable to persuasion and open to conviction, I hope to make him consent to some modifications in the Calcutta Bill. And if I can persuade him, it will not take me long to reach Lord George Hamilton, for Lord George takes his cue in every important matter from Sir Henry Fowler.

I have mentioned all these facts to keep you informed, as you ought to be kept informed, of what I am endeavouring to do for those who have honoured me by appointing me their delegate. Success is uncertain, but I will spare no possible endeavours to secure it. I am going to speak on this Calcutta Bill at Westminster on the 22nd January, and at Lewisham on 29th January. But I depend more on my interviews than on speeches in the present crisis. You are right in trying to get up great meetings and frequent meetings in every ward in Calcutta about this Bill. Also in trying to submit a monster Memorial to Lord Curzon on his arrival in Calcutta. He will not promise anything in reply, but it is well that he should be impressed with the idea that there is a feeling of alarm and of despair among the educated and uneducated people of Calcutta in reference to this Bill. I could not see him, because he left almost immediately after your telegram reached me; but I managed to send him a cutting from the *Manchester Guardian* containing my letter.

I have written to my friend Surendra Nath Banerjea that he should not leave Calcutta now. He should fight hard in the select Committee and in the Bengal Council; his presence is indispensable there; and speeches here will do no good now. If you decide on sending another delegate, send my friend Ananda Mohan Bose. I know of no public man among our Calcutta friends who has more persuasive eloquence in conversation, or truer wisdom and more fervent patriotism than Bose. If he come, we will work side by side, on the same plan and with the same object, as we did in the first half of 1898. If he cannot come, I will do all I can, and will not spare myself.

I will write to you again after a fortnight.—With kind regards and best wishes, I am, yours sincerely,

ROMESH C. DUTT.

54 PARLIAMENT STREET, LONDON, S.W.,
6th Jan. 1899.

MY DEAR RAJA BINAY KRISHNA,—I have just time to send you a short letter by this mail. Since writing to you, I have seen both Sir Charles Elliott and Sir Steuart Bayley, and I explained to them the utter absurdity of giving the Municipal Corporation only four representatives out of twelve in the Executive Committee. They both saw the injustice and absurdity of the thing, though they cannot help me directly. I left a copy of the Memorial with each of them, and they promised to look into it.

Sir Henry Fowler is not in town, but he has written to me from Wolverhampton, promising to make an appointment to see me when he returns to London, which will be in February if not before. I enclose his letter in original for your perusal. I have no doubt I shall be able to convince him of the injustice and the inexpediency of virtually destroying representation in Calcutta. I appealed to him as a Liberal to save us from this. This apparently has touched him, for he promises "full and careful consideration."

According to the advice of Sir Steuart Bayley, I have also written to Lord George Hamilton asking for an interview. I had originally intended to move Lord George after convincing Sir Henry Fowler, but from what Sir Steuart Bayley said, there was the risk of Lord George feeling slighted if I went to his political opponent first. This was evidently in Sir Steuart's mind, and he decidedly advised me to ask for an interview from Lord George at once, and when I have seen Sir Henry Fowler and Lord George Hamilton I shall have done all that it is possible to do in the way of interviewing, arguing, and influencing. It is useless to seek interviews with other Cabinet Ministers —they invariably refer one to the Indian Ministers. Sir Steuart Bayley thinks I may possibly succeed in inducing Lord George in writing to India advising concessions. If I fail in this, my last resource will be to bring on a debate in the House in February when the House meets.—Yours sincerely,

ROMESH DUTT.

54 PARLIAMENT STREET, LONDON, S.W.,
27th January 1899.

MY DEAR RAJA BINAY KRISHNA,—I am delighted to see from telegrams that important and crowded meetings continue to be held in Calcutta against the Municipal Bill. Please go on holding such meetings from time to time until the Bill is disposed of one way or another. You can hardly conceive what good you are doing by holding such meetings. The impression produced here in official circles is *excellent;* the officials feel that the proposed legislation is opposed by the mass of the citizens of Calcutta, and they begin to doubt the wisdom of alienating the people. And on the other hand, the people of Calcutta too are educated by such meetings, and the monstrous proposals of the Government become widely known and widely condemned. So please continue holding such meetings—fight to the bitter end the great constitutional battle which you have undertaken—and whether you succeed, or whether you fail, your name will be remembered as that of a leader who remained true to his country when other zamindars proved unpatriotic and false. My own idea is, and it is based on what I have seen and heard here, that the Government will not pass the Bill in its present shape if we are true to ourselves, and oppose it *bitterly, vehemently, and universally to the very end*. But if we grow lax now, all is lost.

I am making good use of Mr. N. N. Ghose's excellent pamphlet. I distributed some 500 copies at the Manchester Free Church Meeting which I addressed last Sunday, as you will see in *India* of this week. I am also going to distribute another 500 copies at the Lewisham meeting which I am going to address next Sunday. I have sent 6500 copies to the British Committee for distribution at various meetings that may be held from time to time. Both myself and the Editor of *India* have privately sent copies of the pamphlet to influential people, and this week's *India* has an excellent analysis of the book. Lastly, I have sent a copy to Mr. Herbert Roberts, whom I am going to coach for making a speech on the subject in the House next month, as I coached him last year in respect of the Sedition Law. I enclose Mr. Roberts's letter for your perusal.

I saw the Right Hon. Leonard Courtney last Tuesday, and am going to see Sir Charles Dilke on the 8th February. I expect to see both Sir Henry Fowler and Lord G. Hamilton early in February, and will try to persuade Lord George to remove the most objectionable clauses. The British Committee will meet on the 31st of this month, and I will attend, of course, explain to them the course I have pursued during these three months, and receive from them all help (if any) that they can render in the matter.—Believe me, yours sincerely,

ROMESH C. DUTT.

54 PARLIAMENT STREET, LONDON, S.W.,
3rd February 1899.

MY DEAR RAJA BINAY KRISHNA,—I am glad to get your letter of the 12th January, and thank you for the enclosures. By the series of meetings you have held in Calcutta you have redeemed the reputation of the citizens, proved their zealous regard for their municipal rights, and enormously strengthened our cause in this memorable struggle.

Here I have completed my preparations, and the Parliament meets next week. I spoke at Lewisham last Sunday and distributed Ghose's pamphlet. I have, on the one hand, asked for early interviews from Lord George Hamilton and Sir H. Fowler, to try and persuade them to modify the Bill, and, on the other hand, am going to help Mr. Herbert Roberts to prepare his amendment to the Queen's Speech, so as to bring some pressure on Lord George to grant the modification required. And if I can induce Sir Charles Dilke and Mr. Leonard Courtney to take a part in the debate—I will see them all before the debate comes on—the pressure is likely to be effective.

I have thought it proper to explain to you fully my plans. Virtually I have three strings to my bow. In the first place, I will try argument and persuasion with Lord George Hamilton, and may succeed, as Sir Steuart Bayley has supported my views. In the second place, I will put pressure on him through Mr. Roberts's amendment to the Queen's Speech. In the third place, I will try to make that pressure effective by inducing some stronger men in the House than Sir W. Wedderburn or Herbert Roberts to take part in the debate. These are my plans for the immediate future; of course they will undergo developments with every new turn in the course of events, and I shall have a busy time of it during the next few weeks.

My repeated speeches and letters to the *Guardian* and the *Times* have had some effect on the public opinion in this country; not a voice is raised to defend the Bill, and even an Anglo-Indian has written to the *Manchester Guardian* attacking the Bill. I have no doubt you will be pleased to read this article, which I enclose; for it will show that your labours in Calcutta and my labours in London have not been in vain. Continue your labours, and have a large meeting at least once a fortnight, till the Bill has been disposed of one way or other, and I will continue to take every possible action here.

I attended the meeting of the British Committee last Tuesday; Wedderburn, Hume, Caine, and other members were present. The Committee will, of course, do all they can to help the cause. Mr. Caine drafted the amendment to the Queen's Speech which Mr. Roberts is to move; and Sir William Wedderburn suggested that a small leaflet, containing in one or two pages the opinions of previous Lieutenant-Governors on the Calcutta Corporation, should be prepared and distributed in the House of Commons just before the debate. The rest of the work, of course, falls on me.—Believe me, yours sincerely,

ROMESH C. DUTT.

54 PARLIAMENT STREET, LONDON, S.W.,
4th Aug. 1899.

MY DEAR RAJA BINAY KRISHNA,—I have received your letter of the 13th July, and have read the Viceroy's letter to the Bengal Government, a copy of which you enclosed. You are probably right in thinking that all hope is now lost, and that the scheme which the Viceroy has dictated, and which Sir John Woodburn has accepted, will be passed into law. Even taking this view of the matter, we owe it to ourselves to make a last and unanimous protest against this confiscation of our rights. Let it be made clear that we do not accept this, that we protest against this, that it is forced down our throats by a powerful and unsympathetic Government. Such a protest will have its moral effect; it will probably be fruitful of some important concessions during the passage of the Bill through the Council, and it will make the Government unwilling to force other reactionary measures on us. More than this, such a protest is what we owe to ourselves; after having fought against the Bill so long, we are bound to make a last demonstration to show that this measure has not our assent, and will not elicit our co-operation.

Rely on my doing here all that can be done. I have come back to London from the sea-side in haste, and I have induced Mr. Herbert Roberts to raise a debate on Tuesday next, when the Indian Budget will be discussed. Sir M. M. Bhownaggree will probably speak for us from the Tory benches; and the debate will at least proclaim the fact that this reactionary measure is being forced on us against the wishes of the nation. I will be in the House of Commons from 2 P.M. to midnight on the Indian Budget night, and I will offer all help and information to our friends that they may require.

It is sickening to me to see the fight that is going on among ourselves at the very moment when we are losing an important privilege and right—the *Patrika* attacking Surendra Nath and Narendra Nath, the *Hitabadi* attacking the *Patrika*, a spiteful and personal dissension in our own camp when we should be united. It makes me sad and disheartened. Why should these personal matters be discussed in the papers at all? How does it strengthen our public cause to know if Surendra Nath made a promise to Nalinaksha or to Ananda Mohan which he did not redeem?

We have all seen differences among Liberal leaders lately—Lord Rosebery, Sir W. Harcourt, Mr. Morley, Mr. Asquith, Sir H. C. Bannerman, &c.—but they are differences in principles. Who ever heard of any of these Liberals dragging to the public

Facts were brought to light in connection with the alarm of plague in Calcutta, which showed that the town was in a terribly insanitary condition, and that the existing constitution of the Municipality was ill-adapted to stand the strain of a grave and sudden emergency, and failed to secure the prompt and continuous executive action which was necessary in view of the fact that the sanitation and conservancy of the great Indian maritime cities had become a matter of international concern. About the same time it came to notice that the collection of the rates had for a long time been defective; that important branches of the accounts had fallen into confusion, and that considerable uncertainty prevailed as to the respective functions of the Chairman and the Corporation. Further, it had for long been recognised as a defect in the existing law that the European community was inadequately represented, and did not exercise the influence to which it was entitled.

The Bill was intended not only to remedy these defects, but also to provide for a responsible municipal executive, and to furnish this executive with a law adequate to the sanitary requirements of the city and to modern standards of municipal administration. In order to enable the heavy and complicated business of the city to be carried on smoothly, the Bill interposed a small working Committee between the Chairman and the main body of Commissioners, and the functions of these authorities, the Corporation, the General Committee, and the Chairman were precisely defined and carefully distinguished. Following the Bombay Act, the Bill vested the entire executive power in the Chairman, to be exercised either independently or subject to the approval or sanction of the Corporation, wherever this was expressly so directed. The General Committee was to stand between the deliberative and executive authorities, and deal with those matters which by their nature were ill-adapted for discussion by the Corporation, and yet were too important to be left to be disposed of by the Chairman alone. The Bill reduced the number of the General Committee from eighteen to twelve members, and provided for the appointment of these from among the general body of Commissioners in equal proportions by (*a*) the elected Commissioners voting in four electoral divisions, (*b*) the Chamber of Commerce, the Trades' Association, and the Port Commissioners, and (*c*) the Government.

Mr. Dutt's position with regard to this important controversy may be condensed as follows:—

(1) That the elected Commissioners fairly represented

the Hindu, Muhammadan, and the European communities according to their respective numbers.

(2) That the Commissioners had worked in the past on the whole without any serious internal dissensions, and shown commendable public spirit.

(3) That though there was much to be done in the future to improve the sanitation of the metropolis, yet Calcutta was healthier than the surrounding country, and the Corporation (as then constituted) was responsible for many improvements.

(4) That the Corporation of elected Commissioners had worked better than its predecessors, the Commissioners and Justices of the Peace appointed by the Government.

(5) That previous Lieutenant-Governors since the days of Sir Steuart Bayley had spoken very highly of the work of the Commissioners, and one of them, Sir Antony MacDonnell, had said "that in some cases their zeal had risen to devotion."

The essence of his views is to be found in a letter to the *Manchester Guardian*, dated the 9th December 1898.

> In Bombay the delegates are empowered [he wrote] to choose two-thirds of the members of the Executive Committee; in Calcutta it is proposed by the present Bill that the delegates should choose only one-third of the members of the Executive Committee. This virtually means that the governing executive body would not represent the delegates, and would not therefore represent the wishes and opinions of the ratepayers. Is this an object which should be aimed at, even in India? Generations of English statesmen and administrators have laboured in England and in India to evoke that "high public spirit" which Sir John Woodburn commends so much, but which it is now intended to crush and stamp out with a light heart and a despotic hand. Macaulay and Bentinck, Munro and Elphinstone, Canning and Northbrook, Ripon and Gladstone all have laboured to spread English education, to create public spirit, and to bring self-governing institutions into existence in India. And when a small and humble and successful beginning has been made, will Englishmen look at the fruit of their labours with distrust and suspicion, and will Lord George Hamilton root out the tree which has taken three generations to grow?

The death of self-government will be the death of good administration in India. You cannot govern India well except with the co-operation of the people; you cannot secure their co-operation without trusting them with some powers.

His own countrymen, specially the citizens of Calcutta, were not unmindful of this devotion, and the great services which he rendered in the cause of the civic rights of the metropolis.

The *Indian Nation* wrote :—

That English public opinion, even English Parliamentary opinion, has been roused on the subject of the Calcutta Municipal Bill, is a result for which we should be grateful to Mr. R. C. Dutt. He has been working single-handed in England, but he has been speaking and writing and interviewing and conferring almost unremittingly. And all his agitation has been conducted in an honest, gentlemanly manner, never by a concealment of the true or a suggestion of the false or an imputation of motives. His aim has been to convince, not to intrigue. The agitation in Calcutta, conducted mainly by the energy of Raja Binay Krishna, has of course helped him materially.

The *Amrita Bazar Patrika* wrote :—

Mr. Dutt is giving up his entire time to the agitation, interviewing members of Parliament from Lord George Hamilton and Sir Henry Fowler downwards; and if any measure of success follows the debate in the House, it will be largely due to the tact, skill, and untiring energy of Mr. Dutt.

Raja Binay Krishna of Sobhabazar wrote :—

We may all again be permitted to express our sincere thankfulness to you for the earnest manner in which you are devoting your time and energy for our motherland. The sight of a single individual toiling against odds and in a foreign land to protect civic rights has raised you greatly in our estimation.

Babu Nalin Bihari Sirkar, perhaps the most capable and public-spirited Indian that has sat on the Municipal Board within recent years, wrote to him :—

11 Clive Street, Calcutta, *2nd March* 1899.

My dear Mr. Dutt,—Allow me now to tender you our heartfelt thanks for all that you are doing there on behalf of the residents of Calcutta against the proposed municipal law. Raja Binay Krishna has been good enough to read to me from time to time your letters to him, containing brief but very interesting accounts of your work in England in connection with the Calcutta Municipal Bill agitation. We really feel that if you had not been in England now, our cause would have suffered grievously. I look upon your presence there as quite providential; and I cannot say how much we are all indebted to you for your powerful advocacy in the cause of Local Self-government in Calcutta. Born and bred in Calcutta, you will long be remembered as one of its great worthy citizens, who has nobly fought for justice and fair-play in the matter of city government. May you live long and prosper is the hearty prayer of every Hindu resident of Calcutta at the present moment.

Mr. Dutt, as a last resource, approached Lord Curzon himself, and the Private Secretary wrote back in 1899:—

I am desired by the Viceroy to thank you for your suggestion, which he knows to be based upon a sincere desire both for harmony between the Government and the native community in Calcutta, and for the future good administration of the city; but he does not see his way to give you any hopes, as the matter was no longer open.

In September 1899, twenty-eight elected Commissioners, including all the prominent and most experienced men, resigned their seats in the Council as a protest against the Bill. Thus closed this memorable controversy.

As far as academic arguments are concerned, the opponents of the amending Bill appear to have held a strong position; but how far in practice, the metropolis of India, which aspires to be one of the foremost cities of the Empire, and whose efficient government is an integral part of the government of the Indian Empire itself, has profited by the new legislation, the future alone can decide.

While busily engaged with his political campaigns, Mr. Dutt's pen had not remained idle. During these two years he conceived and carried out the remarkable task of translating into English verse the most important portions of the ancient epics of the "Ramayana" and the "Mahabharata." Of this memorable work an account is given in the next chapter.

Towards the close of the year, in October, he received an invitation, through his friend the late Mr. W. C. Bonnerjea, to preside at the next session of the Indian National Congress to be held at Lucknow. He cheerfully accepted the offer, and set sail for India after nearly three years of arduous work in England.

8th September 1899.

MY DEAREST BIMALA,—I am coming at last—with no "Mahabharata" or "Ramayana" in hand—for the best of reasons that the work is done. I placed my "Ramayana" in the hands of my publishers this week, and it will be out before I leave for India.

LONDON, *27th October* 1899.

MY DEAREST BIMALA,—You have heard of course that I am coming to preside at the Congress at Lucknow. So immediately on landing I shall be marched off to Lucknow. But after that I am resolved to take complete rest for months. No work will take me away from the comfortable fireside, be it at Sylhet or Midnapur.—With love to all, your loving father,

ROMESH.

In May 1899, he was elected Fellow of the Royal Society of Literature of the United Kingdom.

CHAPTER XVII

TRANSLATION OF THE EPICS

DURING the years 1898 and 1899, Mr. Dutt worked at what Professor Max Müller considered the almost impossible task of translating into English verse the kernel of the great Epics of ancient India. But Mr. Dutt was never deterred by the difficulty of any task, which, after mature consideration, he took up. He went on with his work, and when the "Mahabharata" was completed, he presented a copy of it to the Oxford Professor. Professor Max Müller was so charmed and astonished with the result that he readily consented to write an introduction.

The "Mahabharata" appeared in August 1898, and exactly a year afterwards his "Ramayana" saw the light. In his luminous epilogues to these two works, Mr. Dutt explains both the scope of the Epics and the method pursued by him.

In the epilogue to the "Mahabharata" he wrote :—

The work went on growing for a thousand years after it was first compiled and put together in the form of an Epic; until the crystal rill of the Epic itself was all but lost in an unending morass of religious and didactic episodes, legends, tales, and traditions. The modern reader will now understand the reason why this great Epic—the greatest work of imagination that Asia has produced—has never yet been put before the European reader in a readable form. A poem of ninety thousand couplets, about seven times the size of the "Iliad" and the "Odyssey" put together, is more than what the average reader can stand; and the heterogeneous nature of its contents does not add to the interest of the work.

But, although the old Epic has thus been spoilt by unlimited expansions, yet, nevertheless, the leading incidents and characters of the real Epic are still discernible, uninjured by the mass of foreign substance in which they are embedded, even like those immortal marble figures which have been recovered from the ruins of an ancient world, and now beautify the museums of modern Europe. For years past I have thought that it was perhaps not impossible to exhume this buried Epic from the superincumbent mass of episodical matter, and to restore it to the modern world. For years past I have felt a longing to undertake this work, but the task was by no means an easy one. Leaving out all episodical matter, the leading narrative of the Epic forms about one-fourth of the work; and a complete translation even of this leading story would be unreadable, both from its length and its prolixness. On the other hand, to condense the story into shorter limits would be, not to make a translation, but virtually to write a new poem; and that was not what I desired to undertake, nor what I was competent to perform.

There seemed to me only one way out of this difficulty. The main incidents of the Epic are narrated in the original work in passages which are neither diffuse nor unduly prolix, and which are interspersed in the leading narrative of the Epic, as that narrative itself is interspersed in the midst of more lengthy episodes. The more carefully I examined the arrangement, the more clearly it appeared to me that these main incidents of the Epic would bear a full and unabridged translation into English verse; and that these translations, linked together by short connecting notes, would virtually present the entire story of the Epic to the modern reader in a form and within limits which might be acceptable. It would be, no doubt, a condensed version of the original Epic, but the condensation would be effected, not by the translator telling a short story in his own language, but by linking together those passages of the original which describe the main and striking incidents, and thus telling the main story as told in the original work. The advantage of this arrangement is that, in the passages presented to the reader, it is the poet who speaks to him, not the translator. Though vast portions of the original are skipped over, those which are presented are the portions which narrate the main incidents of the Epic, and they describe those incidents as told by the poet himself.

Accepting the dictum of Stopford Brooke — that prose no more represents poetry than architecture does music, and that translations of poetry are never much good, but at least they should always endeavour to have the musical movement of poetry and to obey the laws of the verse they translate—Mr. Dutt decided to render his translation into verse.

One of my greatest difficulties in the task I have undertaken has been to try and preserve something of the "musical movement" of the sonorous Sanskrit poetry in the English translation. Much of the Sanskrit Epic is written in the well-known *sloka* metre of sixteen syllables in each line, and I endeavoured to choose some English metre which is familiar to the English ear, and which would reproduce to some extent the rhythm, the majesty, and the long and measured sweep of the Sanskrit verse. It was necessary to adopt such a metre in order to transfer something of the truth about the "Mahabharata" into English, for without such reproduction or imitation of the musical movement of the original, very much less than a half truth is told. My kind friend, Mr Edmund Russell, impelled by that enthusiasm for Indian poetry and Indian art which is a part of him, rendered me valuable help and assistance in this matter, and I gratefully acknowledge the benefit I have derived from his advice and suggestions. After considerable trouble and anxiety, and after rendering several books in different English metres, I felt convinced that the one finally adopted was a nearer approach to the Sanskrit *sloka* than any other familiar English metre known to me. . . .

It would be too much to assume that even with the help of this similarity in metres, I have been able to transfer into my English that sweep and majesty of verse which is the charm of Sanskrit, and which often sustains and elevates the simplest narration and the plainest ideas. Without the support of those sustaining wings, my poor narration must often plod through the dust, and I can only ask for the indulgence of the reader, which every translator of poetry from a foreign language can with reason ask, if the story as told in the translation is sometimes but a plain, simple, and homely narrative. For any artistic decoration I have neither the inclination nor the necessary qualification. The crisp and ornate style, the quaint expression, the chiselled word, the new-coined phrase, in which modern English poetry is rich, would scarcely suit the translation of an old Epic whose predominating characteristic is its simple and easy flow of narrative. Indeed, the "Mahabharata" would lose that unadorned simplicity which is its first and foremost feature if the translator ventured to decorate it with the art of the modern day, even if he had been qualified to do so.

For if there is one characteristic feature which distinguishes the "Mahabharata" (as well as the other Indian Epic, the "Ramayana") from all later Sanskrit literature, it is the grand simplicity of its narrative, which contrasts with the artificial graces of later Sanskrit poetry. The poetry of Kalidasa, for instance, is ornate and beautiful, and almost scintillates with similes in every verse; the poetry of the "Mahabharata" is plain and unpolished, and scarcely stoops to a simile, or a figure of speech unless the simile comes naturally to the poet. The great deeds of godlike kings sometimes suggest to the poet the mighty deeds of gods; the rushing of warriors suggests the rushing of angry elephants in the echoing jungle; the flight of whistling arrows suggests the flight of sea-birds; the sound and movement of surging crowds, the heaving of billows; the erect attitude of a warrior suggests a tall cliff; the beauty of a maiden suggests the soft beauty of the blue lotus. When such comparisons come naturally to the poet, he accepts them and notes them down, but he never seems to go in quest of them, he is never anxious to beautify and decorate. He seems to trust entirely to his grand narrative, to his heroic characters, to his stirring incidents, to hold millions of listeners in perpetual thrall. The majestic and sonorous Sanskrit metre is at his command, and even this he uses carelessly, and with frequent slips, known as *arsha* to later grammarians. The poet certainly seeks for no art to decorate his tale, he trusts to the lofty chronicle of bygone heroes to enchain the listening mankind.

And what heroes! In the delineation of character the "Mahabharata" is far above anything which we find in later Sanskrit poetry. Indeed, with much that is fresh and sweet and lovely in later Sanskrit poetry, there is little or no portraiture of character. All heroes are cast much in the same heroic mould; all love-sick heroines suffer in silence and burn with fever; all fools are shrewd and impudent by turns; all knaves are heartless and cruel, and suffer in the end. There is not much to distinguish between one warrior and another, between one tender woman and her sister. In the "Mahabharata" we find just the reverse; each hero has a distinct individuality, a character of his own, clearly discernible from that of other heroes. No work of the imagination that could be named, always excepting the "Iliad," is so rich and so true as the "Mahabharata" in the portraiture of the human character, not in torment and suffering as in Dante, not under overwhelming passions as in Shakespeare, but human character in its calm dignity of strength and repose, like those immortal figures in marble which the ancients turned out, and which modern sculptors have vainly sought to reproduce. The old Kuru monarch Dhrita-rashtra, sightless and feeble, but majestic in his ancient grandeur; the noble grandsire Bhishma, "death's subduer," and unconquerable in war; the doughty Drona, venerable priest and vengeful warrior, and the proud and peerless archer Karna, have each a distinct character of his own which cannot be mistaken for a moment. The good and royal Yudhishthir (I omit the final *a* in some long names which occur frequently), the "tiger-waisted" Bhima, and the "helmet-wearing" Arjun are the Agamemnon, the Ajax and the Achilles of the Indian Epic. The proud and unyielding Duryodhan, and the fierce and fiery Duhsasan stand out foremost among the wrathful sons of the feeble old Kuru monarch. And Krishna possesses a character higher than that of Ulysses; unmatched in human wisdom, ever striving for righteousness and peace, he is thorough and unrelenting in war when war has begun. And the women of the Indian Epic possess characters as marked as those of the men. The stately and majestic Queen Gandhari, the loving and doting mother Pritha, the proud and scornful Draupadi nursing her wrath till her wrongs are fearfully revenged, and the bright and brilliant and sunny Subhadra, these are distinct images pencilled by the hand of a true master in the realm of creative imagination.

And if the characters of the "Mahabharata" impress themselves on the reader, the incidents of the Epic are no less striking. Every scene on the shifting stage is a perfect and impressive picture. The tournament of the princes in which Arjun and Karna—the Achilles and Hector of the Indian Epic—first met, and each marked the other for his foe; the gorgeous bridal of Draupadi; the equally gorgeous coronation of Yudhishthir, and the death of the proud and boisterous Sisupala; the fatal game of dice, and the scornful wrath of Draupadi against her insulters; the calm beauty of the forest life of the Pandavs; the cattle-lifting in Matsyaland in which the gallant Arjun threw off his disguise and stood forth as warrior and conqueror; and the Homeric speeches of the warriors in the council of war on the eve of the great contest—each scene of this venerable old Epic impresses itself on the mind of the hushed and astonished reader. Then follows the war of eighteen days. The first few days are more or less uneventful, and have been condensed in this translation often into a few couplets; but the interest of the reader increases as he approaches the final battle and fall of the grand old fighter Bhishma. Then follows the stirring story of the death of Arjun's gallant boy, and Arjun's fierce revenge, and the death of the priest and warrior, doughty Drona. Last comes the crowning event of the Epic, the final contest between Arjun and Karna, the heroes of the Epic, and the war ends in a midnight slaughter, and the death of Duryodhan. The rest of the story is told in this translation in two books describing the funerals of the deceased warriors, and Yudhishthir's horse-sacrifice.

"The poems of Homer," says Mr. Gladstone, "differ from all other known poetry in this, that they constitute in themselves an encyclopædia of life and knowledge, at a time when knowledge, indeed, such as lies beyond the bounds of actual experience, was extremely limited, and when life was singularly fresh, vivid, and expansive." This remark applies with even greater force to the "Mahabharata"; it is an encyclopædia of the life and knowledge of ancient India. And it discloses to us an ancient and forgotten world, a proud and noble civilisation which has passed away.

For the rest, the people of modern India know how to appreciate their ancient heritage. It is not an exaggeration to state that the two hundred millions of Hindus of the present day cherish in their hearts the story of their ancient Epics. The Hindu scarcely lives, man or woman, high or low, educated or ignorant, whose earliest recollections do not cling round the story, and the characters of the great Epics. The almost illiterate oil manufacturer or confectioner of Bengal spells out some modern translation of the "Mahabharata" to while away his leisure hour. The tall and stalwart peasantry of the North-West know of the five Pandav brothers, and of their friend the righteous Krishna. The people of Bombay and Madras cherish with equal ardour the story of the righteous war. And even the traditions and tales interspersed in the Epic, and which spoil the work as an Epic, have themselves a charm and an attraction, and the morals inculcated in these tales sink into the hearts of a naturally religious people, and form the basis of their moral education. Mothers in India know no better theme for imparting wisdom and instruction to their daughters, and elderly men know no richer storehouse for narrating tales to children, than these stories preserved in the Epics. No work in Europe, not Homer in Greece, or Virgil in Italy, not Shakespeare or Milton in English-speaking lands, is the national property of the nations to the same extent as the Epics of India are of the Hindus. No single work except the Bible has such influence in affording moral instruction in Christian lands as the "Mahabharata" and the "Ramayana" in India. They have been the cherished heritage of the Hindus for three thousand years; they are to the present day interwoven with the thoughts and beliefs and moral ideas of a nation numbering two hundred millions.

The following extracts are from his epilogue to the "Ramayana":—

The "Ramayana," like the "Mahabharata," is the growth of centuries, but the main story is more distinctly the creation of one mind. The "Mahabharata" grew out of the legends and traditions of a great historical war between the Kurus and the Panchalas; the "Ramayana" grew out of the recollections of the golden age of the Kosalas and the Videhas. The characters of the "Mahabharata" are characters of flesh and blood, with the virtues and crimes of great actors in the historic world; the characters of the "Ramayana" are more often the ideals of manly devotion to truth, and of womanly faithfulness and love in domestic life. The poet of the "Mahabharata" relies on the real or supposed incidents of war handed down from generation to generation in songs and ballads, and weaves them into an immortal work of art; the poet of "Ramayana" conjures up the memories of a golden age, constructs lofty ideals of piety and faith, and describes with infinite pathos domestic scenes and domestic affections, which endear the work to modern Hindus. As an heroic poem the "Mahabharata" stands on a higher level; as a poem delineating the softer emotions of our everyday life, the "Ramayana" sends its roots deeper into the hearts and minds of the millions in India.

And yet, without rivalling the heroic grandeur of the "Mahabharata," the "Ramayana" is immeasurably superior in its delineation of those softer and perhaps deeper emotions which enter into our everyday life, and hold the world together. And these descriptions, essentially of Hindu life, are yet so true to nature that they apply to all races and nations.

There is something indescribably touching and tender in the description of the love of Rama for his subjects and the loyalty of his people towards Rama—that loyalty which has ever been a part of the Hindu character in every age. Deeper than this was Rama's duty towards his father and his father's fondness for Rama; and the portion of the Epic which narrates the dark scheme by which the prince was at last torn from the heart and home of his dying father is one of the most powerful and pathetic passages in Indian literature. The stepmother of Rama, won by the virtues and kindliness of the prince, regards his proposed coronation with pride and pleasure, but her old nurse creeps into her confidence like a creeping serpent, and envenoms her heart with the poison of her own wickedness. She arouses the slumbering jealousy of a woman and awakens the alarms of a mother, till—

> "Like a slow but deadly poison worked the ancient nurse's tears,
> And a wife's undying impulse mingled with a mother's fears!"

The nurse's dark insinuations work on the mind of the queen till she becomes a desperate woman, resolved to maintain her own influence on her husband, and to see her own son on the throne. The determination of the young queen tells with terrible effect on the weakness and vacillation of the feeble old monarch, and Rama is banished at last. And the scene closes with a pathetic story in which the monarch recounts his misdeed of past years, accepts his present suffering as the fruit of that misdeed, and dies in agony for his banished son. The inner workings of the human heart and of human motives, the dark intrigue of a scheming dependant, the awakening jealousy and alarm of a wife and a mother, the determination of a woman and an imperious queen, and the feebleness and despair and death of a fond old father and husband, have never been more vividly described. Shakespeare himself has not depicted the workings of stormy passions in the human heart more graphically or more vividly, with greater truth or with more terrible power.

It is truth and power in the depicting of such scenes, and not in the delineation of warriors and warlike incidents, that the "Ramayana" excels. It is in the delineation of domestic incidents, domestic affections and domestic jealousies, which are appreciated by the prince and peasant alike, that the "Ramayana" bases its appeal to the hearts of the millions in India. And beyond all this, the righteous devotion of Rama, and the faithfulness and womanly love of Sita, run like two threads of gold through the whole fabric of the Epic, and ennoble and sanctify the work in the eyes of the Hindus. Rama and Sita are the Hindu ideals of a perfect man and a perfect woman; their truth under trials and temptations, their endurance under privations, and their devotion to duty under all vicissitudes of fortune, form the Hindu ideal of a perfect life. And if trial and endurance are a part of a Hindu's ideal of a man's life, devotion and self-abnegation are still more essentially a part of his ideal of a woman's life. Sita holds a place in the hearts of women in India which no other creation of a poet's imagination holds among any other nation on earth. There is not a Hindu woman whose earliest and tenderest recollections do not cling round the story of Sita's sufferings and Sita's faithfulness, told in the nursery, taught in the family circle, remembered and cherished through life.

The ideal of life was joy and beauty and gladness in ancient Greece; the ideal of life was piety and endurance and devotion in ancient India. The tale of Helen was a tale of womanly beauty and loveliness which charmed the Western world. The tale of Sita was a tale of womanly faith and self-abnegation which charmed and fascinated the Hindu world.

The modern reader will now comprehend why India produced, and has preserved for well-nigh three thousand years, two Epics instead of one national Epic. No work of the imagination abides long unless it is animated by some sparks of imperishable truth, unless it truly embodies some portion of our human feelings, human faith and human life. The "Mahabharata" depicts the political life of ancient India, with all its valour and heroism, ambition and lofty chivalry. The "Ramayana" embodies the domestic and religious life of ancient India, with all its tenderness and sweetness, its endurance and devotion. The one picture without the other were incomplete; and we should know but little of the ancient Hindus if we did not comprehend their inner life and faith as well as their political life and their warlike virtues. The two together give us a true and graphic picture of ancient Indian life and civilisation; and no nation on earth has preserved a more faithful picture of its glorious past. To trace the influence of the Indian Epics on the life and civilisation of the nation, and on the development of their modern languages, literatures, and religious reforms, is to comprehend the real history of the people during three thousand years.

Professor Max Müller, in his introduction to Mr. Dutt's "Mahabharata," says:—

It is easy to see how round the nucleus of this war an immense mass of poetry, both popular and artificial, was accumulated, but it was not so easy a task to sift this enormous mass, and to extract from it what may have been the original story. This task has been boldly undertaken and carried through, as far as I can judge, with great success, by Mr. Romesh Dutt in his "Mahabharata" condensed into English verse. He has himself given an account of the principles by which he was guided in his work. He has, as much as possible, taken a number of verses of the original and rendered them faithfully into English. He has left out on the very largest scale, but he has not added; and the impression which his bold undertaking leaves on the reader, is certainly that something like what we here read in English may have been recited in India when the war between the Kurus and the sons of Pandu was first sung by the ancient bards of the country.

As a mine of information the "Mahabharata" is inexhaustible, and will for a long time remain unexhausted. We are all the more grateful to Mr. Romesh Dutt for having given us a kind of photographic representation, a snap-shot, as it were, of the old poem—the longest poem, I believe, in the whole world—and having enabled students of literature to form for themselves some kind of idea of what our Aryan brothers in India admired and still admire in the epic poetry of their country.

The translations were reviewed in most of the leading journals and reviews, and Mr. Dutt received many letters from distinguished literary men and his personal friends about them. He presented specially bound copies of both the "Mahabharata" and "Ramayana" to Queen Victoria, who in graciously accepting the present directed the following letter to be written to him:—

WINDSOR CASTLE, *8th March* 1899.

DEAR SIR,—I have laid before the Queen the copy of your "Epic of Ancient India" which you have been good enough to offer for Her Majesty's acceptance. I am desired to express to you the thanks of Her Majesty for this interesting work.—I am, dear Sir, yours very faithfully,

ARTHUR BIGGE.

From officials connected with the Indian Administration he received the following letters:—

6th April 1900.

DEAR MR. ROMESH DUTT,—I am much obliged to you for sending me a copy of the epic "Ramayana" in English. The "Mahabharata," into which I occasionally dipped, was very instructive, as bringing before me the peculiar ideal which the Hindu race tried to cultivate and attain.

I was very glad to be able to allude to you in the recent debate in the House of Commons, as I shall always be glad to

hear from one of your exceptional experience and moderation, and who, whilst anxious to improve British administration in India, does not depreciate its best work.—Believe me, yours truly,
GEORGE HAMILTON.

MY DEAR MR. DUTT,—I have to thank you for the handsomely bound volume of your work, "Epic of Ancient India," which you so kindly sent me. I will read it with utmost pleasure. Your labour and trouble in translating such a classical poem will be repaid, for it will bring home to many, who before were wholly ignorant of the fact, what Indian civilisation and literature were when we were comparative savages.—Believe me, yours truly,
GEORGE HAMILTON.

LAHORE, *25th April* 1900.

DEAR MR. DUTT,—Let me thank you for the very dainty companion volume to that which I already possess. It has reached me by the last mail. The presentation of these ancient Epics, in a readable and therefore a condensed form, to European readers is in the nature of a public service. It acquaints English students with a good many of the bases of Indian history, thought, religions, and life, and helps to strip off the mask from the mysterious and sometimes almost unintelligible features of the past.—Yours faithfully,
CURZON.

24th September 1898.

DEAR MR. ROMESH DUTT,—Your letter has just reached me, and I hasten to say that it will give me much pleasure that you should dedicate to me your translation of the "Mahabharata." I am gratified by your wish to do so.—Believe me, yours very truly,
RIPON.

From the Lieutenant-Governor of Bengal :—

3rd January 1901.

DEAR MR. DUTT,—The last mail brought me a beautiful copy of the new edition of your "Epics," and I hasten to thank you. The gift would have been complete with the author's signature, and I hope some day that may be added to it.

Your labour must be amply repaid; not yet have the great Indian epics been presented to the English in a form so winning. Everything that makes us know more of each other makes us like each other better, and I thank you for your share in this best of works.

With my best wishes for the new year, and renewed thanks for your beautiful gift,—Believe me, yours very sincerely,

J. WOODBURN.

Amongst acknowledgments from men of letters the following will be of interest :—

THE ATHENÆUM, *27th June* 1899.

MY DEAR SIR,—I duly received your kind note, and to-day I have the pretty volume, for which pray accept my best thanks. I have hastily sampled the contents. I find everywhere musical and accomplished verse, which I shall read carefully and with interest when I get into the country. I will then write my impressions and thanks. I think it is doing a great service to English readers to familiarise them with the great Indian epics, which have been the delight of so many generations of mortal men, and for me in particular everything connected with India has especial interest. Thanking you again for your kind gift,—I remain, yours very truly, LEWIS MORRIS.

21st April 1899.

DEAR SIR,—I can assure you that I am much honoured by your letter, and greatly gratified by having presented to me so charming a volume. It is certainly on the face of it one of the most graceful books of the time, and I congratulate you on the taste and judgment of its general form.

Absorbed as I am now with pressing matters, I have only been able to sip passages in leisure half-hours ; but I am already much struck with the vigour and grace of your verses, and with the ease and harmony of the rhythm. Like so many others, I am only a believer on trust of the merits of the "Mahabharata," and have never had the courage to face its immense cantos for myself. I shall read your work through with great expectation and interest, and will write to you again when I have so done.—Yours very truly, FREDERIC HARRISON.

PARKSTONE, DORSET,
1st March 1899.

DEAR SIR,—I thank you very much for sending me your beautiful translation of the "Mahabharata," which I have heard much of, but have never before become acquainted with. If, as you say, your translation is almost a literal one, it is indeed a great poem. I am surprised at the clear sequence of the story, which is in itself interesting, but more especially in the force and simplicity of the language and the beautiful, often poetical and lofty ideas.

I must also express my admiration of your beautiful, poetical, and rhythmical version in what is to you a foreign tongue. It is perfectly clear and harmonious, and is a pleasure to read; and I am sure that, if better known, it would become a favourite with English readers. I only regret that it has not been issued in a more worthy form, with better paper and a little more margin. You have showed excellent judgment in giving what you do translate in full, with brief connecting prose summaries. I think, however, you should give in notes, or in a glossary at the end, the meaning of the various untranslated Sanskrit words you introduce in your translation. Also the proper names are so numerous that I think, at the commencement of each book, the names of all the persons mentioned should be given, with their positions, titles, and relationships, as in the *dramatis personæ* of a play. I should like to see a new edition, with illustrations of the chief scenes like that you have as a frontispiece.

I seldom go to London now, but shall have great pleasure in receiving a visit from you here, should you ever be in the vicinity.—Believe me, yours very truly,

ALFRED WALLACE.

PARKSTONE, DORSET,
8th March 1899.

MY DEAR SIR,—Very many thanks for the copy of the large edition of your translation of the "Mahabharata." It is very elegant and well worthy of the great poem, and I hope will have a large sale. I waited to finish reading the poem before writing to you, and I have also read the earlier books over again with even greater pleasure than at first. One wants to know the characters and all the chief ideas of such a poem before it can be duly appreciated, hence a second reading is necessary. I have noted, while reading, a number of places where I think the wording can be improved or the meaning better expressed, and also a few press errors. I enclose you notes of all these, with new readings suggested in many cases, which I hope may be of use to you in correcting for a new edition.

The "Story of Savitri" is the gem of the whole poem, and I cannot recall anything in poetry more beautiful, or any higher teaching as to the sanctity of love and marriage. We have really not advanced one step beyond this old-world people in our ethical standards. How fine and lofty, too, is Krishna's exposition of a king's duties at the end of Book III. Draupadi's plaint and Dhrita-Rashtra's kindness are also very fine, and the acceptance of slavery by these warlike princes on a point of honour is grand, though we may consider it excessive.

The least satisfactory part of the poem is the fact of Draupadi, after having accepted Arjun, becoming the wife of Judhishthir. Considering her character, that seems very extraordinary. Was she married to Arjun or Judhishthir? I cannot believe that she became the wife of five in common. I wish you had translated the main part of the wedding ceremony. Also the great game of dice, which must surely lend itself to some fine poetry. But, even as you give it, it is a grand poem.—Believe me, yours very faithfully, ALFRED WALLACE.

24th June 1899.

DEAR SIR,—I thank you heartily for your gift of the interesting abridgment of the "Mahabharata," which you have been good enough to send me. I am reading it with much enjoyment, having long had a great curiosity to know something of the famous Indian Epic, and being debarred by my ignorance of Sanskrit from studying it in the original. You have rendered no small service to English lovers of primitive literature in enabling us to form an idea of the great Oriental parallel to the "Iliad."

If as I go on I find that any of the observations which occur to me in reading your spirited version seem worthy of being conveyed to you, I will write them to you.—Believe me, faithfully yours, JAMES BRYCE.

As examples of the many criticisms to which the translations gave rise, we may quote the following from the *Journal of the Royal Asiatic Society* (July 1899):—

It should be judged as a literary effort, not as historical criticism. And as literary effort, it is certainly a very great success. A generous admiration for the original, and a warm sympathy with its tone, a striking command of vigorous and flowing and idiomatic English, a fine sense of rhythm, and a real power of poetic imagination have combined to render this selection just what it is intended to be—a most interesting and attractive way of introducing to English readers what the author considers to be the essence of the grand old Indian poem.

CHAPTER XVIII

PRESIDENT OF THE NATIONAL CONGRESS

MR. DUTT was elected to be the President of the Fifteenth Indian National Congress held at Lucknow in December 1899. On his nomination the *Indian Nation* remarked :—"A better selection could not be made. By his learning, experience, position, sobriety, and soundness of judgment, he seems to be specially marked out for the honour which it has been decided to confer upon him." The *Tribune* observed :—"Now the whole country will have the opportunity of showing its sense of appreciation of his devoted labours, and we doubt not but that it will rise to the occasion."

Some surprise was felt, and not a little hostile criticism levelled at Mr. Dutt for accepting the Presidentship of the Indian National Congress. But Mr. Dutt had always the courage of his convictions. As he explained in his presidential speech, he honestly believed—

> That the National Congress is the only body in India which seeks to represent the views and aspirations of the people of India as a whole in all large and important and imperial questions of administration, and thus does a service to Government the value of which cannot be over-estimated. It is a gain to the administration to know what we feel and what we think and what we desire, though our demands cannot always be conceded. It is a help to responsible administrators to know in what direction our wishes and aspirations tend, though they may not always agree with us. I honestly believe, therefore, that you are helping the cause of good administration and good government in India by your deliberations year after year.

And he was not the only retired servant of Government who saw in the Indian National Congress a legitimate and highly useful and patriotic organisation deserving of the sympathy and careful consideration of Government. In 1896, no less a personage than Sir Richard Garth, a retired Chief Justice of the highest judicial tribunal in India, considered it necessary to defend this movement from the attack of Sir George Chesney in language much more forcible and unrestrained than that of Mr. Dutt. "There is no subject, I consider, upon which the English Press and the English public have been so cruelly and persistently misled," said Sir Richard. And again :—

The Indian National Congress is a large, influential, and important assembly of earnest and patriotic gentlemen who, since 1885, have at the close of each year met at one or other of the large centres in India, such as Calcutta, Madras, or Bombay, to discuss their political views and opinions. They consist of delegates from every part of India who are duly elected at a number of divisional headquarters. We are told that at the Congress meeting in Allahabad in the year 1888, fully three millions of men took a direct part in the election of these delegates, who themselves numbered no fewer than 1248. The constitution of this important body was thoroughly representative; it consisted of Princes, Rajahs, Nawabs, fifty-four members of noble families, Fellows of Universities, members of Local Boards, and professional men, such as engineers, merchants, bankers, journalists, landed proprietors, shopkeepers, clergymen, priests, Professors of Colleges, zamindars, and others.

I will tell you what they have done. They have dared to think for themselves, and not only for themselves, but for the millions of poor ignorant people who compose our Indian Empire. They have been content to sacrifice their own interests, and to brave the displeasure of Government in order to lend a helping hand to those poor people. They have had the courage and the patriotism to denounce abuses which have been condemned by public opinion in India and in England, and to which the Indian Government appear to cling with a tenacity which seems utterly inexplicable. They have dared to propose reforms which, despite the resistance of the Government, have been approved by Parliament, and to endeavour to stay that fearful amount of extravagance which has been going on in India for years past, and has been the means, as some of our best and wisest counsellors consider, of bringing our Eastern Empire on the verge of bankruptcy.

Mr. Dutt's presidential address received unanimous praise both for its substance and its tone from critics of all phases of political opinion. It was taken up chiefly with the consideration of economic and agrarian topics relating to the welfare of the masses, but questions of administrative and fiscal reforms also passed under his comprehensive survey. These views will find a place in a subsequent section. The Anglo-Indian press was hardly less complimentary than the Indian. The *Englishman* said:—

The public always expect something good from Mr. Romesh Dutt, and in his address at Lucknow, as President of the Congress, it has not been disappointed. We hope later to have an opportunity of examining this able and moderate address at greater length. In the meantime, in these days of famine, the observations of so experienced an administrator as Mr. Dutt on the chronic poverty and indebtedness of a large proportion of the rural population in India call for more than passing notice.

The *Statesman,* in the course of a long leading article, said:—

While we miss from the presidential address, delivered yesterday at the annual meeting of the Indian National Congress at Lucknow, the glowing periods we have become accustomed to look for on these occasions, Mr. Romesh Chunder Dutt's speech is very far from being either characterless or ineffective. Taking it as a whole, perhaps the most noteworthy feature of the address is the tone of calm assurance that pervades it. Not only is Mr. Dutt convinced that the phase of reaction through which Indian administration is at the moment unfortunately passing is destined to prove ephemeral, but he feels confident that, in spite of it, the value of the work that is being done by the Congress is appreciated by the Government. That such a conviction should be entertained by a man of Mr. Dutt's large experience, is enough in itself to show how great an advance has been made since the time, not so very distant, when the Congress was denounced by nine officials out of ten as a centre of disloyalty. But though the President took what to many of his hearers may not improbably have seemed an optimistic view of the situation, and though he declared the main object of his address to be practical suggestion rather than criticism, he was sufficiently outspoken in his condemnation both of the recent backslidings and some of the chronic defects of British policy in India.

The *Statesman* then went on to support Mr. Dutt's views on the land revenue assessment and its relation to famines, and his proposal that Indians should be admitted to the Executive Councils, a proposal adopted ten years later by Lord Morley.

The correspondent of the *Pioneer* wrote (3rd January 1900) :—

Mr. Dutt, who it must be remembered is the only Indian gentleman who has ever attained to the rank of Commissioner in the Indian Civil Service, and who held that position for many years, is a tall, commanding-looking man, with an impressive personality and particularly intellectual physiognomy. His delivery is quiet, but intensely convincing. The impression at once conveyed by it is that Mr. Dutt most thoroughly believes in the truth of whatever he may be speaking, and that he is resolved that his hearers shall do the same. . . . It was a very interesting speech ; and as thoughtful and carefully prepared in its subject matter as it was eloquent and convincing in its delivery.

The *Times of India* (1st January 1900) :—

We have nothing but praise for the general tone of Mr. Romesh Chunder Dutt's admirable presidential address at the Lucknow meeting of the Indian National Congress. It was restrained in language, moderate in the aspirations it expressed, and evidently animated by a sincere desire to offer friendly and helpful criticism upon the policy of the British administration in India. Disagreement from many of Mr. Dutt's opinions need not prevent us from recognising the calm attention he has brought to bear upon the important questions he discussed. Two years' intimate acquaintance with some of the best phases of public life in England, acting upon a habit of mind already moulded by long experience of administrative work, seems to have enabled him to ascend from the ordinary Congress level of heated controversy to a cooler point of outlook. If all the orators who make the Congress hall ring with their bitter harangues could absorb something of the temperate spirit of Mr. Dutt, there would be less disposition in other quarters to condemn the tendencies and the influence of the Congress—so far as it has any influence at all.

Madras Standard (27th December) :—

Public opinion with one voice will, we are sure, declare that none was greater than the address delivered by the President of the Fifteenth Indian National Congress. With characteristic modesty, Mr. Dutt says that his speech is "the plain words of a plain man," and indeed if this means the methodical marshalling of facts and the most powerful arguing from incontrovertible data, the description he gives of his speech is apt. Mr. Dutt uses his facts and arguments not for the purpose of criticism, but to prove the soundness of his own remarks and suggestions.

India (29th December 1899) :—

That he has a command of the English tongue such as most Englishmen seek in vain is true. But he is far from having thereby lost his kinship with the people of India, and he has taken as the main subject of his address, not the many real grievances of his educated countrymen, not even the evils which directly affect all classes, *but the wrongs and sufferings of the agricultural population.* It was a wise choice; for there is no one better able to deal with it; and there is no question which more profoundly touches the well-being of India. . . .

But all who admire sound sense beautifully expressed will do well to read the whole speech for themselves. Mr. Dutt is one of those rare men who can keep an even mind amid conflicting motives. His official career has not made him draw away from his own people. His ardour for the popular cause has not made him forget the lessons of his official experience. While India has such leaders, who shall say that her hopes are vain?

The remarkable effect of this speech, in setting an example in moderation and sobriety, was not lost on future Presidents; and the change in the tone of the Anglo-Indian press was, for a time at least, no less remarkable. An illustration of this was afforded, a year later, when Mr. (afterwards Sir Narian) Chandravarkar presided over the National Congress at Lahore. The *Times of India* on that occasion spoke of the Congress and its President in terms of respect which contrasted strikingly with the ordinary comments of the Anglo-Indian press, before Mr. Dutt's address had compelled their admiration, and, it must be confessed, with the customary attacks of later years.

No one can read the report of the address delivered at the opening of the Lahore Congress yesterday, by the Hon. Mr. Chandravarkar, without feeling that the deliberations of that body claim the respectful attention of all—whether Englishmen or natives, officials or non-officials—who are interested in the well-being of India. That proposition may be laid down upon the broad general ground, that it is foolish and unjust for any intelligent person to turn aside with indifference from any reasoned statement of the opinions of any man, or class of men, who in good faith, and in command of authentic sources of information, endeavour to enlist public interest in the well-being of the country.

As regards the spirit of Mr. Dutt's address and his perfectly loyal attitude to Government, there was thus no question, though as regards the substance of his charges against the Indian administration, specially on the connection which he traced between the Land Revenue policy of Government and famines, there were naturally various dissentient voices, both official and non-official. Mr. Dutt's views and the criticisms which were offered against them will be considered in detail in later sections. I shall only mention here the criticism of his speech made by the Secretary of State, Lord George Hamilton, in an address before the Northbrook Society.

I read the other day a remarkable speech by no unfriendly critic of British administration in India. He admitted frankly and fully that British administration had conferred great benefits on India and that it was conducted for the people; but he wished to substitute another phase, that government in India should be conducted by the people.

Mr. Dutt was not slow in defending his standpoint.

I am much flattered by this allusion to my speech by a friendly critic [said he], but may I ask permission to point out that nowhere in my speech have I proposed to substitute the present form of government in India by a system of government by the people? I stated that administration for the people, not by the people, had failed in Europe; but I added that the conditions of India are different, and I admit freely and fully that we want a strong centralised government here. In that strong centralised government I desired to have some representation of the popular element; I proposed the appointment of one Indian member in each Provincial Executive Council, and of three Indian members in the Viceroy's Executive Council, so that the Viceroy, who has the benefit of consulting experienced English administrators in his Executive Council, should also have the advantage of hearing the views and opinions of a few Indian members in the same Council before he decides on questions affecting the interests of the people of India. This proposal of mine may be acceptable to the authorities, or it may not; but the proposal certainly does not amount to substituting the present form of government in India by a system of government by the people.

At the close of the Congress Mr. Dutt was entertained to dinner at the Prince of Wales Hotel, Lucknow, by Nawab Mehdi Hasan Fateh Nawaz Jung, who was one of the speakers at the Anti-Congress demonstration held about the same time. In the course of the after-dinner speech, in which he proposed the health of the delegates, coupled with the name of Mr. Dutt, the Nawab said :—

Although he was separated from his hearers on political questions, he was glad to give an hospitable welcome to the leaders of the Congress, several of whom, including the President, he had had the pleasure and privilege of knowing for many years, and all of whom represented the feelings of a large section of the educated community. While he disagreed with many of their views, he would have been very sorry indeed to have associated himself with the petition to the Lieutenant-Governor, asking His Honour to disallow the Congress to be held in Lucknow, for they were fully entitled to set forth their opinions and had every right to claim an hospitable welcome from a city inhabited by men of the Muhammadan faith whose hospitality was proverbial.

On the 6th of January Raja Binay Krishna invited Mr. Dutt to an evening party at his house in Calcutta, and gave him a great ovation. Mr. Oldham, Member of the Board of Revenue, the Hon. Mr. Justice Gurudas Banerjea, Raja Pyari Mohan Mukerjea, and other leading citizens of Calcutta were present.

Mr. Dutt had a long audience with Lord Curzon on

his return to Calcutta, and pressed two points upon the Viceroy. In the first place he pleaded for some reasonable limits to the Government demand from land, both in Raiyatwari and in Zamindari tracts—limits which would control the operations of Settlement Officers, and could be enforced by impartial tribunals. Lord Curzon listened courteously to the facts and arguments urged, promised to give them consideration, but was not prepared with an immediate reply. In the second place Mr. Dutt pleaded for some share for his countrymen in the control and direction of the administration, some room in the Executive Councils of the Viceroy and of the Provinces. There was some debate on this point, and Lord Curzon closed it by asking the question which he has often asked since: "After all, is not the rule of one man the best form of rule for India?"

Mr. Dutt followed up his verbal representations with five open letters to Lord Curzon, written from February to May 1900, on Land Assessment in India. The five letters dealt with the Central Provinces, Madras, Bombay, Bengal, and Northern India respectively. His Congress speech and these open letters fairly launched him into that memorable controversy about Land Settlements and the poverty of the agricultural classes, which engaged him during most of his stay in Europe.

On the 23rd February 1900, a great demonstration was held in Calcutta, and Mr. W. C. Bonnerjea, on behalf of the citizens of Calcutta, presented him with an address, the important passages of which were as follows:—

We are aware that one of the principal reasons of your early retirement from the Indian Civil Service was a desire to be more useful to your country, and an anxiety to direct the attention of our rulers to the aspirations and grievances of the people of India from a position of greater freedom. The way in which you have employed your time since your retirement has fully justified the wisdom of that step. You have, within a short time, done much, through the press and the platform, to inform the enlightened public opinion in England on some of the most momentous questions of Indian administration. . . . For these

CHAPTER XIX

1900 AND 1901

"FAMINES" AND "ECONOMIC HISTORY"

I

I HAVE hardly arrived here before I find myself in the very thick of my work. There was an important debate in the House of Commons two days ago, about the Indian famine and land assessments referred to in my Congress speech.

The debate of which Mr. Dutt speaks in this passage took place on the night of the 3rd April, when Sir William Wedderburn moved that :—

In view of the grievous sufferings which are again afflicting the people of India, and the extreme impoverishment of large masses of the population, a searching inquiry should be instituted in order to ascertain the causes which impair the cultivators' power to resist the attacks of famine and plague, and to suggest the best preventive measures against future famines.

In the course of this debate Mr. J. M. Maclean observed :—

They all acknowledged that the Indian Government was doing exceedingly good work in coping with the famine. But what they complained of was, that it had become the habit of the Indian Government and the India Office too much to treat any famine that occurred in India as an act of God for which nobody was responsible, to say that there were no deep-seated causes which brought about famines of this kind, and that those causes ought not to be inquired into with the view of providing a permanent remedy for this deplorable state of things.

It was also during this debate that Lord George Hamilton said:—

A good deal of the speeches that had been made had been devoted to the question of land assessment, and the member for Flint had reproduced several of the arguments and figures which a well-known Bengal gentleman, Mr. Romesh Dutt, recently used in a speech delivered by him as President of the National Congress. Mr. Dutt was a gentleman who had served with distinction in the Indian Civil Service. He had the pleasure of his acquaintance. He had communicated with him on various matters, and when, therefore, he saw that Mr. Dutt had made definite statements of fact in order to show that the land assessments in certain parts of India were too high, he at once paid the most careful attention and gave the most careful investigation to these figures and statements.

The Secretary of State's criticisms of Mr. Dutt's statements, and Mr. Dutt's reply, will be referred to later.

Another capable and well-informed critic, Sir A. MacDonnell, now Lord MacDonnell, in closing the debate upon the United Provinces budget for 1899–1900, also challenged some of the statements made by Mr. Dutt in his Congress speech. Reference has been made to these criticisms also in the section on Mr. Dutt's economic views.

Apart from any direct benefit to the country which Mr. Dutt might have rendered by calling the attention of the ruling authorities to these grave and important agrarian problems, the Indian public appreciated the indirect advantages that must arise by so able an advocacy of their cause. Even the *Pioneer* was appreciative:—

Mr. Dutt has set in motion an interesting and instructive controversy. It is not every one who can induce a Lieutenant-Governor to take up a challenge publicly thrown down.

And Mr. Dutt was not the man to let the grass grow under his feet.

The whole official world in England and India [he wrote to his brother] is overwhelmed by my charge against the Indian

Government about over-assessments of lands. I hear that the India Office here is quite upset, and is looking up figures and documents. I will give them no rest, but will prove the charge to the hilt. I am going to bring out a popular and readable book on the subject, including my letters to Curzon and a lot of valuable documents and proofs. That book will be in the hands of every Englishman and every Indian who wishes to study the Indian land questions.

II

In July 1900 the book styled "Famines in India" appeared, and Mr. Dutt distributed the book widely to public men of all shades of public opinion with a covering letter :—

I feel persuaded that Englishmen of all parties are anxious to take effective measures to prevent, as far as is humanly possible, such terrible calamities in the future. It is in the hope of indicating the real causes of the poverty and wretchedness of the Indian cultivator and labourer, and of suggesting means to improve their condition and making them more resourceful and self-relying, that I have published this work in the present year. And I trust that the present century will not expire without some steps being taken, as was done in the last century, to improve the condition of the people of India.

Many appreciative and able criticisms of the book appeared. Of the important part it played in educating the British democracy to take interest in Indian subjects, the *Daily Chronicle* observed :—

The great extent and severity of the present famine, following so rapidly upon that of 1896–7, conclusively shows that something requires to be done towards preventing famines in India. What that something is the English democracy, knowing little of India, cannot be expected to divine. But we are all aware nowadays that without the driving force of the democracy behind, a government does nothing. The Cabinet Minister shuffles his responsibility on to the shoulders of the "man in the street." It is necessary, therefore, for the man in the street to learn something about Indian famines, their cause and remedy, in order that he may cast the weight of his vote into the proper scale. For this purpose nothing could be better than the book on Indian famines which Mr. Dutt has just published in the form of some open letters to Lord Curzon. It is thoroughly informed, well-reasoned and temperate; it tells the inquiring man exactly what he ought to know.

The same paper praised the moderation of Mr. Dutt's demands :—

Mr. Dutt is wise; he has learnt the wisdom of moderation. There was a time when his panacea for famines was a permanent settlement for the whole of India, but that was a hopelessly Utopian project which he has now discarded as being outside the region of immediate possibility. Englishmen, who are a practical race themselves, will commend this evidence of practicality in Mr. Dutt. He now contents himself with setting up the more moderate standard of Northern India. That is a perfectly fair and reasonable proposal. What the Government does in two provinces, which are not thereby made too prosperous, should be done in the remainder of India. It may be argued that the Government must have the revenue somehow, and if it does not fall on the people in one way it will in another. But a sufficient saving could be effected by treating the Indian Army on its proper footing, as part of the Imperial Army. We are now paying 5s. a day to Australian troops in South Africa, but until recently we refused the Indian soldier his ordinary pay of 3d. a day when serving outside India, and even now, in times of peace, we make India pay for Imperial as well as local necessities. These are some of the inequalities in our government of India which Mr. Dutt rightly lays bare, while his statement is not so partisan as to cause distrust in his judgment.

The *Times* had the following notice of the book :—

Mr. R. C. Dutt's volume is extremely opportune at the present time, and his position, that an excessive land tax renders the agricultural population unable to face two or three successive years of drought, calls at least for careful examination. The subject is one upon which it is difficult to dogmatise, not only owing to the various circumstances of the geographical and political divisions of the Indian continent, but because there is unlimited scope for individual discretion in enforcing systems which in themselves differ widely in different provinces. It is, however, most desirable that the main features should be succinctly stated within a reasonable compass, and without technical details. Should Mr. Dutt succeed in eliciting from the

Indian Government a brief and popular answer, he will have done much service to a cause which he and all friends of India must have at heart, even though some of his positions may be shaken.

The *Manchester Guardian*:—

> The practical value of the letters lies perhaps in their specific suggestions for reform rather than in the exposition they give of the working of the system criticised. One of the gravest defects inherent in the rent doctrine, and one with which Mr. Dutt only partially deals, is that it affords a stimulus instead of a check to expenditure. And in the case of India the expenditure lies outside the country, and the existence of an automatic incitement to extravagance strikes at any hope of fiscal balance and sanity.

The *Daily News* quoted the authority of the Finance Member of the Bombay Council (1900), who said, "Bombay has been accustomed to poverty, but such dire grinding destitution as we are now suffering from is simply overwhelming"; also of Sir William Hunter, who in the Viceroy's Council declared, "The fundamental difficulty in relieving the peasantry of Deccan arose from the fact that the assessments did not leave enough food for the cultivator to support himself and family withal throughout the year"; and, further, of Sir Charles Elliott, "The majority of the Indian cultivators do not know from year's end to year's end what it is to have their hunger satisfied." It then observed, "The famine question resolves itself into a question of reform and reconstruction in every department of the Indian service, and first and chiefly in the system, or rather systems, of rent and revenue."

As examples of the high intellectual standpoint of Anglo-Indian journalism may be quoted the criticisms which appeared in the columns of the *Pioneer* and the *Civil and Military Gazette*. The former remarked:—

> Mr. Romesh Chunder Dutt, C.I.E., is indebted to the Government of the Empress for position, income, and decoration; yet he does not find it inconsistent with his self-respect to promulgate false impressions about the administration of that Government of India which would amount to a political danger if they were not open to the readiest possible correction.

The *Civil and Military Gazette* said :—

But for British rule in India, Mr. Dutt, with all his ability, could not have hoped to rise above the position, perhaps, of Amil under some Muhammadan or Mahratta Sardar. His salary might have been 50 rupees a month with pickings. To the British Government he owes education, opportunity, high office, dignity, large pension, and the freedom to malign it.

Here are some of the opinions of private friends and critics. Prince Kropotkin wrote :—

Thank you very much for the book. It is one of those which are sure to produce a deep impression. . . . The conditions of your agricultural populations are awfully, terribly similar to those of Russian peasants, and I now will often think that whatever we do in Russia, for awaking the consciousness of the agrarian evil—and anywhere in Europe as well—will be in an indirect way for hundreds of millions of people whom we cannot approach without feeling love for them.

Lord Curzon, who was then Viceroy of India, wrote :—

SIMLA, *30th August* 1900.

DEAR MR. DUTT,—I have received the copy of your book which you have been good enough to send me. It will be most useful to me to have in so concise a form a reasonable and well informed statement of the views of the school of opinions whom you represent. . . . —Yours faithfully, CURZON.

The following is from Sir John B. Phear :—

MARPOOL, W. EXMOUTH,
15th August 1900.

DEAR MR. ROMESH CHUNDER DUTT,—Pray accept my very cordial thanks for the copy of your very valuable book "Famines in India," with which you have kindly presented me. It deals with a subject, namely, Government Revenue, in which I have always taken considerable interest, and it is impossible, I think, to exaggerate the importance of the economic questions which you invite the Government to solve. I quite acquiesce in the view presented by you in the last sentence of your preface.

India is plainly suffering from impoverishment caused by the *continuous* drain out of the country of industrious products without return, the burden of which by reason of the revenue system falls mainly on the cultivating peasant. To moderate the drain means to lessen the gain of the foreign ruling class—to re-adjust the land revenue system or rather systems, and to put them upon a fair and equitable footing throughout, means to diminish the total revenue, and to render great reduction of expenditure necessary. Who is prepared to undertake or to initiate this double task?

I see only too clearly the magnitude of the existing evil; but I confess that I am not sanguine as to any serious abatement of it being effected under a non-parliamentary Government.—Believe me, dear Mr. Dutt, with reiteration of thanks, yours very truly,

J. B. PHEAR.

From the late Chief-Justice of Bengal:—

DEAR SIR,—I congratulate you heartily upon the book you have lately published, "Famines in India." I sincerely hope that it may be thoroughly read and appreciated both here and in India. If you will allow me to say so, I think you have been far too merciful to the Government of India and your branch of the service. But for the selfish and utterly mistaken greed and avarice of the Government, and their persistent obstinacy in clinging to the old system of temporary settlements, famines would have become far less severe, if they had not in great measure disappeared long ago. . . . I hope the Indian Press will take the question up, and the English Press too, but the latter are so lukewarm upon Indian matters that I fear it is no use to look for any help from them.—Yours truly,

RICHARD GARTH.

From a former Secretary to the Bengal Government:—

DEAR MR. DUTT,—I have to thank you for a copy of your excellent book on "Famines in India," which I have read with great pleasure and interest. You make out an unanswerable case, which is all the stronger for the moderation with which it is put forward. I am inclined to lay stress upon this, as I think that the diatribes of such reformers as Mr. Hyndman offend equally against good taste and accuracy of fact, and thus do more harm than good. Your book (like your Presidential Address to the Congress) is entirely free from this blemish, and must commend itself to the sober judgment of all who take an interest in the subject.

You are quite right in putting excessive land revenue assessments in the foreground as a main cause of the impoverishment of India, *both because it is well to concentrate attention upon one much needed reform, and because reduction of land assessment must necessarily lead to retrenchment in expenditure.* I have long been of opinion that the Permanent Settlement ought to be made general throughout India (except perhaps in some specially backward provinces); but I fear there is little prospect of this. But I should hope that your book will have some influence upon Lord Curzon, who, with all his faults, is at least a strong Viceroy with a will and policy of his own. . . . —Believe me to remain most sincerely yours, H. J. REYNOLDS.

MY DEAR SIR,—I am much obliged to you for a copy of your book on Indian famines. It is a subject which I, in common with all serious Englishmen, view with deep despondency and almost with despair. But it is also a subject on which I have no personal knowledge. . . .—I am yours faithfully, FREDERIC HARRISON.

PARKSTONE, DORSET,
1st August 1900.

DEAR SIR,—Many thanks for sending me your book on "Famines in India"; with its numerous appendices and statistics, it is of great value, and will be an indispensable book of reference on various questions relating to the social and economic condition of India, and our (mis)government of it.—Yours very truly, ALFRED R. WALLACE.

III

Professor Max Müller died on the 29th October 1900, and on November 23rd Mr. Dutt, at the English Goethe Society, delivered a short address. In the course of the speech he said:—

I do not exaggerate facts, Sir, when I state that, for a period of half a century, my countrymen have looked upon Professor Max Müller not only as the best interpreter of ancient Indian literature and philosophy and religious thought in Europe, but also the truest friend of the people of modern India. For half a century they have watched his literary labours with admiration;

they have hailed his noble vindication of modern India with gratitude; and they have regarded him with feelings of affection and of love, heightened by the long distance from which they contemplated his sympathetic work. And the few of my countrymen who had the privilege of approaching him and knowing him personally, have found in him a true and devoted friend.

On the 20th November he wrote an important letter to the Government of India, reviewing some of the principles laid down in the Government Resolution of the 5th October on the Nagpur Settlement.

His last act of the year was the joint memorial which he, together with several well-known Anglo-Indian officials, presented to the Secretary of State on the 21st December, praying for a limitation of land tax in India. On the 20th he wrote home to his friend, Mr. B. L. Gupta: "I am trying also to get a few retired civilians to join me in a moderate and respectful representation to the Secretary of State on this subject. Reynolds, late Secretary of Bengal, agrees with me exactly, and he and some others have promised to join me."

But, in spite of the busy life he led, he did not find it easy to suppress the promptings of his heart for his home and the dear ones he had left behind.

4th January 1901.

MY DEAREST KAMALA,— . . . I was amused to read of baby's taking kindly to Mr. Sen, mistaking him for me. It will be a happy day indeed for me when I am able to come and be amongst all your children again. And I am resolved it must be next winter, if not earlier. I am not happy, even in the midst of all my work, separated from all of you. I feel lonely at times, and think that life was never meant to be all work and no social and domestic enjoyment.—I am, your loving father,

ROMESH.

At the end of 1900 he spent a few days in Wales and was a guest of Lord Stanley of Alderley, and early in January he went to Sir John Phear's splendid place in Devonshire. Sir John was a good Liberal, and he organised two meetings, at which Mr. Dutt spoke.

The one was at Exeter, where he spoke on "Famines and their Causes and Remedies," Sir John Phear taking the chair, and the other at Exmouth.

He was elected delegate by the Lewisham Liberal and Radical Club to the general meeting of the National Liberal Federation held at Rugby. At one of the sessions of the Federation, on the motion of Mr. Dutt, seconded by Miss Garland, it was resolved :—

That this meeting deplores the succession of severe famines which have caused the deaths of millions of people in India in recent years, and considers it necessary to prevent the recurrence of such severe calamities by moderating the land tax, extending irrigation works, and relieving as far as possible the annual burdensome drain on the financial resources of India, which impoverishes the people of that country.

A Conference of all the Indians resident in the United Kingdom was held in the Westminster Palace Hotel, under the presidency of Mr. Dadabhai Naoroji, on the 24th May 1901, when resolutions about the financial and agrarian poverty in India were discussed. Mr. Dutt was present, and made a speech.

On Monday, 24th June 1901, Mr. Dutt joined in the discussion that followed the reading of a paper by Mr. S. S. Thorburn, late Financial Commissioner of the Punjab, entitled "Agricola Redivivus," describing the genesis and history of the Punjab Land Alienation Act. The Right Hon. Leonard Courtney presided, and amongst those present were Lord Reay, Lord Stanley of Alderley, Sir James Lyall, Sir Charles Stevens, and others. Mr. Dutt said :

He would not judge a Bill which he had not seen. But on broad economic grounds he maintained that failure must attend any effort which sought to save the cultivators by confiscating their rights and lowering the value of their property. Economic laws which operated elsewhere operated in India. It was sometimes said that cultivators in India were like children. They might be ignorant and superstitious, but, taken generally, they were conscious of their own interests and keen in defending them. What they wanted was a moderate assessment and clear rights, which they were able to defend. He did not wish to make any remarks about the Punjab Act, but the extension of this Act to the rest of India would be a calamity.

On the 29th June Mr. Dutt spoke before the Fabian Society, at Clifford's Inn, on the causes of the poverty of the agricultural classes.

All the time he was compiling materials for his next great work, "The Economic History of India." On the 10th May he wrote to his brother :—

> I at last see my way to compile something like an economic history of India in two or three volumes, as I have secured a magnificent collection of Indian Blue Books and State papers in 200 stout folio volumes, full of valuable information. An economic history dealing only with the people during the 150 years of the British rule will supply a real need, and will reveal facts which are very often passed over in silence in political histories. But it is a work of years, and I do not know when, if ever, it will be compiled.

On the 18th July 1901, he left England for Norway, and took a short holiday in that delightful and interesting country. He returned to England on the 2nd of August.

On the 16th of August the Indian Budget debate took place, and Lord George Hamilton once more challenged the opinion that land assessment had anything to do with famines, quoting in support the opinion of the last Famine Commission. "At the same time," he observed, "I readily admit that it may be that the rise under resettlement may sometimes be too sudden, and that here and there assessments may have been too high. And it is further an undoubted fact that the indebtedness of the occupier in many places is a serious economic and political danger."

Mr. Dutt went to Glasgow on 2nd September 1901, and returned to London on the 12th. At Glasgow, in connection with the Glasgow International Exhibition, a course of lectures on India was arranged by the Glasgow International Assembly. Sir John Jardine delivered the first lecture, and Mr. Dutt the second. He took as his subject : "Indian Industries, Trade and

Agriculture, Railways and Irrigation, Land Revenue Administration and Finance."

On the 12th October, he spoke in the Town Hall, Liverpool, when Sir Edward Russell presided over a distinguished assembly, among whom were Mr. and Mrs. W. C. Bonnerjea. The chairman said :—

There was a great deal indeed to lament in the past in the apathy with which such occurrences as they had to deplore had been regarded. It was almost a proverb in this country that Indian affairs had not received the attention to which their magnitude and the extent to which India was bound up with our honour and credit entitled them. Let them make at the very outset the resolution that that meeting should be the beginning of a different state of things, at all events, as regarded themselves.

The speeches at Glasgow and Liverpool were two of the most important delivered by Mr. Dutt in England, and in them he compressed most of his economic and agrarian views. Of the Glasgow speech, Mr. (now Sir) Horace Plunkett of Dublin (Department of Agriculture and Technical Instruction) remarked :— "I learned more about Indian economics from your interesting Glasgow lecture than I ever knew before."

On the 18th November he wrote to his brother :—

MY DEAR BROTHER,—I am glad you liked my Glasgow speech. Since then you may have read my Liverpool speech. I have succeeded in doing one thing. Liberal newspapers in this country and even officials in India feel that the land tax in India is oppressively severe, and causes poverty and famines. Even Sir A. MacDonnell in his Famine Report speaks of the heavy land tax, and its rigorous exaction as a cause of the unblessedness of the cultivators. And I quoted him in my Liverpool speech as the triumph of my agitation on this subject which had been neglected before.

I am certain to come to India this winter (perhaps in January) as soon as my "Economic History," vol. i., is in the press.—Yours affectionately, ROMESH.

On the 23rd November a Conference of the Indians residing in the United Kingdom was held at Palace

Chambers, Westminster, under the chairmanship of Mr. Dadabhai Naoroji. Its object was to adopt a memorial to the Secretary of State for India in regard to the Bombay Land Revenue Amendment Act. The first resolution was moved by Mr. Dutt.

About this time there was formed in London the Indian Famine Union, with the object of inquiring into the causes of Indian famines and adopting measures for their prevention. It was at the instance of this body that a memorial was addressed to the Secretary of State for India early in January 1902, to institute inquiries into the economic condition of India. Its signatories were a very impressive list, and contained the names of some of the foremost men in England, such as the Archbishop of Canterbury, the Bishop of Liverpool, and the Dean of Manchester.

In the same year he had an important controversy with the Secretary of State, Lord George Hamilton, about the Bombay Land Revenue Bill. He at first strenuously opposed the passing of the Bill, and after the Bill was passed in India he pressed for the suspension of the Bill for two years, on the analogy of a similar postponement in the case of the Assam Labour Act. But his efforts did not bear any immediate fruit.

He was more fortunate, however, in his intercession with the Secretary of State on behalf of Mr. Rangachari, an eminent scientist and scholar, for the Professorship of Sanskrit in the Presidency College, Madras, a post which the Local Government had proposed to be abolished. After the appointment, Mr. Rangachari, the editor of the *Hindu*, wrote to Mr. Dutt thanking him warmly for the eminent service he had rendered to the cause of education in Madras.

IV

The book upon which he was working so hard appeared early in 1902, under the title of "Economic History of British India," and received an appreciative welcome. We quote a few of the press reviews.

The *Daily News* :—

Mr. Dutt is to be congratulated on his undertaking. While there has been a surfeit of books on Indian war and policy, the economic history of the people of India has yet to be written. Mr. Dutt has brought his narrative down to the year of Queen Victoria's accession. We trust he may continue it to these first years of a new century. It is startling to think that the impressive language in which Edmund Burke deplored the "economic drain" of India's resources a hundred and twenty years ago may, with but a few incidental alterations, be applied to the outflow of to-day.

The *Manchester Guardian*, in the course of a lengthy article, said :—

In several respects this will rank as the most valuable of recent books on British India. Presenting a close record of agriculture and land settlements, trade and manufacturing industries, finance, and administration from the rise of British power in 1757 to the accession of Victoria, it furnishes clues to much that is otherwise mysterious in the present condition of our great Eastern Empire. Following the records of the Company and the reports of the House of Commons Committees, Mr. Dutt has woven an intelligible history of the economic policy of the Company, the accuracy and impartiality of which can hardly be questioned. The net result is somewhat to exonerate our recent policy at the expense of the past, under which the spoliation of the peasantry and the destruction of the finer native industries may be said to have formed part of the system of government. Mr. Dutt's book, however, is by no means framed as an indictment of British rule; no writer has accorded a fuller or more enthusiastic testimony to the labours of such enlightened and public-spirited administrators as Munro, Malcolm, and Elphinstone, and to the excellent intentions which have animated not a few of the most unsuccessful experiments. If we have failed, as assuredly we have, to maintain the conditions of an assured livelihood for great masses of the population of India, it is because we have built upon the evil policy bequeathed by a trading company, whose primary object was to draw profits for shareholders out of the taxation and trade of the country which had been placed at their disposal.

But, as will be seen from the following, all the criticisms were not equally favourable.

The *Times*:—

If the general character of natives really were as it appears in Mr. Dutt's pages, not only would there be no need now of a British Empire, but that empire would never have been permitted by the natives to be formed. If we could think away this strong element of bias we should be able to appreciate the scholarly character of much of Mr. Dutt's book. But it cannot be got rid of, it determines every quotation, it warps every argument, it vitiates the book. The literary skill and research which he has devoted to his object, prove Mr. Dutt to be capable of writing history if he could for a moment put his politics aside. But the work before us is not a history; it is merely a collection of historical arguments for the use of a political sect.

The *Times of India*:—

There is only one serious complaint that we have to make against Mr. Dutt's latest contribution to the discussion of Indian economical problems. He does not say it in so many words, but the idea seems to have gained possession of his mind that the British in India, like the Bourbons in France, have learnt nothing and forgotten nothing. He tells again the story of the plundering and injustices of the latter part of the eighteenth century as though they were the beginnings of a policy which has been maintained, with none of its vices mitigated, until the present day. *Sicut erat in principio*—and the same condemnation is passed upon England's work in India to-day as is passed upon the *régime* of the Company, when the avowed purpose of the administration was trading for profit in the first place, and decent government—at a long interval—only in the second. Mr. Dutt would not have been a less vigilant champion of his country's interests than he is, if he had remembered that even in the drawing of an indictment it is necessary to distinguish between major and minor offences, and that while India under the Company was not always as ill governed as it was before Cornwallis' day, India under the Crown has been administered with an honest desire to do justice by its people. He, however, makes no distinction between the beginning and the end of the story.

Mr. Dutt, however, protested against this criticism of the *Times of India*, and pointed out that his work professed to be only a history of the pre-Victorian period, and not a history of the entire period of British rule in India.

If this fact [he further wrote] had appeared anywhere in your review, your readers might have understood the reason for the omission which you have so repeatedly commented upon. Nevertheless, if I am able to complete this great work, your readers will have no cause to complain that I have left any important portion of the story untold. I shall not consider it fair to myself, or to my readers, to write a single chapter of the "Victorian Age" without examining all the vast materials that are available to me, here and in England, for the period covered by that chapter; and no Economic History of India is worth the name which does not take note of the more modern mill industry of India, as well as of "tea, coffee, coal, and sugar" of which you make mention.

A curious passage at arms occurred in connection with the statements made by Mr. Dutt in his work. A writer, signing himself "G.," wrote to the *Times of India*:—

Mr. A. Rogers, late Bombay C.S., in his letter to you of the 20th ultimo, published in the *Times of India* a few days since, refers to Mr. R. C. Dutt's recent communications to the *Pioneer* on the land revenue question, and after pointing out that there are in them "certain misleading statements which in the interests of truth must not be allowed to go forth to the world as actual matters of fact," remarks on what he holds to be one such, relating to the increase of land revenue in this Presidency during the first year of British rule, as under:—

"Another of the half truths common to Mr. Dutt's writings is contained in the following words:—'In Bombay the revenue of the territories acquired from the last Peshwa in 1817 was increased within a few years from eight to fifteen millions of rupees.'

"Mr. Dutt (must we say designedly?) omits to mention that by the treaty of Bassein in 1819 and subsequent agreements, the whole of the Province of Gujrat, vast in extent and unsurpassed in fertility, came into British possession, and the increase of revenue he adduces as a proof of the rapacity of our methods of administration is due to extension of territory and not, as he leaves it to be inferred, to oppressive taxation of the land already in our possession. The public may now be left to judge of the reliability of an author who uses such arguments as these."

It is much to be regretted that Mr. A. Rogers, who takes so sympathetic an interest in the well-being of the Bombay cultivators, and whose long and varied experience of revenue matters gathered in the Presidency entitles his opinion on such questions to respectful consideration, does not always, perhaps through excess of zeal, sufficiently weigh his words or make sure of his facts before he writes to the papers. The only treaty of Bassein known to Indian history, and given in Aitchison's "Collection of Treaties," 3rd ed., vol. vi., part i., p. 53, is the celebrated treaty of 1802, and the acquisition of Gujrat and the conquest of the Peshwa's dominions were both almost complete before the middle of 1818.

Then the writer goes on to quote from the Government Administration Report of 1822–23, to show the "oppressive character of the land revenue demanded during the first few years of British administration," and remarks :—

Mr. Dutt's statements are more than amply borne out by the facts being, indeed, under-statements of the position of things as it then existed rather than otherwise, and that there is absolutely no foundation whatever for Mr. A. Rogers' allegation as to their historical incorrectness.

Mr. Dutt was detained in England a few days longer than he had originally planned, because he was determined to finish the proof correction of his "Economic History" before sailing for home. On New Year's Day 1902, he wrote home: "It has been cold and wet and windy and miserable in London this December, and I am longing for the blue skies of India and to see you all after this long separation."

He set sail on board the *Mombassa* on the 9th January, and reached Madras early in February.

CHAPTER XX

1902 AND 1903

THE DELHI DURBAR, INDIAN TOUR, AND LANCASHIRE CAMPAIGN

I

At Madras Mr. Dutt received a great ovation. A reception was given to him and to his fellow-passenger, Sister Nivedita (Miss Margaret Noble), and an address was read to him in the Hall of the Mahajan Sabha, by Mr. G. Subramaniya Iyer, sometime editor of the *Hindu*. In reply he made a graceful reference to Sister Nivedita's work :—

I received your telegram a few days ago at Colombo, kindly inviting me and my gifted fellow-passenger, Sister Nivedita, to speak at a public meeting on our arrival at Madras. I felt an unspeakable joy that you should have thus accorded your hearty greetings to a lady who is now one of us, who lives our life, shares our joys and sorrows, partakes of our trials and troubles, and labours with us in the cause of our Motherland. I also felt gratitude at the honour you had done me personally by giving me this welcome after my prolonged absence.

His address contained a noble exhortation to his countrymen to work, to persevere, and to have faith in the future destiny of India. In this speech he also referred to the Government Resolution of January 1902, on Land Settlements :—

In the few words I have addressed to you I have purposely refrained from alluding to the important Resolution which the Government of India have recorded on the subject of the Indian land revenue. I feel greatly honoured by the reference which has been made to my humble work in this very important Resolution, and the courtesy with which His Excellency's Government has dealt with my suggestions almost disarms criticism. The paper was placed in my hands only this morning, and I have not read even a tenth part of the Resolution yet, and you will pardon me therefore if I am wholly unable on the present occasion to express any opinion on this most important subject.

He was not, however, silent very long. His first reply to the Resolution appeared in the columns of the *Pioneer* on March 12th, and this was followed by three other letters which appeared in quick succession. This controversy is dealt with in a later chapter.

In November he gave evidence before the Police Commission, presided over by Sir Andrew Fraser, and submitted a written note containing suggestions for the reform of the police system. The following passages from the note are important, for, as the *Bengalee* observed, his remarks are a complete and categorical answer to the sweeping and unfounded charges against the character of the Indian people, which witnesses like Mr. E. H. Munro, formerly a police official and then a missionary, had chosen to prefer.

I have mentioned these facts because I have seen strange inferences drawn from the dishonesty of the police by men who do not know our society, and have never had any means of knowing it. I have seen it stated that the police in India are of the people, and that the police is dishonest because the people are so. Those who make such sweeping charges do not know, or do not consider, that by the inadequate scale of pay we have fixed for the police service, we draw to that service by a natural selection a class of men not fit for their high responsibilities, and that we train them in dishonesty by giving them ample powers, and an undue degree of protection when they are detected in wrong-doing. The same causes led to the same results among the East India Company's European servants, among District Magistrates and Collectors, a hundred years ago, and also among the Subordinate Judicial Officers fifty or sixty years ago. A higher pay and better prospects have improved all services, European and Indian; the police remains an exception because it continues to be badly recruited and inadequately paid. To consider the subordinate police service as fairly representative of the Indian people is to misapprehend the true bearings of the case, and thus unwittingly to blacken the character of the nation. And it is sweeping and reckless charges of this nature which widen the gulf between the European and Indian communities, and, as I said as Commissioner of Burdwan seven years ago in my published report, make the task of administration more difficult than it need be.

It was in this year that he wrote articles for the supplement to the "Encyclopædia Britannica," on the foremost Bengalis of the nineteenth century. He reviewed the careers of Raja Ram Mohan Ray, Pandit Iswar Chunder Vidyasagar, Michael Madhusudan Dutt, Bankim Chunder Chatterjea, Kristodas Pal, and Sir Romesh Chunder Mitter. Throughout life he never lost an opportunity of doing honour to the great leaders of his country. In 1904, he presided over the anniversaries of Raja Ram Mohan Ray and Pandit Iswar Chunder Vidyasagar, and the high tribute he paid to the memory of the three men whom he considered the greatest sons of Bengal is worth quoting :—

The memory of Iswar Chunder Vidyasagar does not require to be perpetuated by such gatherings as this, for it is deeply engraved in the history of the land, and in the hearts of the nation. But nevertheless it does good to us, it is an education to us, to contemplate the lives of our great leaders in the past, and to derive from such contemplation fresh strength and courage in the performance of those duties which lie before us in the present. And among such leaders who shaped our progress, and shaped our thoughts and aspirations, I know of none greater than Raja Ram Mohan Ray, who worked in the early decades of the nineteenth century, and Pandit Iswar Chunder Vidyasagar, who flourished in the middle of that century, and the gifted and lamented Bankim Chunder Chatterjea, whose genius shed a lustre over the last decades. It is often said that we have no national king among us to lead us and direct us, to help and encourage us in our social and religious and literary endeavours. But in Bengal, we do recognise a kingship in thought and culture, and there is not one among us present here who does not pay his homage to the memory of those kings of men who lived and died among us in the nineteenth century.

II

In December 1902, he visited the famous Delhi Durbar held by Lord Curzon to celebrate the accession of His Majesty King Edward VII. to the throne of the British Empire. During his stay in Delhi he was the guest of the present writer, whom the Viceroy had placed in charge of the Indian Press Camp, and he thoroughly enjoyed the magnificent pageant.

DELHI, *7th December* 1902.

MY DEAREST AMALA,—I am at Delhi at last! The weather is delightfully cold and bracing, Ganen and Sarala and the children are in perfect health now, and I feel stronger and healthier than I have during the last six months. They have given me a tent all to myself, and I need hardly say made me comfortable and happy. If Khirod comes to Delhi during the long Christmas holidays, I can promise him joy and comfort!

It is a city of tents now, outside the town; the great waste fields which you saw round the town are now levelled and watered, laid out in roads and lighted with electric light, and crowded with fine carriages and horses, elephants and camels. The Viceroy's residence shines out white and dazzling among a forest of white tents, and the L. G.'s camp, the Assam Camp, the Burma Camp, the Bengal Camp, and all other camps lie in all directions, each crowded with white tents laid out in roads, planted with palms, lighted with electricity!

I am leaving Delhi to-morrow for Muzaffarnagar, where a zamindar has invited me, and thence I go to Saharanpur, where I lecture on the Epics of India, the District Judge presiding! I come back to Delhi after about a week, and I shall stay on here probably till near the end of this month, to see the entry of the Viceroy and the Rajas, &c. But I won't stay till the end of the Durbar.

So write to me to this address, and let me know all about yourself and the children and about Khirod's plans. I am anxious to return to Calcutta before the end of this month to see Bimala and Boli, who I hope will stay in Calcutta till the first week of January. I am writing to Kamala about this, but if you know anything about Bimala's plans, and the duration of her stay in Calcutta, let me know.—Your ever loving father,

ROMESH.

Mr. Dutt was, however, disappointed that no great

SARALA, FOURTH DAUGHTER

political or financial concession marked the historic occasion :—

The spectacle has not satisfied or impressed the people of India. "What has been conceded to us?" asked the people, and people are not satisfied with a remission of interest upon loans to Native States, and a vague promise of financial relief in the indefinite future.

The concluding portion of his letter to the *Daily News* on the Durbar is worthy of quotation :—

I have heard what few Englishmen now living in India have—three Proclamations read and published in India, those of 1858, of 1877, and of 1903. Between 1858 and 1877 lay the age of Canning, and Lawrence, and Northbrook, the age of Peace, Retrenchment, and Reform. Frontier wars and annexations were avoided; Mysore was rendered back to native administration; the greatest acts of Indian legislation—the Penal Code and the Civil and Criminal Procedure Codes—were passed; the Bengal Rent Act saved the cultivators of the soil from harassment and oppression; a permanent settlement of the State demand from the soil was recommended for all India; education was encouraged, and the Universities of Calcutta, Madras, and Bombay were established. Between 1877 and 1903 falls the period of Imperialism, the age of repression and distrust at home, and wasteful wars beyond the frontiers of India. With the brief exception of Lord Ripon's administration (1880–1884) this age has brought no great remedial measures in India to the impoverished people. Within this period we have seen two Afghan wars and one Burmese war swelling the Indian debt by over twenty-five millions; we have seen the taxes of India forced up from thirty-five to forty-five millions, and call this the "prosperity of India"; we have seen the army expenditure increased from twelve to eighteen millions; we have seen the liberty of the Press restricted, municipal self-government repressed, the higher services virtually closed to the people of India, railways multiplied and irrigation neglected; and we have witnessed frequent and devastating famines, more widespread and intense than any of which history keeps any record. People in India ask to-day if the Durbar of 1903 is the high-water mark of this tide of Imperialism, and if hereafter we shall make for retrenchment and some real relief to the suffering and silent millions. Is there no statesman in England in this generation, Tory or Liberal, like Sir Stafford Northcote or Sir Charles Wood, who can make a clean sweep of this wasteful and exhausting Imperialism, and stand up for real reforms and redress to the people of India? Is there none who has the power and the determination of cutting down with a merciless hand the annual drain of nearly half the revenues of India into the office at Whitehall? Is there none who can abolish the salt tax, limit the land tax, reduce the military expenditure, promote Indian industries, open the Executive Councils and the higher services to the people, and give them a real share in the administration of their own affairs? If these reforms are denied, then the Durbar of 1903 is a mockery and a delusion, and, to quote Lord Curzon's words, India will continue to be a land "of diminishing plenty, of empty prospects, and of justifiable discontent."

III

In the early months of 1903, Mr. Dutt went on an extensive tour in Southern India, chiefly with the object of making the acquaintance of the leading Indians of Deccan, and making a first-hand study of the economic and agricultural condition of that part of the Indian continent.

In January he visited Coconada, and conferred with Mr. Ganjam Venkataratnam Pantulu and other local celebrities about the condition of the agriculturists of the Deccan. He also went out to some villages, and collected first-hand information from the raiyats themselves. During his stay of four days he found time to deliver a lecture on "the Ancient Indian Epics and their Influence on our Modern Progress," which was very much appreciated.

From Coconada he went to Raj Mohendry, where he delivered an address on the "Ancient Epics," which was described by the local correspondent as "attractive and thrilling."

He visited Hydrabad on 2nd February, and delivered a lecture on "Ancient India" in Shapurwadi Hall. Bishop Vicano presided, and the first noble of the State, Nawab Zafar Jang Shamshul Mulk Bahadur, nephew of His Highness the Nizam, and Military Minister, sat on the daïs. The hall was crowded. Mr. Shapurji, the leading Parsi of Deccan, was at home, and the Nizam's band discoursed music at intervals. The next morning Mr. Dutt had a long interview with His Excellency Maharaja Sir Kishen Prasad, Prime Minister.

There could be no stronger proof of the universal esteem in which he was held than the cordial welcome which was accorded to him on the occasion of his visit to the premier Muhammadan principality in India.

In March Mr. Dutt went to Gujrat to make personal inquiries into the condition of the agriculturists, and after visiting Kheda, Ahmedabad, Broach, and various villages in the Surat District, was the guest of Mr. Jeemanji Lungibhai at Surat. There he received an address from the agriculturists—an event without precedent. The address contained the following passages:—

> Allow us agriculturists of Gujrat to express the gladness and joy of our hearts at your unexpected visit to us on your mission of inquiry into the condition of Indian agriculture. We have heard of your efforts to bring to the notice of the ruling authorities the disadvantageous conditions of assessment and tenures obtaining in the various provinces of our ancient country. We are happy to observe that the ability and research, the earnestness and thoroughness with which you advocated the cause, evoked the consideration of the highest authority in the country.
>
> High intelligence, great experience in important administrative posts, deep study, and extensive learning, with a clear grasp and comprehension of the innumerable complicated problems involved in this question of the development of a vast country, aided by a hearty devotion to the one single purpose in view and a keen sense of the responsibility of speech, together with your justly earned reputation as a loyal British subject, no less than an Indian patriot citizen—these, we say, have obtained for your writings and opinions an admiration amongst your countrymen and an esteem and consideration amongst our rulers which, whilst showing a bright promise of the future, indicate in the present the urgent necessity of steady perseverance in the efforts already begun. May God give you and your coadjutors the joy and the glory of success, and good results in your noble championship of the interest of the agriculturist community.

This may not be the language of the agriculturists themselves, but the address at any rate shows in what high esteem he was held by the leaders of public opinion in Gujrat, as almost in every other part of India, and how the people considered him to be the devoted and disinterested champion of their cause.

His reply to the address contained some noteworthy passages:—

> Believe me, when I tell you that there is no work which I have undertaken in my life which is more deeply interesting to me than to see with my own eyes how the cultivators of the different provinces of my country live in their homes and till their fields. It is a work which interested me greatly during the period of over a quarter of a century when I was in service, and the interest has grown upon me with every passing year, since I retired from service in 1897. No trouble and expense incident to this inquiry are commensurate with the reward that I reap. Occasionally the sun and the dust of March are trying to me, and long drives in bullock carts over rough country roads are sometimes too much for my old bones. But when at the end of such journeys I arrive at remote villages, see the cultivators with their women and children collected before me, speak to them in the Hindustani language, which people in Gujrat generally understand, inspect their fields and homes, their bullocks and buffaloes, and ascertain facts relating to the produce they reap, the revenue they pay, the incomes they make and the debts they have incurred, I feel that never in my life have I done a better day's work, or have been more amply rewarded for my work. I speak to you honestly when I say that I would sooner have missed the brilliant spectacle of the late Delhi Durbar, which I saw three months ago, than the far more interesting pictures of village life in Gujrat which I have witnessed during my recent inquiries, and which will remain impressed on my mind as long as I live. I am drawn to the sober, industrious, peaceful, and honest men and women before me, as to my kith and kin; I do not think I could have felt for you, and worked for you, more, if I had been born in one of those humble peaceful village huts which I am daily visiting.

And men of his stamp have been described as "arm-chair politicians" in one of the most recent and ambitious publications on Indian affairs.

His final words of caution and encouragement to the agriculturists to avoid exaggeration and have faith in the justice of the British Government were highly characteristic.

At Satara he received another important address :—

Throughout your career you have been actuated by one supreme motive, that of bringing the rulers and the ruled together; and, in furtherance of that, you have been devoting your time and energy, not to speak of money, in making yourself personally acquainted with the actual state of the various parts of this vast British Indian Empire, a step calculated to enable your views and suggestions to weigh with those who have cheerfully accepted from Providence the sacred trust of such a large dependency. Viewed from that point, we doubt not your visit to the interior of the Deccan would be of immense benefit to all.

Your constant and pointed efforts towards the revival of a love for the history of this ancient land of Bharat have filled the readers of your highly appreciated works on India, both in prose and poetry, original or translations, including your latest production, the interesting and charming "Lake of Palms," with a genuine feeling for inquiry into what India was and what she is now, and cannot fail to awaken in her sons a sense of duty demanded of them by their contact with the most enlightened and liberal country of the West.

We feel as if we are in the presence of an example of a patriotic and enlightened self-sacrifice of which the whole country is proud, and we only pray that you may be blessed with a continuing vigorous energy for the purpose of bringing together the rulers and the ruled in the interests of India's prosperity under the British rule, which is one of the first aims and objects of this Union Club.

Of these last days in India he gives the following account in a letter to his friend Mr. B. L. Gupta :—

It is twelve days since I left Calcutta, but within this time I have not had twelve hours to myself to sit down and write to my friends. They detained me a day at Jubbulpur to tell me all about the Central Provinces land settlements, and at Bombay the Maharaja of Darbhanga wanted me about his Police Commission business. Since then I have been taken to several villages in Gujrat to see how the agriculturists live; all village Hampdens here know that I have been fighting their battle for the last few years; all are eager to show me their homes, their fields, and their cattle. Coming back from Ahmedabad to Baroda, I hoped for a few days' peace here, but what with the Gaekwar's birthday Durbar, what with a lecture which they forced me to deliver yesterday, and what with dinners and entertainments in the Palace every day (in honour of the Thakore of Gondal, who is here) I have had little time left to me. The Resident is gushingly kind to me—sought me out and made my acquaintance at the Durbar, and has invited me to breakfast with him to-day before I have had time to call. I leave Baroda to-morrow for Surat and Broach, and after seeing some agricultural villages there I return to Bombay. Thence I go to Poona and a few other places before leaving for Europe. My steamer does not start till the 6th April, and that gives me time to do Bombay thoroughly.

A farewell meeting was held at Bombay on the 3rd April 1903, in honour of Mr. Dutt, on the eve of his departure for England. The Hon. (afterwards Sir) P. M. Mehta presided.

Mr. Dutt left the shores of India again with a heavy heart. From the Apollo Hotel he wrote to his daughter Sarala:—

Yes, I shall miss you all very much after being constantly with you all for the last twelve months; I now feel more like going in exile than I ever did before. However, I hope to come more frequently to India now than I have done within the last six years, and then it will be a continuous change—

"From toil to rest,—and joy in every change."—BYRON.

To his eldest daughter Kamala he wrote:—

Your home, with all the love that surrounds me there, has been a dream of joy and happiness to me; and though I tear myself away from all that for a time, I will return again and again in the midst of my labours to bask in the sunshine of that undying love.

He left Bombay on the 4th April, and reached London on the 24th.

IV

From London he wrote to his friend Mr. Gupta and to his brother, reviewing the past work of his life and mapping out his future.

MY DEAR BIHARI,—I have not yet seen any one in London, nor have I regularly commenced my work. But I hope to do so as soon as we are settled down in our new house. I am also going to lecture at University College from next week, if I can form a class. The great work before me is the second volume of my "Economic History,"—the Victorian Age (1837–1900), and if I can finish that in the present year my life's literary work is done! I may write novels and political articles after that, but am not likely to engage in any great work again at this age! My "Ancient India," and "Epics," and "Economic History" will remain the most important productions of my rather prolific pen during the maturest period of my life, between forty and sixty.—Yours affectionately ever, ROMESH.

MY DEAR BROTHER,—I have received your very kind letter written on my birthday. So I am fifty-five now, and entitled to retire from work. Well, I will retire in this sense, that after my "Economic History" is completed (next month), I will not undertake any such big literary work again. My fame as an English writer may live or perish early; but so long as it lasts it will be connected with three works—my "Civilisation," my "Epics," and my "Economic History." If I live much longer and have literary leisure, I will of course go on with small works henceforth, including an adaptation of my novels into English and such like recreation. No heavy task again after one is fifty-five.—Yours very affectionately, ROMESH.

It should be mentioned here that as usual he completed what he had undertaken, and his review of the economic and material progress of India during the Victorian era appeared early next year (1904). The book received a very flattering reception, and his two volumes of the "Economic History of British India" still remain the most exhaustive and scholarly treatises on the subject. It was of the last work that so acute a critic as the late N. N. Ghose, of the *Indian Nation*, wrote: "A book like this does more work than cart-loads of Congress speeches."

At a meeting held at the Westminster Palace Hotel on 15th July 1903, Mr. Dutt read a paper on the "Peasant Proprietors of India." In this paper he pointed out, that out of the five recommendations made by himself and the other memorialists to the Secretary of State, three had been practically acceded to by the Government, and the remaining two—that assessments should be made within definite limits, and enhancements made only on the grounds of the rise of prices—had not been accepted, the result being that there was still a great deal of difference in the legal and economic status of the Madras raiyat as compared to his more favoured brother of Bengal.

During the course of the debate which followed, Mr. Wagle said: "He himself was a peasant proprietor, and belonged to a family of peasant proprietors. At the Bombay revision settlement, commenced in 1866, Col. Henderson, Settlement Officer, enhanced the land revenue in his district by 93 per cent. to 230 per cent.; and no Court in the land had jurisdiction to revise or rectify the acts of the Settlement Officer. Under the old Hindu and Muhammadan rule, the land tax was paid, once for all, and the cultivator was free to use pasture lands, fire-wood and timber from forests, and made his own salt. Now he was taxed for his land, taxed for grazing cattle in forests, taxed for the use of timber, taxed for his salt."

In July Mr. Dutt's protest against the saddling of the Government of India with a part of the cost of maintaining the army in South Africa, appeared in the *Manchester Guardian*:—

What comments my countrymen will make on the honesty of the present Government! The Government keeps 25,000 men in South Africa because it is good training ground, and will charge India with a portion of the cost because the army may be wanted in the Indian North-Western Frontier! Has Imperialism come to this? Schoolboys in India will see through this trickery, this endeavour to screen a crude injustice by means of sophistry. Has India asked for any help from the British army within the last forty-five years? Has not India, on the contrary, lent her army to Great Britain in recent years, in China and South Africa? Should not England, in justice and equity, pay a portion of the cost of the Indian army instead of India paying a part of the expenses of the British army?

Sir Henry Campbell-Bannerman spoke manfully on the subject, and exposed and ridiculed the plea of the Government in the House of Commons. But is there any possible way of preventing such acts of financial injustice towards India? The people of India are never consulted under the "free" Government under which they live. The Secretary of State for India, paid by India, is a member of the British Cabinet, and cannot oppose the joint action of the Cabinet. And this Council consists of members selected by him and paid by India. Where, in the entire machinery of the Indian Government, can the Indian people find any protection against injustice and the sacrifice of their interests? Thirty years ago another act of financial injustice was incidentally discussed by a select Committee of the House of Commons, of which Henry Fawcett was a member and Lord Lawrence was a witness. "Why should they not," asked Mr. Fawcett, speaking of the members of the India Council, "if they thought that this expenditure was wrong, say: 'We are receiving salary from the revenues of India; we care nothing about the political pressure that may be brought to bear upon the Secretary of State; no power on earth shall induce us to sanction an expenditure of money which we think is wrong, so far as the interests of India are concerned?'"

Is it too much to hope that the Liberal statesmen who are so vigorously denouncing the present injustice will organise some means of preventing it in future, and safeguarding the just rights of India? Is it too much to expect that a Liberal Government will find it possible in the near future to induce some popular element in the financial administration of India? Five years ago I made a modest proposal in my evidence before Sir Henry Fowler and his colleagues on the Currency Committee, to the effect that a small committee of representative Indians should be formed to advise the Viceroy and his Finance Minister in all financial matters, to prevent waste and reduce taxation, and to strengthen the hands of the Indian Government in their discussions with the British Cabinet on pecuniary questions.

Mr. Dutt was present at the meeting convened by the British Committee of the Indian National Congress and the London Indian Society at Caxton Hall, to protest against the proposal to tax the people of India for maintaining a British garrison in South Africa, and for the increased cost of recruiting the British army. The chair was taken by Sir Charles Dilke, M.P., and among those present were Sir W. Wedderburn, Lord Welby, Sir M. Bhownaggree, M.P., Mr. T. R. Buchanan, M.P., Mr. Naoroji, and a large number of representative Indians and Indian officials. Mr. Naoroji proposed the first resolution, protesting against the proposal, and Lord Welby seconded, and Mr. Dutt moved the third resolution, which read as follows :—

This meeting is of opinion that, looking to the extreme poverty of the Indian masses, and their consequent sufferings from famine and pestilence, these fresh burdens will inevitably increase the distress and mortality among the population; that the imposition of these new and crushing charges will be a perversion of England's duty to India; and that no final decision should be passed until a full hearing has been granted to those who can give authentic expression to the feelings of the Indian people with regard to these proposals. This meeting appeals to the British public to prevent this undeserved blow being struck at the unrepresented and helpless people.

In his speech he pointed out that the fundamental weakness of the position lay in the fact that the India Council in London was unable to protect the interests of India, even if strongly supported by the Government of India and the public opinion of that country.

In the beginning of November Mr. Dutt delivered a series of addresses on Indian subjects in Lancashire. On 3rd November he addressed the Women's Liberal Association, West Houghton, on India. On 4th November he delivered an address at the Pembroke Forum on "India, Present and Future." On 5th November he spoke at Chorley on "Labour and Wages in India." The same evening he addressed a meeting in the schoolroom at All Saints' Church on "India and the British Empire." On the 6th November the last meeting of the Lancashire series took place, and he spoke at the Unitarian Church Hall, Liverpool, on the "Fiscal Policy of India."

On the 25th November Mr. Dutt addressed a meeting at the South Place Institute, Finsbury, on the "Tariff Question in India," saying in the course of his speech :—

The young mill industry of India required protection for a time, just as England protected her own mill industry in the early years of the nineteenth century, and as the Colonies were protecting their rising industries. To force the exports of grain and raw material still further by preferential tariffs would be cruelty to India. India would be more prosperous if she was compelled to export less of her food supply, and if she imported less of manufactured articles.

Sir Henry Campbell-Bannerman, to whom he sent a copy of this speech, sent through his private secretary the following reply :—

DEAR SIR,—I am desired by Sir Henry Campbell-Bannerman to thank you for your letter, and for the report of your speech on the tariff question in India, and I am now to add that whilst Sir Henry is not prepared to offer an opinion as to all the details of a highly technical question, he is in complete sympathy with your view that there is no justification for the imposition of an excise duty on any class of goods which can be shown not to enter into competition with imported duty-paying goods.—I am, yours faithfully, W. T. S. HEWETT.

In the meanwhile he had received a pressing invitation from the Gaekwar of Baroda to help him in the administration of that most progressive of Indian States, and he left England on the 10th December 1903, for India.

Thus came to a close Mr. Dutt's labours of nearly seven years in England. If the fate of India has now been indissolubly linked with that of England, the patriotic efforts of an Indian who, more than any other man, has helped to make the cause of India familiar to the democracy of England, and created a healthy Indian atmosphere in that country, are not to be lightly passed over. The story of these days, with the constant round of speeches and protests, does not perhaps make very interesting reading, nor were the long and dreary days which he spent in his self-appointed task in a foreign country, removed from his home and relatives, at an advanced stage of his life, very exhilarating for him. But the thing had to be done—it was of supreme importance to India. And who but the strong and selfless men of the earth are to do the work which demands constant sacrifice and apparently brings no reward? Such men have the faith and courage of their convictions, and Romesh Dutt knew that his labours were not to be in vain. Many fortuitous circumstances, and notably the revival of Liberalism in England, have been responsible for the memorable concessions to Indian aspirations which have recently been made, but it may safely be said that history will see in this seven years' struggle by Mr. Dutt one of the most potent causes heralding the new day in India.

CHAPTER XXI

FIRST PRINCIPLES OF POLITICS

I

IN criticising the policy of the Indian Government of his day, Mr. Dutt was not unaware that his position as a retired servant of that Government imposed upon him some disabilities, and might make his action savour of ungraciousness in the eyes of the world. Nor was he ignorant that the position he had taken up was likely to stand in the way of his future advancement in any career of usefulness and influence depending upon the support or patronage of Government. But he had as much faith in the honesty of his own convictions as in the Englishman's love of fair-play and justice. He was too close and clear-sighted a student of the history of British political institutions not to know that freedom of thought was the one great hall-mark which distinguished England from almost all the civilised nations of modern Europe. In his preface to "India under Early British Rule," he thus explained his position:—

> For one who has himself spent the best and happiest years of his life in the work of Indian administration, it is an ungracious and a painful task to dwell on the weak side of that administration, the financial and economic policy of the Indian Government. I have undertaken this duty, because at the present moment the economic story of British India has to be told, and the deep-seated cause of the poverty of the Indian people has to be explained.

Similarly, in moving at a conference of Indians in 1898, a resolution against the Sedition Law, then before the Viceroy's Council, he observed:—

subject. Licking the dust off their feet will not move them from this policy; unsparing criticism and persistent fighting can, and will do it. Englishmen understand fighting, and they will yield to persistent fighting—not to begging.

Thirdly, it is admitted perhaps that my Land Revenue agitation has done some good. It has forced Government to correct past mistakes, to revise assessments in Bombay, Madras, and the Central Provinces, and to frame rules of remissions and suspensions when crops fail. And our personal interests sink into insignificance compared with these results. Assure the Honourable Member of the Board that I am doing all I can to help my friends forward; and I am working also for larger results, compared with which our personal prospects sink into utter insignificance.

His bold and outspoken attitude was appreciated by even such critics as Lord George Hamilton and Lord Curzon.

The *Pall Mall Gazette* voiced the opinion of the best informed section of the British public when, in 1904, reviewing his work, "India in the Victorian Age," it said, "These suggested remedies for Indian poverty might or might not be effective. But at any rate the Indian case is argued here with ability and moderation, and the loyalty of the writer to the Empire is beyond dispute."

Mr. Dutt, as his readers know well, was never slow to make the most ample and unstinted acknowledgment of the blessings of British rule. In the preface to his "Victorian Age," he has said:—

The Indian Empire will be judged by history as the most superb of human institutions in modern times.

And again:

Englishmen can look back on their work in India, if not with unalloyed satisfaction, at least with legitimate pride. They have conferred on the people of India what is the greatest human blessing—peace. They have introduced Western education, bringing an ancient and civilised nation in touch with modern thought, modern science, modern institutions and life. They have built up an administration which, though it requires reform with the progress of the times, is yet strong and efficacious. They have framed wise laws, and have established Courts of Justice, the purity of which is as absolute as in any country on the face of the earth. These are results which no honest critic of British work in India regards without high admiration.

We all remember his famous eulogy of the Civil Service, delivered during the course of his Congress speech at Lucknow:—

I have had the honour of passing the best years of my life in the Indian Civil Service, and I shall be the last person on earth to question either the ability or the honesty of purpose of those able and hardworking men who form that magnificent service. I will say this, that, take the Indian Civil Service with all its faults and all its shortcomings, for hard work and honesty of purpose there is not a finer body of administrators in the world.

To the honest intention and devotion of the rulers he bore equally unequivocal testimony:—

I have said repeatedly, and I firmly believe, that there is a sincere desire in the higher administrators to promote and safeguard the interests of the people, and many of them whom I have the honour of knowing are men who are incapable of passing an order which they consider detrimental to the good of the people of India.

Equally warm and whole-hearted were his expressions of gratitude to Lords Morley and Minto:—

In spite of all that has been said and written to the contrary, I honestly believe that India has never had any better or truer friends than Mr. John Morley and Lord Minto, who have the progress of the country as much at heart as any one here. . . . I honestly believe it, because I have closely studied their acts. I have tried to probe the motives of their conduct, and to decipher the reasons for the action taken by them during the past two years. I do not think that any of us, who are so loud in our professions of enthusiasm for the progress of the country, if we had been placed in the circumstances which the higher officials occupy to-day, would have acted very differently.—*Lucknow Speech*, 1908.

In the same speech, the following unreserved and just acknowledgment occurs of the services which the Government are rendering to the country :—

Silently, and without proclaiming their noble deeds, the Government are doing their best to help us in this and other matters.

In all his important speeches he took good care to place his political creed and that of the educated Indians on a perfectly unequivocal footing. He described it in his great speech at the Lucknow Congress, and again in almost identical language in his farewell speech at Calcutta in 1900.

We identify ourselves [he said on the latter occasion] with the British rule, and pledge our support to that rule at every sacrifice. And we demand under the British rule a larger share in the administration of our own concerns. This is my creed, and this is your creed, and there is not an educated Indian at the present day who does not in his heart subscribe to this creed. Educated India has identified itself with the British rule, and educated India seeks, through the continuance of the British rule, that larger measure of self-government and representation which it is our aim and endeavour to secure.

If in his political writings and utterances he seemed at any moment to press a point too warmly, and if a tone of bitterness on rare occasions marred the strong optimism of his political views, it must be ascribed to the heat of argument or the fatigue of disappointment. And it should be remembered that during the years 1897–1904, when most of his political writings saw the light, the Indian horizon was darkened with famine and plague, and that a spirit of liberalism and sympathy did not mark the administrative measures of the Government. As he said in his Calcutta speech (1900) :—

Gentlemen, the prospect before us is not inspiring. We are living in reactionary times; we have achieved nothing of late; we have lost a great deal of what we possessed before. I have felt this as well as any of you; I have made my humble endeavours against the tide of reaction; I have struggled to save the wrecks of our established rights; I have seen the object of my endeavours snatched away from me almost at the moment of triumph; I have been beaten, defeated, swept away by the overwhelming tide. It would be idle to pretend that I did not feel the disappointment as bitterly and acutely as any one of you; but I can truly declare before you that I have never, in bitterest moments of disappointment, been filled with despair.

In the same strain are the remarks made by him in the course of his speech at Madras in 1902:—

India has seen little change during these five years. A century has ended and a new century has begun, but we have seen no sign of progress—rather the reverse. There is no sadder chapter in the economic history of India than the story of these five years, commencing with the famine of 1897, and proceeding on to the famine which has not yet ended. Never in India's history were the mass of the people more resourceless, more crippled as manufacturers, more indebted as agriculturists. Never were greater misfortunes and deaths crowded together within so brief a space. Never did a civilised, fertile, and industrious country present a scene of more widespread poverty and desolation.

Yet there was never any doubt of his undaunted optimism and his faith in the future:—

We cannot fail in our endeavour—the future is with us; and, looking at the progress of nations all over the British Empire in every part of the world, I for one feel confident that we too are destined to move onwards as limbs of that great Empire, and that we too shall secure some measure of progress and self-government under the imperial rule of England.—*Madras Speech.*

II

He firmly believed that progress in India would have to be on the lines of the modern civilisation of the West, but that as our national life is so indissolubly wedded to the past, a too violent wrenching would be likely to destroy the very roots of our national existence.

Those nations whose past has no connection with the present do not live. The ancient Babylonians, the ancient Egyptians and Greeks, do not live. They are mixed up with everything new. They have changed their religion; even their races have mixed. It is only in India and China that the whole history is one connected whole.

A nation which has a past has a future. My countrymen had never been wanting in having a manly admiration of the past, and though it had on occasions gone to the extent of superstition, all the same I regard that feeling as ennobling and health-giving. It is a duty which devolves upon the educated Indians to try to explore their past and to see what they had actually achieved in the past, generation after generation, in order that they might base their endeavours and build their future hopes on them.

For my countrymen the study of ancient Indian history has a deeper value as a preparation for the duties of Indian citizens in the present day. Our successes, and still more our failures, in the past have lessons for us in the present. A knowledge of our national strength in the past inspires us in our endeavours; a knowledge of our national weakness is still more helpful to us in correcting our mistakes and seeking proper remedies. All history is instructive in this way; but the genius of the Indian nation is not the genius of the West, and a knowledge of Indian history is peculiarly fitted in the present day to guide us and to warn us, and to lead us onward in the path of progress.—*Speech on Indian History*, 1903.

Again:

A correct appreciation of the past would make us better citizens in the present; it would fill our minds with a manly admiration of the true glories of the past, and it would, at the same time, disabuse our minds of much of that prejudice and vain-gloriousness which impedes our social and political progress in the present time.—*Speech at Hydrabad*, 1903.

With this we may connect his view of the path of Indian progress in the future:—

All efforts of living society are simultaneous; and reforms in India, political, social, educational, religious, and economic, must go hand in hand. As we have worked since the days of Raja Ram Mohan Ray, so we must work in the future, for national progress and advancement in all directions simultaneously. . . . No movement was genuine unless it pervaded all the departments of human activity. One can as well say to a plant that it may grow into a tree without spreading branches in all directions. Any movement, if it is genuine, must grow in all directions.—*Letter to the Press*, 1904.

In making his suggestions, and pressing the Indian cause, he was never forgetful of the impotence of abstract theories in the domain of practical politics, and the futility of "crying for the moon," as Lord Morley called it. In reply to the charge made against his Congress speech, that he wanted to substitute "in the place of a government for the people, a government by the people." he said:—

Theories, as such, have no attraction for me; I always endeavour to find out what is practicable under existing circumstances; and all that I claim under the existing circumstances of India is that we should have a voice, a share, in the control of the administration of our own concerns.

In a similar vein he had written in the preface to "India under Early British Rule":—

The people of India are not fond of sudden changes and revolutions. They do not ask for new constitutions, issuing like armed Minervas from the heads of legislative Jupiters. They prefer to work on lines which have already been laid down.

A signal example of this spirit was his recommendations to find some measure of fixity in the land tenure system prevailing in each province of India, instead of recommending the permanency of settlement which obtains in Bengal; and the practicality of his suggestion was greatly appreciated by the British public, who, as the *Manchester Guardian* pointed out, are a practical race.

He was also thoroughly imbued with the necessity of observing moderation, and avoiding exaggeration in all his statements. The advice which he gave to the Gujrati agriculturists embodied a lesson which he never forgot to offer to himself:—"We have a good case; do not spoil it by exaggeration and violent declamation. Be patient, be firm, be strong and persevering!" Still more clearly and more emphatically did he impress upon his countrymen the supreme need of veracity and accuracy in all their political representations. In his farewell speech at Bombay in 1903, he said :—

> We, who are of the people and are in touch with the people, have thus the duty imposed upon us to represent their cases and their circumstances *fully and fairly before the Government;* and we shall be false to that duty, if by a single word or a single syllable we exaggerate or minimise the evils which we witness, or which we feel. Let no sense of false patriotism ever induce us to utter one word exaggerating the evils which we witness; and let no fear of displeasure ever prevail upon us to suppress or minimise the miseries of our fellow-countrymen. The consciousness that we are representing what is true, and striving after what is right, will sustain us through years of disappointment; and truth will prevail in the end. If we are mistaken either in our observations, or in our inferences, we shall fail, and shall deserve to fail. But if we are right, an enlightened and a rational Government can never deny to us for ever those measures of redress which the circumstances of the country and the people demand of them.

We may conclude our summary of this part of the subject by mentioning the last, and perhaps the most important, article of his political faith. He did not believe that the future of India was to be won by an attitude of mendicancy, and that the toil and the burden of the day were to be thrown on the shoulders of the administrators of the country alone. He knew full well that on the capacity of the Indians themselves must ultimately depend the character and extent of the political concessions which they are destined to get from their rulers. In the fine speech at Madras already quoted, he gave eloquent expression to his views on this point :—

> More than this, the future of India depends on us, and on us alone. I am old enough to be able to look back thirty or forty years, when a few solitary voices, in a few remote places disconnected with each other, asked for some feeble concessions for the people. I have lived to see the whole of the educated people of India united by one common aim,

striving for one common object, demanding that priceless boon of self-government which no civilised government can for ever deny to a civilised nation. I have heard the same note sounded in Madras and in Bombay, in Calcutta and in Lucknow; I have seen the best, the foremost, the most moderate and thoughtful men in India banded together to obtain for their countrymen a real share in the administration of their own concerns. . . . Do you think this fact has no significance? Do you think that the spread of this feeling, this idea, this ambition, among the entire body of our educated men—which has taken place within our own memory—means nothing? Why, gentlemen, I see in this one fact the strongest promise for the future, the strongest guarantee for administrative reform and political advancement. *It is this slow, silent, steady, irresistible advance which makes nations, not particular Acts of legislation, or measures of administration. The most liberal Acts would be useless and valueless and even hurtful if we had no strength, no faith, no capacity for progress.* The most retrograde Acts will fail to impede us, if we have trust and faith in ourselves, if we are true to our country and our cause.

He went further than this: he held that the pursuit after political rights, the struggle for political emancipation, is of higher value than the results actually attained:—

One of the most famous English philosophers has said that if an angel from the skies came down with two gifts, one the gift of truth, the other the pursuit after truth, he would have chosen the latter. This should be our cult also, for it is the pursuit after the rights of citizenship which really makes the citizen.

I have always regarded concessions in the light of milestones, which show the exact distance we have travelled from year to year, and decade to decade. They only mark the progress made, they are not progress itself. One of the greatest concessions the people of England obtained was in 1832, when the Reform Bill was passed. Do you think the people made any large progress in that year? No! Their progress had been made for over fifty years, and when they got that concession it was a milestone showing that they had gone so far. Whether we get Local Government, or an expansion of the Councils, it will show that the authorities really appreciate that we have made some progress, and that they are making some concessions in accordance with our demands.—*Speech at Lucknow*, 1908.

As regards the slow and halting course of real progress in India he has the following :—

Their progress must necessarily be slow. After all, there had been political ideas abroad only during the last twenty or thirty years. And what was this period in the lifetime of a nation? If the rate of progress was not as rapid as some of the more impatient enthusiasts would have it, or if in the place of hope they had received disappointment, they ought not to get fretful and abandon their attempts to obtain what they wanted by peaceful and loyal and constitutional agitation. Nowadays, there was a good deal of talk and clamour and ostentatious oratory. He was honestly convinced that under the British Government the people had made progress in their political condition. They had now some measure of representation and political self-government already granted to them; and the further progress and the larger share they asked for would come to them in course of time as they proved their fitness for it. The Government did not retard their progress, but gladly facilitated it and helped them to make it. Of course their rulers made blunders, as they themselves made blunders. There was a saying in England that he who made no mistakes did nothing. But the privileges granted by Government should be given gradually and slowly and cautiously, so that they might be of use to the people; for they knew that if Government showered on them privileges like the showers of their October rain, it would not be to the advantage of anybody. Reforms made in a day tumbled down as rapidly. They ought not to forget the lessons taught by the history of the French Revolution, and the political condition of England after the period of Cromwell's Protectorate in England. They illustrated that hasty reforms ended in disasters.

CHAPTER XXII

AGRARIAN AND ECONOMIC VIEWS

I

THE central idea in the whole field of Mr. Dutt's political creed was the necessity for raising the material condition of the proletariat in India. The importance of the topic and the absorbing interest which it had for him was expressed both in his speeches and in his political writings. Throughout his whole span, from the days when as a comparatively junior officer in the ranks of the Civil Service he raised his voice on behalf of the peasantry of Bengal, to the last days of his life, the subject commanded his deepest sympathy and evoked his sternest energies. It may safely be asserted that the annals of Indian political controversy do not contain the record of a more memorable championing of the cause of the voiceless agriculturist than the fight which Mr. Dutt made in their cause. The importance of the subject is admitted on all hands.

> The well-being of the agricultural community in India [runs the famous Resolution of Lord Curzon], constituting as it does so overwhelming a proportion of the entire population of the Indian continent, and contributing so large a quota to the Indian revenues, cannot fail to be to the Government a matter of the most intimate concern, as one of the highest national importance, transcending the sphere of party or sectional controversy, and demanding at once the most exhaustive scrutiny and the most liberal treatment.
>
> The gravest difficulty which English administrators have to face in India [said Mr. Dutt in his "England and India"] lies in the extreme poverty of the Indian population. Four-fifths of the population of India depend upon agriculture, and administrators who have passed their lifetime among the Indian cultivators are

aware of their state of almost helpless poverty and indebtedness. And their poverty, their chronic indebtedness, and their want of resource form one of the gravest problems which we have to face.

Similarly, in his Glasgow speech (1901):—

I do not think there is a question of graver import connected with any part of the British Empire than the present (economic) condition of India.

The appeal which the sight of poverty and distress made on his feelings has thus been described by him:—

If there is one subject which should be above the sphere of party controversies, and should appeal to the humanity of all, it is the subject of those famines which are desolating the country so frequently in recent years. And if any of you, gentlemen, have visited relief centres as I have recently done, and seen hundreds and thousands of starving and tottering men and women, our brothers and our sisters, crawling along the roads, resting under trees, lying down on the wayside perhaps to die before the hand of relief can reach them, you will have felt, as I felt, that this calamity, this overwhelming scene of human suffering and distress and death, cries to Heaven for a permanent redress.—*Madras Speech*, 1902.

II

In the concluding chapter of "India in the Victorian Age" he gives a summary of his conclusions on the material condition of the Indian people:—

The income of the people of India, per head, was estimated by Lord Cromer and Sir David Barbour in 1882 to be 27 rupees. Their present income is estimated by Lord Curzon at 30 rupees. Exception has been taken to both these estimates as being too high; but we shall accept them for our present calculation; 30 rupees are equivalent to 40 shillings; and the economic condition of the country can be judged from the fact that the average income of the people of all classes, including the richest, is 40 shillings a year against £42 a year in the United Kingdom.

The taxation, per head of population, is nearly 4s. 8d. per head. This is a crushing burden on a nation which earns very little more than its food. He is taxed 40 per cent. more than the taxpayer of Great Britain and Ireland.

Leaving out exceptionally rich districts like Backerganj, Delhi, and Ahmedabad, and exceptionally poor districts like Fyzabad, the wages of the able-bodied agricultural labourer range from 4s. 8d. to 6s. 8d. a month. Except in very rich districts, therefore, the agricultural labourer does not get even 3d. a day; his average earnings scarcely come to 2½d. per day. Some deduction should be made from this, as he does not get employment all through the year; and 2d. a day therefore is more than he hopes to get throughout the year. The appalling poverty and joylessness of his life under such conditions cannot be easily pictured. His hut is seldom re-thatched and affords little shelter from cold and rain; his wife is clothed in rags; his little children go without clothing. Of furniture he has none; an old blanket is quite a luxury in the cold weather; and if his children can tend cattle, or his wife can do some work to eke out his income, he considers himself happy. It is literally a fact, and not a figure of speech, that agricultural labourers and their families in India generally suffer from insufficient food from year's end to year's end. They are brought up from childhood on less nourishment than is required even in the tropics, and grow up to be a nation weak in physique, a prey to plague or famine.

Agriculturists who have lands are better off. They are better housed, better clothed, and have more sufficient food. But a severe land tax or rent takes away much from their earnings, and falls on the labouring classes also. For where the cultivator is lightly taxed, and has more to spare, he employs more labour, and labour is better paid. In Backerganj, where the land is lightly rented and the cultivator is prosperous, the labourer employed by him gets 10s. 8d. a month. In Salem, where the land is heavily taxed, and the cultivator is poor, the labourer he employs earns 4s. 8d. a month.

But, as is well known, Mr. Dutt's chief argument in support of his contention as regards the growing poverty of India is the frequency and severity of famines, in recent times.

One cannot read without a feeling of sadness and of humiliation this melancholy record of famines in India under British rule. There were reasons for famines in the last century and in the early years of this century. When an old system of government breaks down, and the country passes under a new power, wars and disorders are inevitable. When the Moghal power broke down in India, the Mahrattas and Afghans contended for supremacy, war and devastation followed. And when the British nation entered into the arena they, too, took their part in many wars which impeded cultivation and harassed the population of peaceful villages. In the words of Sir Thomas Munro, wars were added to unfavourable seasons to bring on recurring famines in India. We may also add to these reasons the misrule of the servants of the East India Company, and the unhappy blunders which were perhaps inevitable when a new race of rulers found themselves suddenly called upon to administer the land revenues of a strange and newly conquered country.

But these causes have long ceased to operate. In 1858, the administration of the country passed from the East India Company to the Crown, and since then India has enjoyed profound peace, undisturbed by a single war within her natural frontiers. The land is fertile; the people are peaceful and loyal, industrious and frugal, and generations of British administrators have been trained in the duties of Indian administration. And yet famines have not disappeared. Within the last forty years, within the memory of the present writer, there have been ten famines in India, and, at a moderate computation, the loss of lives from starvation and from diseases brought on by these famines may be estimated at fifteen millions within these forty years. It is a melancholy phenomenon which is not presented in the present day by any other country on earth enjoying a civilised administration.—"*Famines in India,*" pp. 13-16.

III

Mr. Dutt then proceeds to analyse the underlying causes of the poverty of the masses in India.

As the reader is already aware, famines and the economic causes of famines loom largely in his writings, and an exposition of the causes of famine really resolves itself into an examination of the causes of the poverty of the masses. The reason, obviously, why Mr. Dutt chose to examine the general economic question of the poverty of the masses under the special phenomena of famines is, first, because it was the appalling extent of the famines which forced the question of Indian poverty so prominently upon the attention of the public, and, secondly, because he wanted to place the discussion on

His Highness The Maharaja of Baroda.

a practical and tangible basis, so as to be able the more effectually to enlist the attention and sympathy of the British public. In stating the results of his examination, he rejected some of the theories which have usually been advanced :—

Superficial explanations have been offered one after another, and have been rejected on close examination. It was said that the population increased rapidly in India, and that such increase must necessarily lead to famines; it is found on inquiry that the population has never increased in India at the rate of England, and that during the last ten years it has altogether ceased to increase. It was said that the Indian cultivators were careless and improvident, and that those who did not know how to save when there was plenty, must perish when there was want; but it is known to men who have lived all their lives among these cultivators, that there is not a more abstemious, a more thrifty, a more frugal race of peasantry on earth. It was said that the Indian money-lender was the bane of India, and by his fraud and extortion kept the tillers of the soil in a chronic state of indebtedness; but the inquiries of the latest Famine Commission have revealed that the cultivators of India are forced under the thraldom of money-lenders by the rigidity of the Government revenue demand. It was said that in a country where the people depended almost entirely on the crops, they must starve when the crops failed in years of drought; but the crops in India, as a whole, have never failed, there has never been a single year when the food supply of the country was insufficient for the people, and there must be something wrong, when failure in a single province brings on a famine, and the people are unable to buy their supplies from neighbouring provinces rich in harvests. —*Preface to "India under Early British Rule."*

After rejecting these superficial explanations, he remarks :—

Deep down under all these superficial explanations we must seek for the true causes of Indian poverty and Indian famines. . . . The sources of a nation's wealth are Agriculture, Manufacture, and Commerce, and these are conserved by a sound financial administration. While British rule in India has brought the manifold blessings of peace and a wider civilisation, it has not widened the sources of the national wealth of the country from an Indian point of view, and has therefore not improved the material condition of the mass of the people to any marked extent. The mass of the people depend on agriculture. There has been extension of cultivation, and intensively also land perhaps yields more now than it did before. It is not denied that the prices of agricultural produce have gone up. Still the agriculturists are no better off than they were before.—*Preface to "India under Early British Rule."*

The causes of Indian poverty according to Mr. Dutt are threefold :—

(1) Agriculture has now to support a larger population than before, on account of the gradual decay and extinction of the indigenous industries of India and the swelling of the ranks of agriculturists by men who before supported themselves by commerce or manufacture.

(2) The system of administration is now more expensive and complicated than used to be the case before, and as necessarily a great deal of money is spent outside India, the agriculturists on whom the main burden of taxation falls have to pay a comparatively large portion of their income, and get no indirect returns as they formerly did.

(3) The fiscal policy of Government and the system of land revenue assessments adopted over a large portion of India are such as to make it impossible for more than bare necessities to be left to the tillers of the soil.

The first two contentions may be left for the present, as they will be dealt with in the next section. For the present we will try to follow in some detail the chain of argument by which Mr. Dutt seeks to establish the close relationship of the later land assessment policy of Government with the poverty of the agriculturists, and consequently with the diminution of their famine-resisting powers.

In his preface to "India in the Victorian Age," he gives the following summary of the evolution of the land assessment policy of the British Government, beginning from the commercial policy pursued during the early days of the East India Company's rule, through the broad and the sympathetic policy of Lord Cornwallis and Lord William Bentinck, to the more calculating and profit-seeking policy of later years.

The history of the Land Revenue administration in India is of the deepest interest, because it is intimately connected with the material well-being of an agricultural nation. In the earlier years of the British rule, the East India Company regarded India as a vast estate or plantation, and considered themselves entitled to all that the land could produce, leaving barely enough to the tillers and the landed classes to keep them alive in ordinary years. This policy proved disastrous to the revenues of the Company, and a reform became necessary. The Company then recognised the wisdom of assuring to the landed classes the future profits of agriculture. Accordingly, Lord Cornwallis permanently settled the Land Revenue in Bengal in 1793, demanding from landlords 90 per cent. of the rental, but assuring them against any increase of the demand in the future. The proportion taken by the Government was excessive beyond measure; but cultivation and rental have largely increased since 1793; and the peasantry and the landed classes have reaped the profits.

A change came over the policy of the East India Company. They were unwilling to extend the Permanent Settlement to other provinces. They tried to fix a proper share of the rental as their due, so that their revenue might increase with the rental. In Northern India they fixed their demand first at 83 per cent. of the rental, then at 75 per cent., then at 66 per cent. But even this was found to be impracticable, and at last, in 1855, they limited the State demand to 50 per cent. of the rental. And this rule of limiting the Land Revenue to one-half of the rental was extended to Southern India in 1864.

The rule of the East India Company terminated in 1858. The first Viceroys under the Crown were animated by a sincere desire to promote agricultural wealth in India. Statesmen like Sir Charles Wood and Sir Stafford Northcote, and rulers like Lord Canning and Lord Lawrence, laboured with this object. They desired to fix the State demand from the soil, to make the nation prosperous, to create a strong and loyal middle class, and to connect them by their own interest with British rule in India. If their sound policy had been adopted, one source of national wealth would have been widened. The nation would have been more resourceful and self-relying to-day; famines would have been rarer. But the endeavours to make the nation prosperous weakened after the first generation of the servants of the Crown had passed away. Increase of revenue and increase of expenditure became engrossing objects with the rise of Imperialism. The proposal of Canning and of Lawrence was dropped in 1883.

The reader will no doubt clearly grasp the two distinct

principles which were held by the two different schools of administrators. One was the school of Lord Canning and Lord Lawrence, of Lord Halifax and Lord Iddesleigh, who urged a permanent settlement of the Land Revenue. They knew that land in India belonged to the nation and not to a landed class, that every cultivator had a hereditary right to his own holding, and that to permanently fix the Land Revenue would benefit an agricultural nation, and not a class of landlords. The other school demanded a continuous increase of the Land Revenue for the State, by means of recurring land settlements, in course of which the State demand was generally increased at the discretion of Settlement Officers.

The Marquess of Ripon was the Viceroy of India from 1880 to 1884, and he proposed a masterly compromise between the opinions of the two schools. He maintained the right of the State to demand a continuous increase of the Land Revenue on the definite and equitable ground of increase in prices, but he assured the cultivators of India against any increase in the State demand unless there was an increase in prices. He assured to the State an increasing revenue with the increasing prosperity of the country as evidenced by prices. And he assured to the cultivator a permanency in the State demand reckoned in the proportion of the field produce taken as Land Tax. Lord Ripon's scheme happily combined the rights of the State with that security to cultivators without which agriculture cannot flourish in any part of the world. But Lord Ripon left India in December 1884; and his wise settlement was negatived by the Secretary of State for India in January 1885. The compromise which had been arrived at after years of inquiry and anxious thought in India was vetoed at Whitehall; and a nation of agriculturists was once more subjected to that *uncertainty* in the State demand which is fatal to successful agriculture.

The Half-Rental Rule still remained in theory. But in practice it had been violated. The expenses of the Mutiny wars had vastly added to Indian liabilities, and demanded increase in taxation. Commerce could not be taxed against the wishes of British merchants and British voters; the increased taxes therefore fell on agriculture. Accordingly, from 1871, a number of new taxes were assessed on land, in addition to the Land Revenue. If the Land Revenue was 50 per cent. of the rental, the total assessment on the soil, including the new taxes, came to 56 per cent., or 58 per cent., or even 60 per cent., of the rental.

It will appear from these facts which I have mentioned as briefly as possible, that agriculture, as a source of the nation's income, has not been widened under British administration. Except where the Land Revenue is permanently settled, it is revised and enhanced at each new settlement, once in thirty years or once in twenty years. It professes to make 50 per cent. of the rental or of the economic rent, but virtually takes a much larger share in Bombay and Madras. And to it are added other special taxes on land which can be enhanced indefinitely at the will of the State. The land assessment is thus excessive, and it is also uncertain.

Then he further points out in his preface to "India under Early British Rule":—

The Land Tax in India is not only heavy and uncertain, but the very principle on which it is raised is different from the principle of taxation in all well administered countries. In such countries the State promotes the accumulation of wealth, helps the people to put money into their pockets, likes to see them prosperous and rich, and then demands a small share of their earnings for the expenses of the State. In India the State virtually interferes with the accumulation of wealth from the soil, intercepts the incomes and gains of the tillers, and generally adds to its land revenue demand at each recurring settlement, leaving the cultivators permanently poor.

Next he considers the incidence of Land Revenue claimed by Government in different parts of India compared with the rental of the land and its gross produce.

In Bengal the Land Tax was fixed at over 90 per cent. of the rental, and in Northern India at over 80 per cent. of the rental, between 1793 and 1822. It is true that the British Government only followed the precedent of the previous Muhammadan rulers, who also claimed an enormous Land Tax. But the difference was this, that what the Muhammadan rulers claimed they could never fully realise; what the British rulers claimed they realised with rigour. The last Muhammadan ruler of Bengal, in the last year of his administration (1764), realised a land revenue of £817,553; within thirty years the British rulers realised a land revenue of £2,680,000 in the same province.

In Bengal the Land Tax now bears a proportion of 28 per cent. on the rental of estates plus 6¼ per cent. of other taxes also assessable on rent; in Northern India, 50 per cent. on productive rental of estates plus other taxes; in Central Provinces 60 per cent. plus other taxes; whereas in Bombay and Madras the State takes one-third of the field produce, which may approximate to 100 per cent. of the economic rent of the field.

In Bengal 80 per cent. of the gross produce is retained by the cultivator, 14 per cent. is paid to the landlord as rent, and 6 per cent. to the Government as Land Tax. This tax has been permanently fixed since 1793. In Northern India the cultivator also gets 80 per cent., but the landlord 10 per cent. and Government 10 per cent. The assessment is made for thirty years. So it can be changed to the advantage of Government. In Bombay and Madras, where the Government is also the landlord, the cultivator gets only 70 per cent., in the Central Provinces barely 60 per cent.

The difference between the position of the Bengal raiyat and his less favoured brethren in Southern India is thus drawn:—

In Bengal the rental increases about 6 per cent. in seven years; in the North-West Provinces and Central Provinces it has increased 15 to 48 per cent. in the same period. In Bengal the peasantry are protected by the Tenancy Act; in the other parts of India the peasantry are not so protected; the State is the landlord and obtained enormous enhancements. In Bengal the money which is received as rent from the cultivators remains with the zamindars in the country, and is spent in fostering local trades and local industries, and in promoting education and various charities; in other parts of India the money received as rent from cultivators is Imperial revenue, and mostly goes out of the country in Frontier wars or in Home charges.—*Paper on "Peasant Proprietors of India."*

In brief, his position therefore would seem to be:—

(1) The Land Tax of India as a whole is excessive, and the principle underlying the system does not compare favourably with the system in vogue in other civilised countries.

(2) The land assessment in Southern and Central India is excessive compared to the assessment in Bengal and Northern India, and the former bear an unfairly larger share of the burden of the State. Assessment being excessive and periodical in these parts, not only is very little left to the agriculturists, but there is hardly any motive either to save or to improve their holdings.

His next step is to establish a connection between the resourcelessness of the agriculturists and famines.

There is no doubt that famines are directly caused by the failure of the autumnal rains, over which man has no control. But the intensity and frequency of recent famines are greatly due to the resourceless condition and chronic poverty of the cultivators caused by the over-assessment of the soil, on which they depend for their living.—"*Famines in India.*"

He then points out that in the Central Province, the most sparsely populated part of British India, the people have suffered the most from recent famines, whilst Bengal, the most thickly populated, has lost not a single life through famine since the Permanent Settlement.

Before going on to consider the remedial measures suggested by Mr. Dutt, it is necessary to advert to his contention, that agriculture bears a disproportionately heavy burden of taxation, and that from every point of view it is a fatal blunder to tax the agricultural community of India too heavily. Happily, so far as theory goes, there is very little room for any difference of opinion about the justice of this contention.

The net revenues of India for the current year (1901) have been estimated at forty-two millions sterling. Roughly speaking you can say that twenty millions out of this comes from Land Revenue, twenty millions from other taxes including salt, and two millions from opium. In other words, the trades and industries of the country bring little revenue, because the trades and industries are on the decline—one-half the revenue of the country is tax on land and tax on salt, and is raised from the food of the poor. If you examine the figures thus closely, you will find how little reason there is for congratulation of the increase of revenues in India; that increase does not mean increasing prosperity, but only an oppressively increasing taxation on the food supply of the people. Twenty-six years ago, our present Prime Minister, Lord Salisbury, was Secretary of State for India, and condemned in the strongest terms this undue taxing of the food of the people. He wrote in 1876:—

"*So far as it is possible to change the Indian system, it is desirable that the cultivator should pay a smaller proportion of the whole national charge.* It is not in itself a thrifty policy to draw the mass of revenue from the rural districts where capital is scarce. . . . The injury is exaggerated in the case of India, where so much of the revenue is exported without a direct equivalent."

These remarks of Lord Salisbury apply with greater force than they did twenty-six years ago. We are "bleeding" the agricultural population of India at a time when they are suffering from repeated, continuous, and widespread famines; and we are exporting a larger portion of that revenue out of India without a direct equivalent to-day, than you did twenty-six years ago. —*Mr. Dutt's Speech on the "Economic Condition of India," delivered at Glasgow*, 1901.

He has two other arguments to show the unwisdom of taxing the agricultural population too heavily

If we took less from agriculture in ordinary years, Government will probably have to spend less during famine, any slight decrease of revenue will be a set off against the Famine Fund.

Similarly if the agriculturists were better off than they are now, they will be better consumers of the products of British industry. An export of forty-nine million of pounds to a population of three hundred millions means a consumption of three shillings per head of the population. If the people of India consumed goods at the rate of five or six shillings a year per head of population—and this is a moderate estimate even for a poor Asiatic nation—exports into India would be doubled, and England would carry on a trade with India exceeding your trade with any other country in the world. Therefore, I say that the trade interests of England and those of the people of India are closely allied and not divergent.—*Ibid.*

IV

For the improvement of the material condition of the agriculturists, he suggested the following modifications in the land assessment policy of Government:—

The suggestions I have made are, I believe, moderate and practicable, and do not contemplate any change in the different land systems which prevail in the different provinces of India. For the sake of convenience I will sum them up below:—

(*a*) Where the State receives Land Revenue through landlords, and the revenue is not permanently settled, we ask that the

"Saharanpur Rules," limiting the State demand to one-half the rental, may be universally applied.

(*b*) Where the State receives Land Revenue direct from cultivators, we ask that the rate may not exceed one-fifth the gross produce of the soil *in any case*, and that the average of a district, including dry lands and wet lands, be limited to one-tenth of the gross produce, which is approximately the revenue in Northern India.

(*c*) Where the State receives Land Revenue direct from cultivators, we ask that the rule laid down by Lord Ripon, of permitting no enhancement at recurring settlements except on the ground of an increase in prices, be universally applied.

(*d*) Where the Land Revenue is not permanently settled, we ask that settlements be made not oftener than once in thirty years, which is the general rule in Northern India and Bombay.

(*e*) We urge that no Cesses, in addition to the Land Revenue, be imposed on the land except for purposes directly benefiting the land; and that the total of such Cesses may not exceed six and a quarter per cent. (one anna in the rupee) in any province of India.

(*f*) We urge that, now that the protective railway lines have been completed, a million tens of rupees be annually spent out of the Famine Insurance Grant on protective irrigation works; that these works be undertaken, as recommended by the Famine Commission of 1898, "without expectation of direct return" from the outlay; and that the cultivator be left the option of using the water when he requires it, and paying for it when he uses it.

(*g*) And lastly, we urge that in the case of any difference between cultivators and Settlement Officers in the matter of assessment, an appeal be allowed to an independent tribunal not concerned with the fixing and levying of the Land Tax.

It will be obvious to any reader that it is not possible to improve the condition of the Indian cultivator without granting him some security from uncertain demands and harassing claims, which are a ruin to agriculture and a bar to all improvements. And it will be obvious that the security contemplated in the above rules, and the limitations on Land Revenue prescribed therein, are not possible without some check on the growing and ruinous expenditure of the Indian Government. We cannot moderate the revenue demand without moderating the expenditure; we cannot give relief to the overtaxed cultivator without economy and retrenchment.—*Preface to "Famines in India."*

A summary of his recommendations over a wider range is to be found in the preface to his "India in the Victorian Age":—

> The evils suggest their own remedies. The Excise tax on Indian mill industry should be withdrawn; the Indian Government should boldly help Indian industries for the good of the Indian people, as every civilised Government on earth helps the industries of its own country. All taxes on the soil in addition to the Land Revenue should be repealed, and the Land Revenue should be moderated and regulated in its operation. The Public Debt, unjustly created in the first instance, is now an accomplished fact; but an Imperial guarantee would reduce the rate of interest, and a Sinking Fund would gradually reduce its volume. Civil and military charges incurred in England should be borne, or at least shared, by Great Britain, as she shares them in the case of her colonies. Civil charges in India should be reduced by a larger employment of Indians; military charges in India should be repressed with a strong hand; and India should pay for an army needed for her own requirements. All further extension of railways from State loans, or under guarantee of interest from the taxes, should be prohibited. Irrigation works should be extended, as far as possible, from the ordinary revenues. The annual economic drain from India should be steadily reduced; and in carrying out these fiscal reforms, representatives of the people of India—of the taxpayers, who are alone interested in retrenchment in all countries—should be called upon to take their share and offer their assistance.

V

It is not a matter of surprise that such views as these should have evoked a host of criticisms, culminating in the famous Resolution on Land Revenue policy issued by the Government of Lord Curzon. But it ought to be recognised that the views were not novel, and that Mr. Dutt was by no means singular in holding them. In his works on "Early India" and "India in the Victorian Age," he quoted in full opinions of the great administrators and statesmen like Cornwallis, Canning, Munro, Elphinstone, Lawrence, and others, who were the great pioneers of British liberal principles in Britain's dependency in the East. It would be useless to multiply such quotations; but, regarding his question of over-assessment, the following views of Bishop Heber coincide so fully with those of Mr. Dutt that they deserve a place here:—

> Neither native nor European agriculturists, I think, can thrive at the present rate of taxation. Half the gross produce of the soil is demanded by Government, and this, which is nearly the average rate wherever there is not a Permanent Settlement, is sadly too much to leave an adequate provision for the present, even with the usual frugal habits of the Indians, and the very inartificial and cheap manner in which they cultivate the land. Still more is it an effective bar to anything like improvement; it keeps the people, even in favourable years, in a state of abject penury; and when the crop fails in even a slight degree, it involves a necessity on the part of the Government of enormous outlays in the way of remission and distribution, which, after all, do not prevent men, women, and children dying in the streets in droves, and the roads being strewed with carcasses. *In Bengal, where, independent of its exuberant fertility, there is a Permanent Assessment, famine is unknown.* . . .
>
> I am convinced that it is only necessary to draw less money from the peasants, and to spend more of what is drawn within the country, to open some door to Indian industry in Europe, and to admit the natives to some greater share in the magistracy of their own people, to make the Empire as durable as it would be happy.

But it was not only philanthropic administrators of the last century who held such views. It has already been stated that they were supported by experienced and competent Anglo-Indian officials of his own day, and a memorial was presented, in December 1900, to the Secretary of State for placing the Land Revenue administration on a sound and equitable basis:—

> In view [so ran the memorial] of the terrible famines with which India has been lately afflicted, we, the undersigned, who have spent many years of our lives among the people, and still take a deep interest in their welfare, beg to offer suggestions to your Lordship in Council, in the hope that the Land Revenue administration may be everywhere placed on such a sound and equitable basis as to secure to the cultivators a sufficient margin

of profit to enable them better to withstand the pressure of future famines.

The only hope for the cultivators throughout the greater part of India is, therefore, that they should be put in such a position as to enable them to tide over an occasional bad season. To place the cultivators in such a position we consider it essential that the share taken as the Government demand on the land should be strictly limited in every province.

The memorial was written by an experienced Revenue Officer, Mr. Puckle of Madras, and it bore the signatures amongst others of such experienced officers as J. H. Garsten, late Member of Council, Madras; H. J. Reynolds, late Revenue Secretary to the Government of Bengal and late Member of the Legislative Council of the Governor-General of India; A. Rogers, late Settlement Officer and Member of Council in Bombay. Mr. Dutt was himself a signatory in this memorial, and the suggestions made were almost identical with his recommendations quoted above.

His views gained also the support of the most capable Indian publicists of the time. In the Viceregal Council, in the Budget debate of 1900, the Honourable (afterwards Sir) P. M. Mehta made an impressive speech on the growing poverty of the agriculturists, and quoted the authority of Sir Theodore Hope and the Deccan Agriculturists Relief Act Commission to show that "the rigidity of the revenue system was undoubtedly one of the causes of the raiyats' indebtedness."

During the same debate the Honourable A. Charles supported Mr. Mehta's views, and pressed "for a settlement to be finally and at once made, and that all future revisions should solely depend on a manifest, steady, and tangible rise in prices over a reasonable number of years, so as to produce the conviction that the old order has substantially given place to the new." The Honourable Mr. B. K. Bose and the Honourable Maharaja of Darbhanga at the same session of the Imperial Council also urged for a moderation of land revenue assessments.

At the session of the Congress following Mr. Dutt's presidential address in 1889, Dr. Chandravarkar, the President, confined himself almost exclusively to agrarian and economic topics, and made an observation which will bear repetition :—

His Excellency the Viceroy has more than once assured that this important subject is now engaging his "independent investigation." But His Excellency put the question to the Mahajan Sabha of Madras the other day :—"Supposing that we did reduce the assessment throughout India by 25 per cent., is there a man among you who would guarantee me that he honestly believed that there would be no more famine, no more poverty, no more distress?" No one would be so bold as to give a guarantee on that condition, and no one, I take it, thinks that a mere reduction by 25 per cent. in the assessment throughout India will stamp out poverty, for the poor will always be with us. But what is put forward is that if the assessments be reduced 25 per cent. in the Madras and Bombay Presidencies and in the Central Provinces, wherein revision assessments have been raised more than 25 per cent., the relief given will be sufficient to dispense with the necessity of direct famine relief to that extent. At present where Government levy high assessments in good years, they have to refund the sums so levied by opening relief works when famine visits the land.

Lastly, in 1905, Mr. Gokhale in his Budget speech quoted figures, and showed that whereas in England and other European countries the burden of tax on land in relation to produce is well below 10 per cent.; in the case of India, taking land revenue alone, over most areas it is about 15 per cent., and in some portions as high as 20 per cent. "The agricultural producer is terribly handicapped," he observes, "and his position is getting harder every day."

Mr. Dutt also claimed the partial support of the "Indian Famine Commission of 1900."

We had urged again and again that in Southern India—in Madras and Bombay—where the State levied the tax direct from the peasant proprietors the assessment was too heavy; that in many cases it swept away the whole economic rent of the land; that it made the cultivator unable to save anything even in good years against years of bad harvest; that it left him resourceless and indebted and an easy prey to famines. On the other hand the apologists of the Indian Government had denied this charge; they denied any connection between land assessments and

had been two most serious famines in Bengal, and on both occasions the condition of those under the Permanent Settlement was in no degree better than that of those who were in the neighbouring districts which were only temporarily settled. Then Mr. Dutt asserted that rents were low in Bengal, and never exceeded one-sixth of the gross produce, or about 16 per cent. He could not understand what induced Mr. Dutt to make that statement. The condition of the raiyats under the Permanent Settlement in Bengal was most unsatisfactory. They paid the highest rents of any land occupiers in the whole of India, and the State got the smallest amount of land revenue from them. He had made inquiries, and had been informed that in no case did the rents represent only 16 per cent. of the gross produce, but that the grain produce rents in Bengal in most cases were over 51 per cent., and even went up to 70 and 75 per cent. Mr. Dutt seemed to think that in the Central Provinces the Government of India were exacting an exorbitantly high land revenue. He was very reluctant to dogmatise as to what was and what was not a reasonable land revenue, and he should be very sorry to say, that in the past they might not here and there have placed the land assessment too high. But the rules and principles which had been laid down, and which regulated the revenue officers, were framed in a spirit of justice and equity, and so far as he had been able to make inquiry, in comparing the land revenue of British India with the land revenue of the Native States, in every single instance the land revenue of the adjoining Native States was assessed higher than that of British India.

In reply, Mr. Dutt wrote two letters, one to the *Times*, and the other to the *Manchester Guardian*. The latter journal had the following comment on the Secretary of State's speech, and Mr. Dutt's rejoinder:—

During the recent debate in the House, Lord George Hamilton combated statements previously made by Mr. Dutt unfavourably contrasting the rents paid to the Government in Madras with those charged by private owners in Bengal. The Secretary of State announced that the result of his inquiries was to show that Mr. Dutt's statements were entirely erroneous, and he even asserted that the rents paid in Bengal were the highest in India. Mr. Dutt, however, stands to his guns. He declares that having been for more than twenty-five years employed as a Revenue Officer in various parts of Bengal, he took note of the produce of fields, and of the rents which the cultivators generally paid to zamindars. He found that the proportion was one-sixth in many districts, and less in other districts. He supports his statements and his conclusions by figures quoted from Sir William Hunter's "Statistical Account of Bengal," showing that in a number of districts selected at random the proportion of rent to produce varied from less than one-sixth to less than one-eighth. This testimony of an Indian official, and an eye-witness, confirmed by an acknowledged British authority on India, cannot be reconciled with the unhesitating declaration of Lord George Hamilton, that in no case are rents in Bengal as low as one-sixth of the total produce. It is impossible to resist the conclusion that Mr. Dutt is right when he asserts that the Secretary of State is misinformed, and it is to be hoped that Lord George Hamilton will accept the challenge thrown down by Mr. Dutt to institute an inquiry through the district officers of Bengal. In Northern India, according to Mr. Dutt, the rents generally obtained by private landlords from cultivators are one-fifth of the gross produce. Under the Government in British India the maximum rental is one-third. Under the circumstances, Mr. Dutt's contention may well be believed that Bengal has escaped the severer famines which devastated Madras solely by reason of the greater ability of the raiyat to provide against the absence of the rainy day.

II

The points raised by Lord George Hamilton were elaborated and more forcibly put in the famous Resolution of Lord Curzon on the Land Settlement policy of Government, published in January 1902. It was urged in the Resolution that :—

(1) As regards the condition of cultivators in Bengal, who are the tenants of the landowners instituted as a class in the last century by the British Government, there is still less ground for the contention that their position, owing to the Permanent Settlement, has been converted into one of exceptional comfort and prosperity. It is precisely because this was not the case, and because, so far from being generously treated by the zamindars, the Bengal cultivator was rack rented, impoverished, and oppressed, that the Government of India felt compelled to intervene on his behalf, and by the series of legislative measures that commenced with the Bengal Tenancy Act of 1859, and culminated in the Act of 1885, to place him in the position of greater

security which he now enjoys. To confound this legislation with the Permanent Settlement, and to ascribe even in part to the latter the benefits which it had conspicuously failed to confer, and which would never have accrued but for the former, is strangely to misread history.

(2) The Government of India indeed know of no ground whatever for the contention that Bengal has been saved from famine by the Permanent Settlement, a contention which appears to them to be disproved by history; and they are not therefore disposed to attach much value to predictions as to the benefits that might have ensued had a similar settlement been extended elsewhere.

(3) Sufficient stress has not been paid in the recommendations of Mr. Dutt and the memorialists for placing a limit on the demands of the zamindars from their raiyats:—

If it is the interests of the raiyat that are at stake, and that stand in most urgent need of protection, that protection is not less necessary when his payments are made to a Native landlord in the form of rent, than when they are made in the form of Land Revenue to the British Government.

The Government of India will welcome from their critics upon future occasions a co-operation in these attempts to improve and to safeguard the position of the tenant which they have not hitherto as a rule been so fortunate as to receive.

In stating that the Permanent Settlement is not to be held responsible "even in part" for the benefits which have accrued to the raiyats in Bengal, it is questionable whether the Resolution has done full justice to that historic measure. For it is well known that one of the principal points on which Lord Cornwallis directed investigation to be made before resorting to permanent legislation, was concerned with "the measures necessary to prevent the raiyats being oppressed," and although the inquiries made were not sufficient to justify legislation, yet by sections 7 and 8 of Regulation I. of 1793 and section 67 of Regulation VIII. of 1793, ample provisions were made for subsequent legislation. Thus Mr. Rampini, in his introduction to his standard work on the Tenancy Act, remarks:—"It is on these declarations made in connection with the Permanent Settlement of the Land Revenue that all subsequent agrarian legislation in Bengal has been based." In fact, the evils which subsequent legislation corrected were the making not of the Permanent Settlement, but of the notorious enactments, the Haftam (Regulation VII. of 1799) and Pancham (Regulation V. of 1812).

In his replies to the Resolution of the Government, Mr. Dutt pointed out that:—

(1) He did not recommend the extension of the Permanent Settlement.

The question of Permanent Settlements does not arise in this discussion. Believing as I do, that a Permanent Settlement of the land revenues would be in the highest degree beneficial to the people, and would add to their wealth, prosperity, and staying power, I nevertheless refrained from urging such a settlement in my Open Letters, because the India Office has rejected the proposal so late as 1883. And the retired officers who submitted their Memorial to the Secretary of State did not ask for a Permanent Settlement. We asked for such concession as were probable, and were consistent with the present land policy of the India Office and the Indian Government.—*Reply to Lord Curzon's Land Assessment Resolution.*

(2) That he had not said that the Permanent Settlement had saved Bengal from famines, but that the Bengal raiyat is better able to withstand a famine than his less favoured brethren of Southern India.

Since that date famines have been rare in Bengal, and *there has been no famine within the permanently-settled tracts causing any loss of life.*

Within a period of over a hundred years there has been no famine in Permanently-Settled Bengal causing loss of life; while loss of life has been lamentable and frequent in every other province of India in spite of all relief operations. The contention, therefore, that the Permanent Settlement has saved Bengal from the worst results of famines is not disproved, but proved by history as completely and unanswerably as any economic fact can be proved.—*Reply to Lord Curzon's Land Assessment Resolution.*

(3) He had not stated that the prosperous condition of the Bengal raiyat was due to the Permanent Settlement alone. He had distinctly referred to the beneficial results of the Tenancy Act.

I myself rendered some humble assistance in the framing of the Rent Act of 1885, and my services on the occasion were kindly acknowledged in the *Calcutta Gazette* by the then Revenue Secretary of Bengal, Mr. Antony MacDonnell (now Sir Antony MacDonnell), the most distinguished Indian administrator of the present generation. I shall be the last person, therefore, to deny that the Rent Acts of Bengal were needed for the protection of cultivators, or that they completed the good work done by the Permanent Settlement.—*Reply to Lord Curzon's Land Assessment Resolution.*

(4) But he further points out that even before the Tenancy laws, the effect of the Permanent Settlement was described by competent observers to be wholly salutary. He is able to quote the opinions of such high authorities as Colebrook, Sir William Bentinck, Sir Thomas Munro, the Marquess of Wellesley, Lord Minto, Marquess of Hastings, Sir Charles Wood and Sir John Lawrence in support of his view. Sir John Lawrence wrote :—"I recommend a perpetual settlement, because I am persuaded that, however much the country has of late years improved, its resources will be still more rapidly developed by the limitation of the Government demand." In 1813 Lord Minto said :—"To ameliorate generally the conditions of the natives, it is our firm conviction that no arrangement or measure will tend so speedily and effectually to the accomplishment of those important objects as the establishment of a permanent settlement."

Such were the opinions [concludes Mr. Dutt] of three generations of distinguished administrators and able statesmen in India, of men who built the Empire, and valued the contentment and happiness of the people.—*Reply to Lord Curzon's Land Assessment Resolution.*

As regards the charge that Mr. Dutt and the other memorialists had not pleaded for a limitation of the zamindar's claims against the raiyat, it should be remembered that they were well aware that Government was already engaged in such beneficial legislation, and one of their principal demands was that the Government as landlord should impose the same limitations on its demands as it fixed on private landlords. There is a note of impatience in this section of the Government Resolution which is not in keeping with the studied dignity of that document as a whole, and is specially unfortunate in its application to Mr. Dutt; for it might have been known to the Government of India that there was hardly an officer of his time, except perhaps Sir Antony MacDonnell, who had fought so strenuously and so consistently on the side of tenants against landlords as Mr. Dutt.

It is important, therefore, to realise clearly that Mr. Dutt, though he defended the Permanent Settlement, did not by any means hold a brief for the zamindars, as opposed to the interests of the tenants. As he himself wrote in February 1899, to the *Pioneer*:—

I hold no brief for zamindars, or taluqdars, or malguzars, or landlords of any class. I hold and have held all through my official life that the actual cultivator of the soil should be lightly assessed. The cultivators are the nation in India, and if they are well off the nation is prosperous and resourceful, and famines would not be the terrible calamities that they are now.

He again made his position quite clear on this point in a letter addressed to Sir Antony MacDonnell on the 14th September 1900, in reply to a letter received from the Lieutenant-Governor of the North-Western Provinces.

I am as strong an advocate now [wrote Mr. Dutt] of the cultivator's rights to moderate assessments and fixity of tenure as I was fifteen years ago. I will never lend my support to landlords' demands to indefinite enhancements and excessive rents, and I will never cease to admire, and to support in such humble manner as I can, your endeavours to define and safeguard the interests of the poor cultivating population of Northern India as you *have* safeguarded the interests of the Bengal raiyat. I am in frequent communication with many public men in India, including, of course, some prominent landlords both in Bengal and in Northern India, but you can accept my assurance that the obvious desire of landlords to be left unfettered, in the matter of enhancing rents, and dealing with their raiyats as they like, has never received my support, and shall never receive any support, direct or indirect, from me, in whatever capacity I may work for my country.

My principal object in writing the Open Letters to Lord Curzon and in publishing them in the shape of a book was to draw attention to the state of things in Southern India. In the Central Provinces things are not as you left them; Mr. Fuller[1] has influenced the revenue policy—not beneficially—under the administration of your successors, and things are not as they should be. Happily that province has a good Chief Commissioner now; I know Mr. Fraser,[2] who went out to India in the same year with me, and I am sincerely hopeful he will set things right again. In Madras and Bombay they have drifted without any settled plan or purpose, and it *is* a fact that the revenue demanded by the Government from the cultivators is excessive. You tried to make a rule for Bengal (see p. 107 of my "Famines in India"), fixing one-fifth of the gross produce as the maximum of rent in Bengal. Such a rule, together with Lord Ripon's rule stopping enhancements except on the ground of increase in prices, would be the saving of Bombay and Madras cultivators.

In his letter of the 8th August, to which reference has just been made, Sir Antony MacDonnell, then Lieutenant-Governor of the North-Western Provinces, complained:—

I wish you had made it clearer that I do not think forty per cent. of the rental a fair share to be ordinarily taken by the Government at a resettlement. When the rents are reasonable, and when deductions from the rental are made for unexhausted improvements, and for *Sir* land, out of which the landlord, if he cultivates himself, gets as much as a tenant can, I think the Government is entitled to a share which should approximate to fifty per cent. If a fifty per cent. assessment gives a large enhancement of revenue, our practice here is to take less than fifty per cent., so that the enhancement shall not press heavily on the proprietor. And we also mitigate the burden by a progressive enhancement, which is so adjusted as to reach the full assessment, when considerable, in the eleventh year of a thirty-year settlement.

The same point was referred to by Sir Antony in his Budget speech 1899–1900. On the latter occasion

[1] Afterwards Sir Bampfylde Fuller, Lieutenant-Governor of Eastern Bengal.
[2] Afterwards Sir Andrew Fraser, Lieutenant-Governor of Bengal.

Mr. Dutt replied in the columns of the *Champion*, Bombay, and remarked :—

The correction seems to me to be merely a verbal one. When the British Government does an act, I always assume that it does it because it considers it just and fair. When the British Government accepts forty per cent. of the landlords' assets in the North-Western Provinces, I assume that the British Government considers that proportion just and fair, considering all circumstances. When Sir Antony MacDonnell asserts that fifty per cent. of the landlords' assets is theoretically the fair share of the Government, the assertion does not affect my main argument. Without speaking of the "theoretical share" of the Government, my argument would still be this, if the Government of the North-Western Provinces thought it expedient to take forty per cent., why should it demand sixty per cent. in the Central Provinces?

Mr. Dutt, however, subsequently acknowledged the mistake he had made, and in replying to Sir Antony's letter, said :—

I am greatly indebted by your very kind note of the 8th August. I think you will find in the footnote on p. 27 of my book on "Famines in India" that I have now clearly explained that fifty per cent. and not forty per cent. is considered as a fair share to be ordinarily taken in the North-Western Provinces by Government as revenue out of the rental.

While speaking of these criticisms, mention must be made of the just objection which Sir Antony took to Mr. Dutt's reference in his letters to the days of the "Hindu Arcadia." Sir Antony averred that if comparison had to be made with the state of things in the past, we ought to confine ourselves to historical times, and we may compare the revenue assessments under British rule with the revenue demand of Akbar, as noted in the "Aini Akbari." In a letter to the Bombay *Champion*, Mr. Dutt urged in reply that it was not fair to take the Moghal demand on paper to represent the actual collections of the time, and showed that even if we did accept these figures, we find that actual collections for Northern India had risen to 123 millions at the close of the nineteenth century from a demand of 77 millions in the sixteenth century. It is much to be wished, however, that these problematical comparisons with what might have been the case in Muhammadan and Hindu times had been avoided in a serious controversy, and Mr. Dutt had remained content with his old position—that to judge of the merits of British administration we should not be satisfied by simply proving its superiority to a state of things which prevailed under an Oriental form of government.

We may now proceed to those sections of the Government Resolution which deal with Mr. Dutt's proposals for the limitation of the amount of Land Revenue claimed by Government, for the extension of the period of settlements in tracts not permanently settled, and lastly for limiting the grounds for enhancements of rents to a rise in prices only. It was pointed out in the Government Resolution :—

That in areas where the State receives its land revenue from landlords, progressive moderation is the key-note of a policy of the Government, and that the standard of fifty per cent. of the assets is one which is almost uniformly preserved in practice, and is more often departed from on the side of deficiency than of excess. It is admitted, however, that in the Central Provinces, which have been for a shorter period under British rule, and where much higher assessments, amounting in some cases to over seventy-five per cent. of the actual income, were inherited from the Mahratta Government, there has been a progressive reduction of assessment; but it has not yet reached the very moderate level that is common in the North-Western Provinces. In time, as population increased, and more labour and expenditure are devoted to cultivation, the share taken by Government may be expected still further to diminish.

That in areas where the State takes the land revenue from the cultivators, the proposal to fix the assessment at one-fifth of the gross produce would result in the imposition of a greatly increased burden upon the people.

In reply it was pointed out by Mr. Dutt that the rule about the half-rent produce and one-fifth gross produce from the raiyats was meant to be a maximum which should not be exceeded in any single case, as there appear to have been some cases (*e.g.* of some taluqs in Madras where the Land Revenue was thirty-one per cent. of gross produce, and in Gujrat where the Land Revenue was twenty per cent.) where the Land Revenue must have exceeded this limit. It was also urged that a declaration of the maximum which the State would take as Land Revenue would have this further advantage "that the cultivators would know and understand clearly what the State demands, and what they are entitled to keep." For the declaration that "there is a growing tendency to approximate to the fifty per cent. standard, and that assessments have ceased to be made up on the prospective assets," Mr. Dutt expressed gratefulness to Lord Curzon.

Adverting to the period of settlement, it is pointed out in the Resolution that except in the Punjab and the Central Provinces thirty years is the accepted period of settlement at the present time.

> Where the land is fully cultivated, rents fair, agricultural production not liable to violent oscillations, it is sufficient if the demands of Government are re-adjusted once in thirty years, *i.e.* once in the lifetime of each generation. Where the opposite conditions prevail, where there are much waste land, low rents, and a fluctuating cultivation, or, again, where there is a rapid development of resources owing to the construction of roads, railways or canals, to an increase of population or to a rise in prices, the postponement of re-settlement for so long a period is both injurious to the people, who are unequal to the strain of a short enhancement, and unjust to the general taxpayer, who is temporarily deprived of the additional revenue to which he has a legitimate claim. Whether these considerations, justifying a shorter term of settlement than thirty years, apply with sufficient force to the Punjab and the Central Provinces at the present time; and if they do apply at the present time, whether the force of their application will diminish with the passage of time, are weighty questions to which careful attention will be given by the Government of India upon a suitable occasion.

In reply Mr. Dutt pointed out that the Punjab and Central Provinces were not less fully cultivated and not less developed in 1865 (when Lord George Hamilton ruled the shorter period for these provinces), after half a century of British rule, than the Bombay Province was in 1837, after twenty years of British rule, or the North-Western Provinces were in 1833, after thirty years of British rule. He added:—

If Lord Curzon succeeds, before laying down his office, to extend the thirty years' rule to the Punjab and the Central Provinces, His Excellency will have satisfied the memorialists, and earned the gratitude of millions of cultivators in those provinces.

Lastly, with regard to the grounds justifying an enhancement of rent, the Government Resolution laid down:—

To deny the right of the State to a share in any increase of values except those which could be inferred from the general tables of price statistics—in itself a most fallacious and partial test—would be to surrender to a number of individuals an increment which they had not themselves earned, but which had resulted, partly from the outlay of Government money on great public works, such as canals and railways, partly from the general enhancement of values produced by expanding resources and a higher standard of civilisation.

Mr. Dutt's rejoinder on this point is perhaps one of the most convincing passages in this famous controversy:—

This decision is disappointing. Increase in value is indicated by the table of prices. Lord Ripon's rule suggested, the rule framed by the memorialists also suggested, that the Government should obtain an enhancement of revenues when there was such increase in prices. And they reasonably urged that the Government should claim no increase when prices had not increased. *All the real advantages which the cultivator secures from new roads or lines of railway are shown in a rise in prices.* I was a District Officer in Midnapur ten years ago, when there was no railway line in the district. I am writing the present letter from the same place, which is now connected by rail with Calcutta,

AMALA, THIRD DAUGHTER

Bombay, and Madras. And prices have increased owing to this connection. A high official who has been here all these years informs me that rice was selling at 16 seers the rupee ten years ago and is now selling at 12½ seers the rupee. When such increase takes place in temporarily settled tracts, it is a legitimate ground for enhancement of revenue at the next settlement. When no such increase has taken place, the cultivators have derived no advantages; and to claim an increase of revenue at a settlement is to drive them deeper into debt and poverty. And not to define, clearly and intelligibly, the grounds on which the State is entitled to an increase of revenue from lands, is the most efficacious method that human ingenuity could devise for keeping them eternally in the gloom of uncertainty and the slough of despond.—*Mr. Dutt's Second Reply to Lord Curzon's Land Resolution.*

He further pointed out that by not defining the grounds under which Government would claim enhancements, Government had placed the raiyats of their own estates in a less satisfactory position than was held by the raiyats of private zamindars:—

As between private landlords and tenants the Rent Acts of Bengal lay down clearly and definitely the grounds of enhancement, and Courts of Justice will allow no enhancement of rent except on those specific grounds. As between the State and the peasant proprietors no such definite grounds of enhancement of the Land Tax are laid down, and no appeal to Courts of Justice is allowed.

IV

We may next turn to the discussion of the accuracy and adequacy of Mr. Dutt's analysis of the causes of Indian famines.

In the preliminary section of the Resolution it is stated that "it is not necessary to discuss the economic fallacy that any alteration in the system or scales of assessments can permanently save an agricultural population from the effects of a climatic disaster." "Nevertheless," proceeds the Resolution, "if prevention of the inevitable consequences of drought be an ideal incapable of attainment, mitigation is manifestly an object worthy of the closest attention of the Government. It cannot but be their desire that assessments should be equitable in character and moderate in incidence; and that there should be left to the proprietor or to the cultivator of the soil—as the case may be—that margin of profit that will enable him to save in ordinary seasons, and to meet the strain of exceptional misfortune."

Again, "Nor can it be denied that upon the incidence of the land revenue collections must the prosperity of agricultural classes in a great measure depend."

It has been seen that both Mr. Dutt and the other memorialists made it amply clear that the direct cause of famines is undoubtedly climatic, and thus there would hardly seem to be much substantial difference between Government and their critics on this important point. Accordingly in his reply Mr. Dutt pointed out:—

In these passages, the Government of India have fully recognised the cardinal principle which I have urged so often in recent years, that in an agricultural country like India, the prosperity and well-being of the nation greatly depend on the incidence of the Land Revenue being moderate and equitable; and that land assessments should be made so as to leave to the proprietor, or the cultivator, of the soil a margin of profit which will enable him to save in ordinary years to meet the strain of exceptional bad harvests. I could not wish for a more emphatic confirmation of the opinions which I have so frequently advanced; and I gratefully acknowledge that there is no difference in principle between the views I have urged and the views so authoritatively laid down in this Government Resolution.—*First Reply to Lord Curzon's Land Resolution.*

The following arguments are however advanced in the Resolution, to prove that there cannot be any material connection between the occurrence of famines and the existing Land Revenue assessment of the areas concerned:—

(1) There has been a progressive reduction of assessments, extending throughout the last century, and becoming more instead of less active during its second half. If, then, the severity of famine be proportionate to the weight of assessments, the famines in the earlier part of the nineteenth century ought

to have been incomparably more serious than towards its close; whereas the contention is familiar that the reverse has been the case.

(2) The Famine Commission do not support the theory that the most highly assessed parts have suffered most from famines.

(3) The total Land Revenue demand of India is insignificant compared to the total agrarian losses caused by droughts during famines.

It has been calculated that no reduction of the Land Revenue demand, short of its total abolition, and not even its abolition itself, could enable any community to hold up its head against a calamity so vast and so appalling.

(4) It is not of course disputed that if the Government were largely to abate its demand, and if the amount of such abatement were fairly distributed amongst the cultivating classes, and were saved up by them instead of being thoughtlessly spent, or absorbed by an increase of population, or appropriated by a particular section, a reserve would be created that might enable those classes better to withstand the losses caused by failure of the rains. But, unfortunately, neither in the past nor in the present circumstances of the country can any warrant be found for the belief that the revenue so relinquished by Government would constitute a famine relief fund in the hand of the people.

In illustration, a reference may be made to Bihar, which is permanently settled at a very light revenue, estimated as equivalent to a concession of at least eighty lakhs of rupees a year to the inhabitants. These advantages, however, have been monopolised by the land-owning section of the community, while the Bihar tenants remain among the most heavily rented in India, and, as the experience of two famines in the last thirty years has shown, have displayed the least capacity of resistance to the shock.

(5) It is manifest that any one who shuts his eyes to the industrial and economic forces that are at work in India at the present time, and that are patent upon the surface of agrarian life, who does not take into account the ever-increasing subdivision of holding (arising from the land-hunger of the peasant population and the inveterate reluctance of the raiyat to move even to the smallest distance from his natal place), the decline of industrial occupations other than agriculture, the rack-renting to which tenants are subjected by the more inconsiderate class of landlords and especially by middlemen of various degrees, the usurious rates of interest demanded by the money-lending class, the speculative expenditure upon litigation, the proneness

to extravagance on festival occasions, and the numerous payments in the form of petty bribes among the raiyats themselves, but who concentrates his entire gaze upon one aspect alone of their poverty, will carry away a most distorted impression both of the malady which he has set himself to diagnose, and of the remedies which it is in the power or is the duty of Government to apply.

As regards the references to past famines, it might be observed that the range covered by the illustrations in the Resolution would appear to be more limited than that of the historical review of famines made by Mr. Dutt, with the object of establishing the fact that famines have been more severe in Southern and Central India than in Bengal. It might also be urged that economic laws are only tendencies, and it is only over long periods and wide areas that their real trend becomes manifest. Mr. Dutt also disputes the proposition that leniency in land assessment reacts prejudicially on the raiyats.

> The experience of every revenue officer in Bengal directly contradicts this theory. Within my memory—within the last forty-three years since the first Rent Act was passed in Bengal—the indebtedness of the Bengal cultivators and the power of the money-lenders have decreased in consequence of the provisions against the undue enhancement of rents; and this has been so even in Bihar since the passing of the last Rent Act. It is excessive assessment and rigorous collection, not leniency, which drive the cultivators to serfdom under money-lenders, and this is proved by the report of the last Famine Commission.—*Third Reply to Lord Curzon's Land Resolution*.

In any case it is clear that the position of Government is, not that there is no connection between Land Revenue assessments and the famine-resisting powers of the raiyats, but that the connection is remote, and the poverty of the agricultural class is attributable to other and more potent and direct causes. The real difference between Government and their critics would therefore appear to be that, while the Government of India hold land assessments to be a negligible and unimportant factor in the discussion of famines and their remedies, Mr. Dutt and his supporters hold the reduction of the Land

Tax to be most important, not in preventing famines, but in adding to the famine-resisting powers of the people. According to the critics of Government, under the present circumstances of the agricultural community in India, the only practicable way of helping the agriculturists is to relieve them to some extent of the burden of rent which they have to pay either to a private landlord or to Government. Without denying that the spread of education, agricultural and general, the organisation of credit, the cultivation of the habit to save, the multiplication of occupations, and a diversion into industrial and commercial channels of the congested agricultural population of the country, are perhaps more permanent remedies for the removal of the poverty of the agricultural classes, they maintain that in the existing condition of the agricultural industry in India, steeped as the tenants are in poverty, ignorance, and debt, these civilising forces will take considerable time to reach them ; but in the meanwhile the only practical way to relieve them would be to lighten the burden of taxation of their lands. Hence the importance of the subject, and the necessity of "fixing one's gaze on this aspect of the question." So Mr. Reynolds wrote to Mr. Dutt :—

> You are quite right in putting excessive rent assessments in the foreground as a main cause of the impoverishment of India, both because it is well to concentrate attention upon one much-needed reform, and because reduction of land assessments must necessarily lead to retrenchment in expenditure.

Though it is obviously not the business of Romesh Dutt's biographer to pass judgment on the relative merits of the arguments advanced on either side, it may nevertheless be permissible to point out that the famous controversy was fruitful of many important results. It brought about a full and exhaustive statement of the present policy of Government, and gained for the raiyats some substantial concessions, particularly with regard to enhancements on the ground of prospective rise in prices, which Sir Antony MacDonnell acknowledged, in a letter to Mr. Dutt, to be "the great error of the old method of settlement." It also cleared a good deal of misapprehension, and showed how in recent settlements moderation had been the key-note of the policy pursued by Government. For his courage in starting the controversy, and the ability and grasp of details which he showed in advocating his views, Mr. Dutt is entitled to the gratitude both of the Government and the people.

CHAPTER XXIV

VIEWS ON INDUSTRIAL AND FINANCIAL QUESTIONS

I

FROM Land Assessment, Mr. Dutt passes to the next factor which, according to him, has contributed to the poverty of the Indian people, viz. the contraction of the indigenous industries and manufactures during the early years of British rule. The following summary of his views on this subject is taken from the prefaces to the two volumes of his "Economic History."

India in the eighteenth century was a great manufacturing as well as a great agricultural country, and the products of the Indian loom supplied the markets of Asia and of Europe. It is, unfortunately, true that the East India Company and the British Parliament, following the selfish commercial policy of a hundred years ago, discouraged Indian manufacturers in the early years of British rule in order to encourage the rising manufactures of England. Their fixed policy, pursued during the last decades of the eighteenth century and the first decades of the nineteenth, was to make India subservient to the industries of Great Britain, and to make the Indian people grow raw produce only, in order to supply material for the looms and manufactories of Great Britain. This policy was pursued with unwavering resolution and with fatal success; orders were sent out to force Indian artisans to work in the Company's factories; commercial residents were legally vested with extensive powers over villages and communities of Indian weavers; prohibitive tariffs excluded Indian silk and cotton goods from England; English goods were admitted into India free of duty or on payment of a nominal duty.

The British manufacturer, in the words of the historian, H. H. Wilson, "employed the arms of political injustice to keep down and ultimately strangle a competitor with whom he could not have contended on equal terms"; millions of Indian artisans lost their earnings; the population of India lost one great source of their wealth.—"*India under Early British Rule.*"

When Queen Victoria ascended the throne in 1837 the evil had been done. But, nevertheless, there was no relaxation in the policy pursued before. Indian silk handkerchiefs still had a sale in Europe; and a high duty on manufactured Indian silk was maintained. Parliament inquired how cotton could be grown in India for British looms, not how Indian looms could be improved. Select Committees tried to find out how British manufactures could find a sale in India, not how Indian manufactures could be revived. Long before 1858, when the East India Company's rule ended, India had ceased to be a great manufacturing country. Agriculture had virtually become the one remaining source of the nation's subsistence.

British merchants still watched and controlled the Indian tariff after 1858. The import of British goods into India was facilitated by the reduction of import duties. The growth of looms and factories in Bombay aroused jealousy. In 1879, a year of famine, war, and deficit in India, a further sacrifice of import duties was demanded by Parliament. And in 1882 all import duties were abolished except on salt and liquor.

But the sacrifices told on the Indian revenues. In spite of new taxes on the peasantry, and new burdens on agriculture, India could not pay her way. In 1894 the old import duties were revived with slight modifications. A 5 per cent. duty was imposed on cotton goods and yarns imported into India, and a countervailing duty of 5 per cent. was imposed on such Indian cotton fabrics as competed with the imported goods. In 1896 cotton yarns were freed from duty; but a duty of 3½ per cent. was imposed on cotton goods imported into India; and an excise duty of 3½ per cent. was imposed on all goods manufactured at Indian mills. Coarse Indian goods, which did not in any way compete with Lancashire goods, were taxed, as well as finer fabrics. The miserable clothing of the miserable Indian labourer, earning less than 2½d. a day, was taxed by a jealous Government. The infant mill industry of Bombay, instead of receiving help and encouragement, was repressed by an excise duty unknown in any other part of the civilised world. During a century and a half the commercial policy of the British rulers of India has been determined, not by the interests of Indian manufacturers, but by those of British manufacturers. The vast quantities of manufactured goods which were exported from India by the Portuguese and the Dutch, by Arab and British merchants, in the seventeenth and eighteenth centuries, have disappeared. India's exports now are mostly raw produce—largely the food of the people. Manufacturing industry as a source of national income has been narrowed.—*Preface to "India in the Victorian Age."*

Mr. Dutt was, however, not unaware that it was not alone the selfish policy pursued during the early years of British rule which was responsible for the decay of the Indian industries. In the preface to "India under Early British Rule" he said that "the invention of the power-loom in Europe completed the decline of the Indian industries," and his later pronouncements on the subject contain a completer statement of the case :—

It would be a needless waste of time to refer to-day to those causes which led to a decline and decay of Indian manufactures from the middle of the eighteenth to the middle of the nineteenth century. The internal wars among contending nations in India was one principal cause; the commercial policy of England in those days was a second potent cause; and the discovery of power-looms in England was a third.—*Surat Speech*, 1907.

In the writings of this middle period, however, he did not formulate any constructive scheme for the revival of indigenous industries, and his views on the industrial position of the present and prospects of the future were certainly not as hopeful as those held at a later period. For instance, as regards the new industries, like indigo and tea, which have grown up during British rule, he had the following :—

Gentlemen, you hear very little in this country of this decline of the old national industries of India. Your attention is naturally attracted to those industries only in which British capital is employed. You read of tea and coffee, of indigo and jute, of coal mines and gold mines, which are worked by British companies. We wish well to all these industries, for they give employment to hundreds of thousands of Indian labourers. But you cannot improve the condition of the people of India without fostering their own industries, carried on by themselves, in their towns and villages. You cannot add to the wealth of the Indian people except by wise legislation, tending to promote and help their own national undertakings.—*Glasgow Speech*, 1901.

Similarly, as regards the rise of imports and exports, he said :—

Figures often mislead us unless rightly explained. We have been told that the trade of India has increased by leaps and bounds, and the increase of trade must mean the prosperity of the people. We have been told that the total value of India's exports and imports has increased from Rs.20,000,000 to over Rs.200,000,000 within the present reign. The export of tea from India has risen from nothing to 150,000,000 pounds; the export of cotton has increased from nothing to 11,000,000 hundredweight; the production of jute has increased from almost nothing to 1,000,000 tons; the export of wheat has risen from nothing to 750,000 tons; coal is produced every year to the extent of 3,000,000 tons, and there is increase in the production or export of various other articles which form articles of trade. Twenty thousand miles of railway have been constructed, and steamers ply in all the navigable rivers of India.

We have no desire to minimise the prosperity of the English trade with India which these figures indicate; but when they are brought forward to prove that the material condition of the industrial and agricultural population of India has improved, a great fallacy is committed. Among the many blessings which England has conferred on India, the encouragement of Indian industries is not one. The increase in the value of imports into India really means that the manual industries of India have died out in an unequal competition with the steam and machinery of England. And the increase in the value of exports from India means that vast quantities of food and raw material have to be sent out from India to pay for imported English goods.—*Glasgow Speech*, 1901.

For his later and more optimistic—perhaps juster—views on the subject, with due recognition of the present policy of Government of encouraging indigenous industries—reference should be made to a later section.

The following remarks regarding the relative claims of the further extension of railways and the construction of irrigation works are taken from his Glasgow speech, 1901 :—

I now turn from the important subject of the Land Tax to the railways and irrigation works of India. The construction of railways has, I need hardly remark to this audience, been highly beneficial in India, as it is beneficial in every other part of the world. It has shortened distances, made travelling and traffic cheaper, and, what is of great importance, it has made transport of food grains from one province to another in times of distress quicker and easier. Nevertheless, railways in India have been constructed with doubtful wisdom out of the revenues of the country, or under guarantees of profits out of such revenues. When the State undertakes railway construction or guarantees profits out of public revenues, the concern is never as paying as when undertaken by private companies on their own risk. And so it happens that the entire railway system in India has resulted, not in profit, but in a total loss of 40 million pounds sterling to the revenues of India. This loss has added to the public debt, and the taxpayers of India are paying, year after year, a heavy tax as interest on the debt thus piled up. During the last year there was no loss, because the railway earned much by conveying vast quantities of food grains to the famine-stricken provinces. What was a wide-spread calamity for the people was a gain to the railway. We all hope the famine will not last long, and I much fear the profits of the railways will disappear with the famine. In any case it is extremely doubtful if the Indian railways will ever make sufficient profits to wipe off the past loss of 40 millions; and generations of Indian taxpayers will continue to bear the burden of taxation in consequence of this loss.

The total length of railways in India open to traffic by the end of 1898 was 22,500 miles. In that year the Indian Famine Commission stated in their published report that the lines required for famine protection purposes had been completed, and that preference should be given to irrigation works in the future. The advice was unheeded. There is a continuous pressure put on the Indian Government by capitalists and speculators for the construction of fresh railway lines out of the Indian revenues. And thus in spite of the advice of the Famine Commission of 1898 and the earlier Commission of 1880, the Indian Government has shown more activity in the construction of railways than irrigation works. The total length of railways open to traffic up to the end of 1900 was 25,000 miles.

The railway system does not add one single blade of corn to the food supply of the country, while irrigation works double the food supply, save crops, and prevent famines. Nevertheless, while 225 millions sterling have been spent on railways, only 25

If we turn from the sources of wealth to the distribution of wealth, the same depressing picture is presented to us. The total revenues of India during the last ten years of the Queen's reign 1891–92 to 1900–1 came to 647 millions sterling. The annual average is thus under 65 millions, including receipts from railways, irrigation works, and all other sources. The expenditure in England during these ten years was 159 millions, giving an annual average of nearly 16 millions sterling. One-fourth, therefore, of all the revenues derived in India is annually remitted to England as Home Charges. And if we add to this the portion of their salaries which European officers employed in India annually remit to England, the total annual drain out of the Indian revenues to England considerably exceeds 20 millions. The richest country on earth stoops to levy this annual contribution from the poorest. Those who earn £42 per head ask for 10s. per head from a nation earning £2 per head. And this 10s. per head which the British people draw from India impoverishes British trade with India. The contribution does not benefit British commerce and trade, while it drains the life-blood of India in a continuous, ceaseless flow.

For when taxes are raised and spent in a country, the money circulates among the people, fructifies trades, industries, and agriculture, and in one shape or another reaches the mass of the people. But when the taxes raised in a country are remitted out of it, the money is lost to the country for ever; it does not stimulate her trades or industries, or reach the people in any form. Over 20 millions sterling are annually drained from the revenues of India; and it would be a miracle if such a process, continued through long decades, did not impoverish even the richest nation upon earth.

The total Land Revenue of India was 17½ millions in 1900–1. The total of Home Charges in the same year came to 17 millions. It will be seen, therefore, that an amount equivalent to all that is raised from the soil, in all the Provinces of India, is annually remitted out of the country as Home Charges. An additional sum of several millions is sent in the form of private remittances by European officers, drawing their salaries from the Indian revenues; and this remittance increases as the employment of European officers increases in India.

The 17 millions remitted as Home Charges are spent in England, (1) as interest payable on the Indian debt; (2) as interest on railways; and (3) as Civil and Military Charges. A small portion, about a million, covers the cost of military and other stores supplied to India.

A very popular error prevails in this country that the whole Indian debt represents British capital sunk in the development of India. It can be shown that this is not the genesis of the Public Debt of India. When the East India Company ceased to be rulers of India in 1858, they had piled up an Indian Debt of 70 millions. They had in the meantime drawn a tribute from India, financially an unjust tribute, exceeding 150 millions, not calculating interest. They had also charged India with the cost of Afghan wars, Chinese wars, and other wars outside India. Equitably, therefore, India owed nothing at the close of the Company's rule; her Public Debt was a myth; there was a considerable balance of over 100 millions in her favour out of the money that had been drawn from her.

Within the first eighteen years of the administration of the Crown the Public Debt of India was doubled. It amounted to about 140 millions in 1877, when the Queen became the Empress of India. This was largely owing to the cost of the Mutiny wars, over 40 million sterling, which was thrown on the revenues of India. And India was made to pay a large contribution to the cost of the Abyssinian war of 1867.

Between 1877 and 1900, the Public Debt rose from 139 millions to 224 millions. This was largely due to the construction of railways by Guaranteed Companies or by the State, beyond the pressing needs of India and beyond her resources. It was also largely due to the Afghan wars of 1878 and 1897. The history of the Indian Debt is a distressing record of financial unwisdom and injustice; and every impartial reader can reckon for himself how much of this Indian Debt is morally due from India.

The last items of the Home Charges are the Civil and Military Charges. This needs a revision. If Great Britain and India are both gainers by the building up of the British Indian Empire, it is not fair or equitable that India alone should pay all the cost of the maintenance of that superb edifice. It is not fair that all the expenses incurred in England, down to the maintenance of the India Office and the wages of the charwoman employed to clean the rooms at Whitehall, should be charged to India. Over forty years ago one of the greatest of Indian administrators suggested an equitable compromise. In a work on "Our Financial Relations with India," published in 1859, Sir George Wingate suggested that India should pay all the expenses of Civil and Military Administration incurred in India, while Great Britain should meet the expenses incurred in England, as she did for her Colonies. Is it too late to make some such equitable adjustment to-day? India's total Civil and Military Charges, incurred in England, come to 6 millions, a sum which would be considerably reduced if it came from the British taxpayer. Is it too much to expect that Great Britain might share this burden, while India paid all the Civil and Military charges incurred in India?

These are the plain facts of the economic situation in India. Given these conditions, any fertile, industrious, peaceful country in the world would be what India is to-day. If manufacturers were crippled, agriculture overtaxed, and a third of the revenue remitted out of the country, any nation on earth would suffer from permanent poverty and recurring famines. Economic laws are the same in Asia as in Europe. If India is poor to-day, it is through the operation of economic causes.

As to the special disadvantages which, according to Mr. Dutt, the existing system of administration both in England and India imposes on any attempt to carry out a policy of financial retrenchment or constitutional reform, Mr. Dutt makes the following observations in the preface to "India under Early British Rule."

The statesman and administrator in India labours under peculiar difficulties. Three successive Governors-General, Lord Wellesley, Lord Minto, and Lord Hastings, desired to place a permanent limit to the Land Tax of India, but the East India Company overruled them, and would consent to no limit to their demands. Three Viceroys under the Crown, Lord Canning, Lord Lawrence and Lord Ripon, pressed again for some limitation of the Land Tax, but the Secretary of State for India rejected their proposals. Three times within the present generation have the Indian tariffs been altered, under the dictation of British manufacturers, against the interests of India, and sometimes against the opinions of the majority of the Viceroy's Council. Three times within this period have endeavours been made to grant adequate protection to Indian labourers, recruited for the tea-gardens of Assam, who cease to be free men and free women after they have once signed their contracts, sometimes under misapprehension or fraud. The penal laws which chain them to the gardens still remain on the Statute Book, the proposals recently made by the Honourable Mr. Cotton, Chief Commissioner of Assam, to assure them adequate pay were whittled down in the Viceroy's Council, and their operation was then suspended for two years by Lord Curzon, because British shareholders in the tea concerns objected to them. Administrators in India are helpless on such occasions. Remedial measures, placing equitable limits on the taxes of India, have been vetoed by the Home authorities, and protective measures needed for the welfare of the people of India have been sacrificed, when they were supposed to touch the interests of any class of capitalists or manufacturers commanding votes in Parliament.

Nor are the Indian administrators strong in the support of the Indian people. The Indian Government means the Viceroy and the Members of the Executive Council, viz. the Commander-in-Chief, the Military Member, the Public Works Member, the Finance Member, the Home Member, and the Legal Member. The people are not represented in this Council; their agriculture, their landed interests, their trades and industries, are not represented; there is not, and never has been, a single Indian Member in the Council. All the Members of the Council are heads of spending departments, as was lately explained by Sir Auckland Colvin and Sir David Barbour before the Royal Commission on Indian expenditure. The Members are high English officials, undoubtedly interested in the welfare of the people, but driven by the duties of their office to seek for more money for the working of their departments; there are no Indian Members to represent the interests of the people. The forces are all arrayed on the side of expenditure, there are none on the side of retrenchment. "The tendency is," said Sir David Barbour, "ordinarily for pressure to be put on the Financial Department to incur expenditure. It is practically pressure. The other departments are always pressing to spend more money; their demands are persistent and continuous." There is no counterpressure to reduce expenditure, to moderate taxation, to safeguard the agricultural interests of the people, to encourage their industries and manufacturers. Thus the constitution of the Indian Government makes an alien rule still more isolated and weak. Every grave question is virtually decided *ex parte*. The Members of the Council are able, wise, experienced, and conscientious men; but the wisest judges will fail to decide cases rightly if they hear the evidence of one party only. And the Indian Government, with every honest desire to do its duty, is unable to secure the material welfare of the people, because it is not in touch with the people, does not accept the co-operation of the people, cannot by its constitution act in the interests of the people.

III

Here, again, in the field of Finance and Industry, Mr. Dutt based his opinions on the views of an earlier generation of English administrators who had devoted their lives to the welfare of India. These opinions are quoted at length in Mr. Dutt's works, and a few extracts will be useful to show that Mr. Dutt's ideas, though they are perhaps not based on an adequate consideration of all the issues involved, certainly did not originate from any racial or sectarian bias and short-sightedness in him. Montgomery Martin, in his "Eastern India" (1838), observed :—

For half a century we have gone on draining from two to three and sometimes four million pounds sterling a year from India, which has been remitted to Great Britain to meet the deficiencies of commercial speculations, to pay the interests of debts, to support the home establishment, and to invest on England's soil the accumulated wealth of those whose lives have been spent in Hindustan. I do not think it possible for human ingenuity to avert entirely the evil effects of a continued drain of three or four million pounds a year from a distant country like India, and which is never returned to it in any shape.

The Hon. John Shore (afterwards Lord Teignmouth), in his "Notes on Indian Affairs" (1837), said :—

The fundamental principle of the English had been to make the whole Indian nation subservient, in every possible way, to the interests and benefits of themselves. They have been taxed to the utmost limit; every successive province, as it has fallen into our possession, has been made a field for higher exaction.

Sir George Wingate, in his work on "Our Financial Relations with India," 1859 :—

If, then, we have governed India not merely for the natives of India, but for ourselves, we are clearly blamable in the sight of God and man for having contributed nothing towards defraying the cost of that government. Our fair share, represented by the degree in which British interests have decided our Indian policy, be it great or small, should have been duly paid, but this has never been done, and now there is a heavy debt which has been running up against us for many years to be settled. England was powerful, and India at her feet, and little chance had the weak of enforcing payment from the strong. . . .

With reference to its economical effects upon the condition of India, the tribute paid to Great Britain is by far the most objectionable feature in our existing policy. Taxes spent in the country from which they are raised are totally different in their effects from taxes raised in one country, and spent in another. In the former case the taxes collected from the population at large are paid away to the portion of the population engaged in the service of Government, through whose expenditure they are again returned to the industrious classes. They occasion a different distribution, but no loss of national income, and hence it is that in countries advanced in civilisation, in which the productive powers of men are augmented by mechanical contrivances and a judicious use of the powers of nature, an enormous taxation may be realised with singularly little pressure upon the community. *But the case is wholly different when the taxes are not spent in the country from which they are raised. In this case they constitute no mere transfer of a portion of the national income from one set of citizens to another, but an absolute loss and extinction of the whole amount withdrawn from the taxed country. As regards its effects on national production, the whole amount might as well be thrown into the sea as transferred to another country, for no portion of it will return from the latter to the taxed country in any shape whatsoever.* Such is the nature of the tribute we have so long exacted from India.

It is hardly necessary to point out how close the resemblance is between these views and the opinions formulated by Mr. Dutt.

It is not proposed here to examine in detail the soundness or otherwise of the above views judged on a broad and scientific review of economic and financial data which the present relations of England and India present; but I believe it has to be conceded that these views are perhaps open to the following criticisms :—

(1) They hardly make sufficient allowance for the gradual change in the economic and financial policy of the Government of India. As has already been stated, Mr. Dutt in the later years of his life made adequate acknowledgment of this fact.

(2) They do not take adequate note of the fact that from the very nature of the present political relations of England and India, it is unavoidable that some portion of the Indian revenues must be spent in England. It was no special virtue of the Moghal Emperors, who were settled in India, that they spent their revenues in India, and it is no charge against the British Government that a part of the Indian revenue has to be spent in England, which is the seat of a vital portion of the administrative machinery of the country.

(3) And lastly, sufficient allowance has hardly been made of the fact that a very large portion of the so-called "tribute" is only a return for valuable services received by India. As Sir Theodore Morison has pointed out in his recent work on "The Economic Transition in India," "the answer to the question, 'What economic equivalent does India get for foreign payments?' is that India gets the equipment of modern industry, and she gets an administration favourable to economic evolution cheaper than she could provide it herself."

It would appear, therefore, that the permanent value of Mr. Dutt's laborious researches into the past economic relations of England and India, lies not so much in the account which he gives in the two volumes of his Economic History of the selfish and shortsighted mercantile policy of the earlier British rule in India, as in the strong and unanswerable plea he makes out in these works for the adoption of a more generous policy for developing the nascent indigenous industries of the country, for a fairer adjustment between India and the sovereign country of the civil and military charges, and for a remodelling of the machinery of government, both as regards the internal constitution of the Government of India and its relations with the Home Government, so that it may lead to closer economy in the expenditure of the revenues of the country.

CHAPTER XXV

VIEWS ON ADMINISTRATIVE REFORMS

MR. DUTT finally passes to the elaboration of those reforms in the general administrative machinery of the country, which, by associating a few educated and capable children of the soil in the administration of their country, will, according to him, bring the British Government more in touch with the people, and make administration itself more efficient and less expensive. A brief outline of his views is given by him in his preface to "India in the Victorian Age":—

This form of administration, shaped by Warren Hastings and Cornwallis, and improved by Munro, Elphinstone, and Bentinck, requires some change after seventy years. Education has spread within these seventy years; educated men are a growing power in India. They demand a fair share in the higher services of their own country; they desire to have a voice in the highest Councils of the Empire. It is easy to disregard this demand, to alienate the educated and influential sections of the Indian population, to increase discontent and disaffection in the country, and to weaken the Empire by continuing an exclusive rule. It would be wiser, on the other hand, to array the rising forces on the side of the Government, to make educated and influential men in India partakers in the control of the administration, to make them represent their own interests, industries, and agriculture, and to make them responsible for improving the material condition of their countrymen and the prevention of famines. To quote once more from John Stuart Mill: "It is an inherent condition of human affairs that no intention, however sincere, of protecting the interests of others, can make it safe or salutary to tie up their own hands. By their own hands only can any positive and durable improvement of their circumstances in life be worked out."

The people of India are not fond of sudden changes and revolutions. They do not ask for new constitutions, issuing like armed Minervas from the heads of legislative Jupiters. They prefer to work on lines which have already been laid down. They desire to strengthen the present Government, and to bring it more in touch with the people. They desire to see some Indian members in the Secretary of State's Council, and in the Viceroy's Executive Council, representing Indian agriculture and industries. They wish to see Indian members in an Executive Council for each province. They wish to represent the interests of the people in the discussion of every important administrative question. They seek that the administration of the Empire and its great provinces should be conducted with the co-operation of the people.

As to the inclusion of Indians in the Executive Councils of the Empire, he made the following suggestions :—

There are Executive Councils in Bombay and in Madras; similar Executive Councils may be formed in the North-West Provinces and the Punjab, in the Central Provinces and in Bengal, and at least one member of an Executive Council should be an Indian gentleman with experience in administrative work, and representing the views of his countrymen. It is usual for a member of an Executive Council to have a portfolio, *i.e.* to have one department of work assigned to him; and the work which I would assign to the Indian member is Land Revenue, Agriculture, and the Industries. There is no department of work in which an Indian member can make himself more valuable to the voiceless millions of cultivators and artisans. The addition of one Indian member will not weaken Provincial administration. It will strengthen such administration, make it more sympathetic, and bring it into somewhat closer touch with the people.

And, gentlemen, am I aspiring too high when I hope for similar seats for Indian members in the cloudy heights of Simla? Am I urging anything unreasonable when I propose that the Viceroy, who has the benefit of consulting experienced English administrators in his Executive Council, should also have the advantage of hearing the views and opinions of a few Indian members in the same Council before he decides on questions affecting the interests of the people of India? Am I urging anything unwise when I propose that the Viceroy, when he considers measures affecting the condition of the indebted cultivators, the operations of the plague and famine relief, the rules of land revenue settlements, the questions affecting Hindu and Muhammadan customs and manners, should have by him, in his own Executive Council, a few Indian gentlemen who represent the views, the opinions, and the feelings of the people? An Executive Council cannot be much enlarged without loss of efficiency, but surely the Viceroy's Council could make room for three Indian gentlemen, one to represent Bengal and Assam, another to represent the North-West and the Punjab, and the third to represent Bombay, Madras, and the Central Provinces. The selection should rest, of course, with the Viceroy himself, for anything like election into an Executive Council would be absurd; and the three Indian members should be entrusted with the departments of Agriculture, Industries, and Land Revenue of their respective provinces.—*Presidential Address to the Indian National Congress*, 1899.

There is a Legislative Council in each large Indian Province, and some of the members of these Councils are elected under the Act of 1892. The experiment has proved a success, and some expansion of these Legislative Councils would strengthen administration and bring it more in touch with the people. Each Indian province is divided into twenty or thirty or more districts, corresponding to English counties, and each district has a population of a million or more. The time has come when each district might elect its own member for the Legislative Council of the Province. A province with thirty districts and a population of thirty millions may fairly have thirty elected members on its Legislative Council. Each district should feel that it has some voice in the administration of the province.

The higher services in India, which were theoretically declared open to the people in 1833, in 1853, and by Queen Victoria's famous proclamation of 1858, should be practically open to the people, and not reserved for English boys seeking a career in the East. In the great Indian Civil Service, as well as in the Education, Engineering, Postal, Telegraph, Police, and Medical departments, Indians should find it possible to obtain high employment. We want Englishmen in all these departments, we welcome them to help us, but we do not wish them to monopolise all the higher services to the virtual exclusion of the children of the soil.

In each Indian district there is a District Officer who is the

millions of Indians have been educated in English and vernacular schools in India; thousands of them have travelled in Europe and completed their education in England. Steam and telegraph have brought the people of India closer to England; loyal and influential political bodies have taught them the methods of constitutional agitation; and the very spread of the idea of imperial federation has inspired them with the hope that India, though only a dependency, has deserved, and will receive, some measure of self-government, along with the other parts of England's world-wide empire.

A feeling of unrest is perceptible in India, *not of unrest under the British rule, but of unrest under a form of government framed forty years ago, and which no longer suits the circumstances of the present day.* There is danger in exaggerating this feeling, but it were folly to close our eyes to it altogether. And the secret of this feeling of unrest is this, that educated Indian opinion and sentiment and ambition are struggling against that cast-iron form of administration which has not expanded with the times. Indian opinion seeks to be heard, and is not heard; Indian feeling seeks to be represented, and is not represented. It is easy to condemn this desire as discontent, or even disloyalty, but Englishmen must know that it is neither one nor the other. It is a natural feeling produced by antiquated methods of government after the country has outgrown those methods. It is a feeling which Englishmen would have felt to-day if the old system of representation had not been reformed by the Acts of 1832, 1867, and 1884.

England now *stands at the parting of the ways* in regard to Indian administration. She can continue to rule India regardless of the wishes of the people, and according to the method constructed forty years ago. She can continue to keep the door closed against any real representation of Indian opinion and Indian feeling in the government of the country. She can refuse to allow to the people of the country a real and legitimate share in conducting and directing the administration. She can turn a deaf ear to the growing demand to make the administration more liberal, more in touch with the people, more in consonance with the progress of the times. And she can decline the counsels and the co-operation of the people in her endeavours to ameliorate their condition, to readjust finances, and to face scarcities and famines. England has the power to proceed on these lines if she thinks it a wise course.

There is yet a second course which England can adopt. *Without yielding in the slightest degree her hold over India she may yet admit the children of the soil into a larger share of administrative power.* Strong in maintaining order among the various races and nationalities of India, she may yet seek to minimise the chances of disorder and the causes of discontent by allowing some system of representation to those races. Determined to hold the balance evenly among the different Indian communities, and to rule with firmness as well as with justice, she may still invite the natural leaders of those communities to partake more largely in the work of administration, and to enlighten the Government with their views and opinions on questions affecting their welfare. And maintaining her strong rule over the great continent peopled by nearly three hundred millions of men, she may yet allow that vast population some carefully guarded system of representation, some method of being consulted and heard in the management of their own concerns.

It is impossible to read this strong arraignment at the bar of the British nation and to follow the course of legislation during the last few eventful years without feeling that his manly and strong voice was not raised in vain. And no more convincing proof of the impression which Mr. Dutt's views made on the political philosophy of Indian questions can be found than in the memorable words which Lord Minto used in his speech at the United Service Banquet at Simla (October 1910), in reviewing the course of legislation during his viceroyalty, on lines so strikingly similar to the just and moderate demands of Mr. Dutt.

But the problem with which the Government of India was confronted in 1906 [said His Excellency] was something more genuine and therefore much more serious. It was the assertion of a political awakening. There were two ways of dealing with it. It was open to the Government of India to say we will not listen to these new ideas; they are opposed to the stability of British rule, or to recognise the justice of them as the product of years of British administration and adaptation of British political thought. *We had come to the parting of the ways*, and to my mind there has never been a shadow of a doubt as to which was the right road to follow. It was perfectly open to us either to refuse to recognise the signs of the times, or to recognise them and attempt to deal with the new conditions. *I can only say, gentle-*

men, that if we had adopted the former course we should have gone back on all that we have said and done in the past, and alienated from the cause of British administration many who had been brought up in its doctrines, and built their hopes upon a belief in its justice. We should have driven them into the camp of the enemy to become the traducers of British rule. We should have perpetuated a discontented India.

CHAPTER XXVI

LITERARY PREFERENCES

MR. DUTT contributed to the *Wednesday Review*, 23rd August 1905, an article describing the literary influences of his life. We reproduce it in full:—

Sir Walter Scott was my favourite author forty years ago. I spent days and nights over his novels; I almost lived in those historic scenes and in those mediæval times which the enchanter had conjured up. Scott has, in fact, created a world of his own—a somewhat idealised, but a vivid and, on the whole, faithful picture of the mediæval world in Europe. The other writers who come close to him in creative imagination can be counted on one's fingers. Charles Dickens has portrayed with admirable truth and admirable humour a London world; Balzac has reproduced with unsurpassed power a Parisian world; and Emile Zola has drawn with equal force some phases of lower French life and society.

I do not know if Sir Walter Scott gave me a taste for history, or if my taste for history made me an admirer of Scott; but no subject, not even poetry, had such a hold upon me as history. The first great work that fascinated me—it is thirty-four years since I first read it—was Gibbon's "Roman Empire." The vast extent of his canvas, the grandeur and variety of his scenes and subjects, and his power of graphic and vivid delineation make the work almost unique in historical literature—nations and tribes, Romans, Gauls, Germans, Arabs, Moghals, and Turks—august emperors, barbarian leaders, and bold Christian Crusaders, march past before our eyes. The progress of the human race from the decline of ancient civilisation, through the dim light of the Middle Ages to the time when the broad sunshine of modern civilisation was breaking in Italy and Spain and in Flanders, is depicted with a power and comprehensiveness which has never been excelled.

I longed for other historical works, but seldom found his equal. Grote is painstaking, accurate, and profound, but lacks sympathy and the power of graphic representation. Guizot's "History of Civilisation" is philosophic and thoughtful, and gives one an insight into the mediæval times. Buckle is full of theories, and his pictures of certain ages of France and Spain are powerful. I read the thirty odd volumes of Sismondi's "France" in French, and his short work on "Italian Republics" in English; both are great works. Macaulay and Carlyle depict scenes and characters in brilliant colours, but are rather painters and narrators than historians. I never learnt German well enough to read the great works of modern German historians in the original. Our education is incomplete unless we learn the three great modern languages—English, French, and German. My Sanskrit Professor, the late Dr. Goldstucker, often used to say: "Never trust what one nation tells you; read the writings of all the three and judge for yourself."

No great work on the history of the last five centuries has yet been written—a Gibbon on modern Europe has yet to arise. Historical writers in recent times have been delving for fresh facts and materials; when these are collected, I have no doubt a proper history of modern Europe will be written. In the meantime we have full and accurate and often graphic accounts of particular ages. In England Freeman and Froude, Lecky and Gardiner are industrious workers, but the nineteenth century produced no great English historians.

The worst fault of French historians is that they are too dramatic. The worst fault of English historians is that they are too narrow, and often too reserved. The French historian loses himself in striking dramatic incidents, whether they be of great national achievements or of great national crimes. The English historian does not do sufficient justice to great British achievements, and does not care to speak of great British crimes. The Frenchman is eloquent on the glories of the French Revolution, as well as its crimes and massacres. The Englishman does not do sufficient justice to the great battle which England, under Elizabeth, fought for freedom and humanity, and he is silent on the crimes and massacres in Ireland, worse than those of the French Revolution or of Jhengiz Khan and Tamurlane. The French writer over-paints his picture; the English writer does not paint sufficiently well to produce a vivid impression. The best historian of the English people is Green; the best historian of the French people is Michelet.

Among American historians, Prescott and Motley are my

favourites; but, long before I knew their works, Washington Irving was the delight of my boyhood. The Americans have produced the best lives of Napoleon Bonaparte. I believe they will produce the best history of modern Europe, because they can write with a degree of impartiality which an Englishman, a Frenchman, or a German cannot command.

Byron and Sir Walter Scott were my favourite poets forty years ago; their simple, lucid style—what modern critics call want of depth—is intelligible even to boys. Years after, I read Homer and Shakespeare, the former in Pope's translation, for I never learnt the European classics. And I then understood that a great poet is a great creator. Homer has created a world, a reflection of an ancient world which has passed away, but the picture will live for ever. And Shakespeare, too, has created a world of his own—a world of strong living characters, animated by human feelings, moved by human passions. I never much admired Milton. The English have no genius for epic poetry. Brilliant pictures of hell and paradise do not make an epic, and discussions on Free Will and Predestination are more worthy of a Puritan preacher than a poet. Nor have I learnt to fully appreciate later English poets, even Tennyson or Browning. Modern poets seem intent on coining well-turned phrases, quaint words and chiselled verses; the grand imagery of the older poets is wanting. The knights of Tennyson's "Idylls of the King" are like tapestry figures, woven with exquisite skill and art, compared with the bold, life-like figures of Scott, hewn out of solid marble. Shelley alone combines the exquisite melody and beauty of verse which is modern, with that wealth of imagery and glow of passion which are of the past. What whole-hearted protest against wrong, what agonising wail of pain, what depth of feeling and frenzy of passion and melody of verse! If he had lived longer, Shelley might have taken a more comprehensive view of life, and poetry is many-sided, like life itself.

France is not rich in poetry. Since the time of the old masters Racine and Corneille, France produced no great poet till the nineteenth century. Voltaire was the greatest literary man of the eighteenth century; the thrones of Europe trembled before him; the superstitions of Europe withered under the fierce light of his genius; and modern history, in the sense in which we understand it, was created under his formative touch. But Voltaire was no true poet; his "Henriade" is stilted, and his dramas are tiresome. Rousseau had the soul of a poet though he seldom wrote verse; his burning prose inspired nations. The greatest French poet of the nineteenth century is Victor Hugo, whose poetry sounded like a trumpet-blast through modern Europe.

Goethe and Schiller I can only admire through translations, but even in translations they are great and glorious. Like Voltaire and Rousseau in France, like Byron and Shelley in England, they are of that brilliant galaxy which heralded or represented that great movement in Europe which had its political manifestation in the French Revolution. And with these great names may I mention those of some humbler poets who were the delight of my boyhood, and who charm me still? Robert Burns's poetry throbs and pulsates with life and feeling; Thomas Moore's "Irish Melodies" still linger in my ear; Longfellow's simple verses still stir me to action.

I learnt Sanskrit long after I learnt English, and what a change from the poetry of the West to the poetry of the East! What repose and softness, what warm tints and brilliant lights, what scenes of loveliness and images of beauty! The East is the home of poetry, as of philosophy and great religions; to the East belong the noblest flights of human imagination and loftiest aspirations of human faith.

Kalidasa fascinated me from the first; I liked his "Kumara" even more than his world-renowned "Sakuntala." The two together form the highest plane of poetry that the gifted bard of Ujain ever reached. And the two characters, Sakuntala in her hermitage and Uma in her mountain solitudes, are among the loveliest creations of human imagination. Bhavabhuti is more powerful, but has not Kalidasa's soul, nor his delicate sense of loveliness. Bharavi is sublime at times, but is often stilted.

But for real poetry of the highest order, go to the grand old Indian Epics. The imagination of man has compassed nothing finer or grander than the "Mahabharata." It is a world more vivid, more varied, more splendid in its scenes and incidents than the "Iliad." And all the characters stand before us clear and bold and distinct, pulsating with life—Karna and Arjuna, Bhisma and Drona, Bhima and Duryodhana, Gandhari and Draupadi—each is a living character with the passions and ambitions, the virtues and often the dark crimes, of heroic men and women. The vast canvas is filled up with nations from the East and from the West. The story is instinct with deeds of valour and determination, and of wrongs done and wiped out in blood, and the whole picture is that of a world three thousand years old, but which still lives in the verse of the immortal bard.

No two men probably agree in their estimates of the two greatest poets. My own standard, as I have said before, is that the greatest creators are the greatest poets. And judging by this standard, which others may or may not accept, I reckon the poet of the "Mahabharata" to be the greatest among the poets of all nations; and the poet of the "Iliad" is the second. Third perhaps—but a long way after the other two—stands the poet of mediæval faith and mediæval civilisation, the immortal Dante. But both Dante and Shakespeare suffer by comparison with the older poets, because they succeed best in portraying human beings in agony, or under the frenzy of passions. The dignity of man, in strength and in repose, is seen best in the Old Masters. And the world created by them is incomparably vaster, richer, and more varied.

As an heroic poem, the "Ramayana" will not compare with the "Mahabharata"; as a poet, Virgil will not compare with Homer. It is a pity Virgil was led away by the story of a Trojan founding Rome, instead of collecting songs and legends of the ancient Romans, and other Latin tribes, and weaving them into a real epic, reflecting a real ancient world. It is a pity Valmiki was similarly led away by the story of a war in Ceylon, instead of composing a real epic out of the traditions and tales and legends of the Kosalas and the Videhas. We miss in the wars of the "Æneid" and the "Ramayana" that truth to nature, that fidelity to ancient customs, that loyalty to old traditions which make the "Iliad" and the "Mahabharata" unique as works of imagination. Nevertheless, the earlier portion of the "Ramayana" excels in soft domestic touches and the portraiture of tender domestic life. And Sita is the noblest ideal of womanhood that the literature of the world has produced.

Perhaps I am unfair to Firdusi in omitting him from the list of great masters, but I have never read him in the original. Firdusi laboured for twenty years to collect together the traditions and tales of ancient Persia, and has woven a picture of old-world life and heroism which will endure for ever. I have read the "Nibelungenlied" in an English translation, a portraiture of mediæval German life, but a poor portraiture compared with the epics of the East. If we except Homer, or if we reckon him an Asiatic that he was, we may truly say that epic poetry belongs to the East. Europe has not produced one great epic poem.

It is strange, but it is true, that I learnt to appreciate Bengali literature after I had learnt to appreciate Shakespeare and Scott, for Bengali literature was not much esteemed forty years ago. In old Bengali literature there is one poet who stands head and shoulders above all others, and that is Mukundaram. He is a true poet, a true creator, and his portraiture of humble, peaceful

Bengal village life will live for ever. Kasiram and Kirttibas will be remembered for their translations of the old Indian Epics. Bharat Chandra excels in command of words and mastery of versification, but fails in truth, pathos, simplicity—in all that is true poetry. The nineteenth century produced two great writers in Bengal. Madhusudan's imagination is brilliant, but his inspiration is not drawn from nature, but from books—mainly from two books, the "Ramayana," and the "Iliad." Bankim Chunder is wiser in drawing from nature, and his portraiture of modern Bengal life is as vivid, as powerful, and as true as the creations of the greatest masters in fiction.

I have said nothing of philosophy yet, though I was fond of it in my younger days. Sir William Hamilton's Lectures attracted me first, but John Stuart Mill and Bain soon replaced him in my estimation. I then turned to those lucid masters of English thought, Locke and Hume, and even sometimes to the profound thinker, Hobbes. Lewes's "History of Philosophy" opened out the whole world of philosophy to me, and I tried to grasp from that popular but somewhat superficial work the leading ideas of Descartes and Leibnitz, of Kant and Hegel, as well as of the older philosophers of Greece. But European histories are imperfect, and take little count of Eastern thought; and it was late in life that I learnt something of those noble systems of philosophy which India produced twenty-five centuries ago, the Sankhya and Vedanta.

Political Economy, as a more practical science, engaged my attention later than Philosophy; and Adam Smith and Ricardo and John Stuart Mill opened out a new world to me. As a student in London I often saw and heard John Stuart Mill, and had the honour of knowing Henry Fawcett more intimately, and I was a faithful believer in their doctrines. But later in life, as a practical administrator, I saw the limitations of these doctrines, and perceived how the greatest European writers failed to grasp the economic conditions of Eastern life. Sismondi and Laveleye, and other European writers, do not understand the Indian land system; even Mill, who was thirty years in the India Office, speaks of the system of England and Ireland, France and Italy, but does not venture to touch on Indian problems in his "Political Economy." The East must produce its own thinkers, its own historians, its own economists.

I never had any regular and systematic religious training, but a Hindu boy never lacks religious instruction at home. My mother, who was a pious Hindu, and deeply religious by nature and instinct, told us, when I scarcely knew my alphabet, those sacred legends in which religious lessons are conveyed in the East. My father and uncle—though not Christians—often read to me, when I could understand English, passages from the Bible and religious poetry. Among the earliest works which fell into my hands were Paley's Sermons and Blair's Sermons, and in those days I often attended the lectures of the great Brahmo teachers, Devendranath Tagore and Keshab Chunder Sen. It was many years after that I learnt to turn to those deep and sublime religious works of ancient India—the "Upanishads" and the "Bhagavadgita." I then felt impelled to make this ancient storehouse accessible to my countrymen generally; I translated the "Rig Veda" into Bengali with the help of learned men; and I published, with Bengali translation, a comprehensive work of selections from the entire range of the Hindu Scriptures.

Religion is a sentiment more than a doctrine or creed, and I often feel a regret that this sentiment, ingrained in the Indian heart, is not fostered by the modern system of education. Readings from the Hindu Scriptures and Epics for Hindu boys, from the Koran for Muhammadan boys, and from the Bible for Christian boys, might be provided in every large educational institution. One or two hours in the week might be allotted to these readings, and good and venerable teachers, reading from these sacred volumes, would soon gather round them all the boys of an institution, and perhaps hundreds of listeners from outside, on the appointed days. And the lessons of duty and charity and unselfishness which these sacred works inculcate in various shapes and in various legends would create deep impressions on the minds of young learners, would help to form their character, and would shape their future conduct and life.

the misanthrope or the pessimist either in the man or the writer. Perhaps one of the truest things about him was said by Babu Rabindra Nath Tagore, the greatest living poet of India :—

> One always saw a smile on his face ; the smile was born of the depth and plenitude of his powers. His mind and body were steeped in perfect health, and in his dealings with other men it was the completeness of his nature which spread such a feeling of unutterable charm.

Of his geniality, his love for his home and children, and the romantic attachment he had for his brother Jogesh Dutt and his friend B. L. Gupta, I have already spoken. His heart hungered for the society of good men and women, and it was no common sacrifice for him that almost throughout his life he had to live a solitary life. His moral rectitude was an integral part of him ; it was manifest in all his words and deeds ; his was one of those large, sincere spirits which women instinctively trust. His nature was deep, chivalrous, sympathetic, lovable ; marked by self-control and by avoidance of ostentation in every form. Here again Babu Rabindra Nath has truly said :—

> The most striking feature of his character was that, with boundless enthusiasm, he possessed a severe classical repose, a combination rare in these days. His indomitable energy and unconquerable will drove him to his life mission of serving his country, but in no single instance did they overflow the bounds of self-restraint and dignified action. Whether in the domain of literature, or in the field of administration, or in the service of his country, all his wonderful energy was in full flow, but the bonds of self-restraint never snapped—this indeed is the sign of real strength.

His generosity in private life was remarkable. He was the mainstay of most of the members of his family. He materially helped his sisters and their families. The terms in which his eldest brother recognised the help he had received from him have already been quoted. Another example of his generosity is furnished by an incident which occurred quite early in his career, shortly after his first return from England. His father's cousin, Babu Raj Kissen Dutt, was hard pressed for funds to support his son, who was being educated in England. Babu Raj Kissen's own brothers, who were in affluent circumstances, refused help, but Mr. Dutt at once came forward with what assistance he could render. On this occasion his grateful relative wrote :—

MY DEAR NEPHEW,—I cannot sufficiently express the lively sense of gratitude which I feel for the noble and generous assistance which you have so timely rendered to a poor despised man like me, but permit me to give you an extract from the letter I have this day addressed to my son, to show in some degree my genuine feelings for your disinterested kindness, which I shall always remember with thankfulness.—Believe me to be, your most affectionate uncle, RAJ KISSEN DUTT.

26th June /77.

This morning I went to Jogesh to inquire if any reply had been received from Romesh. I went with a heavy heart expecting a refusal, because Jogesh had told me a few days before that he was not certain whether Romesh would advance the amount, being very much out of pocket on account of his new house. I was used to rebuffs from our relatives, not only in money matters, but in all other kinds of friendly assistance, but disappointment in my last hope would have made me mad. I could hardly meet your wants by the sale of our clothes and furniture, and even if I could I would have been left actually starving and penniless after the remittance, because I am without employment now, and I doubt whether I could in a hurry sell my clothes and furniture so well as I expected. For these reasons I spent several days in deep anxiety, and went to Jogesh this morning with a melancholy heart, and asked him whether he had received any reply from Romesh. He answered in the affirmative, and I waited with great trepidation whilst he was getting out Romesh's letter. What was my astonishment, joy, and gratitude when I read the letter. Romesh had instructed Jogesh not only to pay Rs.500 at once, but accompanied his generous instructions with such noble and encouraging words that it made my heart full, and deprived me for a time of my power of speech. I restrained with difficulty tears of gratitude starting into my eyes. Jogesh gave me the amount at once, and I merely said that I could not find words to express the deep sense of gratitude that

I felt. I would like to give you a copy of Romesh's letter, if I could, but it was addressed to Jogesh, so I could not take it. However, I shall repeat the sentiments expressed in it as far as I remember. Romesh says that Jogesh is already aware of the state of his purse on account of the new house that he is building, but were his circumstances much worse than they are now, he would not hesitate for a moment to render the assistance asked for. That he can well understand the noble sacrifices which Nakaki (your mother) has made, and the deep solicitude with which Nakaka has accumulated the means for the education of his son. He desired Jogesh not only to pay the amount at once, but directed him not to take any bond, receipt, promise, or engagement of any kind for the repayment of the money; that he would not only decline to take any interest, but wished it to be understood that he would not take back the amount until and unless Upen is successful, and returns with flying colours. That he would be extremely sorry if Upen were prevented from trying his last chance for the want of such a paltry sum as Rs.500, and that he would not only wish success to Upen with all his heart, but would be as glad to hear of it as Nakaka and Nakaki, if not more.

He wrote a long letter, but I do not remember the whole of the contents now, but his sentiments were clothed in such noble and eloquent language as quite overpowered me with a lively sense of gratitude, and I fervently thanked God in my heart for putting such generous sentiments into his noble mind.

I hope that by zeal and diligence you will prove yourself worthy of the expectations of your noble benefactor.

Of his great unselfishness and freedom from any tinge of jealousy, the letter he wrote to Mr. Surendra Nath Banerjea just before his death will bear ample testimony :—

What a wonderful revolution we have seen within the lifetime of a generation! What a change in the thoughts and ideas of a nation! and what a noble part you have played in leading that change! One by one all our fellow-workers are dropping round us—Bonnerjea is gone! Ananda Mohan is gone! Lal Mohan is gone! and we too shall soon pass away. But the History of India of the nineteenth century and early twentieth century will cherish the names of a band of patriotic workers, none nobler, truer, more persistent and more patriotic than yourself.

No man was ever more entirely free from the jealousy that is a besetting fault of literary and public men. He was always prepared to give a cordial welcome to younger men working in the cause which he had at heart: as witness the following words used in proposing the election of Mr. Gokhale to the Presidentship of the Twenty-first Indian National Congress, in 1905:—

Gentlemen, I do not know how you received that speech, but when for the first time I read that speech, I felt within myself that that was the coming man for India. The power of eloquence, the power of debate, the great moderation and lucid statement of facts, which characterised that splendid speech in the Viceroy's Council showed that we had at last got a champion who would do justice to his country and countrymen. Year after year we have watched the proceedings of the Viceroy's Council, and I think I am reflecting the opinion of every one of you present, when I say that our cause could not have found a more eloquent, a more upright, and a more able advocate than in the Hon. Mr. Gokhale. I shall not forget even in the few moments which are allowed to me to mention the services which Mr. Gokhale lately rendered by his splendid series of speeches in England at a time when the old Government was crumbling down, and when the new Government was being formed. You may have heard and read in the papers some accounts of the efforts which Mr. Gokhale made to represent our cause, the cause of all India, before all classes of the English community, from the merchants of Lancashire to those people who are about to hold the reins of the Empire. I believe that the fruit of these endeavours we shall see before long.

We cannot conclude this section better than by quoting the impression which his ideals and the firm and unflinching manner in which he acted up to them, created in the minds of two of his most intimate acquaintances, both foreigners, an Englishwoman and an English military officer. Colonel Meade (sometimes Resident of Baroda) wrote after his death:—

But above all I believe your father was a man of the highest and best ideals, who lived up to what he believed, *and was incapable of doing a wrong action.*

Miss Noble wrote:—

Romesh Chunder Dutt was a man of his own people. The object of all he ever did was not his own fame, but the uplifting of India. He was one who stands amongst the fathers of the future, one who dreamt and worked at great things untiringly; yet left behind him before his country's altar no offering so noble, no proof of her greatness so incontrovertible, as that one thing of which he never thought at all—his own character and his own love!

BOOK III

CHAPTER XXVIII

WORK IN BARODA

(*August* 1904 *to July* 1907)

I

HIS HIGHNESS the Gaekwar of Baroda had as early as 1895, when Mr. Dutt was officiating Commissioner of Burdwan, opened negotiations with him and requested him to enter the Baroda State service. On that occasion Mr. Dutt expressed his gratitude for the Gaekwar's kind offer, but requested to be allowed to consider the matter after he had retired from Government service. The Secretary of the Gaekwar replied: "His Highness was greatly pleased and gratified by your letter, and desires me to express his thanks for your generous willingness to accede to his wishes after your retirement from Government service."

The offer was renewed nine years later after Mr. Dutt's return to Calcutta in 1904. Such an invitation to help in the administration of one of the foremost native States Mr. Dutt could not refuse, and he entered the State service as Revenue Minister of Baroda in August 1904, and held that appointment until July 1907. Whether Mr. Dutt was altogether wise in accepting it has been questioned by some of his critics. It was contended that what was a great gain to the Baroda State was a heavy loss to the whole of India, and that Mr. Dutt's energies would be absorbed in the details of administration instead of being devoted to the continued advocacy of the cause which he had hitherto served in so distinguished a manner. There was doubtless something to be said for this view, but on the other hand it should be remembered that the appointment gave him an opportunity of testing the efficacy and value of his own suggestions and views in the most advanced native principality in India.

At a dinner given at Belvedere in honour of the Maharaja Gaekwar, the then Lieutenant-Governor of Bengal, Sir Andrew Fraser, in referring to this appointment made the following observations :—

> I may be permitted perhaps, as now identified with Bengal, and as a member of the Indian Civil Service, to refer to a fact which has undoubtedly given some satisfaction in this province, namely, that His Highness selected as one of his councillors an old member of the Bengal Civil Service. Mr. Romesh Chunder Dutt joined the Civil Service the same year as I; and when I last met him in this city he showed me a photograph of myself taken as a very young man while we were still probationers together in London. I knew him well then; and it was a pleasure to me to renew my acquaintance with him in Calcutta. When Mr. Dutt was appointed by His Highness to the office to which I have referred, he wrote to me a courteous letter informing of his appointment and containing this sentence, which gave me real pleasure. "I need not add," he says, "that it will be my endeavour to perform my duties at Baroda with that method and regularity in work, and that equal regard for the interest of all classes of the people, which I have learned under British administration, and which it is the desire of the British Government to see everywhere." With such sentiments as these there is no doubt that Mr. Dutt goes to Baroda in full sympathy with its distinguished ruler.

Mr. Dutt's first impressions of Baroda are given in letters to members of his family.

BARODA, 23*rd August* 1904.

MY DEAREST AMALA AND SARALA,—Arrived at last. And I have seen the Gaekwar, and taken charge of my duties, and am an official again! No romance in a Native State, no driving four-in-hand, no *sowars* in front and rear, but all severely simple as in British territory. I am now living in a house of the Maharaja's and using his carriage and pair, but this is only temporary. I have to rent a house, buy my furniture, keep my servants, get my carriage and horse! All very prosaic, is it not? besides all this will run away with a month's pay or more. As if I was still only a Commissioner of Burdwan, and not the presiding genius in an historic Hindu State.

However, there are compensations. The place is pleasant—cooler and drier than Calcutta, the Maharaja is a nice man, and I am virtually my own master. And the pay is not to be despised—by a poor man. . . . How funny to feel that seven years' political work and book-writing have passed away, and I am a sober, quiet official again. I saw the State offices to-day; they are like a big collectorate, with many departments and many rooms full of records and clerks. I made the acquaintance of the heads of offices to-day, and saw my own room, comfortably fitted up with office furniture. The highest officers of the State are the Prime Minister and myself—both on the same pay—and the idea of the Gaekwar is to divide the supervision of all State affairs between us two, giving me the Revenue and Finance and other Departments of which I have special experience. I have also suggested to him the formation of a Council. If I can in a few years remodel the administration of Baroda, and make it a model State in India, my work shall not have been done in vain.—I am ever your loving father,

ROMESH.

And so, as was his habit, he quietly settled down to work. The spirit in which he worked and the high ambitions which surged in his breast will be seen from the letters which follow :—

BARODA, 14*th October* 1904.

MY DEAR BROTHER,—Your letter of 8th October reached me in due time. I have been busily at work in all the Revenue departments here, reorganising and reforming; and I am glad the Maharaja has so far acceded to all my moderate suggestions about Income Tax and Customs duties, &c. But the greater Land Question looms ahead! All Western India is watching my Land measures in Baroda, to see if I have the courage to practise what I have preached to the British Government these seven years! There was an "open letter to Mr. Dutt" in the *Times of India* yesterday which voiced the general expectation that the radical Land Revenue Reformer should now reduce his enlightened theories into practice! Well,—the radical reformer will *not* fail in his duties. In a year or two the public will see a great Land Reform in Baroda, or Mr. Dutt will not be here!

I will send you a copy of my Income Tax and Tariffs Resolution in a day or two, as they may interest you.—Yours affectionately ever,

ROMESH.

BARODA, *14th November* 1904.

MY DEAR PRASANTA,—. . . . The fact is, all the important work in the State is in my hands. All other officers from the highest to the lowest are content with routine office work—I am the only man here who takes the initiative, assumes new responsibilities, presses for reforms, carries out new ideas, and works for the progress and advancement of the State. All the merchants and mill-owners are crowding round me; all the agriculturists are petitioning to me for redress; it is funny that even ignorant bazar women gossip to ladies, to whom they bring their things for sale, that a Calcutta Babu has come who is organising everything, and so long as he is at Baroda things will go on all right! It is a fearful responsibility to have the destinies of the people of a State in your hands; but I will not spare myself nor move from the path of my duty; and, God helping, I hope to bring some light and joy and comfort to the homes of the poor, and also add to the trade and the manufacture and wealth of the State itself, if I am spared to work here for a few years steadily and well. I am thankful to say I am enjoying good health, and my new work and high responsibilities inspire me with new zeal and hopes. One thing I am careful in doing. I try my best to prevent my reforms being published in newspapers, or trumpeted to the world. It would spoil my work, and possibly excite alarm, if my early endeavours in this State were so talked about. If I succeed in my endeavours, the result will reveal itself to the world, and Baroda will be a model State in India, not only in education and methods of administration which the Gaekwar himself has initiated, but also in the prosperity of the agriculturist people, the briskness of trade and enterprise, the starting of new mills and new industries. There is not one single mill of any kind conducted by private enterprise within the State. I shall be very disappointed if I do not succeed in starting a dozen—not by the State, but by encouraging private enterprise—before five years are over. And my ambition is to see Baroda a brisk centre of trade in Western India (after Bombay and Ahmedabad) within a very few years. —Yours affectionate,

ROMESH C. DUTT.

To Sister Nivedita, whom he called his "God-daughter," he wrote in a still more enthusiastic and confidential tone.

MY DEAR NIVEDITA,—I am trying to strike out new lines of progress, to develop new policies and reforms, and am determined to move forward and to carry the State forward. I am trying to gather together the scattered forces which were present here, to encourage enterprise and talent in younger men, to welcome new ideas and new schemes, to initiate progress in all lines, and to make Baroda a richer and a happier State. I go among the people, print and publish my schemes, face the Maharaja with my proposals, and manage to have my way in a manner which old officers of this State pronounce quite "unconventional"! I am trying to relieve the agriculturists of excessive taxation on their land, I am endeavouring to get together capitalists to start new mills and industries, and if I can build up the Legislative Council I will make the work of the State proceed in the interest of the people, and in touch with the people. Everything shall be open and above-board,—nothing done in dark tortuous, secret, autocratic ways. Dreams! Dreams! some will exclaim. Well, let them be so,—it is better to dream of work and progress than to wake to inaction and stagnation. This last shall never be my vocation, it is not in my nature.

Pardon all this declamation; the fact is that my pen sometimes runs away with me, and I think so much of reforms by night and day, that sometimes these ideas will come out in spite of myself. Don't show this foolish letter to any one, or show it only to such as will be charitable enough to appreciate even my boyish enthusiasm.—Ever your loving godfather,

ROMESH CH. DUTT.

His appointment was watched with keen interest both in India and in England. "Mr. Dutt's English friends heard with pleasure of his appointment to the Council of the Maharaja of Gaekwar," said the *Manchester Guardian*. "The Maharaja no doubt knew," said the same paper, "that Mr. Dutt's advent would mean changes with regard to some indefensible customs, and it is to his credit that he is fully supporting his new Amatya by his approval and co-operation."

II

The nature of the reforms carried out by Mr. Dutt under the orders and direction of the Gaekwar are embodied in the annual Reports of the State for the three successive years during which he served there. Of his first Report for the years 1902-4, the *Statesman* remarked:—

The State of Baroda, second in importance to Hydrabad only, has long been famous for the enlightened and progressive character of its administration. Nor has this reputation suffered since the Maharaja Gaekwar placed its Revenue, Finance, and Land Settlement Departments in the hands of Mr. Romesh Dutt, who has found time, amidst his manifold labours, to compile a Report on the Administration of Baroda during the years 1902–4, which stands in refreshing contrast to most official reports that it is our hard lot to read and review from time to time. His is more than a work of reference; it is a book that can be read and enjoyed. It bears testimony not only to the conditions prevailing in the dominions of the Gaekwar, but also to the literary ability of his Revenue Minister. In brief, it amply fulfils the promise contained in the preface, namely, "to present in a concise form all figures and tabular statements which are essential or useful, and to narrate all facts which are important or interesting." It tells us, within the limits of a handy volume, all that we want to hear.

The following extracts from these Reports will give us a good idea of the reforms in the inauguration of which the new Minister had a hand.

(1) Administrative Reforms.

Separation of Judicial and Executive Functions.

For several years past His Highness the Gaekwar has endeavoured to bring about a separation of the Judicial and Executive duties. The Taluka Executive officers (Vahivatdars) used to try all criminal cases in years past, while the Taluka Judicial officers (Munsiffs) took cognisance of civil cases. This arrangement was open to many objections. In the first place, the Vahivatdars were unable to devote that degree of attention to their executive and revenue work which it needed, when much of their time was taken up in trying criminal cases. And in the second place, the exercise of criminal powers spoilt them as revenue officers, and armed them with an authority which was inconsistent with the discharge of their revenue duties.

After a careful consideration of all opinions, and with his intimate knowledge of the actual work of administration as it is carried on in districts and Talukas, the Maharaja came to the conclusion that a separation should be effected. The officer who is virtually the prosecutor should not be the judge. The officer who is virtually the plaintiff in the matter of revenue demands should not exercise magisterial powers. The officer who is the head of the District, or the Taluka, should be free from the suspicion of doing executive work with the help of criminal powers. On these considerations His Highness resolved on a separation of functions.

The policy was cautiously and gradually carried out. It was directed that three-fourths of the criminal cases should be tried by Munsiffs, and one-fourth only should be tried by Vahivatdars. The bulk of the criminal work was thus made over to trained judicial officers who performed no executive or revenue work; a small portion of the work was still left in the hands of the executive and revenue officers. This state of things continued till the end of the year under report.

Since then a complete separation has been effected. The work of revenue and executive officers has largely increased in this year of scarcity and famine, and the Maharaja has directed that they should be relieved of all criminal work. From the current year, therefore, all criminal and civil work will be performed by judicial officers; the revenue and executive officers will devote all their time to their legitimate duties.

This important reform attracted the attention of the Government of India, and Colonel M. J. Meade, the Resident, wrote to the Dewan :—

MY DEAR SIR,—In the Baroda Administration Report for 1902–4 reference is made to the separation of the judicial and executive functions; and, as you are aware, this important measure has much interested the Government of India. I should be greatly obliged if you will give me some information on the subject, and let me know how long ago the idea was started, how the separation was effected in Baroda, how the judicial and executive functions are now being separately performed, and what measure of success has attended this change in the method of administration.—Yours sincerely,

M. J. MEADE.

Amongst other judicial reforms, the creation of the Honorary Village Munsiffs and the organisation of Judicial Conferences may be mentioned.

With the same object in view, an Honorary Village Munsiff, with power to decide suits up to the value of Rs.60, was appointed in August 1903. Intelligent patels or village headmen have been empowered to try cases relating to petty thefts of agricultural produce, assault, simple hurt, conservancy, &c., and to award punishments extending to a fine of Rs.5 or imprisonment for forty-eight hours. The results of these experiments are watched with keen interest. And it is the desire of His Highness to extend this system of obtaining co-operation of the villagers themselves in settling their own petty differences, and of saving the people from the trouble, the expense, and the demoralising effects of attending Law Courts.

Lastly, with the object of keeping the administration in touch with the people, His Highness the Maharaja Gaekwar directed a Judicial Conference to be held in every district. The District Judge was to preside, and Munsiffs, Magistrates, and Pleaders were to attend. Many interesting facts were elicited at the Conference held last March, and amendments of laws were suggested which are still under consideration.

Amongst other reforms in the system of administration may be mentioned the decentralisation of the Revenue department carried out in 1904–5. The department was divided into two sections, and a responsible officer was placed in charge of each section. The pay and prospects of both the Judicial and Revenue services were also improved, and none but graduates were held to be eligible for these gazetted services.

But the most important reform in this department was the creation by the Maharaja early in 1904–5 of an Executive Council to supervise the entire administration of the State. The Council assisted the Maharaja in preparing the programme of the Famine Relief operations of that year, and after the Gaekwar's departure for Europe, directed and controlled the administration of the State in all departments of work. In Mr. Dutt's Report for the year 1904–5 it is stated: "The Council meets twice in the month, and each session generally lasts for three or four days. It is gratifying to record that, while every member of the Council acts and votes with perfect independence according to his own judgment, the deliberations of the Council have been uniformly marked by harmony and mutual courtesy." In the absence of the Maharaja, the Dewan is the President of the Council.

(2) Revenue Reforms.

As was to be expected, the most notable reforms were in the Revenue departments. The abolition of taxes on various professions known as Veros, which were mostly paid by the poor, and the substitution in their place of an Income Tax payable by the richer classes and officials, were the earliest reforms introduced by the new Minister. The minimum of taxable income was at first proposed to be Rs.150 a year, but it was raised successively to Rs.300, Rs.500, and then to Rs.750 from 1907–8, before Mr. Dutt left Baroda. The rate of tax was one pice in the rupee for every class of income, and assessments were made by Government servants with the help of a Panchayet in the town or village concerned.

As was explained in the first Report, the advantages of this new system were that—

> (1) It made a clean sweep of all the numerous and oppressive Veros, except rent for homestead lands and the pilgrim tax. (2) It exempted the poor from taxation. (3) It imposed on the richer classes a proportionate burden which they had evaded before. (4) It imposed on official classes their fair share of the burden which they had escaped.

His next step was to do away with a whole series of Customs duties harassing to trade, and to limit duties to a few principal articles only. Octroi duties were abolished in all small towns in the State, and the vast body of Nakadàrs or Customs officers who had been previously maintained was reduced by about 150 officers, and the pay of those retained was improved. It is satisfactory that in Baroda, as in other civilised countries, the experiment had the desired result, and the reduction of the number of duties actually brought in an enlarged revenue, as it led to an expansion of business and trade.

In the important department of Land Revenue Assessments he showed the same anxiety for the tiller of the soil as he had done while criticising the system prevailing in British India. He recommended that—

(1) The Land Revenue demand of a Taluka should be fixed after considering what the Taluka had paid in the past taking good years with bad, and can pay in the future without detriment to agricultural prosperity.

(2) No enhancement should be made unless there has been a rise in prices, or there are other reasons, like the increase of produce or of cultivation, justifying an enhancement.

(3) No cultivator should be asked to pay more than one-half of the net produce of his field.

By net produce is meant the average produce of a field minus the cost of cultivation, which last includes the fair wages of the cultivator and his family labouring in the field, and also a fair rate of interest on his agricultural stock, such as plough, bullocks, &c. Thus if a field yields an average annual produce of the value of Rs.60, taking good years with bad years, and if the cost of cultivation, including the wages of labour and the interest on the agricultural stock, comes to Rs.40, the net produce of the field is Rs.20. And under the rule laid down by Sir Charles Wood, the Government demand should be Rs.10, or one-sixth of the total produce of the field, which is also the maximum Land Tax according to the Institutes of Manu. If a field is very fertile and yields Rs.100 a year, taking good years with famine years, and the cost of cultivation, including wages, &c., is only Rs.50, the net produce is Rs.50, and the limit of the Government demand is Rs.25, or one-fourth of the total produce. On the other hand, if the field is very poor, and yields an average produce of Rs.40 only, and the cost of cultivation, including wages, &c., is Rs.30, then the net produce is Rs.10 only, and the Government demand is limited to Rs.5, which is one-eighth of the total produce.

Those who had anticipated to see a cooling down of the ardour of the irresponsible critic when placed in the responsible position of the chief Revenue Minister of one of the foremost Indian States must have been greatly disappointed. For what could be more fearless and outspoken than the following letter which he addressed to the Gaekwar recommending a moderation of the Land Tax in the resettlement of the Padra Taluka :—

BARODA, 11*th Jan.* 1906.

YOUR HIGHNESS,—I had expected to see your Highness yesterday, and to speak again on the Padra Settlement question; but I had to come away at 2.30 to attend the Council.

Your Highness will therefore permit me to put my remarks on paper.

In the first place, we are all endeavouring to improve the administration of the State and the condition of the people. Your Highness is encouraging various industries in the State, and extending primary education to all classes with profuse liberality. But all endeavours in this direction will be vain unless we moderate the land assessment where it is excessive as each Taluka comes up for revision of settlement. Land assessment is more intimately related in India, as Colonel Bairdsmith said more than forty years ago, "to the everyday life of the people, and to their growth towards prosperity or towards degradation" than any other cause that can be mentioned. If land assessment is moderated, as each Taluka comes up for revision of settlement, the State of Baroda can be a populous, prosperous, and thriving State. But if land assessment remains cruelly severe, as it did under the former Gaekwars, Baroda will continue to be a scantily populated, impoverished, resourceless State. This is the simple truth; it is my duty as a trusted officer to state this truth plainly, and your Highness will then decide the question as you think best.

In the second place, the enormous difference between our rates and those prevailing in the contiguous British tracts has already been noticed by British officers. A Member of the Bombay Council has referred to it from his place in the Council, and the Resident of Baroda has spoken of it to our officials. It is for your Highness to decide whether this fact, so little creditable to the administration of a Native State, should be permitted to exist, and to be published to the world.—With sincere respects, I remain, yours sincerely, R. C. DUTT.

(3) LOCAL SELF-GOVERNMENT.

Now we come to that far-reaching system of Self-Government which Mr. Dutt succeeded in organising in the State, and which posterity is likely to consider amongst the most solid of his achievements in the service of the State. Local autonomy in Baroda begins, as it should do, in the Village; the Village Boards being the first units of the fabric of Local Self-Government of that State. The Village Boards lead up to the Taluka Boards, the Talukas send up representatives to the District Boards, and these in their turn send up Councillors to the State Legislative Council. The following extracts from an article on the revival of village self-government in Baroda, contributed by Mr. Dutt, and which appeared in the *Hindusthan Review* in December 1909, after his death, describes the system clearly :—

Five years ago, His Highness the Gaekwar entrusted me with the duty of introducing Local Self-Government in this State. The first question was to form electorates for the election of members of the Taluka Boards. In Bengal and elsewhere, some property or other qualification has been prescribed for voters; but in Baroda the good work done by Mr. Elliot before me made my work easy. I reorganised the Village Boards, embracing all villages in my scheme without any selection, and groups of these Village Boards were formed into electorates. Fifteen or sixteen Village Boards were grouped to form an electorate, and returned one member. The method was simple; it was understood and appreciated by the people; it gave Village Boards a status and position, and it avoided the necessity of collecting large numbers of ignorant cultivators at polling booths to their own astonishment and to the amusement of sight-seers.

The next step was to entrust these Village Boards with such public works as were legitimately their own. The proceeds of the Local Cess, after some deductions, were distributed to District Boards, and these in their turn distributed the money to the Taluka Boards under them. On an average, each Taluka received ten thousand rupees for public works, and this was distributed to those villages where public works, and generally drinking water wells, were most needed. As a rule, the money allotted was given to the Village Boards, and they executed the works with a degree of efficiency and economy which surpassed all expectations. Large sums were added to the Local Cess by Government in a year of water famine for construction of wells; and the Gaekwar signalised the jubilee of his accession to power by a generous gift of five lakhs of rupees for the construction of wells. Virtually all these sums were distributed to Village Boards, the people felt they were getting more than an adequate return for the Cess they paid; and there was no room for complaint or criticism when they did their own work. I cannot help thinking that much public criticism would disappear if the people were more largely entrusted with their own concerns.

Nevertheless, allotments of money for such public works could only be made to a small number of villages in a year; the rest of the Village Boards sat with their hands folded, expecting their turn to come, for out of ten thousand rupees a year for public works only ten or fifteen villages could be served in a year—the others had to wait. The credit is due to another officer of the Bombay Civil Service for remedying this state of things, and providing all Village Boards with some funds every year. Mr. Seddon, whose services have been lent to the Baroda Government for Settlement and other work, took this step for the development of village institutions, and proposed an annual allotment to every village. The Council of Baroda decided that, after deducting portion of the total income for the expenditure of the District and Taluka Boards, and for large works, the rest should be distributed among Village Boards, for their petty village works, in proportion to the Cess they paid. . . . Thus in Baroda the villagers will, for the first time, have it in their power to remove their own simple wants by their own efforts year after year.

The next important step has quite recently been taken by the Council of Baroda by entrusting deserving Village Boards with small civil and criminal powers. They are empowered to dispose of small suits (loans, &c.) up to Rs.25, and they will punish petty offences with fines up to Rs.5. No fees are required, no records (except a register) are to be kept, no lawyers will appear, and no appeals are permitted. The District Officer and the District Judge are vested with powers of revision in cases of grave injustice. These rules have received the sanction of His Highness the Gaekwar.

In matters of education, Village Boards have as yet no power, as the Education Department in this State, as elsewhere, has taken over the management even of primary schools. But an Education Commission is sitting, and the question of control over primary schools is one of the most important problems for its decision.

The Taluka Boards and District Boards are thus described in the first Report:—

As regards the constitution of the Taluka Boards, it has been provided that all the villages in a Taluka shall be divided into a number of groups, and each group of villages shall return a member to the Taluka Board. Similarly, each separate municipality in the Taluka shall return a member. And lastly, all the alienated villages in the Taluka shall have the privilege of choosing a member. The persons thus elected shall form not less than one-half of the total number of members, the other half, or less than half, being nominated by Government. Of the nominated members not more than half shall be Government servants; and the Naib Subah shall be the chairman of the Taluka Board.

As regards the constitution of the District Boards, it has been provided that each Taluka Board within the District shall elect one or more members of the District Board, and each Municipality with a population of over ten thousand, situated within the District, shall also send up a member. These, with one member elected by alienated villages, shall be the elected members of the District Board, and their total number will be not less than one-half of the total number of members. The other half, or less than half, shall be nominated by Government; and among nominated members not more than one-half shall be Government servants. The District Officer shall be chairman of the District Board.

The duties vested in Taluka Boards and District Boards are:—The construction of roads, tanks, wells, and water-works; the management of dharmasalas, dispensaries, and markets; the supervision of vaccination, sanitation, primary education, and arboriculture; the undertaking of relief measures on a small scale in times of famine; and generally such other public duties within their respective jurisdictions as may be entrusted to them. The proceeds of the Local Cess, and such other funds as may be assigned for the purpose from time to time by His Highness the Maharaja, shall be devoted to the performance of these works.

The last superstructure of this edifice is the State Legislative Council. It is described in the first Report as consisting of eighteen members, including the Dewan, who is the President. One-third of the members are elected thus:—

4 returned by the four District Boards.
1 „ „ Baroda Municipality.
1 „ „ Sardars of the State.

The remaining two-thirds consist of *ex officio* members and members nominated by Government. Bills passed by the Council require His Highness's sanction, and the Maharaja has the power to veto any Bill. It is thus practically an advisory Council only.

The extension of the principle of Self-Government embraced the further development of the municipalities. It was decided that the administration of the municipalities, instead of being in the hands of a government servant, should be carried on by a body of Commissioners, to be partly elected and partly nominated. The town of Baroda and eight other large towns were first selected for this experiment. In place of specific grants, such as were made from State funds to these District towns, sources of revenue yielding sums adequate for their present expenditure were generally assigned to them. Where such sources were not available, specific grants were continued. It was hoped that there would be no need for these District towns to impose fresh taxation if the sources of revenue assigned to them were carefully developed. The boon of Self-Government was thus granted to these towns without any addition to taxation.

(4) EDUCATION.

The following remarks occur in Mr. Dutt's first Report:—

In no department of administration is the far-sighted liberality of His Highness the Maharaja Gaekwar more conspicuous than in education, and in none are the results more real and tangible. The percentage of the State Revenue spent on education is 6.5 in Baroda, against 1.17 in Bengal, 1.44 in Bombay, 1.33 in Madras, and about one per cent. in all British India. And the percentage of children under instruction to the total population is 8.6 in Baroda, against 4.0 in Bengal, 6.2 in Bombay, 3.09 in Madras, and less than three per cent. in all British India. Seven annas is spent on education per head of population in Baroda against about an anna in British India.

It was in January 1903, immediately on his return from Europe, that His Highness decided to introduce Compulsory Education in one part of his State, and selected Amreli Taluka for the purpose. The rules framed were that all boys between the ages of seven and twelve, and all girls between the ages of seven and ten, should attend schools. The guardian of a child of this age, absenting for ten consecutive days, or for fifteen days in any month, would be liable to a fine of two annas. No fees were charged at all. But children wishing to stay on after passing the age limit might do so on payment of a monthly fee of one anna. Children of aboriginal tribes like Bhils and Kols were supplied with books at State expense. There were fifty-two schools of this class. The result, numerically, has been very satisfactory. Out of a total population of 52,828 in the fifty-two villages of the Taluka, no less than 5201 children, or nearly the entire juvenile population within the age limit stated above, attend the compulsory schools. The success of this scheme has induced His Highness the Maharaja to direct the preparation of a Bill on Compulsory Education, which was published in the *Official Gazette* in July 1904.

In 1905 free and compulsory education was ordered to be extended over the entire State. The annual grant necessary for this purpose was increased to nearly five lakhs of rupees, and was divided between the Education Department, which looked after towns and large villages, and the Local Boards, which looked after ordinary villages. The rule adopted was that all boys between seven and twelve, and all girls between seven and ten, should go to schools under penalties for non-attendance, and receive instruction in reading, writing, and arithmetic in the first three standards. In that year there were over two thousand Village Boards constituted by the Local Self-Government Act of 1904, and the idea was to establish a Village School or Gramyashala under each Village Board. The total number of such schools already established up to that year (excluding those in towns) exceeded fourteen hundred.

(5) Industry and Manufacture.

The fostering and encouragement of indigenous industries was one of the principal features of Mr. Dutt's administration as Revenue Minister of the State. In his first Report he frankly acknowledged the backward condition of industrial enterprise in Baroda :—

> On the whole, it must be admitted that our record of trades and industries in Baroda is a poor one. The old industries are mostly on the decline; industries under new methods have not yet achieved a notable success; and State enterprises have been, commercially, failures. New cotton mills have not sprung up at Baroda as they have at Ahmedabad; and trades and manufactures are not brisk here as at Broach or Surat.

. . . .

It will be our own fault as administrators if we fail to bring about those favourable conditions under which trade and manufacture prosper, to remove that feeling of uncertainty handed down from the past which deadens enterprise, and by liberal fiscal measures and a wise continuity of policy to create that feeling of security under which the people are always prompt to work out their own salvation. A wise administration will give them all the help and instruction that is needed, and will remove all hurtful and needless restrictions; and there is every hope that Baroda will, in the near future, take its legitimate place as a centre of the manufacturing industries of Western India.

He gave this important matter his unremitting attention, and in his second Report for 1904–5, he had the satisfaction of noting that signs of improvement were already perceptible :—

The hand-loom industry received a great impetus in the last year; a new and simple loom, called the Sayaji loom, has been invented in our Weaving School, the number of hand-looms at work has doubled in Petlad and Vaso towns, and a hand-loom weaving company has been formed at Nehsana. Mill industry showed an equally satisfactory progress in the last year, and the transfer of the State Spinning and Weaving Mill at Baroda to private hands has given an impetus to private enterprise. Two new mills have been commenced at Baroda, and a ginning factory, with weaving apparatus, has been established at Kadi. It may be added that the dyeing factory at Petlad is showing continued progress; the chocolate factory at Billimora has been reopened in the current year; the State sugar factory at Gandevi has been transferred to private hands; and the valuable concession made to the cultivators of these parts, by bestowing on them the ownership of all date trees growing on their holdings, is likely to help the sugar industry. Students were sent last year to Europe, America, and Japan, to learn mechanical engineering and other useful professions; the services of a silk expert were borrowed from the Bengal Government in the current year for the extension of sericulture in this State; and the pearl-fishery of the Dwarka sea-coast is under investigation by an expert whose services have been lent by the Ceylon Government.

The demand for labour naturally increased with the revival of industrial enterprise, and wages and the condition of the labouring classes also visibly improved.

III

The *Indian World* (Calcutta) made the following observations on Mr. Dutt's administration of Baroda :—

It is as an administrator and a statesman that Mr. Dutt's memory will long be cherished in Indian homes. His famous scheme on the separation of judicial and executive functions in India, the introduction of free primary education into the State of Baroda, the bringing of a cumbrous and complicated system of taxation into line with a progressive and up-to-date revenue policy will carry his name down to distant generations of Indians.

The scheme for the separation of the judicial and the executive functions is generally recognised as a counsel of perfection, but it was left to a native State and an Indian statesman to give effect to this great administrative reform for the first time in the history of India.

As regards free primary education, there is no difference of opinion between the rulers and the ruled so far as British India is concerned, but it is want of money again that stands in the way of the idea being carried through. Only in the small State of Baroda the determination of an enlightened prince and the administrative skill of a man of Mr. Dutt's position have found means and scope for the realisation of this great dream. It may not bulk so largely before the public eye to-day—the introduction of free education in an Indian State. But this experiment is bound to be followed in other States till the gods of Simla will find the force of public opinion too irresistible to shelve it any longer. Once free education is introduced all over India, half of our moral, social, political, and sanitary problems will get themselves solved in no time. Then will come the time to appreciate the merit of Mr. Dutt's memorable departure in that line.

On his fiscal policy at Baroda the time has not come to pronounce any definite opinion. But if the reduction of taxation, the abolition of vexatious imposts, and the equalisation of the incidence of taxation, lead ever to prosperity and happiness, Baroda is soon destined to become an object-lesson of a growing and contented State. The future prosperity of Baroda will be the best permanent memorial of Mr. Dutt's administrative and fiscal policy. And if the contentment and prosperity of the people indicate social and political advance, Mr. Dutt's memory will be preserved in the annals of India for many centuries to come.

CHAPTER XXIX

HIS COSMOPOLITAN HOME AT BARODA

I

It was a new and cosmopolitan life which Mr. Dutt led in Baroda during the three years of his residence in that city. It made a call on his wider and all-Indian sympathies, and nothing affords such a convincing proof of the breadth of his nature and of his personal magnetism than the ease with which he took root in Baroda, and made for himself a real home in that land, so distant and so different from Bengal. He gathered round him a circle of intimate friends who, though not his kith and kin, were nevertheless attached to him by ties almost stronger than that of blood. From the very beginning he was anxious to be of the people, and neither to feel nor to be felt as an alien. In this he more than succeeded, for when he died a few years later in Baroda, it will be hardly an exaggeration to say that there was no man more universally loved than he was. On his death, Mrs. Mehta, the lady whom Mr. Dutt loved as his own daughter, wrote a touching letter to Mrs. Bose (Mr. Dutt's eldest daughter), in which she said :—

> In Baroda I had no parents, no relations to look after us, but since he came there I never missed my relations. His house was like my parents' house. He, too, treated me always as his own daughter.

His official duties no doubt engrossed the greater portion of his time, and the multifarious duties of an office, which was virtually that of Chief Minister, made a heavy drain both on his mind and body. But Mr. Dutt was not the man to bury himself in the dust and dreariness of mere official routine. The prospect of being of some service to the people, and of at last seeing some of his cherished theories about good and sound government being translated into practice, inspired him to continuous and whole-hearted endeavour; but the softer, and perhaps more dominant, side of his nature made insistent demands for the fellowship of good men and women; and we find that, during his stay in Baroda, he succeeded in drawing round him the intellect, the manhood, as also the beauty and the grace of the womanhood, of the entire portion of that part of the Indian continent.

II

And first, let us try and describe his home. He lived most of his time alone, his wife and daughters joining him but rarely. His eldest daughter, Kamala, and her daughters stayed with him for about six months in the cold weather of 1905–6, and his wife and his second daughter, Bimala, were with him for a month in 1905. Those were great days in Baroda when Mr. Dutt had his family staying with him. Such tennis and badminton parties, concerts and moonlight "Garba" songs and picnics, had never been seen in Baroda before, and those who took part in them are not likely to forget their joyous experiences. Mr. Dutt himself was the exhilarating centre of all these delightful parties. In the following note to Mrs. Bose, Mrs. Mehta describes the days she spent in Baroda at the time:—

Among Mr. Dutt's private friends were Mr. Kershaspji, his wife and the two daughters; Mr. and Mrs. Tyabji and Sharifah, our family, Mr. Manubhai, Merwanji and his daughters. Amongst our small circle at Baroda his personal influence was very great. His constant aim was to bring together members of different communities, men as well as ladies, and for this he used to have various at-homes and parties at his own place. These gatherings were most enjoyable, because he himself took part in them so very enthusiastically, and tried to make every one happy. If one saw him play badminton, or bridge, or his favourite game of *skat*, one could never guess that that was the

HOUSE OCCUPIED BY MR. DUTT AS REVENUE MINISTER OF BARODA

author of so many learned books. With a child he used to play like a child. The Garba parties and the musical evenings were very pleasant too. He always made us sing "Bharater jay," and he himself would always join in the chorus. Oh, the trouble he took to teach my husband to learn those few lines of the chorus! He would never miss a single social entertainment, in spite of all the work he had to do at the office. He was loved by the people also, because he was a man of very wide sympathy, and of a very open liberal mind. He used to appreciate the work of the meanest of the clerks, and even a peon was not afraid to go to him to tell his grievance, because people knew that they would not be ill-treated by him. He heard everybody's complaint, and tried to help every one. He was respected for his diligent work and loved for his wide sympathy. The whole of Baroda mourned his loss. To myself, my husband, and my children he was very kind. He often used to tell me that he looked upon me as one of his granddaughters, and he treated me just like Surama and Pratima (Mr. Dutt's granddaughters).

I remember the days when you were in Baroda with your family, how we used to spend evenings after evenings at your place playing cards and singing Gujrati and Bengali songs. Oh! it makes me so sad to think of those happy days, for those days would never come back, because the main link is broken! But I am sure there is one consolation. He has left us one legacy. It is the nobility of his character that we would never forget. Let us for ever remain as sisters.

Mrs. Bose also has jotted down her own reminiscences:—

When I was staying with father, we had two tennis and badminton days in the week; the Kershaspjis had one day and the Tyabjis took another. After our games we used to have light refreshments and songs. My girls used to sing Bengali songs. Mrs. Mehta and Misses Kershaspjis sang in Gujrati, while Miss Bhore, the Lady Superintendent of the local Girls' School, sang Mahratti songs. Sharifah used to play the *bin*, and to its accompaniment sang Hindi songs. These musical evenings used to be most enjoyable, and we seldom broke up before 8 or 9 P.M. They all used to say that nowhere else did they feel so much at home as at father's.

Everybody used to call father "Babu Dewan." They all

in every village and town, and the highest ladies join the performance in their houses as the lowest congregate in the streets. We had musical parties in my house about that time, and ladies of all races — Gujratis and Mahrattas, Parsis and Musalmans —often left their instruments in the drawing-room, and joined in a Garba dance and a merry Garba chant on the terrace under the clear light of the Indian autumn moon!

But his life in Baroda was not all sunshine. He was very often left quite alone, and the gloom of loneliness hung heavy upon him, and this, despite all his efforts, he found it very difficult to shake off. In these moments of depression he felt like an exile from his home. After his daughter went away in 1905, he wrote this charming letter to his granddaughter:—

20th February 1905.

MY DEAREST SUSAMA,—Is it a *kokil* singing with her first timid, sweet voice from a neighbouring bush after a long dreary winter? Or is it my pet Moyna writing to me again her welcome letters after a long cruel silence? I am delighted to see your handwriting again, and to receive your most loving wishes after such a long interval. I am delighted to know that the pretty little Moyna has not quite forgotten her old nest, though she has built a delightful little nest of her own in Beadon Street.

You have no doubt heard all about me from your *didima* (grandmother), *mejomashima* (aunt), and your *param bandhu* (dear friend). We had a delightful time here when they were here—skat every night, and sometimes nice gatherings and singing. Just before they left I went with the Maharaja on a long tour, far into the Peninsula of Kathiawar, if you know where that is. I was present at the marriage of the Prince of Gondal, and saw your mother's friend Miss Dey there. Thence I went to different parts of the Baroda State scattered about in that peninsula, and also visited some neighbouring States like Limdi and Badhwan. Everywhere they had heard of me and of my appointment at Baroda, and they welcomed me and garlanded me, and desired me to come again and again. Our long tour has been fruitful of good results; the Maharaja has remitted large sums of money due from distressed cultivators, and the people are thanking him and blessing him, and are attributing this good and graceful act to the advice and influence of the new Minister appointed from Bengal.

At last when I came back to Baroda, lo! and behold! my

house was solitary. Like the winter birds which visit India annually, the wild duck or the curlew, all my visitors had taken to their wings at the first approach of summer and had vanished with all their sweet songs and gaudy plumage and merry joyous notes. And so I settled down to my official work again, addressing to my unending Duty those lines that Sir Walter Scott addressed to his unfailing Harp:—

> "When on the weary night dawned wearier day,
> And bitterer was the grief devoured alone.
> That I o'erlive such woes, Enchantress! is thine own!"

Thank God, my health has been very good—this very dry climate suits me very well. I have never been laid up for a single day with rheumatism since I came here. My future plan is very uncertain. I should like to avoid the heat of the summer, and to go to Darjeeling and meet you all in May. But August and September are worse months here, and it would be wiser to take leave in September and go to Darjeeling then. However, I have not settled anything yet; only I hope that sometime or other during this year I will see your sweet loving faces again. In the meantime the Maharaja is going to Europe, probably next month, so that all the responsibility of managing this Raj will rest on the Dewan and on myself. So you see, I shall have plenty of work here, while you, little temptress, are tempting me away with the prospect of "bezique, picnic, singing, and music!" My life has been full of such sudden changes, from hard solitary toil to the joys of a dear loving home, such as few mortals on earth are so proud of as I am; and then from a sweet home and a troop of loving children back to solitary work again. I must say I appreciate this change, and can sing with Byron's Corsair:—

> "From toil to rest, and joy in every change!"

My kindest and warmest regards to your father-in-law and mother-in-law, to Prasanta and his sister, and believe me ever your loving Bardada, ROMESH CH. DUTT.

And after his daughter Kamala left him in 1906 he wrote:—

BARODA, *30th April* 1906.

MY DEAREST KAMALA,—I got your telegram and Pramatha's last evening, and am glad to learn that you are all well. I am quite well too, only this vast house is voiceless now. I come back from office about eleven o'clock, have two hours' rest after breakfast, work in my cool room downstairs in the afternoon, and have a solitary stroll in the evening unless the Mehtas come or I go anywhere. After six months of boisterous and joyous life I resume my accustomed solitude. But it will not be for long. You will have heard from your mother that my three months' leave on half-pay has been sanctioned, and I will probably leave Bombay by the *Egypt* on the 23rd June for Europe. It will be a welcome change and rest for me.

Write to me also about your meetings and gatherings. I will read the accounts with double joy in my solitude.

I met Meherbai and Shirinbai yesterday, but the whole station is dull and partakes of my solitary life. Every one tells me: "You *must*, *must*, *must* bring back Mrs. Bose next cold weather." I say to myself, "I wish I could."—With love to all, your loving father, ROMESH.

In May 1906 he wrote to his friend Mr. B. L. Gupta:—

I shall be delighted to have your company, for it is a lonely, cheerless life I am leading here.

III

His most intimate friends were the Mehtas and Tyabjis. What his feelings were towards Sharada, the wife of Dr. Mehta, and Sharifah, the daughter of Mr. Tyabji, is best told by the following poem which he wrote in their memory in the year of his death as a New Year's gift to his adopted children:—

One, a mother young and beauteous,
  One, a nobly gifted maid,
Blessed me with their sweet affection,
  Sang to me and often played,—
Till my soul was drunk with music,
  Till my heart was wrapt in love,
Ever, even as my daughters,
  They shall my affection prove!

One, a gentle Hindu mother,
  One, a duteous Moslem maiden,
In their loves they were united
  Like two creepers perfume-laden!

Sister streams that sweetly mingled,
  Sister blossoms on one stem,—
Creeds might differ, love of duty,
  Love of country blended them!

They were of the Western region,
  I was from the farthest East,—
How their truth and tender sweetness
  Filled my heart, my cottage blest!
Earth hath streaks of light and sunshine,
  Life hath gleams that cheer and bless,—
May the memory of their kindness
  Never in my heart grow less!

This is the place for a few letters which passed between Mr. Dutt and his adopted children, and which show their intimate comradeship and their free and loving exchange of ideas.

BARODA, 21*st September* 1906.

MY DEAR MR. DUTT,—Thanks for your kind letter which I received the other day. I did not write to you during the last month thinking that the letter might not reach you as you were coming on the 26th of this month. But now it seems that we'll have to wait for you almost a month or so. But for one thing I am glad because the longer you stay here the better it is for your health, and now you have to look after your health first.

I have received those lovely postcards. Little Lila likes them very much, and even while sleeping she keeps them under her pillow. She remembers you very much, and asks me to write and tell you to come back soon.

There is nothing particular going on here at present. The long-expected exhibition comes off on the 20th of the next month. I wish it had been postponed a little longer so that you might have seen it. I hope it will be a grand success. Baroda people are really waking up. At our meeting last month nearly 300 ladies attended, and we had a small exhibition of *swadeshi* things which are mostly useful to women. The lectures went off very nicely indeed. I also gave a short lecture, and the ladies appreciated it very much. Poor Mrs. Tyabji and Sharifah could not attend the meeting, because it was within a week of Mr. Badrudin's death. India has really lost three of her greatest men within the last few months, Mr. Bonnerjea, Mr. Tyabji, and Mr. A. M. Bose. All of them worked conscientiously for our country, and were all of them really great and good men. . . .

For the Presidentship of the Congress there has been a regular quarrel going on. One party, viz. of Babu Bipin Ch. Pal, strongly advocate for Mr. Tilak. I don't know what your own views are. But really to select such a man at such a time is really ruining the great cause itself. We don't know what will be the result of all this fight. I hope some nice experienced man like Mr. Dadabhai Naoroji or Mr. Cotton or yourself, or some man from Madras, is appointed President. A man like you would mend all matters, and bring everything to its proper place.

I have not heard from your people since a long time. I hope they are all well.

Merbai and Shirinbai have come back. Sharifah and Mrs. Tyabji have again gone back to Bombay. We are all doing well. The rains have now stopped. Fever is raging in the city. We have been having so much rain that fever will continue for a long time this year.

Doctor sends his kind regards to you. Hope this will find you quite well.—I remain, yours affectionately,

SHARADA.

On the birth of a boy, Mrs. Mehta named it after Mr. Dutt, and wrote :—

AHMEDABAD, *14th February* 1907.

MY DEAR MR. DUTT,—It is a very long time since I wrote to you last. But I was not strong enough to write letters. Now I am much better. In about a month I'll go to Naosari. I intend stopping at Baroda for a day or so to see all my old friends. I hope you will be in Baroda then. Little Lila is quite well. She remembers Dutt Saheb, and speaks of Pratima and Surama very often. She still thinks that you are in England. Sarala has grown very big, and she talks a lot now. My little boy is quite well. We have named him after you. We are going to call him Romesh. You must be his godfather. You are always so very kind to us, and always treat us as your own children, hence we thought it best to give him your name as a living memory. I hope he'll be worthy of his name, and will follow in the footsteps of his good godfather.

I hope all your people at Calcutta are quite well. I have written to Pratima and Surama to-day. How is the world going on at Baroda?—With kind regards, I am, yours affectionately,

SHARADA.

Mr. Dutt promptly replied :—

BARODA, 15*th February* 1907.

MY DEAR SHARADA,—It is really very very good of you to name your boy after me, and to make me his godfather. Though I have not seen the young gentleman yet, let me accord to him a most cordial welcome to this world of ours, and sincerely wish that he may live long and happily. Let me know the date of his birth, for I must keep a note of it, and let me know if you have completely recovered now.

I have lately returned from a long tour in Amreli District, in course of which I had the pleasure of visiting the ruins of the famous Somnath temple at Prabhas Pattan, and also the sacred temples at Dwaraka, Beyt, Gopi, Prachi, and elsewhere. When it is a little hotter I propose to make a good long stay at Naosari if you are there at the time. None of my daughters or grand-daughters seems likely to come to Baroda this time, so you and I and the Doctor must manage to have some Skat, and you must introduce me to the great and august gentleman my godson!—Yours ever affectionately, ROMESH CH. DUTT.

Mrs. Mehta translated his novel, "Sansar" into Gujrati, and gave it a new name "Sudha Hasini" (Sweet Smiler), and wrote :—

NAOSARI, 13*th April* 1907.

MY DEAR MR. DUTT,—I am sending you a copy of the book "Sudha Hasini." I hope you will like it. The press people really took an awfully long time in getting the book out. However the get-up is not bad, I think. I have sent you only one copy just now; but if you want a few more copies for any of your friends I shall be glad to send them immediately.

We'll read the book together when you come here, which I hope will be very soon. We are all doing well. The weather here is charming; no burning fires during the day-time. I hope this will find you well.—With kindest regards, I am, yours affectionately, SHARADA.

Mr. Dutt then wrote two letters in reply :—

BARODA, 14*th April* 1907.

MY DEAR SHARADA,—I shall be delighted to get your "Sudha Hasini"; she will come to me as one of my grand-daughters in Gujrati clothes, and I will welcome her all the more in her new garb! The book has not reached me yet, perhaps because this is Sunday, and there may be no book-post delivery to-day; at any rate I expect to get it to-morrow.

Kershaspji is going on two months' leave with his family, and will leave Baroda probably to-morrow. I shall be acting for him. Mr. Tyabji and Sharifah are shortly going to Tithal, where they will spend the summer. The Maharaja and family are going to Ooty very shortly, so I shall be all by myself here! I wish I could spend a month or two months at Naosari, but I am afraid Kershaspji's absence from Baroda will compel me to be at Baroda pretty often.

You seem to be in love with Naosari! Do you still wish to return to Baroda, say in June next, or does Dr. Mehta prefer to continue in Naosari for a year or two more! Reply to this after consulting your husband by return of post. More when we meet in about a week's time, I hope.—With love to your children, yours affectionately, R. C. DUTT.

BARODA, *17th April* 1907.

MY DEAR SHARADA,—I have received your letter of the 15th instant. I am glad you have told me of your preference of Baroda to Naosari. I will see if I can do anything.

Yes, I have received "Sudha Hasini," and for the last three days I have read nothing else. The translation is so deeply interesting to me—I see my own characters, my own scenes, my own thoughts, in the garb that you have so well bestowed on them. The gentle, faithful Bindu chats quietly with her husband in Gujrati; Bindu's pompous and garrulous but good-natured aunt boasts of her wealth in Gujrati; the passionate Sarat pleads his love in Gujrati; the meek-eyed Kalitara and her mother-in-law speak in Gujrati all the way to Jagarnath. The proud, insulted, but forgiving Uma consoles her repentant husband in Gujrati, and at last the Sanyasini returns to the embraces of her lord. I go over all the old scenes, recognise all my dear old friends, read again all my old thoughts—clear and vivid as in my own language. You and your sister have given me hours and hours of the greatest joy, and I read and read (as Sarat used to speak and speak) till the hand of the clock indicates midnight. There are so many things I have to tell you about the translation, but I will wait till we meet.

Tell me your honest opinion, Sharada, do you not think I would do well to devote the remaining years of my life in writing such books as the "Lake of Palms"—ay, in compiling a complete history of the Indian people from the earliest times to the twentieth century—than to work and vegetate in Baroda? I am the Amatya here, I am acting Dewan here, people look upon me with feelings of awe and respect—but I feel I am proving false to my higher pursuits, false to my destiny! I have done something in Baroda in these three years; let me plunge back to those pursuits which are dearest to my heart. As you are longing to come back from Naosari to the larger world of Baroda—I am longing also to return from Baroda to the larger world of literature and political work.

Tell me what you think.—With love to your dear children and to all, yours affectionately, ROMESH DUTT.

Incidentally here we might find place for a letter which he wrote to his brother about the same feeling, which seems to have been troubling him, that he was neglecting Sarasvati—the goddess of Wisdom—for Lakshmi, the goddess of Wealth and Prosperity.

BARODA, 16*th December* 1906.

MY DEAR BROTHER,—I have received your letter of the 12th December.

I remember quite well you suggested my writing a continuation of Mill's "History of India." I have a better plan in my head —of writing a History of the Indian people from the ancient times to A.D. 1900! It will be in some six big volumes, and will record once for all an Indian view of India's ancient civilisation, of the condition and the progress of the people under the Muhammadans, and of British administration during 150 years. The idea came to my head one sleepless night some nine months ago —and I hope it won't be a "noble idea that died" with Southey!

I will take up the work the day I retire from Baroda service— and the only question is, when can I retire? I want to scrape together a little more money before I go, and that keeps me hanging on here! But I must not stay here very long; I shall commence my sixtieth year next August, and after that one cannot hope to retain capacity of work many years.

Lakshmi and Sarasvati are always jealous of each other; and in my case Lakshmi is chary of her favours, because, I suppose, she has a shrewd suspicion that I mean to serve Sarasvati in the end!—Yours affectionately ever, ROMESH.

I have only two more of his letters to Mrs. Mehta which will be of interest.

BARODA, 1*st May* 1907.

MY DEAR SHARADA,—With a woman's wit you bring the charge of cruelty against me for thinking of leaving Baroda soon!

What can a "mere man" do, when so assailed! But if I was as clever as you ladies are, I might have brought that charge against you for leaving me alone in this blazing hot month at Baroda—while you are enjoying the cool breezes of Naosari. Sharifah is enjoying her sea-bathing at Tithal, Kamala high up in Darjeeling, and Meherbai and Shirinbai are up at Mahabaleswar. Nice girls you all are, sending down copious streams of sympathy to the lonely, "sun-dried," work-bewildered official at Baroda—but never thinking of helping him with your company and conversation, your music and your song! And now you talk of spending this month at Surat, and of coming here in June—just when I shall be packing up, I suppose—just in time to say good-bye, I suppose, to the wanderer beyond the seas! And then in your own pretty way you will say: "Surely, Mr. Dutt, you cannot be so cruel as to leave just when we have come to Baroda. Now, is not that too bad! Isn't that just like the selfishness of a man, &c., &c." And Sharifah will stand by you and say: "But what can you expect of a man, Sharada?—men will be men—did you ever expect anything better from them!" And you would respond—"But surely we expected something different from Mr. Dutt—he seemed to care so much for us all!" And Sharifah would add—"But it is all seeming, Sharada, it is all outward appearance—did you ever know of a man who ever made a real sacrifice for us? It is all the other way." And thus the dear, angelic creatures will talk and talk about the innate selfishness of men, turning up the whites of their lovely eyes to the sky, and wondering if any man was ever born on earth with such an article as a heart! And poor Mr. Dutt would stand before them, without a word to say for himself—abashed, humiliated, convicted beyond the hope of a reprieve, his only crime being to seek some rest and change after months of continuous work and lonely life!

But this will never do, my dear girl; your nice arguments may be unanswerable—but a nice act would be better. Why not come up to Baroda after the marriage of Manubhai's brother, and have some games and music and singing before I leave Baroda? Now, be prepared for this—for I am coming to Surat to attend the marriage—and I am going to fetch you all back with me—including the fine young gentleman—my namesake, whom I have not yet seen!

I read in the papers that the German Emperor is very fond of Skat. So am I. Only I cannot order my court-ladies to attend on me as His Imperial Majesty does. Or if I do order, the court-ladies in Baroda seem to be more independent than at Berlin, and won't obey my imperial mandates.

I end with one item of news—Princess Padmawati gave birth to a girl this morning.—With kindest regards, yours affectionately,

ROMESH CH. DUTT.

BARODA, *May* 1907.

MY DEAR SHARADA,—Call not my last letter "unkind." Can I ever write unkindly to my own people? Have I ever regarded you and Sumant differently from my own people?

I wanted to make you laugh. And I wanted a spirited rejoinder from you on behalf of your sex. And you have sent a spirited rejoinder! I can imagine your flushed face and sparkling eyes when you wrote that reply! I am simply crushed—speechless like Hem when he was assailed by his sister-in-law, in the "Lake of Palms." Poor fellow, he then had some experience of woman's power, and so have I!

For the rest you will not find a stronger champion of your sex than myself. If you read all my Bengali novels, you will find everywhere woman's virtue, woman's endurance, woman's ennobling influence. You will not find one unkind word about your sex in all my works—English and Bengali. But a little good-humoured fun may occasionally be pardoned even by such austere champions of your sex as yourself and Sharifah.

And now, with a woman's wonderful self-sacrifice, you are coming to Baroda about the end of May, just to help me to pack up my things, I suppose! Well, I must not grumble lest I get it hot again! These are days of suffrage, and we men daren't open our lips! By jove, I should like to see the plight of some of the members of the House of Commons when the suffragettes get hold of them. And yet, do you know, some of the suffragettes are the best of wives and mothers! I was introduced to one last year in London, and she was a most amiable and gentle wife to her husband—a member of Parliament. That proves your case, you will say, about the devotion and self-sacrifice of women! Go which way I like, I cannot refute your reasons, so I had better shut up!

Ask your sister to send me ten copies of "Sudha Hasini." I have promised one copy to the Princess of Gondal, and will send one or two to Miss Dey, of Bha Nagar, and also distribute a few at Baroda.

I don't know if the baby elephant is kept in the elephant house opposite my bungalow. But we can send for it any time. —With kind regards, ever yours affectionately,

ROMESH CH. DUTT.

next mail. I was glad to receive the Dewan's letters, which contained much wise counsel which I appreciate. I hope you are having good news from Bengal. I hope this confidential letter will find you perfectly well and as cheerful as you often are, a gift for which you have to be thankful to heaven and to yourself.—Your sincere friend, SAYAJI RAO, GAEKWAR.

EASTBOURNE, 26/5/1905.

On the sad death of his eldest son and heir-apparent, Prince Fatteh Sing, the Gaekwar wrote to Mr. Dutt when he was in England.

KAPURTHALA HOUSE, MUSSOURI, *4th November* 1908.

MY DEAR MR. DUTT,—Thank you very much for your letter of condolence. I did not expect that my poor son would die so soon. The doctor and the valet, that I had determined to get to look after him, only came a week after his death. I am doing all I can for his wife and children, who are all well.

I hope on your return back, you will pay me a visit at Baroda. Nothing has yet been settled about Indra Raja's marriage. I must soon settle something during the next cold weather.

We are all looking forward to the declaration of reforms the Secretary of State is going to introduce in India. With certain safeguards, I am decidedly inclined to give the people of India a substantial voice in the management of their affairs. The representative principles of government may be introduced into India, taking care at the same time that the backward classes in education are given special facilities to come up to their advanced brethren. This is not a chimera, but can be practically done.

I should open up a certain number of commissioned ranks of Lieutenants and above for the Indians, specially the sons of Indian chiefs who will do credit to the military vocation.

I should, for the native princes, give greater powers and let them introduce railways, telegraphs, in there own territories without reference to the central Government. Over-centralised government is bad for all concerned.

I am leaving this on the 11th instant for Baroda. The change has done us all good. I hope this letter will find you perfectly well. Kindly remember me to Lord Morley and Mr. Gokhale, if that does not involve you to go out of your way.—Your sincere friend, SAYAJI RAO, GAEKWAR.

Prince Kerala Varma of Travancore

enthusiastic admiration. Unfortunately, however, it was not to be so at the time. If ever hereafter you chance to take a trip to the Dekhan, I request you not to miss the old-world majesty and arcadian charm of virgin Travancore, whose children to-day in every vernacular school, study and become moulded by the teachings of your great historical work on our country's remote past.—With best regards, yours very sincerely,

KERALA VARMA.

It appears that he was introduced also to the two Ranis of Travancore, and Prince Kerala Varma, in his second letter, says, "The young Ranis have had such an indelible impression made on their mind by your unique personality, that they are not likely to forget you all through life."

Another of his distinguished admirers was the Prince of Nabha, who in 1905 wrote :–

NABHA, *7th June* 1905.

MY DEAR FRIEND,—Pray forgive the delay in acknowledging your very kind and most welcome letter of 29th May. I am also in receipt of your letter dated the 31st ultimo. I showed your letter to my wife ; she asks me to convey her best thanks to you for your kind appreciation of her humble writings. She says, that if it pleases God she will complete the series with great pleasure, as desired by you. She has already undertaken to write the life of our Guru Sri Guru Nanak Dey Ji. Unfortunately her health is very poor and delicate, which is always a matter of great anxiety to me. I thank you sincerely for your so much interest in this matter, and kind promise to bring out the lives of all the ten Gurus in a collected form, and I hope some day to have the pleasure of receiving you here as my honoured guest.—With my kindest regards, and hoping to hear from you, I am, yours very sincerely,

RIPUDAMAN SINGH.

While travelling on board the *Macedonia*, on his way to England in 1908, he made the acquaintance of the Nawab and Begum of Janjira. To this lady he addressed one of his finest poems in English.

Begum, on thy queenly forehead,
I have read—unfaltering truth ;
In thy heart—a noble impulse,
In thine eyes—a woman's ruth.

. . . . . .

Be it still thy lofty purpose
  For that sacred land to toil,
Help the son of loom and anvil,
  Raise the tiller of the soil.
Trust in duty humbly rendered,
  Trust in India's future star,
And our unborn sons and daughters
  Shall be higher than we are!

Unseen clouds will often darken
  Glamour of the brightest day,
Doubt and discord and disaster
  Oft will bar our onward way;
But the brother and the sister,
  Man great-hearted, woman true,
Proudly sweep aside each hindrance,
  Serve the land their fathers knew!

Caste and creed will often wrangle,
  Tear apart those who are one,
Greed and selfishness will hinder
  What by selfless work is won;
But true-hearted men and women
  Moslem or of Hindu faith,
Love of men their high religion,
  Serve their country until death!

After her return to India the Begum wrote:—

KASRE AHMED, MURUD-JANJIRA,
31st August 1909.

DEAR MR. DUTT,—To-day's post brought me the very book of which I was thinking of going to get from Bombay. How very thoughtful of you, and I shall read it with the greatest pleasure. Many thanks. I read an interesting review of it in *East and West*, and I am sure it must be a charming tale.

Often and often we think and speak of those very pleasant days we spent together on the ship. I am glad you came back to Baroda again. Do you remember our long talks? Those were indeed delightful times. Now, when are you going to fulfil your promise, and visit our little island? We will never allow you to slip through; December or January is the best time, the weather being cold and delightful.

Nawab Saheb sends you his best salams, and asks me to tell

you, he is much looking forward to renewing the friendship which began on board. Both my sisters now live with me. I want you so much to know my elder sister too. Atiya asks me to give you her kind regards and salams, and please accept the same from, sincerely yours, NAZLI RAFIQUA, of Janjira.

A brief reference to one more of his gifted women admirers, and we shall close this section. In presenting a copy of her book of verses, "The Golden Threshold," Mrs. Sarojini Naidu wrote:—

HYDRABAD, 17*th February* 1906.

DEAR MR. DUTT,—I don't know if you remember me at all, but I had the pleasure of meeting you several times in London, and I think you know my father, Aghorenath Chattopadhaya. I believe this will be enough of a reintroduction for me to request that you will do me the honour to accept the accompanying copy of my little book of poems, "The Golden Threshold," as the gift of a poet to a poet, and an Indian woman to one of the great men of modern India. I need scarcely tell you that if you can find time to read my little book how valuable your criticism would be to me.

I have been so fortunate as to win the generous approval of the leading English journals, and the book has just gone into a second edition. Will you be so good as to obtain for me the permission of the Maharaja Gaekwar to send him a copy of "The Golden Threshold"? I had the honour of meeting him several times in Bombay last year.—Believe me, sincerely yours,

SAROJINI NAIDU.

And after Mr. Dutt presented her with a copy of his "Epics," she wrote:—

HYDRABAD, 25*th March* 1906.

DEAR MR. DUTT,— . . . I realise what a much finer, more lasting, more fruitful achievement it is to have made accessible to the world, in this splendid and noble version, the grandest epics of the centuries, than the tinkling little verses such as I had the audacity—it seems to me so now—to send you.—Believe me, sincerely yours, SAROJINI NAIDU.

CHAPTER XXX

THE NEW INDUSTRIAL MOVEMENT

In the later years of his life Mr. Dutt realised, even more fully perhaps than he had done before, the great value and importance of an industrial revival in the country, so that India, instead of being merely a producer of raw materials, should take her place as a manufacturing country with the other industrial and progressive nations of the world. Of course, even when devoting his attention more particularly to the economic and agrarian aspects of the Indian problem, he had repeatedly pointed out that one great cause of the poverty of the masses was the dying out of the old industries and the consequent increase of pressure on agriculture, which was gradually becoming more and more the sole means of subsistence of the mass of the people. He held also that living progress in the life of nations must take place simultaneously in all departments of national life—social, religious, economical, and industrial. But in these earlier days he had not matured any constructive scheme for an industrial revival, nor had he pressed the great and vital importance of the subject either on the Government or the people. In fact, having spent the best portion of his life in Bengal, he had few opportunities of coming in contact with the present-day industrial problems of the country, or of realising the capacity of Indians to adapt themselves to the requirements of the modern industrial world. When he took up his residence in Baroda as one of the principal Ministers of the State, he came almost in touch with the full flow of the industrial tide in India, for in no part of India is industry so advanced and up-to-date as in Bombay and Gujrat. And in the ruler of Baroda himself he found a prince who fully recognised his duty of fostering and developing the industrial enterprises of his people. We have seen how Mr. Dutt took full advantage of his splendid opportunity. In no department of the administration was progress so marked in Baroda during Mr. Dutt's time as in the department of industry.

Then came the great wave of Swadeshism, flooding the country from the Punjab to Cape Comorin, and Mr. Dutt joined the national movement with all his wonted energy and devotion. It was he who was selected to be the President of the Industrial Conference which was held for the first time in connection with the Congress at Benares in 1905, and then again in 1907, at Surat. The Congress had decided much earlier to organise an Industrial Exhibition in connection with the national movement, but it was soon realised that it was necessary to have a permanent organisation for the encouragement of the nascent industrial enterprise in the country; and it was in connection with the Benares session of the Congress that the Industrial Conference was first held.

Mr. Dutt worked hard not only to frame practical rules for the working of the permanent organisation, but also contributed handsomely towards the funds of the working committee.

In his speeches delivered at the conferences of Benares and Surat, he formulated his views on this important subject. He began with a statement of the difficulties that lie in the path of the revival of industrial enterprise in India:—

> In the first place, we have to change an ancient and time-honoured habit, the habit of carrying on industries in our homes and cottages. We must change our old habit of universal cottage industry, and learn to form companies, erect mills, and adopt the methods of combined action if we desire to protect or recover our industries. But the formation of companies and the erection of mills require capital, and the conditions in India are not favourable to the accumulation of capital. Lastly, there is the difficulty about our fiscal legislation, which is oftener controlled by Lancashire than by us in this country. These bear on the difficulties before us. In the first place, we have lagged behind, and have to recover the lost ground. And in the second place,

we have to run the race with the treble disadvantage of want of modern industrial training, want of capital, and want of control over our fiscal legislation.

But his was never a gospel of despair.

I mention these discouraging circumstances not to discourage you, but because we have to face and conquer them. . . . The history of the last twenty or thirty years shows that all is not lost, and that much has been gained. We have now turned over a new leaf in the history of our national progress. Our industrious countrymen soon adopted the Western methods of industry, and competed with Western nations for the markets of India and of the East. Forty years ago we had only 13 cotton mills in all India; the number is probably near 300 in the present day. We had less than 300,000 spindles in all India forty years ago; the number to-day is probably six millions. Our advance in the textile industry has been perhaps more rapid than in other industries, but a general movement is observable to-day all over India to revive old industries, to start new industries, and to give the people in India their ancient place among the industrial nations of the earth.

These are some of the results which we have achieved in recent years, and all classes of men, Hindu and Musalman, Englishman and Parsi, have helped in the onward march. I make bold to say that no other country in Asia, except Japan, has shown such industrial progress within the lifetime of a generation; and no country on earth, labouring under the disadvantages from which we suffer, could have shown more adaptability to modern methods, more skill, more patient industry, more marked success.

And then he passes on to the great development called the Swadeshi Movement :—

Now at the commencement of the twentieth century we are more resolved than ever not to be beaten in this industrial race. I see in the faces of those who fill this hall to-day a strong determination that—God helping—we will work out our own salvation by our own hands. Men educated in English schools and colleges in India, men trained in the Universities of Cambridge and Oxford, have come to share this noble work with practical manufacturers and traders in India. And to-day there is a desire, which is spreading all over India, that by every legitimate means, by every lawful endeavour we will foster and stimulate the use of our own manufactures among the vast millions who fill this great continent.

Gentlemen, I am drifting into a subject which has raised much angry discussion, when I speak of the Swadeshi Movement. And yet I would not be fulfilling the duty which you have laid upon me to-day if I passed silently over that subject which is in every man's thoughts. I speak in the presence of some who are among the leaders of this movement in Bengal, and I speak from personal knowledge when I say that these leaders have tried their very utmost to conduct this movement lawfully and peacefully, to the best interests of the people and of the Government. If there have been any isolated instances of disturbance, here and there, we deprecate such acts. On the other hand, if the Government have, in needless panic, been betrayed into measures of unwise repression, we deplore such measures. But neither the rare instances of disturbance nor the unwise measures of repression are a part and parcel of the Swadeshi scheme. The essence of the scheme, as I understand it, is by every lawful method to encourage and foster home industries, and to stimulate the use of home manufactures among all classes of people in India. Gentlemen, I sympathise with this movement with all my heart, and will co-operate with this movement with all my power.

Gentlemen, the Swadeshi Movement is one which all nations on earth are seeking to adopt in the present day. Mr. Chamberlain is seeking to adopt it by a system of Protection. Mr. Balfour seeks to adopt it by a scheme of Retaliation. France, Germany, the United States, and all the British Colonies adopt it by building up a wall of prohibitive duties. We have no control over our fiscal legislation, and we adopt the Swadeshi scheme therefore by a laudable resolution to use our home manufactures, as far as practicable, in preference to foreign manufactures. I see nothing that is sinful, nothing that is hurtful, in this; I see much that is praiseworthy and much that is beneficial. It will certainly foster and encourage our industries, in which the Indian Government has always avowed the greatest interest. It will relieve millions of weavers and other artisans from a state of semi-starvation in which they have lived, will bring them back to their hand-loom and other industries, and will minimise the terrible effects of famines which the Government have always endeavoured to relieve to the best of their power. It will give a new impetus to our manufactures which need such impetus; and it will see us, in the near future, largely dependent on articles of daily use prepared at home, rather than on articles imported from abroad.

In one word, it will give a new life to our industrial enterprises; *and there is nothing which the people of India and the Government of India desire more earnestly than to see Indian industries flourish, and the industrial classes prosper.*

Therefore, I sincerely trust that the Swadeshi Movement will live and extend in every province and in every village in India. There should be associations formed to stimulate the use of country-made cloth and country-made articles, not only in towns but in rural villages. Such associations should peacefully and quietly extend their operations from year to year, disregarding the jeers of their critics, and braving the wrath of their opponents. Spasmodic and hysterical exhibitions should be avoided, for, as a great English writer remarks, strength consists not in spasms but in the stout bearing of burdens. Mindful of the great work we have to perform, we should work with the calm consciousness of doing our duty towards our countrymen. If we succeed in this noble endeavour, we shall present to the world an instance, unparalleled in the history of modern times, of a nation protecting its manufactures and industries without protective duties. If we fail in this great endeavour, and prove ourselves false to the resolutions we have formed and professed, then we shall deserve to remain in that state of industrial serfdom to other nations from which we are struggling to be free.—*Benares Speech*, 1905.

Professor H. B. Lees Smith, in his "Lectures on Indian Economics," points out that the Swadeshi Movement has received the support of all sections of the Indian community, including the business and non-political community and even the Government. He then gives extracts from the speeches of Sir Vithal das Damodar Thackersey at the Conference held in Calcutta in 1906, and of Dewan Bahadur Ambalal Desai at the third Conference held at Surat in 1907, and of Mr. G. K. Gokhale, who all support the Swadeshi Movement in language almost identical with that used by Mr. Dutt.

And then Professor Lees Smith himself observes:—

While in this way Swadeshi encourages home producers, it at the same time enjoins upon them the need of rising to their opportunities. I have pointed out, and shall have to do so again, that the essential weakness of Indian industry is lack of initiative. Swadeshi preaches the courage and mutual confidence which will enable Indians to strike out fresh paths for themselves. Although many of the enterprises started under its stimulus have failed, and doubtless will fail, the first step towards overcoming a fault is to recognise its existence.

Nor was Mr. Dutt ignorant or slow to acknowledge the assistance which the movement for the revival of indigenous industries had received from Government.

It is some years now since the first Industrial Exhibition was held in connection with the Indian National Congress; and it is only a year ago that the first Industrial Conference was held at Benares, at which I had the honour to preside. From the beginning, the Government of India and the Governments of the different Provinces have given us their hearty support and co-operation in these efforts to stimulate our industries; *and we gratefully acknowledge that the attitude of the Government towards our industries at the present day is one of cordial sympathy.* But, *gentlemen, our future rests with us.* There is no civilised and progressive nation in Europe, or in America, which has not secured its own place in the world's history by its own endeavours, strenuous and persistent, in all departments of national life. The call now comes to us from Japan—ay, from China too and other Eastern lands—and it is the same stirring call, teaching us the great lesson of self-help and self-reliance.

Speaking at Lucknow in 1908, he said: "It affords me great pleasure to say, that the greatest and most practical Swadeshite that I have seen in this province is Sir John Hewett. He is creating in the minds of the people a desire to develop their industries and improve their manufactures."

Later on in the same speech he said: "The Government is working quietly, but none the less steadily, in the encouragement of Indian industries. *Silently, and without proclaiming their noble deeds, the Government are doing their best to help us in this and other matters.*"

But he was well aware that the future rests entirely with the people themselves, that neither Government assistance nor any emotional wave of patriotism will permanently help the *Swadeshi* cause, unless the people are prepared to do silent and steady work themselves to improve their own industries: "Exert not only by words, lectures on platforms, or by writing in the newspapers, but by solid, practical, and substantial work."

CHAPTER XXXI

THE DECENTRALISATION COMMISSION

I

THE appointment, in 1907, of Mr. Dutt to be a member of the Royal Commission on Decentralisation was a signal mark of the trust and confidence reposed in him by the Secretary of State, Lord Morley. Originally Sir Henry Primrose was appointed Chairman, with Sir Frederic Lely, Sir Steyning Edgerley, Mr. Dutt, Mr. (now Sir) W. S. Meyer, and Mr. W. L. Hichens as members. But subsequently, on the resignation of Sir Henry Primrose, Mr. Charles Hobhouse was appointed in his place. In India Mr. H. Wheeler, of the Indian Civil Service, was appointed Secretary to the Commission.

The scope of the inquiries to which the Commission were invited to confine their attention did not directly include any fundamental questions of the Indian administration or any of the pressing topics which arose out of the feeling of general unrest agitating India at the time. This is clearly pointed out in the preamble to the Report.

> We hold, too, that our terms of reference precluded us from inquiring into questions of a purely political nature, questions of general policy, and questions such as the separation of judicial and executive functions, and the constitution and duties of the civil and criminal courts. We have, therefore, only touched upon such matters when, in our opinion, they have a direct bearing upon administrative decentralisation. Nor, again, have we felt ourselves called upon to inquire into the general conduct of the administration, or into alleged grievances against particular departments or individual officers.

But still the Commission inquired into such important topics as the "constitution of provincial governments and the extension of the Council form of government which prevails in Madras and Bombay to other large provinces."

Another important circumstance which heightened the consequence of the deliberations of this body arose from the fact, that India was on the eve of the epoch-making reforms of Lord Minto and Lord Morley, and the Secretary of State was anxious to receive the views of this highly qualified and representative body before giving final shape to his scheme.

While our Report was still under consideration [runs the Report] we were informed by Your Majesty's Principal Secretary of State for India, that motives of high policy would require an early pronouncement by him, on behalf of Your Majesty's Government, on certain important reforms in the system of administration in India. Accordingly at his request we furnished him with the conclusions now embodied in our Report. We have not thought it necessary to point out in each instance, the extent to which the application of our conclusions, independently arrived at, may be affected by the pronouncement of the Secretary of State. We have been content to report these conclusions to Your Majesty in their original form.

It is needless to say that the reforms recommended by the Commission greatly strengthened the hands of the Liberal statesman who was steering the ship of State in such troubled waters and through such dangerous rocks.

The method of work and procedure adopted by the Commission have been described in the Report.

We assembled in India on the 18th November 1907, and, having sketched out for the guidance of witnesses, in so far as we could do this in advance, the matters to which we thought our inquiries would probably be directed, we proceeded to take evidence in the various Provinces. Between November 1907 and April 1908, we held public sittings at one or more places in all the major Provinces, as also in the North-West Frontier Province and Baluchistan. Our public sittings occupied in all 71 days, and involved journeys aggregating 12,300 miles in India, and the examination of 307 witnesses, of whom 119 were non-officials. In each Province we obtained a statement of the views and proposals of the Local Government, and examined a large number of high officials who could speak to matters of general policy, or furnish us with information or suggestions as to the working of their departments, *e.g.* Secretaries to Government, Members of Council in Madras and Bombay, Members of Boards of Revenue and Financial Commissioners and representative officers of the Medical, Sanitary, Public Works, Police, Education, and other special departments. We also examined a number of officials concerned with general district administration, from Commissioners down to Tahsildars, as well as district representatives of the special departments above referred to. These witnesses included a considerable number of natives of India. We likewise examined officials and non-officials, both European and Indian, who have been specially concerned with the administration of district boards, municipalities and other local bodies, as well as other non-officials (mainly Indian) who could speak to local conditions and reforms which had fallen within their observation. The non-official witnesses were selected for us by the Local Governments from men who could give us the most useful and representative views on the subjects into which we were inquiring. Invitations were further issued to the public through the press, as well as directly by ourselves, to various persons believed to be specially interested in the scope of our inquiries, to appear before us in support of their views. We likewise obtained the evidence of the Secretaries to the Government of India in the Home, Revenue, Public Works, Finance and Commerce Departments, and of a number of Imperial officers who deal with matters primarily within the scope of the Local Governments.

It is hardly necessary to remark that the Commission got intimately in touch with the views of the leaders of public opinion in India. Mr. Dutt refers to the plan adopted in a letter to Mr. B. L. Gupta :—

TAJ MAHAL HOTEL, BOMBAY,
15th November 1907.

MY DEAR BIHARI,— . . . We are now fairly launched in our work. We had an informal meeting yesterday. Our chairman, Hobhouse, arrives at Bombay to-day—perhaps has arrived. Then we settle our programme definitely, as well as our questions to witnesses, which will be all published in the papers. Then we move about! Government provides a special train to us wherever we go. One compartment to each member and a

That Commissioners should have some control over the work of all Departments (Education, Public Works, &c.) within their divisions, and should hold Provincial Conferences to which non-officials should be admitted (488 and 523).

That Collectors should have a weighty voice over the distribution of irrigation water, and District Forest Officers should be considered as Assistants to Collectors (544 and 553).

That the Subdivisional system should be universally applied, and Subdivisional Officers should live in their subdivisions (582 and 591).

That in Madras, Tahsildars should not be selected from the clerical ranks; and in Bengal, they should be placed in charge of circles answering to Talukas in other Provinces (600 and 601).

That village Panchayets should be created, and should decide petty cases, execute minor village works, maintain village schools, and manage fuel and fodder reserves (700 to 720).

That District and Subdistrict Boards should have a substantial majority of elected members (789).

That Municipal Councils should have a substantial majority of elected members, and should ordinarily elect non-official chairmen (849 to 852).

It is believed that it was chiefly owing to the strong advocacy of Mr. Dutt that the following recommendation was made by the Commission :—

> We desire to add that this expansion of Provincial Executive Councils would also permit of the strengthening of the administration by the inclusion of specially qualified natives of India.

The chief points in which Mr. Dutt disagreed from the opinion of the majority are given below.

The majority of the Commission recommended :—

That a general Delegation Act should be passed, empowering Government to alter Legislative Acts by Executive Notifications, in order to delegate general powers to lower officials. But Mr. Dutt considered such a General Delegation Act bad in principle, unknown in any part of the British Empire, dangerous in India, and a breach of faith if applied in altering Acts already in existence (416).

That Divisional Commissioners should have the power to invest first-class Magistrates and Subdivisional Officers with criminal appellate powers, and should also appoint Tahsildars. Mr. Dutt thought, however, that to confer criminal appellate powers to first-class Magistrates and Subdivisional Officers generally would create alarm and endanger justice; and to invest Commissioners with powers to appoint Tahsildars would lead to favouritism and a deterioration of the service (512, 516, and 590).

That Advisory Councils are not needed in districts. But Mr. Dutt contended that the present system of district administration, which is a one-man rule, is the real cause of much discontent in India; that an Advisory Council in each district, with some provision to help the Collector in his work, would make administration more efficient and popular (534).

That the Collector should always be President of the District Board. Mr. Dutt pointed to Lord Ripon's Resolution of 1882, directing that official control on Boards should be exercised from outside, and not inside; and urged that there is, and can be, no self-government in India if people are not trusted to manage local matters free from official control inside the Boards (795). His view was, however, that such delegation of power should first be tried in selected and advanced districts, and then gradually extended to other districts.

Mr. Dutt held very strong views on the subject of Decentralisation in the existing system of district administration, and the suggestions which he made to Sir Edward Baker, Lieutenant-Governor of Bengal, in a letter written on 19th April 1909, are worthy of record :—

My main idea, which I have had since I was District Officer myself, is to make the people feel that this Government is their own Government, that it is conducted with their advice and co-operation, that they are to some extent responsible for its success or failure. So far as the Province as a whole is concerned, the expansion of the Legislative Council, and the creation of an

Executive Council with one representative Indian on it, will effectually spread this idea, and we want nothing more at present.

But this idea should be created in Districts also. In district administration we get no active help from the people; even when we are trying to repress crime and punish criminals, the sympathies of the people are sometimes against us. This is lamentable, but very natural,—it is not natural for the people to sympathise with an administration in which they have no share, with an alien one-man rule, the rule of the District Officer without popular advice. This should be remedied. Failing the creation of Advisory Councils, the District Boards should be used as such, and should be convened and consulted on all general matters affecting the districts,—Drainage, Irrigation, Water-supply, relief, repression of crime, Settlements, liquor shops, industries, technical education, pasture lands, forest rules, timber, fuel, new crops, water-rates, feeder lines, and a hundred other subjects.

Little Committees of the Boards may be formed to be in charge of specific important duties, and the Collector can make over many petty inquiries and many petty matters for disposal to a general Committee. If all this cannot be effected by a Government Resolution, the Local Self-Government Act should be modified to permit such decentralisation and delegation of duties.

Members of the Committees should be *unpaid non-officials*, (this is important), but a fee for every attendance will remunerate them for their work and expenses. And the people will feel then that they are taking a share in district administration, side by side with the Collector and his official subordinates.

The Sub-District Board might similarly be used as an Advisory Council for the Subdivisional Officer. But what is more important *is the creation of three or four circles in each Subdivision, each to be in charge of a Sub-Deputy Collector whose number must be increased.* Each circle Sub-Deputy Collector aided by Honorary Magistrates, can dispose of all local petty criminal cases and all revenue work which can be disposed of locally, but his principal work will be that he will be a link between the administration and the village Panchayets under him. And village Panchayets should be universally created and entrusted with small powers to dispose of village cases and other affairs.

My idea is thus to link the people by a chain of civil officers and advisory councils with the Government,—to make the people feel that they are a part of the Empire, a part of the British Raj, responsible for the administration of the Province like the L. G. himself. And the creation of these institutions will be the best means to reform the Police, which will no longer be the only link between the Government and the people.

II

In the letter which Lord Morley wrote to Mr. Dutt after his appointment to the Commission, he advised Mr. Dutt not to take a too narrow and partisan view of his position in the Commission, but to be actuated by a spirit of reasonable co-operation. How far Mr. Dutt fulfilled these expectations, and in what spirit, and with what devotion and ability he discharged his duties, will be best seen from the following appreciation which Sir William Meyer, one of the members of the Commission, sent to the present writer:—

OOTACAMUND, 30*th June* 1910.

DEAR MR. GUPTA,—In reply to your letter of 24th instant, it gives me a melancholy pleasure to send you the note you ask me about my late lamented friend, R. C. Dutt. On this occasion, I have no need to remember the old motto *de mortuis nil nisi bonum*, for what I have said about Dutt is simply true, and there was no *malum* in him.—Yours sincerely, W. MEYER.

"I first made the personal acquaintance of Mr. R. C. Dutt (whom I had of course known well by name before) in November 1907, shortly before the Decentralisation Commission assembled; and from that time until the end of February 1909, when the Commission dissolved, I was in close and intimate connection with him.

"Mr. Dutt's position on the Commission was a delicate one. He was the only Indian member, and his prominent connection with the National Congress must have led to great pressure on the part of his political friends to import their ideas into the Commission's Report. Mr. Dutt absolutely resisted any such tendency. Like most of us, he was necessarily swayed by his own prepossessions and past experiences; but he adopted an absolutely fair-minded attitude, and never hesitated to give up a previously conceived view if he thought that the facts did not warrant it. I was much struck by his full and fair examination of witnesses, by his great interest he took in the Commission's work, and by his constant industry in reading up the voluminous papers that were before us and in writing notes on these and on the principal points brought out in the evidence. Another striking point about him was his mental adaptability. At the outset, for instance, he had little knowledge of the details of the financial relations between the Government of India and the Local Governments; but careful study on these points and of the answers given by witnesses in replies to other members soon put him *au fait* with them, as he showed by his own questions.

"When the Commission proceeded to discuss the evidence put before them and the conclusions to be drawn therefrom in England, Mr. Dutt sat with me on a Sub-Committee whose primary duty was to consider matters giving scope for Decentralisation within the Provinces, and of this Sub-Committee he was, by reason of his fair-mindedness and industry, a most valuable member. The same qualities were shown when the Commission as a whole met to consider the suggestions of its Sub-Committees and the draft of the final Report. Mr. Dutt was necessarily not able to fall in with all the recommendations which commended themselves to the majority; but that he possessed in the highest degree that spirit of give-and-take, of forbearing to press non-essential points, which is necessary in members of an important Commission if its deliberations are to be crowned with success, is evidenced by the fact that he contented himself with inserting foot-notes on points on which he considered it essential to press his individual opinion, and refrained from writing any separate note of dissent.

"As regards our personal relations, Mr. Dutt's genial *bonhomie* and constant sense of humour endeared him to all his colleagues on the Commission. To travel together, as we did, for several months over the Indian continent necessarily brings out the weak points in men's personal characters. Mr. Dutt survived this test most successfully. He was always ready to accommodate himself to the wishes of others, to look on the bright side of things, and to turn off with a jest such discomforts as necessarily occurred every now and then during our journeys. I may confidently speak on behalf of my other colleagues on the Commission, as well as myself, when I say that we regarded his sudden death not merely as a grave loss to India, but as a personal bereavement to ourselves."

The following is the note of Sir Frederic Lely on the same subject :—

ETALES, FRANCE, *22nd September* 1910.

DEAR GUPTA,—Although we were contemporaries in official life, I never met your father-in-law, Mr. R. C. Dutt, personally until we served together on the Royal Commission on Decentralisation. Now that he is gone, it is a melancholy pleasure to remember our intercourse at that time. He amply justified his selection by Lord Morley as the Indian member. His affection for and loyalty to his people were undoubted, and to this was most usefully allied the saving grace of long practical experience and a genial, kindly disposition. He could make and take a joke with any of us, and hence spoke with all the more effect on any subject upon which he felt strongly. His relations with the other members of the Commission were most cordial, some credit for which may be due to both sides, but which certainly would not have been possible without his tact and knowledge of the world. . . .—I am, yours sincerely, F. S. LELY.

CHAPTER XXXII

1906 AND 1908

LATER POLITICAL WORK AND REFORM SCHEME

MR. DUTT paid two visits to Europe during the closing years of his life—the first in the summer of 1906 for three months; the second in 1908, in connection with the Decentralisation Commission, who adjourned to England to wind up their work in that country.

On the 9th June 1906, he left India more for rest and for recuperating his over-worked constitution than for any definite political object, although work of some kind was always before his mind's eye. During the former visit, he wrote to Mr. B. L. Gupta :—

BARODA, *7th May* 1906.

MY DEAR BIHARI,— . . . The reason why I leave on the 23rd June is that I may be in London by the 10th July, and see some people whom I would like to see—Herbert Roberts, Sir H. Cotton, O'Donnell, Rees, &c., &c. If I leave on the 7th July, I arrive at London about the end of that month, when many of the M.P.s have left London, as the Indian Budget debate will take place early this year. It is impossible for me, therefore, to postpone my departure.

. . . .

My plan is to spend two or three weeks in England, and then a month or six weeks in Switzerland, perhaps at St. Moritz, an ideal place for enjoyment, for health, and for making tours all round. Though I have only three months' leave, I will overstay it by six days, leaving Marseilles on the 14th September by the *Arabia*, and reaching Bombay on the 28th September. I have written to secure my passage by that steamer, as the rush of people to India will begin about that time. The Gaekwar is not in Europe; he left Liverpool on the 4th May for America, and

The Honourable G. K. Gokhale.

will probably come round by Japan. I am glad of that, because if he was in Switzerland my holiday would be spoilt—I would not be my own master.—Ever affectionately yours, ROMESH.

But complete rest and cessation from work were not his. The great question of the partition of Bengal was agitating the Indian political world at the time, and as soon as he reached England, this veteran champion of India was on the warpath again. During this season, his able coadjutor was Mr. Gokhale—as in former years he had worked with Mr. Dadabhai Naoroji and Mr. W. C. Bonnerjea. His method of work and agitation remained the same as before—quiet and unostentatious work, more persuasion and argument than public oratory and declamation.

NATIONAL LIBERAL CLUB, WHITEHALL PLACE, S.W.,
28th June 1906.

MY DEAR BIHARI,—Just a line to inform you that I have arrived safely, and am stopping at this club—where Gokhale is also stopping. I have seen Hume and Cotton and Herbert Roberts, and will do what I can for our common cause during my short stay in London. I expect to see John Morley soon. . . .—Yours affectionately ever, ROMESH.

To his granddaughter :—

54 PARLIAMENT STREET, LONDON, S.W.,
25th July 1906.

MY DEAR SUSAMA,— . . . I have not had much rest so far. I reached London on the 25th June—just a month ago—and this month I have given to hard work and politics. I have seen all who could help us in our Indian matters—not only Hume and Sir Henry Cotton and O'Donnell and Gokhale, who have been doing their utmost—but also the Indian Secretary, John Morley; the Parliamentary Under-Secretary, Mr. Ellis; the Permanent Under-Secretary, Sir Arthur Godley; Lord Ripon, Lord Courtney, Sir C. Dilke, and many Members of Parliament. If my countrymen had sent me to England just after the Congress—or even three months ago—I think I could have modified the Partition—not by questions in the House of Commons, which often irritate and produce no results, *but by working quietly and persuasively among men in authority*. . . .

Witnin the short time I have been working, I have created an impression. The Partition will not be undone immediately, because Morley has said it is a "settled thing," but I don't despair of its being modified later on. I had the map of India before me, and explained to Mr. Morley how a Partition can be effected without offending the people. Mind, this is private also. The whole subject of my interview with Morley is confidential. In other matters, Gokhale and I have not been unsuccessful; and for the first time, after more than ten dreary years, some concessions in the way of extended representation in the Legislative Councils has been announced. This is a good beginning. The present Parliament is quite different from any that preceded it; there is a large number of earnest Members who are all for India, and the Labour Party feel for India. Men like O'Grady, Keir Hardie, Robertson, Dr. Rutherford, Hart Davies, Schwann, and others are a much greater power than even our Anglo-Indian friends, Cotton, O'Donnell, &c. The credit is due to Gokhale of having drilled these earnest Members in Indian affairs these three months, and I have also done my best during the month I have been here. On the day before the Indian Budget debate, Gokhale and I were invited to a tea party in the House of Commons, and addressed some fifty or more Members of Parliament who had come to listen to us; and Gokhale has even been invited to the Parliamentary meeting of all nations to be held this week. All things are ready, and we must work earnestly. I will retire from Baroda next year, pass a month or so in Calcutta, and then come and settle down in England, and work with much greater hope of success than I have done within the last nine years under a Tory Government and Lord G. Hamilton! I feel like a war-horse at the sound of the bugle!

But a war-horse, too, must sleep sometimes, I think, and I want some rest. Parliament rises soon, and so to-morrow I leave London for complete rest for a month in Malvern and Buxton, and other quiet places in England.

Poor W. C. Bonnerjea died last Saturday, and Dadabhai is a wreck. Gokhale returns to India soon, and so I feel more than ever eager to come and work in England, with annual visits to India. That will suit my health and suit my purposes.—Believe me, ever yours affectionately, ROMESH.

MALVERN, 31*st July* 1906.

MY DEAR BIHARI,—Your welcome letter of the 12th July reached me out here this morning, for I have left London for a month of country air, mineral baths, and complete rest. Malvern in the west of England is a delightful hilly place, and next week I am going to Buxton in Derbyshire, which is the most bracing place in all England. It is 1000 feet higher than London, has mineral baths, and has splendid Derbyshire moors all round; and it quite braced me up on two previous occasions when I went there. I am already feeling healthier and stronger than when I left India; and two or three weeks of Buxton will completely restore me to my usual strength.

The telegraphic wire keeps you informed of all the news here; Morley's *most sympathetic* speech and some real concessions to India, and W. C. Bonnerjea's death and cremation, which I attended. Morley continues to be a true Liberal, even in the India Office, and is struggling to go as far as he can possibly go without having an open split in his Council and his party. I really believe we are going to have a good time for India after over twenty years of reactionary measures, and I do not despair of the Partition question being reconsidered.—Yours affectionately ever,
ROMESH.

BUXTON, DERBYSHIRE, 8*th August* 1906.

MY DEAR BIHARI,— . . . I am much better and stronger for being out of London, but that pain in the heart still comes when I fatigue myself or walk up-hill, &c., &c. Of course I avoid all that as much as possible, and my London physician, Sir William Broadbent, assured me that it will go off entirely when I am quite restored to my usual strength after prolonged rest. I have therefore come to Buxton, which is the most bracing place in England, and mean to have complete rest here for a month. Unfortunately I have to go up to London to-day, just for a day, to see the Gaekwar, who has returned from America. Then I return to Buxton, and have a quiet time of it here.

I think I have already told you I had not a quiet time in London last month. I worked like a horse to have the Partition upset, making earnest personal appeals to Lord Ripon, Mr. Morley, Mr. Ellis, Sir Charles Dilke, and a host of other influential men. My appeals were successful at last. I have achieved what at one time seemed *impossible*, and was declared *impossible* by Cotton, Gokhale, Wedderburn, and others. Morley had declared the Partition a "settled fact" not to be reversed, but I moved him from his declared opinion. . . .

Yes, there is a rumour of an Indian being appointed Member of the Secretary of State's Council, and my name too has been mentioned as the fittest man. But neither Morley nor any other official has given me the slightest hint yet that I may be chosen.

Perhaps they have not made up their minds—at any rate I do not build the slightest hopes till I have more definite grounds than mere rumour. I know the ten Members of the India Council will bitterly oppose the appointment of an Indian, and specially the appointment of a Congress *walla* and a critic of the Government like myself. Morley himself is most kind, most sympathetic; he gave me over an hour's audience, and the whole time spoke to me confidentially like an intimate friend, and expressed his desire to do all he can for India. But of the appointment of an Indian to his Council he gave no hint.—Yours ever affectionately,

ROMESH.

13th September 1906.

MY DEAREST KAMALA,—My stay in Buxton has quite braced me up, though it was interrupted by business now and then. I had to go to London to meet the Maharaja on his return from America; I had to go to Liverpool to meet Mr. Gokhale and W. C. Bonnerjea's daughter; and yesterday and the day before I was in London again to see Mr. John Morley. These interruptions could not be avoided at a time so critical for our country's progress; and I may fairly claim that I have not neglected work, even when I have stayed away from London for rest and cure. My letters to the *Times* and the *Daily News*, which appeared last week and this week, will probably be copied in Indian papers.

I am grieved to learn that one of our great workers, A. M. Bose, is dead. In this country, W. C. Bonnerjea and Budruddin Tyabji died within the last two months. Those who have led the political work during the past generation are fast passing away; younger men must now take their place, and I hope they will do it worthily.—Your ever loving father, ROMESH.

Mr. W. C. Bonnerjea died in July 1906, and was cremated at Golder's Green. Mr. Naoroji delivered a funeral address, and Mr. Dutt also spoke and eulogised "the great moderation and sterling patriotism" of his departed friend.

Two other notable Indian careers closed in quick succession the same year, and India had to mourn the death of Justice Badruddin Tyabji and Mr. A. M. Bose. A meeting was held by the London Indian Society under the presidency of Dadabhai Naoroji, to express sorrow at the death of Justice Badruddin Tyabji and Mr. Ananda

Mohan Bose. Mr. Dutt paid a high tribute to the unselfish and unsectarian patriotism of the late Justice of the Bombay High Court, and said, "Mr. Tyabji knew that in all large questions the interests of Indians, whether Musalmans, Hindus, Parsis, or any other class, were one and the same, and he never forgot the old maxim 'United we stand; divided we fall.'" In concluding his speech about the many sterling good qualities of Mr. Bose, he observed: "The men of the earlier generation who had worked for India during the last twenty-five years were passing away, and the time was approaching when the work will fall on the shoulders of the younger members. He hoped the example of such men as Badruddin Tyabji and Mr. Bose would inspire them to be always faithful and true to their country, and to work with wisdom and moderation."

He returned to India on the 17th November 1906.

II

His last visit to England was in 1908, in connection with the Decentralisation Commission, who were winding up their work and framing their Report. But the theme which engrossed Mr. Dutt and evoked his most strenuous efforts were the reforms which Lord Morley was introducing in the field of the Indian Administration.

It was a fortunate circumstance [says Mr. Natesan] that Mr. Romesh Dutt was in London all through the summer and autumn of 1908; and his labours on the Commission did not prevent him from taking an active interest in the scheme of Reforms which Lord Morley was preparing for India. Lord Morley himself was ever ready to see and consult all well-informed men, Englishmen or Indians, who could speak from personal experience on Indian questions and Indian administration. Mr. Dutt also interviewed some Members of the House of Lords, including Lord Courtney and Lord MacDonnell, whom he had known for many years. He discussed reform proposals with Members of the India Council; and he was in close touch with several Members of the House of Commons who took an active interest in Indian affairs. All through the summer and autumn of 1908 he exerted himself personally, and through friends, to secure some real reforms for India—to secure some share for Indians in the control and direction of Indian administration.

In all this work Mr. Romesh Dutt laboured hand in hand with Mr. Gokhale, who was doing yeoman's service in the same great cause. No two men were better suited to work together in such a cause than Mr. Romesh Dutt and Mr. Gokhale. Both moderate in their views, practical in their aims and methods, accurate and well-informed in facts, tenacious and persevering in their endeavours, they were in complete agreement in their opinions, and were often strangely similar in their style of expression. Both of them had been Presidents of the Indian National Congress, and both were listened to with attention as to the reasonable demands of their countrymen. Mr. Romesh Dutt had now counted sixty years, Mr. Gokhale was a little over forty; but the elder and the younger man worked as fast friends in 1908, as they have ever done in life, in the cause of their common Motherland.

Even before proceeding to England in 1908, Mr. Dutt in a series of letters placed his views about the burning questions of the day before Lord Morley. About the immediate causes of the outbursts of anarchism and lawlessness in different parts of India Mr. Dutt held strong views, and in these letters, as also in the letters he wrote to the *Times* and other newspapers, he expressed them plainly. But the letters he wrote to Lord Morley about this time are not so important for his views on the question of "discontent" as for the statesmanlike appeal he made for the granting of political privileges to his countrymen. Some extracts from these letters are given below:—

15*th May* 1907.

We, in India, have read with great interest the telegraphic summary of the important statement you made in the House of Commons, two or three days ago, about the present crisis in India. You have done but simple justice to Indian leaders by saying that no persons are so interested in the prevention of disorder as the Indian party. We have pressed for peaceful reforms during the lifetime of a generation, and we know, better than any one else, that the spread of disorder now means the postponement of reforms for another generation.

Referring to the troubles in the Punjab:—

24th May 1907.

All protests of the people against these measures were disregarded, and when at last the public feeling culminated in some petty riots—which would perhaps have led to reforms in a European country—the Government of the Punjab suggested sudden and extraordinary measures against leading men, and were determined not to yield to agitation. It is ever thus in India. Peaceful protests against public measures are seldom listened to, so long as they are peaceful. When they lead to violence, they are disregarded because the Government will not yield in the face of violence; in either case we are not heard. I see no remedy to this state of things until the people are strongly represented both in the legislation and in the administration of each Province, so that their views and opinions may be allowed a proper degree of influence in the administration of their own concerns. I cannot express this better than in your own words—

The best guarantee for justice in public dealings is the participation in their own government of the people most likely to suffer from injustice.

7th June 1907.

It is a matter of sincere gratification to me, and to thousands of moderate men in India, that his Excellency the Viceroy has boldly vetoed the Colonisation Act, and that the Liberal Government has promised inquiry into the grievances of all cultivators in Rawalpindi District. If these are the real causes of dissatisfaction and alarm among large classes of the population, the rigour of the measures adopted by Government against the leaders of these dissatisfied men will perhaps be relaxed. I have never justified or palliated seditious speeches and doings, but perhaps the general feeling of the people will be taken into consideration in dealing with them. And it is a lamentable fact that, but for the recent unfortunate disturbances in the Punjab, the blunders of the Government would never have been noticed or rectified. The history of Ireland will bring many parallel instances to your mind.

Peaceful protests of the people of India have seldom induced the rulers to rectify mistaken legislation—the people are simply ignored and disregarded. When a most unwise amendment to the Bombay Land Act was brought before the Bombay Legislative Council, men like Sir Pherozshah Mehta and the Honourable Mr. Gokhale protested in the most earnest manner against it,

some useful recommendations calculated to bring the Government more in touch with the people. There never was a time within the last fifty years when this was more needed than at present, and perhaps you will permit me therefore to place before you a few observations, for what they may be worth, on the present situation.

It seems to me a great pity that the Government of India did not take some of the leaders of the people into their confidence in framing those great proposals of reform which have recently been published. No one can know better what is good for the people than their own moderate leaders, and nothing is gained by excluding them from all share in framing great measures honestly meant for the good of the people. The way in which the proposals have been framed has been a disappointment to the people at large; the moderate leaders, who had great expectations from the Liberal Government, are humiliated, as they can show no tangible results of their endeavours to their countrymen; while the extremists, who openly profess their want of faith in British administration, are triumphant.

The scheme of the Council of Notables will not bring the Government in closer touch with the people unless it is greatly modified. The Ruling Princes of India can hardly take their places as Councillors side by side with British subjects without some feeling of humiliation, and can hardly advise on questions of British Indian administration with which they are not familiar. The Indian Government, moreover, does not bind itself to consult the Council of Notables openly, or to consult the members altogether, or to accept their advice when it is tendered. It is therefore openly hinted that the Council of Notables is formed, not to obtain the opinions of the people and their leaders freely, but to obtain the support of titled individuals in matters in which Government has already decided on its own policy.

In the same manner the scheme for the expansion of the Viceroy's Legislative Council, which has been published, is calculated to minimise rather than increase the influence of educated public opinion on administration; while on the other hand it proposes to introduce distinctions based on race and religion. All India desires an adequate representation of the Muhammadans on all Councils; but this can be secured by the exercise of the power which the Government possesses to appoint non-official members from any community which is not adequately represented among elected members. But to give the Muhammadans of India a special electorate or a special rate because they are Muhammadans is a policy which will spread discontent among

Hindus, Parsis, Jains, and Christians, and will be a source of political danger in the future.

No scheme has yet been published for the expansion of the Provincial Legislative Councils, and I do hope that some of the real leaders of the people will be consulted before such schemes are formed. No section of the Indian community has worked more honestly and more earnestly during the last twenty years and more, to improve British administration and to make it stronger and more popular, than the moderate leaders of the people. To withhold their reasonable demands, to minimise their legitimate influence, and to virtually set them aside will not strengthen the titled classes, which the Indian Government seems to desire, but will be playing into the hands of those darker spirits who have no faith in British rule, and are already posing as martyrs and heroes after the recent unfortunate State prosecutions. To compare small things with great, if the Indian Girondists fall, a wave of disloyalty and crime will spread over India, and the Government will have before it an endless prospect of fruitless coercion and profitless prosecutions.

Pardon my troubling you with these views. I believe the Government is honestly endeavouring to associate the people of India in the administration of the country, and I believe that this policy, if wisely carried out, will do lasting good to the people and their rulers.

This brought a notable reply from Lord Morley :—

INDIA OFFICE, WHITEHALL, S.W., *25th October* 1907.

MY DEAR SIR,—I thank you for your letter, and am very glad that you were pleased to be in the Royal Commission. I hope that you will take an active part, but of course if it should unhappily take a turn—I mean your part in it—of mere partisanship, it will no doubt prove wholly ineffective. You will not take it amiss that I should say so much as this. If there is to be any effective advance at all, it can only be secured by reasonable co-operation. Irrational demands "for the moon," as I have put it, can only end in futility and confusion, and we may as well face that certainty from the first.

There is nothing of unreason, if I may say so, in your tone about the "proposals." Why don't you and your friends put your criticisms upon them in short, definite, and formulated shape? Then we should know with some sort of precision what ground we were standing or walking upon.

It will be a grievous pity, my dear Sir, if you allow your strong faculties to waste themselves in narrow efforts instead of using them to further a real stage in sensible progress.—Yours very truly,

JOHN MORLEY.

Mr. Dutt wrote in reply:—

BOMBAY, 14*th November* 1907.

I thank you sincerely for the kind advice you have given me in your letter of the 25th October, and I will bear it in mind. I have often been misjudged, as people who advocate reforms always will be; but the reforms I have urged have always been moderate and practicable, and, to quote your words, I never have asked "for the moon." In all my official career of twenty-six years I worked in harmony with my colleagues and superiors, and I have pursued the same conciliatory policy during the last ten years, *i.e.* since my retirement from service. Nevertheless, people who are opposed to all reforms have branded me as an "impatient idealist," while ardent reformers have branded me as lukewarm and half-hearted. *A reformer who is moderate is between two fires. He has no friends, as I have learnt to my cost.*

The situation in India still remains critical, and every coercive measure is adding to the influence of the extremists. Ten years ago the deportation of the Natu brothers, the secret search for a conspiracy against the British rule which did not exist, and the savage sentences passed by Courts in many cases under panic, first gave birth to the extremist party in the Mahratta country from Poona to Nagpur. Later on, the unwise partition of Bengal, and the equally unwise measures which were adopted to distinguish between class and class, creed and creed, gave rise to lamentable disturbances, and strengthened the extremist party in Bengal. Recent events, which I need hardly mention, are strengthening the same party in the Punjab. The large majority of the educated people are still moderate, and are striving to stem the new spirit; but their hands are weakened, as they can as yet show no real advance towards self-government, which is the aim of all moderate reformers. I myself have spoken much during a recent tour in Southern India, and a cutting which I enclose from the leading Anglo-Indian paper of Madras will show that my efforts have been appreciated by Englishmen in India. But my younger countrymen listen to us with doubt and distrust; they ask us what has been gained by our "constitutional agitation" during these ten or fifteen years.

You have very kindly suggested that I and my friends should define clearly and concisely what we want. This has been done by the Moderates before, and will no doubt be done again, and the Government of India knows that all that we ask for is a larger share in the control and direction of our own affairs. District Conferences are being held in different parts of India urging this demand, and I have before me advance copies of a Presidential Speech which will be delivered by an able and moderate thinker at one of the most important District Conferences in Bengal early in December. I take the liberty of enclosing a copy, as the speech gives within the brief space of ten pages the substance of what the Moderates all over India are urging, for political advancement of the people under the rule of England. I honestly believe that a real measure of self-government, such as is at present possible in India, would be an act of true statesmanship, and would allay much of the present unrest.

Mr. Morley's reply was as follows :—

24th November /08.

DEAR MR. DUTT,—I thank you for your obliging and interesting letter. Your view as to Extremists and Reactionaries joining hands in antagonism to reforms is perfectly just. I hope I may have the pleasure of seeing you on an early day.—Yours sincerely,

MORLEY OF B.

On the question of election by separate electorates, his views were quite definite :—

2nd December 1907.

The Provincial Governments of India are now preparing schemes for the expansion of the Provincial Councils, and the schemes are based on distinctions of classes, and castes and creeds. . . .

Government might take power to nominate and appoint six members from classes and castes not adequately represented by election. The total of non-official Members will thus be about twenty.

England has ruled India for a century and a half on the just and correct principle of equality and fairness towards all castes and creeds. The new proposal of creating electorates according to castes and creeds is attended with danger. It will create jealousies and hatreds, accentuate differences in daily life, foment riots and disturbances, and be a source of political danger to the Empire. European Governments do not now form separate electorates for Protestants and Roman Catholics, they wisely ignore religious distinctions in political and administrative matters. The same wise impartiality can be pursued in the East, and the rights of the less advanced classes can be secured in the way indicated above.

Apart from what has been stated above, there are some grave objections to elections by castes and creeds which I indicate below, very briefly.

It is the British Government and British Schools and Colleges which have taught us to disregard caste distinctions in public affairs and in civic life. Is it for the British Government now to undo its past work, and to accentuate and embitter our caste differences by making them the basis of political distinctions? . . .

India is content with election by territorial divisions. The defects of that system can be rectified by vesting Government with larger powers of nomination. It would be unwise to abandon that system, and to throw the apple of discord among the numerous castes and creeds of India by making religious differences the basis of political distinctions. Such a policy would be a bad training for civic life, and would also be a fruitful source of troubles and discord in the future.

We may close this remarkable correspondence with the following stirring appeals he made to Lord Morley :—

CALCUTTA, *20th January* 1908.

May I at the commencement of a new year sincerely wish you comparative rest and peace after your arduous work and continuous anxiety during the last two years? I cordially hope that your labours will end in success in securing peace and good government for India.

For one thing, the Partition has strengthened the hands of the extremists all over India, and is a god-send to them. The despair of influencing administration by persuasion and reason drove thousands of men to the camp of unreason, until a few feather-brained talkers grew to be a formidable party. Thanks to the strong sense of our elder leaders, the great majority of my countrymen stoutly resisted the movement from the beginning, and at last tore themselves asunder from the irreconcilables at the Surat Congress.

Disorder must necessarily be repressed with rigour, but the only true remedy for the present unrest, and the only method of making the administration popular and strong in the future, is to secure the co-operation and concurrence of the people, to make them feel that they are sharers in the administration of their own affairs. Intelligent leaders of the people are consulted in all legislative measures, as there are elected Indian Members in the Legislative Councils. But large changes in the policy of the administration are effected by executive orders, and in such matters the people are kept aloof. Important details in the Land Revenue and Irrigation departments, and in matters concerning the Police, Public Works, Education, Medicine, and Forests, are settled by the Executive Councils of India, Madras, and Bombay, and by the Lieutenant-Governors and Chief Commissioners in other Provinces where there are no Executive Councils. We may run our eye over all this vast executive machinery in this great Empire, and we shall not find a single Indian anywhere who is trusted to take a share in shaping the policy of administration. How much is lost by an alien government both in popularity and in the adaptability of its measures through this needless exclusiveness is known only to those who are of the people, and who feel the pulse of the people.

Why should not the British rule be a popular rule in this loyal country, British officers consenting to share with the leaders of the people the task of settling the policy and the details of administration? Why should not Indian leaders proudly stand by the side of devoted British administrators, and work for the great Empire which they may then both call their own? Such questions receive no response from officials generally, the history of the world seldom records instances of men in power consenting to share it with those over whom they rule. But it is a New Year's hope to me, as it has been my lifelong aspiration. Either such co-operation, or a widening gulf with increasing discontent and disorder, is before us, there is no other alternative.

Then again :—

22nd February 1908.

We have now finished our work in all the Provinces of India except Bombay and the Punjab, and in two months more we shall be leaving for England. Within our limited time and within the limited scope of our inquiries, we have done our best to obtain valuable opinion, official and non-official, in all the Provinces, and the whole evidence, when printed, will, I hope, form a record of some value.

I myself have taken this opportunity to mix freely with my educated countrymen in all the Provinces, and to impress them with my hopeful view of our progress and prospects. I have talked to them familiarly in their own houses, argued with them in their social gatherings, and replied to their many addresses, with the object of rallying them in the cause of Order and Progress. One speech which I made at Lucknow has been noticed in many of the Indian papers, and I take the liberty of enclosing a cutting, containing a telegraphic summary of it.

Everywhere I have been listened to with attention, and even with a desire to accept my assurances, I wish I could add that I produced any genuine conviction. . . .

I have always thought a bold step would also be a wise step at the present juncture, and that it is possible to crush discontent and disaffection underfoot by one or two acts of real and tangible concession. The present time is most appropriate. For two years, ever since the Partition of Bengal, the country has undergone local disorders, alarms, coercive measures and prosecutions. It is time now that a pacific remedy was tried. The nations of India recall the fact that this is the fiftieth anniversary of the late Queen's gracious Proclamation: may not some real acts of grace in this year once more obliterate bitter memories?

In the Spring of 1908 he proceeded to England. In London he had a busy time:—

54 PARLIAMENT STREET, LONDON, S.W.,
26th June 1908.

MY DEAREST KAMALA, . . . Our Commission's work has begun, and will probably be over by October next. In the meantime I am often seeing Lord Morley and the members of Parliament and the India Council about affairs in India, and have great hopes of some real and substantial reforms before long. And engagements are coming so thick and fast, as to be quite bewildering. Attended a party at Sir Charles Schwann's, spoke at a temperance meeting at Sir Herbert Roberts's, spoke at a Reception in honour of Mr. Gokhale and myself, spoke at a dinner of the Royal Society of Literature, spoke last night at a dinner given by Mr. Keir Hardie, and am going to attend an evening party given to-night by the Prime Minister to celebrate the King's birthday. It is getting warm now, and I hope this rush of engagements will not continue. . . .

10th July 1908.

MY DEAR BIHARI, . . . On Monday the 30th June I went to the House of Lords to hear the debate on India. Never was Lord Curzon so discomfited in his life, Lord Morley in his slow, inimitable, well-chosen and pointed words simply pounded Curzon to dust! . . . The fatal effects of that measure are now so universally obvious that every one disclaims responsibility, and Curzon tried to falsify history to save his reputation! I never enjoyed a parliamentary debate as on this occasion. . . . Yours affectionately ever, ROMESH.

7th October 1908.

My dear Bihari,—. . . I am still at Twickenham, and am loth to go to London and its tiresome engagements and distractions, unless I am compelled to do so for the Commission's work. Our work is progressing, and will probably come to an end next month. Many of our recommendations will be in the direction of real and popular reforms, and will help Lord Morley in bringing forward his scheme of reforms.

In the meantime Lord Morley has received the India Government's proposals, and has already appointed a Committee of his Council to consider them, and put them into shape, and he has invited Lord MacDonnell to preside over that Committee. Lord MacDonnell is as keen in the direction of real substantial reforms as Morley himself, so that there is every hope the administration of India will be greatly improved and popularised from the next year.

This morning I went to see Lord MacDonnell by appointment. He remembers how he and I fought side by side for the Bengal Tenancy Bill over twenty years ago, and he received me kindly, and spoke to me candidly. I dare not write on paper all that he said, but I believe, from the top to the bottom, from the constitution of Provincial Governments to the constitution of Village bodies and communities, the administration of India will be changed for the good, and the people will have a real share in managing their own concerns.

It is a wonderfully clever step that Morley has taken in asking MacDonnell to put the proposals to shape. If Morley himself had done it, Anglo-Indians would have protested against a philosopher and Radical of no Indian experience trying dangerous experiments in India! But they cannot say the same of MacDonnell, who has been the most successful administrator in India and in Ireland within the last half-century. And with MacDonnell's support, Morley will push through his schemes, in spite of Anglo-Indian opposition. Morley has immense prestige in this country; both parties have faith in him.

12th November 1908.

My dear Bihari,—. . . The statement in the *Englishman* about my having seen Lord Morley's proposals of reform is absolutely unfounded. The proposals were not yet decided upon when the *Englishman* wrote, and have not been decided upon yet. And I do not think Lord Morley will show them to any one outside the India Office until he announces them in Parliament. Lord MacDonnell was asked to preside over the India

Office Committee, and what I gathered from Lord MacDonnell I mentioned to you (as far as I dared to do in a letter) in a previous communication. I believe there will be a large expansion of real self-government in all institutions, from Provincial Councils to Village Panchayets.

A summary of our Commission's proposals will be in Lord Morley's hands within this month—*i.e.* before he announces his proposals in Parliament. Our completed report will be ready by the end of December. I will leave for India as soon as the Commission's work is over.—Ever your affectionate friend,

ROMESH.

17th December 1908.

MY DEAR BIHARI,—This afternoon I was in the House of Lords, where I had the pleasure of listening to Lord Morley's splendid speech on his new Reforms. You will have seen them all, long before this letter reaches you, so I will not repeat them. But I specially valued his promise of appointing an Indian Member in the Viceroy's Executive Council, of expanding the Provincial Legislative Councils so as to enable them to settle the Budgets and to discuss administrative questions, and lastly his promise of creating Executive Councils in four Provinces which are under one-man rule now. All this will give Indians larger power and influence over executive administration. Other matters which he did not mention in his speech, such as giving greater control over District Boards, &c., to Indians—are in his Despatch, which also you will have seen.

Morley was followed by Lansdowne, who made a feeble halting speech with all the dislike of an Anglo-Indian to radical reforms. But the best speech of the evening was Lord MacDonnell's, who condemned the Partition of Bengal in strong terms, and called it the greatest blunder committed in India since Clive won the battle of Plassey!

It is a pity all this will fall flat in our country because of the alarm and indignation caused by the new law of summary justice and the deportation of so many Bengali leaders. And yet when these coercive acts have been undone or forgotten, the reforms announced to-day will have a permanent effect in improving the Government of India and giving the people a real share in the administration of their own concerns. . . .

He was supremely grateful for the Reforms which the Government of India and the Secretary of State announced, and in the January number of the *Indian Review* of 1909, explained their nature and far-reaching effects.

The Reforms announced by Lord Morley in his Despatch of November, and in his speech of December [he wrote] are solid and substantial, and are precisely in the direction in which the Indian National Congress has demanded Reforms during the last twenty years and more. In one word, the changes announced are calculated to give the people of India a substantial share in the control and direction of their own concerns. The voice of the people will find expression through recognised official channels; the wishes and opinions of the people will influence and shape the internal administration of the country.

Firstly, take the proposed appointment of an Indian Member on the Viceroy's Executive Council. He will have a portfolio—*i.e.* will be the head of an important department of administration, whether it be Home or Revenue, Public Works or Law. More than this, he will have a voice in the deliberation of all great questions, coming from all Departments, for discussion in the full Council. Whether it be Land Settlements or Famine Relief, Primary Education, or the organisation of services, encouragement of industries, or the abolition of Cesses, the Indian Member of average ability will represent the views of his countrymen, and take a share in the discussion. Schemes and changes on such subjects have hitherto been initiated without the consultation of Indian opinion in the highest quarters whence such schemes emanated. This will no longer be so, and I venture to think that on every question of importance, affecting the welfare of the vast population of India, Indian views pressed by the Indian Member will receive full and fair consideration, and will largely shape the internal policy of the Empire.

Secondly, consider the effect of a non-official majority in the Provincial Legislative Councils. In their everyday work, the non-officials will naturally differ in their opinions, and this is fair. But great questions will arise like the imposition of a harassing tax, the withdrawal of a landed right, or the partition of a province, which will find the whole body of non-officials ranged on one side. Lord Morley has pointed out in his Despatch that when this is so, Government must pause, and perhaps abandon new-fangled schemes and innovations distasteful to the entire people. For the first time, the non-official members of Provincial Councils will be invested with an effectual power to oppose schemes brought forward by new Lieutenant-Governors, or over-zealous officials—schemes which the people do not want. Legislation like the present Calcutta Municipalities Act, or the Bombay Land Revenue Amendment Act will henceforth be impossible.

Thirdly, consider the larger powers proposed for Provincial Legislative Councils in the matter of settling the Provincial Budget. The final power of accepting the recommendations of these Councils is still left in the hands of the Government, but we are safe in believing that such recommendations will, as a rule, be accepted. The discussion will go on for days under each separate head, and on each question the Council will have the power to divide. Instead of an academic discourse, and the flow of manuscript eloquence for a few hours during a single day, we shall have a business-like examination of the details of the Budgets by members, the majority of whom will be non-officials, and the virtual settlement of the Provincial Budgets according to the views and wishes of the people.

Fourthly, take the proposed powers for the Provincial Legislative Councils to discuss questions of general interest in relation to executive administration. This will give Members of Council, for the first time, the power to travel beyond Legislative Bills, and to inquire fully into the executive administration of the Province. Any executive action which excites general interest, harsh Plague relief measures, the over-assessment of a district, gross police misbehaviour in a subdivision, inadequate relief operations in times of famine, inundation or other calamities, inadequate provision of village pasture by the Forest Department, unlawful obstruction to a gathering or religious procession, all such matters will form the subject, not of interpellation only as at present, but of debates ending in Resolutions when called for. For the first time the Legislative Councils will have some control over Provincial administration.

Fifthly, consider the results of the formation of Executive Councils in the larger Provinces with one or more Indian members on such Councils. Once more the Indian member will have a portfolio—*i.e.* will be the head of an important department; and he will also have a share in the discussion of all questions coming up from all departments to the full Council. We will suppose the Indian member to be a man of average ability; he will still reflect the views and opinions of his countrymen, and Provincial administration will not hereafter be shaped without consultation of Indian feeling and Indian sentiment.

Sixthly, Lord Morley has insisted in his Despatch that Lord Ripon's Local Self-Government scheme of 1882 should be given full effect to. The scheme has worked indifferently for a quarter of a century, because District Magistrates are chairmen everywhere except in the Central Provinces—the members virtually coming to tender advice. The Despatch insists on the real power and responsibility being vested in the people, official control being exercised from outside and not from within.

Seventhly, the Despatch goes further down, and directs the organisation of Village self-government as the basis of District self-government. What does this mean? Endeavours will be made to reorganise Village Panchayets; groups of villages will send up members to Sub-District Boards; these Boards will send up members to District Boards; members of District Boards and Municipalities and others, formed into Electoral Colleges, will send up members to Provincial Legislative Councils; and they shall send up members to the Viceroy's Legislative Council. A chain of representation will thus be formed from the Village to the Central Imperial Council, and the administration of India will be influenced, and I believe considerably shaped, by the wishes and opinions and the sentiments of the people, for whose benefit the administration exists.

On the 8th of March Mr. Dutt had an important interview with Lord Morley. During the course of this interview reference was made to the inference which the writer in the *Times* — signing himself "Thirty Years' Service"—made from the publication of Mr. Gokhale's note on the Reform scheme. In explaining the real facts of the case, Mr. Dutt said: "But, Lord Morley, what the correspondent in the *Times* suggests is absolutely untrue. Mr. Gokhale laid his suggestions before you like 200 other men of all classes and shades of opinion. You have never refused to see any one—Hindu or Moslem, Englishman or Parsi—who had any valuable suggestion to make. You have considered all opinions and framed your own conclusions." Lord Morley: "That is it. Is it to be said that I am not to see a single Hindu?"

Then the question of the omission of clause 3 about Executive Councils came up. Mr. Dutt informed Lord Morley, that the people of India unanimously objected to the omission of clause 3, and that a great meeting would

success. What a thousand pities you and Ganen were not there, the life and soul of all!

Before joining his post in Baroda, he and his friend Mr. Gupta paid a short visit to Shillong:—

SHILLONG, *7th May* 1909.

MY DEAR GANEN,—Bihari arrived yesterday in good health, and I have got rid of my gout also. The rains have ceased for a time, though it is still sometimes cloudy and often windy. Otherwise the weather is delightful.

I called on the Lieutenant-Governor and on Mr. and Mrs. Lyon also, besides leaving my card at a few other houses.

Yesterday I was asked to a garden-party at the Government House, and met Savage, Kershaw, Lyon, Major Singh, and some other officers--Beatson Bell, &c. I often see De, and Mrs. De took me out for a drive the other evening. Dr. Bose comes almost every morning. Both Bihari and I are simply charmed with Shillong, which seems to be the pleasantest hill station we have seen.

On the 1st of June Mr. Dutt took over charge of his duties at Baroda, and from that date to his death in November of the same year, he served as the Prime Minister of the State, the former Prime Minister, Mr. Kershaspji, having retired. The pay of the appointment was raised to Rs.4000 a month. In accepting this appointment, however, Mr. Dutt had no intention of serving for more than a year. His object was to retire from the State service in the summer of 1911, and to settle down in some healthy and dry place like Bankura, where he had made a country house for himself, and spend the remainder of his days in literary pursuits and other congenial occupations. We have seen how even as early as 1907, he wrote to Mrs. Mehta and his brother Mr. J. C. Dutt of his desire to leave the State service at the earliest opportunity and to serve Saraswati in preference to Lakshmi. But alas for human calculations, his dream of a peaceful retired life in a country residence, broken by visits to his beloved daughters and his dear friends and relatives, was never realised. He died in harness at his post in Baroda.

The last rays of sunshine which brightened his somewhat dreary life in Baroda came in the shape of the appointment of his friend Mr. B. L. Gupta to be the Legal Adviser of the State. It was under his advice that the Gaekwar gave the appointment to Mr. Gupta, and those who know that able and experienced judicial officer will understand that a better choice could hardly have been made. After many years of lonely living he got his friend to live with him, and the two friends made many plans of their future.

After Mr. Dutt's death, Mr. Gupta wrote :—

I never dreamed that I should outlive Romesh, and we had decided to leave the Baroda service in 1911 and go to Europe *via* Japan, and spend most of our time together in travelling and in Calcutta, Bankura, and Simultala! Deluded by this idle hope, I never feared or anticipated the possibility of a dull, dreary old age.

In another letter to the present writer, Mr. Gupta wrote :—

Baroda is quite a different place without him, and my life henceforth will be cheerless and without any interest to me. Yes, I know that Sarala was to have come here, and you were to go to Europe on furlough, after leaving her here. Mr. Dutt and I had even apportioned the rooms of the house.

In reference to the intended visit of his daughter Sarala, Mr. Dutt, on the 30th August 1909, wrote to her :—

I am delighted to get your letter of the 24th August. Your stay with me next year will make my home cheerful and bright and happy; and we shall lead an easy and lordly life. Perhaps you will find another Bengal friend here besides myself—but I must not write anything about what is still uncertain. Guess! . . .

From Baroda there are magnificent tours to be made all round. Mount Abu and Chittor and Udaipur and all Rajputana to the north; Bombay, Poona, the hilly Concan, Mahabaleshwar and all the historic Mahratta country to the south. Westward you could go to delightful Kathiwar and the far-famed Temple of Dwarka on the sea; and eastwards you could do the classic Ujjain and Indore and the matchless valley of the Narbada. It is a chance you will never get in your lifetime if you miss it now, so don't miss it. Make up your mind.

One more bright incident before we come to the fall of the curtain; on October 24th he wrote to his brother:—

> Bihari has joined here as Legal Remembrancer, and is of course stopping with me—which is a great comfort.
>
> Yesterday at the Durbar the Maharaja invested me with the insignia of Dewanship, and then I had an elephant ride with much pomp, pageantry, and music! It is usual on such occasions to present gold brocade cloth, gold mace, gold *Masal* and gold umbrella to the Dewan, besides ring and necklace! All these are useless to me, and I shall be glad if I can get cash instead, as one previous Dewan did, specially as I had to make gifts to the Maharaja's servants worth nearly 2000 rupees!

The end came with something like dramatic suddenness. He was in perfect health, and in the full vigour of mind and body. Those of his relatives who saw him in the spring thought he had never looked younger and healthier. After joining Baroda in June, he wrote to Mr. Gupta, "I am thoroughly enjoying the dry heat here, which suits me exactly, while every one else is complaining!" Even so late as the 21st of August he wrote to Mr. Gupta, "I am enjoying fairly good health, though I long to have some rest in October."

It is true the disease of the heart which killed him had given him warning as early as 1906. On 18th June of that year he wrote to Mr. Gupta:—

> The action of the heart naturally becomes weaker with age, and easy work and frequent rest are needed. I have felt pain in the region of my heart, and occasional palpitation, within the last six or seven months of my hard work in Baroda. I consulted the best doctor at Bombay, and he said my heart was perfectly sound, yet *Nature had given me a warning which I should not neglect.* I have therefore practically made up my mind to retire from Baroda next year, and to take things easy afterwards. For Baroda is not like other Native States in India, where you can take things easy. It is hard grind here, and the hard-worked administrator is not his own master.

Soon after, he went to England to recoup his health, but even there he did not quite succeed in getting rid of the pain. Writing in August 1906, he said, in a letter which has been quoted before, that the pain in the heart still came back whenever he was fatigued. But Sir William Broadbent, whom he consulted, assured him that prolonged rest would quite restore him to his usual health.

And rest and change did cure him, and he had no more of this pain all through 1907 and 1908. In fact, before accepting the Dewanship of Baroda he had himself examined, and his heart was pronounced sound.

But the visit of Lord and Lady Minto to Baroda entailed a great deal of mental anxiety and physical strain on Mr. Dutt, as he naturally had to supervise all the arrangements for receiving the distinguished guests. It was too much for even his iron constitution, and on the very night of the State dinner given to His Excellency (the 15th November), while at dinner, the pain recurred, and this time with great severity. Most other men would have asked to be excused and left the dinner table. But though bathed in perspiration and writhing in agony, his strong and masterful will helped him to struggle through the dinner and get up with the other guests. He would not make a scene or draw attention to himself. But this act of heroic self-control appears to have made recovery impossible; his physicians thought that if he had retired in time he might still have had a chance. He took to his bed the same night, and all the efforts of the best physicians, Doctors Myers, Rauth, and Mehta, and at the last stage Dr. Nilratan Sirkar, and the untiring attendance and nursing of his wife and daughter, failed to arrest the decree of Providence, and he passed away on the 30th November 1909, at about two A.M.

Mr. Gupta, who was with him till the last, has sent the following note about his illness:—

> You must have heard from Ajoy of his father's great suffering and godlike endurance during his last and painful illness. For days and nights together, he could not lie down on a bed or even in an easy-chair in a reclining posture, but had to sit up and stoop in front to give relief to the heart and lungs. There was much difficulty of breathing, and on account of the failing heart the doctors forbade all movement. You can imagine what it is to

remain in one posture day and night with difficult breathing and pain at the heart and with hardly any sleep at all. But though fully conscious and able to speak, he never complained, never exclaimed "I can bear it no longer," never grumbled or fretted at anything. When I gently broke the news to him that I had wired for his wife and son to come, and they had already left Calcutta, that they might help to nurse him and cheer him up, he raised his head, said only "Oh" by way of assent, and smiled. It was not until several days after their arrival that we thought there was not much hope left, for every day the disease took a less favourable turn. When he realised that recovery was hopeless, he called his family round him and asked me to sit down, and said, "I have nothing to say. Have you any questions to ask?" We had nothing to ask.

Visitors poured in all day long, and anxious inquiries were made by the Maharaja and Maharani morning and evening, by messenger or telephone. His Highness called more than once to inquire personally. Latterly we issued a bulletin every morning."

Almost regal honours were accorded to the illustrious dead. His body, as it lay in the death chamber, was visited by all the important men of the State and numerous friends. A look of sublime and perfect peace rested on the lineaments of that noble face, and every one felt that he stood in the presence of a prince among men, who had gone to rest and sleep everlasting after the day's battle had been fought and won. For him the night that cometh and in which no man can work had no terrors, for he had done his full tale of work and the peace of the soul that had passed was mirrored in the face that lay in the still solemnity of death. No tears, no wailings, but peace and silence reigned in that silent chamber of death.

His Highness the Gaekwar, as a special mark of high favour, allowed the cremation to be performed in the cremation ground of Kedareswar, on the banks of the Biswamitra, which is specially reserved for royalty alone. The corpse was laid in a palanquin, and with full military honours, and with forty sowars of the Huzrat cavalry, and eleven horsemen of Choti Khas Baga leading, followed by many Sardars, Darakdars, and officers of State, the procession moved slowly to the river bank. Men of all nationalities—Hindus and Muhammadans and Parsis—bent their heads in reverence, and had a last look at their beloved brother, the *Garib ka dost*, before the funeral pyre was lighted; and the deep silence of the scene was broken only by the addresses delivered by several of his friends and admirers.

Speaking in English, Rao Bahadur Manubhai, R. S. Mahammud Ali, and R. S. Satghare made reference to his fine qualities of mind and character, and to the inestimable value of his services to his motherland. "The land upon which we stand," said the last speaker, "is sacred with his ashes, and future generations will visit this spot in veneration of the memory of the deceased." The most moving speech of all was that of Lala Atmaram, who, speaking in Hindustani, compared the sore disappointment of the people of Baroda at the sudden death of Mr. Dutt—so soon after his becoming Dewan of the State—to the grief of the people of Kausala, when Sree Ram Chandra had to go to the forest as an exile, instead of reigning over them as their beloved sovereign. "However, the memory of his career," said the same speaker, "will be an abiding possession of the whole Indian people."

All the public offices were closed in Baroda city and in the four districts of the State. Most of the shops and the mills also were closed, and so deep was the sympathy of the people that all carriage and tramway traffic was suspended.

All through life Mr. Dutt had pleaded for the unity of India, and no more incontrovertible proof of that growing unity could be found than that he, the son of humble Bengali parents, should receive regal honours at his funeral at the other extremity of his vast country, and that all classes of the community—nobles and commoners, merchants and husbandmen, Hindus, Muhammadans, and Parsis—should join in spontaneous homage to their departed friend and brother.

We corresponded fairly regularly, and the last letter which I had written was not long before his death. Mrs. Meade and I were shocked and grieved to hear that our old friend was no more. We hope that you will kindly convey our sincere regrets and condolences to your mother and the other members of your family. His Highness the Gaekwar, to whom I sent my condolence, sent me your address. I consider your father's death is a public loss. He was a rarely gifted man, far above the average in natural and acquired ability. He had also considerable poetic power and great literary knowledge and experience. He kindly gave me his works while I was at Baroda, and his translations and extracts of the great Indian Epics first brought them home to me, and placed those wonderful stories before my mind. But above all, I believe your father was a man of the highest and best ideals, who lived up to what he believed, *and was incapable of doing a wrong action. His judgment was unbiassed, and while he loved India, as a true son of India should do, he was at all times a loyal servant of the British Government and a true friend of many Englishmen.*—With much sympathy, believe me, yours sincerely, M. J. MEADE.

Mr. J. B. Pennington (late Madras Civil Service) wrote :—

I should like to join with you in deeply regretting his untimely end. We did not agree about everything—who does? But I never met a man with whom it was a greater pleasure to work, and it has always been a real grief to me of late years to have so seldom met. He would have been the first Indian member of the Secretary of State's Council if I could have controlled the election.

Sir Vithaldas Thackersy (Bombay) wired :—

Extremely grieved at sad death. State loses ablest officer and India loses best son.

BARODA, 13*th December*.

Mrs. Ole Bull, the widow of the famous Norwegian violinist, whose guest Mr. Dutt had been in her Norwegian home in 1901, wrote from Cambridge, Massachusetts :—

. . . I do hope there will be a memoir written of Mr. Dutt, that will illuminate the mind of young India as to the wisdom and enthusiasm of his patriotism. It is a very real grief to me that I never had the pleasure of a visit from him here in Cambridge. And how much work there still was for him to do!

It has been one of my greatest privileges to have known him, and had him as my guest. I think the memory of his Norwegian visit, and perhaps also the warm friendship made there with our great Liberal leader, John Lund, was a pleasure to him as it remains to me. His was such a big nature, so beneficent and inspiring.

Sister Nivedita wrote to Mrs. Dutt :—

Few women have so noble a record to cherish as yours, so great a name to carry, so lofty a pride! He was so splendid through and through!

Mrs. Bose, the wife of Dr. J. C. Bose, wrote :—

My greatest grief is that I was not able to see him once before his death, and to minister to his wants as a token of my deep regard and affection for him. During our stay in England we came to know each other so intimately that he loved me as his own daughter, and it is for this reason that I wish to mingle my tears with yours. Oh, where is that ever-smiling face, whose very presence brought us such strength and such peace? May we firmly believe that he is blessing us from the sphere to which he has been removed, otherwise this life will be but a barren wilderness.

In the remotest hamlets and villages of Bengal condolence meetings were held, in which all sections of the community—Hindu and Muhammadan, official and non-official—freely joined to express their sorrow, and to recognise Mr. Dutt's unrivalled services to the country. In other parts of India also, in most of the important cities and towns, representative and largely attended meetings were held. Memorial meetings were also held in London and in Cambridge.

At a special meeting of the Calcutta Corporation, presided over by Mr. A. Earle, afterwards Home Secretary to the Government of India, Rai Radha Charan Pal Bahadur, one of the Municipal Commissioners, paid an eloquent tribute to the memory of Mr. Dutt :—

The transcendent abilities of Romesh Dutt have given his name a world-wide celebrity. Whether as an administrator or as a man of letters, or as an advocate of his country's cause, he energies and talents. As a Government officer and administrator he was in the very foremost class. As a man of letters he was in the very first row among his countrymen. As a scholar, historian, and antiquarian he occupied the same eminent position. As a political worker and leader, with the facts and figures bearing on the revenue and financial questions of the country at his fingers'-ends, he was in the front line too. In fact, his life was a record of distinguished success in every one of the different walks he trod. His political work is the political history of India since he freed himself from the trammels of service in 1897. The passing away of this scholar, statesman, political guide, and man of letters leaves a great void in the country and in the hearts of all Indians.

The Hindu.—A life so full of great achievement in varied directions, and a record so unblemished in the service of his country, was the priceless lot of Romesh Chunder Dutt. In him the country has lost a brilliant writer, a great, courageous, and sincere patriot, one of the warmest friends of the poor raiyat, and one of the staunchest champions of his fellow-countrymen's rights and liberties.

The Statesman.—The death of Mr. Romesh Chunder Dutt will be felt to be a heavy loss to India, not only by his fellow-countrymen, but by the British Government, which he served with so much ability and success, and by all those Englishmen who are acquainted with his very striking career. He was, without exception, the most capable Indian who entered the Civil Service, and his great gifts were freely and handsomely recognised by the Indian Government. The Indian civilian satisfied every test of efficiency, and the Government had the courage and fairness to recognise capacity for administration when they saw it.

Indian Nation.—No review of Mr. Dutt's life can, however, be complete without reference to his individuality. When there is considerable controversy about the incongruity of a blending of the East and West, it is well to point to Mr. Dutt as a splendid embodiment of the two great forces of civilisation. He was essentially an Oriental in instinct and imagination, but his long and intimate contact with the West had rounded those corners of Orientalism which are a survival of the dead inglorious past. Mr. Dutt was the most finished product of the culture of the East and West, and the charm of his company and the elegance of his mental furniture were equally the outcome of Oriental lore and European learning. In him East and West truly "mixt their dim lights like life and death to broaden into boundless day."

From Sister Nivedita's article in the *Modern Review* (Calcutta) we have already quoted briefly. Her tribute is at once so just and so eloquent that we take a further extract as conclusion to this chapter.

It was to do the work that he thought he could do for his country, by writing books, that he renounced his appointment with its large salary at the earliest possible moment, and retired to spend even his pension in the further philanthropy of publishing his works! In London, late in 1900, and throughout 1901, it was the pleasure and privilege of my friends and myself to see much of Mr. Dutt in many ways; and one felt more and more in his calm disinterestedness, in his loneliness, and in his concentration, that as his forefathers had gone to the forest to live the life of the *banaprastha* for the development of the self, so here was one leading the same life in the forest of bricks and mortar for the development of his people. "You ask if I will go with you to so-and-so," he wrote to me once of a journey that I knew to be very disagreeable, "only to speak for ten minutes on India! but I would go into a tiger's cage for that!" Unassuming, simple, generous to a fault, the expression might be modern, but the greatness within was the ancient greatness. Romesh Chunder Dutt was a man of his own people. The object of all he ever did was not his own fame, but the uplifting of India. That gained, what matters it to him, the illustrious dead, whether a book or two more or less live or die? But it matters to his countrymen, matters to all eternity, that they should not fail in his meed of reverent salutation, that the voice of criticism should be hushed, and cleverness stand silent while they carry to the funeral pyre one who stands amongst the fathers of the future, one who dreamt high dreams and worked at great things untiringly, yet left behind him, before his country's altar, no offering so noble, no proof of her greatness so incontrovertible as that one thing of which he never thought at all—his own character and his own love!

CHAPTER XXXV

GENERAL ESTIMATE

I

WITHOUT attempting anything in the nature of a final or authoritative estimate, we may nevertheless, in bringing this book to a close, endeavour to gather up the threads of Romesh Dutt's life, and to present as far as possible at this stage the true lineaments of his career. Those who have written of him have generally viewed him from three standpoints, viz. as a man of letters, as an administrator, and finally, as a publicist and patriot; and this division is as convenient as any other for practical purposes. Yet even the most superficial observer could not fail to remark that the basic and unifying principle of Mr. Dutt's life was only one: the service of his motherland, the uplifting of the Indian nation. And this adds to the difficulty of a review of his worth and the value of his actual achievements; for is not the life of India, however we seek to interpret it, hidden in difficulty and obscurity?

II

We have seen the estimation in which Mr. Dutt himself held his own literary efforts, and the work of such great pioneers as Iswar Chunder Vidyasagar and Bankim Chunder Chatterjea, who have created the modern literature of Bengal. He adopted what may be described as the "national" standard. "The greatest works of the half century about to close," he wrote, "centre round the cardinal idea of service to our motherland. Till the middle of this century, we were taught to regard our ancient religion as a system of superstition, our ancient history as fable, and our own languages as unfit for ambitious literary endeavours. That we have outlived those times, that we have discarded those degrading notions, is due to the endeavours of our own countrymen, to that band of noble-hearted and patriotic men who explained to us our ancient religion, elucidated our ancient history, and created our modern literature." Judged from this standard, the achievements of Romesh Dutt are entitled to a very high place. It would be difficult to point to any other man of letters, European or Indian, who has done so much to bring Indian thought and aspirations in touch with the life and thought of the modern nations of the world. It may be true that in the field of strictly antiquarian research Mr. Dutt did not take any very prominent part. But the study of antiquities and the resuscitation of ancient India are two different things, and there is hardly any other writer who has succeeded in setting the past of India in a light so luminous and inspiring, and so historically true, before Western civilisation. This is a signal achievement, which is certain to have far-reaching effects in shaping the future destiny of the country.

But it cannot be forgotten that the national standpoint is not the only, or even the most important one, in judging of the work of a literary man. Historical criticism, after all, is most concerned with the purely literary and artistic merits of a writer. Indeed, the question will arise whether in the present circumstances of modern India there is scope for the rise of a truly great literary genius. But those who are able to judge have already pronounced that modern India has produced at least one really great creative genius—Bankim Chunder, of Bengal. The height attained by Bankim Chunder, however, Romesh Dutt never reached. His historical novels, though they afford abundant example of literary skill, the delineation of powerful characters, and fine dramatic situations, are yet lacking in that creative and fusing quality of genius which gives life and inevitableness to a true work of art. He is more in his element in his social novels, and although even here, amidst pages of description and a somewhat heavy treatment of the palpable shades of life, one meets somewhat seldom with those subtler graces and poignant touches by means of which art lifts and liberates life, the handling is surer and the *ensemble* more powerful than in the novels of his first period. It should also be remembered that Mr. Dutt was one of the first writers of fiction who dealt with the new phases of the social and intellectual life of modern Bengal, and set an example which has been followed, though not yet surpassed, by other writers. In short, the production of these social novels places Mr. Dutt ahead of all living writers of fiction in India, and gives him a place second only to that of Bankim Chunder.

It need hardly be pointed out that Mr. Dutt himself never hoped to have made any permanent contributions to literature by his writings in English. They belong to what we have described as the sphere of national or patriotic literature; his aim being to render accessible to Europe the riches and glories of his motherland in past times. But still the execution and the substance of his historical writings, his style, his broad outlook, the fine enthusiasm and suppressed emotion which occasionally vibrate through his pages, give him a claim to be recognised as a historian of no mean rank. The great merit of his political writings is their directness and lucidity. There is never the least difficulty in following his arguments or mistaking the meaning of what he wants. His translations of the Indian epics are without question the best renderings in English verse of those masterpieces of the Indian mind. The command of verse, and the faculty to express high thoughts and noble sentiments in a manner which, while preserving the beauty and simplicity of the original, yet appeals to the modern mind, display qualities of a high degree of intellectuality, and place these works on a level with the best attempts so far made to present the poetry of the East in English forms.

III

If the test of a great administrator and of true administrative success under the British Government be the approval and appreciation of the Government, and the love and regard, unstinted and spontaneous, of the people themselves, it is undeniable that Mr. Dutt achieved a signal measure of success. One of the ablest and most broad-minded Lieutenant-Governors of Bengal, Sir Steuart Bayley, had pronounced him to be the most capable executive officer of his time. And in the districts where he served, his memory is still as green and as dear to the people as it was when he worked amongst them. He possessed in a pre-eminent degree the qualities necessary to make a successful Indian administrator—tact, sympathy, firmness, imagination and devotion to duty. The people loved him no less than they feared him. They loved him, because they realised in him a genuine and sincere friend and well-wisher. As Sister Nivedita has so well put it, "one had only to stand in the presence of Romesh Dutt to know what a just and merciful judge, what a wise ruler and father he would be." His strict impartiality and regard for the spirit and authority of the law contributed in no small measure to the success of his administration. There was, moreover, an element of sternness in his character, a bull-dog tenacity so often deemed to be specially characteristic of the British race, and grit and pluck to face difficulties promptly and effectively, which accounted for the complete and successful suppression of crime in his districts. These qualities made him an ideal ruler of an Indian district. As the *Law Journal* rightly observed :—"There have been not many magistrates in Bengal who have combined in their executive capacity so much firmness in upholding the authority of the law with a strong sense of fairness and justice, coupled with a genuine concern for the welfare of the people confided to their care."

It has been sometimes observed, and with some

the temper of mind so necessary to the Indian politician, of taking what one can possibly get without wasting energy in "crying for the moon." But this does not imply that the Indian occupying a post of authority should limit his vision, or that he should betray his country's cause in order to ingratiate himself as a "safe" or "useful" man. There is a wide and impassable gulf between self-seeking sycophancy masquerading in the garb of a "moderate" and the wise reserve and restraint of the true patriot who knows the limitations of his cause, and who, without abating one jot of endeavour for the uplift of his people, takes what he can get, then wraps his soul in patience and bides his time. So much for practicality, moderation, and a sense of historical proportion.

Unselfishness and sincerity form the true tests of an Indian politician, no less than of others all over the world. But the politician who is agitating both for a place for himself and for the public weal, is more likely to compromise his cause in India than his more lucky compeers in other parts of the world. Want of sectarianism and a true cosmopolitan feeling are essential qualifications for a patriot of modern India.

On the intellectual side he must be a man of wide information, learned not only in the wisdom of books, but a man who knows the world, and, above all, has first-hand information about the subjects which he makes his own special department. Some amount of specialisation and reticence add not only to the weight of his opinions, but save him from being mistaken for a professional agitator. Add to these a faculty of imagination, the saving grace of urbanity, the sentiment of "give and take," and a generous and real, not a mere lip-deep, recognition of the debt of gratitude which modern India owes to England, and we have a politician who will not only lead public opinion, but who is bound deeply to influence the course of Indian administration.

Judged by these standards, what place should we assign to Mr. Dutt in the roll of India's great men? Deep and lasting as the influence of his career will undoubtedly be, it is perhaps true that the impress of his great powers would have been more immediately felt had he employed his superabundant energies over less wide a field. For we cannot lay to heart too earnestly the wise monition of Lord Morley, that the Indian patriot has need of the most critical circumspection, and must concentrate his attention on the larger and more lasting issues, and not fritter away his energies on ephemeral topics, which, though they may make a great deal of splash at the time, are yet unfruitful of any lasting result. How far was Romesh Dutt gifted with a true insight into the bases of Indian polity, and imbued with the spirit of moderation and wisdom which we have considered to be the highest qualities of the really great Indian statesman? In the heat of the great controversies in which he engaged Government, or sought to lead public opinion, did he always and sufficiently lay bare the foundation of justice and good intention on which the Government of the day is based? The answers to these questions are not so obvious as some would like to believe. There cannot be any question that he realised to the full that the interests of all that is best and most hopeful in modern India are the interests of the Government of the day, and educated India has accepted and supported that Government from the most primary of all motives of self-interest. On all important occasions he never failed to make full and emphatic acknowledgment of this fact. If in any particular mood of depression or despair he seemed to betray a partisan spirit in or to fail to do sufficient justice to the Government side of the case, it must not be forgotten that the task which he had imposed upon himself was particularly wearisome and depressing, and the cycle during which most of his political writings were composed was not marked by any signal acts of the widening of the door of the aspirations of the people of the country, but synchronised with some of the least sympathetic and least liberal measures which have been passed within recent times. But his language meant no more than the heated protest of a party in opposition—and he certainly showed more restraint than most of his adverse critics; and to believe or to avow that an Indian of the stamp of Romesh Dutt could have a lurking desire, even in the most secret chambers of his mind, to see the bark of India cut adrift from the moorings of the British Empire, and to be plunged again into the political chaos of the dark ages, is to betray ignorance of one of the first axioms of Indian politics of the present day. It may be safely maintained, therefore, that in the main, both in choosing the sphere of his contentions and his method of political controversy, he displayed sound discretion and great political judgment, though perhaps he might have taken the views of the philanthropic school of English and Anglo-Indian statesmen somewhat too much on trust, and imported British methods of hard-hitting in an honest cause too unreservedly and without sufficient regard to the difference in the political atmospheres of the two countries.

But even if there be any question about his political sagacity, surely there can be none about his unselfishness, undaunted courage, fixedness of purpose, and devotion to the highest ideals. The far-seeing political wisdom with which he seized on the main shortcomings of the system of administration in vogue during his time, and the tenacity, courage, and resource which he displayed in fighting his cause, had never been equalled before, and are not likely to be surpassed for generations to come. The charge most commonly made by unsympathetic critics of the Indian nationalist movement is, that its leaders are "self-appointed arm-chair politicians," devoid both of real knowledge of the needs of the proletariat and without any genuine desire to champion their cause. It is to be hoped that the record of the great career which it has been our task to narrate, of the indefatigable devotion of a whole lifetime to the cause of the poor and the unrepresented which earned for him the name of "*Garib ka dost*," of his ceaseless toil even at an advanced age to gain first-hand information from the people themselves whose interests were so dear to his heart, will induce these critics not to make indiscriminate charges so thoughtlessly in the future. For it is not a difficult task to throw dirt on the leaders of a fallen and subject race. to assign motives of self-interest, dishonesty, or disloyalty to actions which will bear quite a different interpretation if for the eye of jealousy and haughty intolerance one only substituted a feeling of real fellowship and genuine sympathy. How few of the critics who are just now clamouring to be heard, and who have all obviously got the last word about Indian aspirations, have made any honest attempt to realise the difficulties of the Indian standpoint! The ideal of an Indian patriot is a seeming paradox. He must fight for the best interests of his own country, and at the same time be genuinely loyal to the British Crown, and work for the continuance and permanence of British rule. That such an attitude is possible is abundantly proved by careers like those of Romesh Dutt. Yet there is a melancholy truth in his remark that an Indian publicist of this type "has no friends." His own countrymen are apt not to cherish a very warm admiration for him, for they think he does not go far enough, and unfortunately in official circles also it is not yet fully realised that the whole future of the British Empire in India is indissolubly connected with the possibility of the country's producing leaders of this type.

The services which Mr. Dutt rendered to the nation are solid and many-sided, and are likely to loom larger with the passing of time. His career was an unanswerable demonstration of the capacity of India to produce a citizen of the highest type of manhood. Born in a country which has been under the sway of foreign dominion for centuries, and is now the home of a residuum of uncoördinated nationalities and religions, his passionate love of country, his unbiassed championing of the cause of India as a whole, and his sinking of all other considerations in the service of his motherland, would have done credit to the son of any more favoured country of the West. No Indian in recent times has been imbued in such a marvellous manner with the strength, the manliness, and the patriotism of the West, and yet has done so much to vindicate the greatness of the achievements of Ancient India, and to implant in the national mind a high and legitimate admiration for her past. In doing this, Mr. Dutt materially fertilised what he justly maintained to be the roots of national progress. And in fighting the cause of India in England, though he was not a pioneer, there can be little doubt that his efforts met with far greater success than fell to the lot of other Indian publicists before his time. And when the time comes for analysing the real sources of the motive power which has brought about the momentous changes in the administration of the country in the last few years, it will be found that the share which Mr. Dutt had in turning the course of the tide is far more considerable than has yet been acknowledged in any quarter. For though the reforms have come because India is ripe for them, and are no doubt the outcome, on the one hand, of the political training which India has received under British rule, and the collective influence of the work of those noble Indian patriots who have, since the days of Raja Ram Mohan Ray, striven to raise their motherland; and, on the other, of the wise political foresight of the rulers themselves, yet it can be justly maintained that of all the individual workers it would be difficult to point to many other statesmen who have fought the battle of India with such complete effacement of self, such intimate and first-hand knowledge of all the different phases of the political progress of the country, such wide cosmopolitan sympathy with all classes of the Indian community, and, finally, with so great a power of placing the issues on the enduring bases of history and international morality. There may have been, during the century just passed, more than one Indian who has risen to greater heights in this or that particular sphere; but there has been none built on a larger mould, none who has so greatly influenced the affairs of his country, or championed her cause before the West with a more impressive combination of knowledge, devotion, and high personal worth.

INDEX

Printed by BALLANTYNE, HANSON & Co.
Edinburgh & London